BIG BORE SIXGUNS

JOHN TAFFIN

Published by

**krause
publications**

700 E. State Street • Iola, WI 54990-0001
Telephone: 715/445-2214

Please call or write for our free catalog of firearms/knives publications. Our toll-free number
to place an order or obtain a free catalog is 800-258-0929 or please use our regular business
telephone 715-445-2214 for editorial comment
and further information.

Library of Congress Catalog Number: 97-73041
ISBN: 0-87341-502-7
Printed in the United States of America

Some product names in this book are registered trademarks of
their respective companies.

Q-Tips ®
Outer's Metal Seal ®
Loc Tite ®
Crisco ®
Windex ®

to DOT TAFFIN

For always understanding.

and

to JOE PENNER

For always helping.

and

to J.D. JONES

For always encouraging.

TABLE OF CONTENTS

ACKNOWLEDGEMENTS

A book like this is not written by one's self. It takes a lot of help from a lot of good people. The following have provided sixguns, pictures, leather, stocks, bullets, ammunition, action jobs, custom work, and just plain old encouragement. I thank them tremendously for all their help.

Charles Able	Ben Forkin	Mike Larsen	Paul Rosenberg
Tedd Adamovich	Sherry Fears	Bob Leskovec	Jay Rutt
Bob Alford	Roy Fishpaw	John Linebaugh	Thad Rybka
Massad Ayoob	Val Forgett	Jim Lockwood	Kelye Schlepp
Bob Baer	Grant Fry	Mike Manning	Ed Schmitt
Bob Baker	John Gallagher	Elmer McEvoy	Ned Schwing
Wayne Baker	Richard Gallagher	Richard McCann	Bob Shapel
Jim Barnard	Randy Garrett	Bud McDonald	Mark Shapel
Roger Barnes	Bill Grover	Don McMinn	Blackie Sleeva
John Bianchi	Mario Hanel	Bobby McNellis	Rosetta Sleeva
Ted Blocker	Mike Harvey	Barbara Mellman	Randy Smith
Hamilton Bowen	Rod Herrett	Walt Minard	Veral Smith
Jay Branch	Jeff Hoffman	Milt Morrison	Robert Smythe
Dick Casull	Pat Hogue	Bob Munden	Jim Stroh
Fred Christensen	Andy Horvath	Terry Murbach	Jim Supica
Jimmy Clark	Teddy Jacobsen	Gary Owen	Hal Swiggett
David Clements	Eddie Janis	Keith Owlett	Allen Taylor
Sherry Collins	Allan Jones	Brian Pearce	Jim Taylor
Tom Conrad	Carter Jones	Jack Pender	Dwight Van Brunt
Jerry Danuser	J.D. Jones	Joe Penner	Jim Wall
Gordon Davis	Mike Jordan	Peter Pi	Mike Wallace
Deacon Deason	Ken Jorgensen	Jay Postman	Dave Wayland
Chris Dolnack	Tony Kanaley	Frank Pulkrabek	Ben Wetzel
Doug Donnelly	Ken Kelly	Howard Rhoades	Syl Wiley
Ed Douglas	Larry Kelly	Jim Riggs	Jim Wilson
George Dvorchak	Paco Kelly	Von Ringler	Corky Wood
Doug Engh	Tony Kojis	Bill Ripple	

INTRODUCTION

Forty years ago, I was straight out of high school and I purchased my first sixgun, a Ruger Single-Six .22. In those days a teenager could be trusted to buy a handgun and ammunition, and no one thought it the least bit unusual to see a bunch of teenagers with their sixguns and rifles heading out to shoot—it was totally normal. Many a pleasant Saturday afternoon was spent running hundreds of rounds through that marvelous little .22 Ruger. To this day, the smell of .22 powder and Hoppe's #9 still bring back pleasant memories. Those of us who shot together became gunwriters and peace officers. Maybe it was the smell of the Hoppe's #9 that affected us.

Within six months of purchasing the .22 Ruger, the big bores beckoned. The .44 Magnum, while announced, had not yet arrived at the local gun shop and, in fact, Ruger .357 Blackhawks were just starting to show. Prewar sixguns, mostly Smith & Wesson double actions and Colt Single Actions, however, were in abundance. For $90, two weeks pay then, I acquired a .38-40 Colt Single Action Army with hard rubber grips and a 4-3/4-inch barrel. The case coloring had turned gray over the half-century plus of its existence, but the big sixgun was in excellent shape and I was well on my way to a lifelong passion. I had yet to discover the mysteries of handloading, and while the price of the .38-40 seemed a bargain, the price of ammunition did not.

Colt resurrected the Single Action Army and I soon had a 7-1/2-inch .45 Colt. Then came Rugers, .357 and .44 Magnum Blackhawks, the sixguns we now call Flat-Tops, and Smith & Wessons in .44 Special, .357 Magnum, and .44 Magnum, and more Colt Single Actions—always more Colt Single Actions. My life's path was set.

Of all men, I am most blessed. Others go to work and dream of shooting and hunting. When I work, I shoot or hunt. Others golf to relax. I shoot sixguns. I don't bowl or fish. I shoot sixguns. I don't attend sporting events. I shoot sixguns. Movies? *Terminator* or *Twelve Monkeys*? No! *Tombstone* or *True Grit*? Absolutely! *The Shootist*? I'll buy the popcorn! Skiing? Boating? Nope. Any vacation I plan revolves around shooting or hunting. Fortunately my wife of nearly four decades—we were married very young!—has always understood.

My interests are very narrow. Ask me about the NFL, the NBA, or MLB, and you will talk and I will probably politely listen; however, mention NRA, S&W, HHI, MNP, or SASS, and we will have a great conversation together. I don't buy new cars, or fancy homes, or even expensive clothes—well, let's not count the boots and Stetsons. Sixguns come first—big bore sixguns. Guns that are inscribed ".357 MAGNUM," ".41 MAGNUM," ".44 SPECIAL," ".45 COLT," ".44 MAGNUM," or "454 CASULL" with barrels that carry "COLT," "FREEDOM ARMS," "RUGER," "SMITH & WESSON," or "TEXAS LONGHORN ARMS," draw me like a moth to a flame.

There aren't a whole lot of things in this life that are important to me, or even interest me. Actually, there are only four: Faith, Family, Friends, and Firearms. They are all linked together and one cannot exist without the other. The greatest joy connected with being a sixgunwriter is not all the big bore revolvers and related equipment I get to test. Important? Yes, but this profession's finest aspect is the great people I meet, who teach me as they impart their knowledge. I hesitate to mention any by name because the list will be incomplete, but special thanks go to those who have had a deep impact upon my life. First and foremost, the Grand Old Man, Elmer Keith, then the others, Skeeter Skelton, J.D. Jones, John Linebaugh,

Hamilton Bowen, Hal Swiggett, and to Robert Smythe, Deacon Deason, and Jack Pender, three Shootists and special Brothers who have gone Home ahead of me and are keeping the campfire burning and the beans and bacon hot, and of course, the editors I have worked for at *Guns* and *American Handgunner*, Jerry Lee, Scott Farrell, and Cameron Hopkins.

In these pages I have set down my thoughts on big bore sixguns and especially my prejudices towards them. I hope you enjoy what I have to say and are able to learn something from my experiences.

Good Shootin' and God Bless.
John Taffin
Boise, Idaho

DISCLAIMER: All loading data contained herein should be used with caution. The author is responsible only for that ammunition he personally assembles for use in his personal sixguns. Because we have no control over your reloading practices, neither the author, editor, publisher, nor manufacturers of components assume any responsibility for the use of any reloading data found in these pages.

CHAPTER 1

THE FIRST
BIG BORE SIXGUNS

The roots of the big bore sixgun run deep—all the way back to the first successful revolver, the five-shot Colt Paterson of 1836. It would be thirty-five years before the first centerfire big bore sixgun would arrive on the scene as the percussion revolver evolved from the Colt Paterson, through the Walker, the Dragoons, and the 1851 and 1860 Army. Along the way would come the Remingtons and the lesser-known manufacturers such as Spiller & Burr, Leech & Rigdon, and Dance Brothers.

This book is mainly about centerfire sixguns, those magnificent big bore revolvers from 1870 to the present. We will only concern ourselves with American sixguns, even though one of the author's first revolvers was a double action Deane & Adams percussion pistol. In the two chapters on replica sixguns we will look at the cap-n-ball, or percussion, sixguns as well as the copies of Colt, Remington, and Smith & Wesson single action sixguns of the last century.

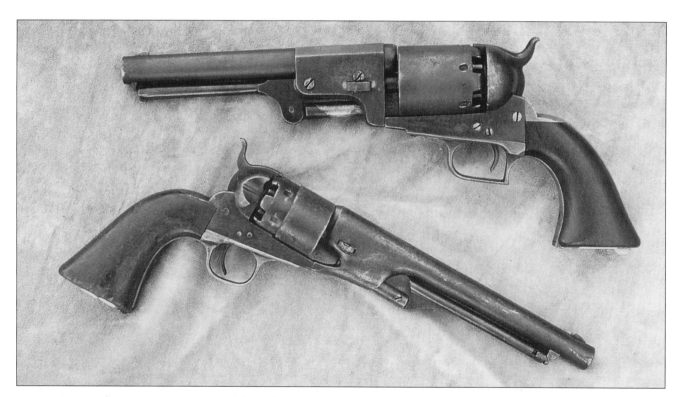

Percussion Colts from the mid-nineteenth century were the forerunners of the centerfire-style big bore sixguns. The First Model Dragoon shot a .44 caliber round ball over a full 50 grains of blackpowder while the trimmer 1860 Army used the same round ball with 40 grains of blackpowder.

The First Model Dragoon, top, combined the power of the Walker Colt with an easier to pack size; the 1851 Navy, middle, is a very rare .40 caliber sixgun; the 1860 Army .44, bottom, was the direct forerunner of the 1873 Colt Single Action Army .45.

In this first chapter we herein confine ourselves to the sixguns that emerged in what was basically the last quarter of the nineteenth century. These were the years after the Civil War, an often violent time when the frontier opened, the gunfighter emerged, cattle drives brought beef from Texas to northern markets, the buffalo were hunted almost to extinction, and the Indians were subdued. By the time the century ended, the telephone, moving pictures, the automobile, and even man-in-flight would all be reality.

While the eastern part of the country was becoming what some would consider civilized, in much of the rest of the country, many a man's day began by buckling on a .44 or .45 caliber sixgun, most often a Colt, Remington, or Smith & Wesson, before the first rays of sunlight and did not end until that same sixgun was unbuckled and hung within reach long after the moon had risen. These same sixguns set the pattern for American sixgunners' taste in big bore sixguns.

Do not expect a collector's treatise as we look at those beginning years. That is far beyond the scope of this short piece; entire books have been written on each manufacturer, and in some cases, each particular model. Also realize that very few specifications for calibers or model types were set in concrete by the factories and many variations were possible. Rather, we will take a general look at the most important big bore sixguns to emerge during this time frame and especially in the great flurry of activity that occurred in the 1870s.

While Colt and Remington first produced cap-n-ball sixguns and then switched over to fixed-ammunition models, Smith & Wesson first began producing a seven-shot pistol that fired the .22 rimfire cartridge before the War Between the States. Smith & Wesson employed Rollin White, who just happened to hold the patent on bored-through cylinders. In the 1860s, it had planned a .44 caliber sixgun, but the War put this model on the shelf until it emerged as the .44 Smith & Wesson American in 1870. The first big bore Smith & Wesson was chambered in .44 caliber rimfire, the same ammunition as used in the Henry Model 1860 and Winchester Model 1866 levergus, however at the suggestion of the U.S. Army, this was changed to a .44 caliber centerfire, the .44 Smith & Wesson. Three years before Colt had its first sixgun firing fixed-ammunition, Smith & Wesson received a military contract for 1,000 six-shot, top-break-design revolvers.

Anyone who has had experience shooting cap-n-ball sixguns will realize what a tremendous step forward this was. The percussion revolvers were accurate and relatively powerful, however, they were, to say the least, slow to reload. In this day of speedloaders for sixguns and high-capacity magazines for semi-automatics, it is easy to forget where it is we came from.

Our government was not the only entity interested in the new .44 from Smith & Wesson. The Russian government placed an order for 20,000 Smith & Wesson Single Actions in a new chambering appropriately dubbed the .44 Russian. In the case of the .44 Smith & Wesson, a smaller caliber heel on the bullet's base resided inside the cartridge case while the bullet proper was the same diameter as the outside of the cartridge case. The .44 Russian bullet was the same diameter throughout its body and was placed inside the cartridge case. Previous cylinders had been bored straight through; the new cylinders were of one diameter for the cartridge case and a smaller diameter at the front of the chamber to accept the bullet. This, in addition to the .44 Russian cartridge, was another significant step forward. This is why .44s are really .43 caliber— they had to be made smaller to fit inside the cartridge case.

The Smith & Wesson .44 American sixgun stayed in production from 1870 to 1874. They are distinguished by a square butt, a smoothly contoured backstrap, and all were furnished with an 8-inch barrel in either .44 rimfire or centerfire.

From 1873 to 1878, Smith & Wesson produced the Russian models. These are distinguished from the American model by a round butt and a pronounced hump at the top of the backstrap not unlike that found on double action sixguns today. The purpose, of course, was to prevent the grip from sliding down into the hand upon the effect of recoil. Both the American and Russian models carried the locking latch on the barrel which extended back to the rear sight area. The Russians were chambered in both .44 Russian and .44 rimfire and carried a spur beneath the trigger for added security in gripping the revolver. Barrel lengths were 6-1/2 or 7 inches.

The Russian contract was a good news, bad news proposition. While Smith & Wesson had a guaranteed income, it could not supply the domestic demand for a

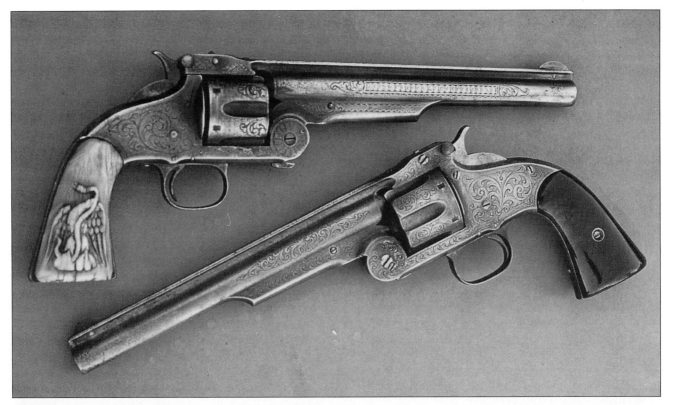

The first big bore sixgun centerfire-style was the Smith & Wesson American. These beautiful examples show factory engraving and are in .44 rimfire and .44 Smith & Wesson American. Note the fine Mexican Eagle ivory stocks.

big bore sixgun and consequently, this market was left for others to fill.

During the late 1860s and early 1870s, Thuer and Richards patents were used by Colt. It did a healthy business converting cap-n-ball sixguns to the new fixed-ammunition style. Remington conversions were also encountered, and the Remington and Colt cylinder backs were cut off and a new section was fitted, or a completely new cylinder was built to accept rimfire cartridges.

In 1872, Colt introduced its 1860 Army cap-n-ball as an open-topped frame, .44 rimfire chambered sixgun. By 1873, Colt was ready with what would be the classic sixgun of all sixguns. Sam Colt is often given credit for the design of the 1873 Colt Single Action Army, but this is not true because Colt had died more than ten years before. The Model P, the Peacemaker, was instead a product of the fertile mind of William Mason.

Smith & Wesson's .44 Russian single action was one of the finest sixguns of all time both in terms of accuracy and workmanship. It did, however, have a couple of drawbacks. The design was top-break, with the hinge at the bottom of the frame front and the break at the back of the top strap. The gun was fragile and, although its simultaneous ejection was fast if one wanted to empty all chambers, the design was a hindrance if one simply wanted to replace a fired cartridge or two—especially on horseback.

In the late 1950s, I had a brand new Second Generation Colt Single Action 7-1/2-inch .45 Colt plus a mate to it that was the same sixgun in its Prewar issue. I soon discovered I had an older neighbor, who also loved single actions. His three single action sixguns all dated back to the nineteenth century. With single action sixguns in common, we immediately became friends. In his modest collection of shooting sixguns, first, of course, was a Colt Single Action that had been expertly converted to a 7-1/2-inch .44 Special and customized further with an 1860 Colt backstrap, triggerguard, and grip. It was also tuned to perfection and fired only one load, the Keith .44 Special. The 1860 parts had come from his second sixgun, a .44 1860 Colt cap-n-ball that now had the Single Action grip parts.

To me, the most fascinating sixgun was his third single action. It was also a .44, but not a Colt. It was, in fact, a .44 Russian—a Smith & Wesson .44 Russian. Up to that time, I had always thought Smith & Wesson only made double action sixguns. After all, who could imagine Roy, or Gene, or Hoppy carrying a Smith & Wesson? The Smith & Wesson Single Action certainly did not have the marvelous feel of the Colt Single Action Army, but even as untrained as I was, I could recognize that this was truly a marvelous piece of engineering.

Smith & Wesson may have arrived first, but when the patent for the bored-through cylinder ran out, Colt

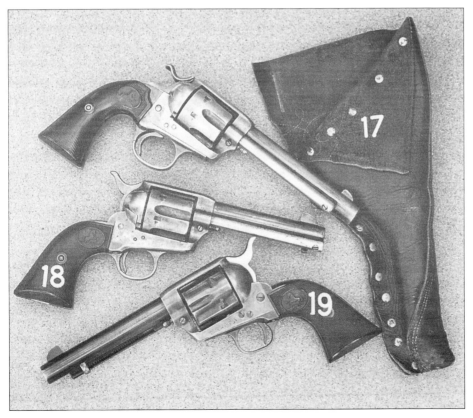

Colt Single Actions of the last third of the nineteenth century were the sixgun of the cowboy, lawman, desperado, and gunfighter: Top, Bisley Model .45 Colt with the comfortable to shoot but slower on the draw ladle-shaped grip frame; middle, a rare .45 Colt with long, fluted cylinder; bottom, a standard 5-1/2-inch .45 Colt. All wear gutta-percha grips of the period. Note the holster built for security not a fast draw.

The gunfighter's gun—the Colt Single Action Army 4-3/4-inch .45 Colt. No gun has ever proven to be faster from the leather.

was ready with its cartridge-style big bore. I'm sure Colt took a good look at Remington's line of cap-n-ball sixguns because the new Colt Single Action Army carried the frame profile of the Remington 1858 instead of the open/top frame of Colt's own 1860 Army. Whatever the case may be, Colt had a winner with a sixgun that is still in production 125 years later in both original and replica form.

The first Colt Single Actions were 7-1/2-inch barreled .45s for the U.S. Army. The original loading for the Peacemaker was a powerful 40 grains of blackpowder under a 255 grain bullet. This was soon cut back to a more manageable 28 grains. From 1873 until 1891, the Army ordered 37,000 7-1/2-inch .45 Colt chambered Single Action Army sixguns for the use of the troops on the frontier.

The .45 Colt was *the* sixgun cartridge for years. A man trapped out on his own with little cover, his 7-1/2-inch Cavalry Model Colt Single Action, and a good supply of ammunition, would certainly be able to give a good account of himself. I would say out to 600 hundred yards, a sixgunner, as my good friend Sheriff Jim Wilson says, "may not hit the enemy but he could certainly keep him pinned down until someone shows up that can shoot!"

In 1877, the first 4-3/4-inch barreled sixguns appeared and the following year saw the introduction of the .44-40 that originally had been chambered in Winchester's 1873 levergun. Now, shooters could have a sixgun and their levergun chambered for the same cartridge. Many in the know stayed with the Colt in .45 Colt and the Winchester in .44-40. In the 1880s, the .38-40 would emerge, chambered in the Colt Single Action

Army. Production standardized with barrel lengths of 4-3/4, 5-1/2, and 7-1/2 inches, with longer barrels available on special order and shorter barrels often without ejector rod assemblies, known as Storekeeper's Models, were also available from Colt on special order.

When production of the First Generation of Colt Single Actions ceased in 1941, more than 350,000 had been produced. Even the experts cannot agree on how many calibers were available, but we do know it was more than thirty. The most popular was the .45 Colt, which was found in more than half of the produced sixguns, followed by the .44-40, .38-40, and the little .32-20.

Approximately 13 percent of the Single Action Army production consisted of the Bisley Model. With its target-style grip and wide hammer and trigger, the Bisley was much easier to shoot, but nowhere as fast from leather as the standard Colt Single Action. The grip of the Bisley Model, which was marked "Bisley Model" in front of the caliber on the left side of the barrel, came up high on the backstrap and very high behind the triggerguard, resulting in the sixgun setting deep in the hand for comfort and control. Frames of the Bisley Colts were 3/16 inch longer from the backstrap to the bottom of the main frame than regular Single Action Armys.

Meanwhile, back at Smith & Wesson, we were about to see a .45 Smith & Wesson introduced to compete with the Colt for the Army contract. The United States Army had adopted the stronger .45 Colt Single Action over the more intricate Smith & Wesson. The Colt was slower to unload than the automatic-ejecting Smith & Wesson, but it carried a more powerful load and had a solid frame. The Colt was certainly better built for use as a persuader because it could be used for rapping someone on the head and one didn't have to worry about bending the frame.

The Smith & Wesson American required two hands to operate the latch on the top of the barrel. Major George Schofield of the 10th Cavalry decided to improve the Smith & Wesson and make it more adaptable to military use, which in those days meant horseback. To this end, Schofield changed the Smith & Wesson latch from barrel to frame, allowing it to be pushed in with the thumb of the shooting hand rather than opened with the off hand. This allowed one-hand operation even on horseback.

In 1873, a test was set up that placed the Schofield Model Smith & Wesson against the Colt Single Action Army. While mounted on a moving horse, the horseman had to empty the sixgun, remove six cartridges from his belt pouch, and reload. It took twenty-six seconds to unload the Colt and it was reloaded in sixty seconds. The improved Smith & Wesson

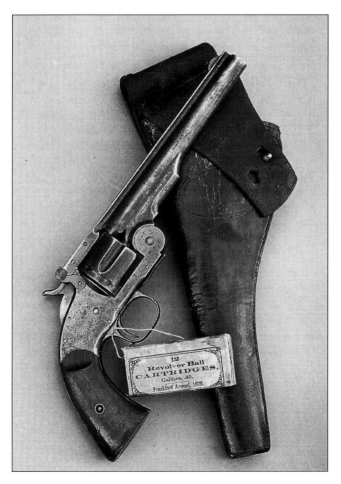

This Second Model Schofield is a military issue caliber .45 Smith & Wesson. Note the two holes on the holster flap to allow its use for either the Schofield or the Colt Single Action.

Schofield took only two seconds to unload and it was loaded in twenty-six seconds. Needless to say, the Army ordered Schofields.

Trouble was waiting in the wings, though. The Schofield Smith & Wesson was in .45 caliber, not the standard .44 of other Smith & Wesson single actions, but the Schofield's cylinder was shorter than that of the Colt Single Action Army .45 Colt. The Colt sixgun could handle the .45 Smith & Wesson ammunition, the ".45 Short Colt," but the Smith & Wesson would not chamber the ".45 Long Colt." When battle units equipped with .45 Schofields received unusable .45 Colt ammunition, the problem was solved by dropping the Schofields. They became government surplus in 1880 and many of the 7-inch Schofields had their barrels cut back to 5 inches, making them quite popular with Wells Fargo agents.

The final Smith & Wesson Single Action would be the New Model No. 3. This beautifully crafted sixgun was chambered mostly in .44 Russian, with a few examples in .44-40 and .38-40. The latch was back on the barrel, the grip frame was rounded, there was a hump on the backstrap, and the barrel length was standardized at 6-1/2 inches. Production lasted all the way into the twentieth century and the eve of World War I.

Remington was also involved in single action sixguns with the Model 1875. It had a 7-1/2-inch barrel, the most popular length with the gun's best customer, the U.S. Cavalry. At first glance, the Remington Single Action looks a lot like a Colt, but there are several differences. The Remington's grip frame is part of the main frame which results in a more solid and possibly stronger sixgun. The triggerguard is separate from the main frame and does not form part of the front grip strap as it does on the Colt. The Remington achieves its most distinctive appearance from a web under the barrel that runs from the end of ejector housing to the front of the frame. The cylinder pin also runs all the way to the end of the ejector tube.

Only about 25,000 Remington Single Actions were produced, 10,000 of which went to the Egyptian government. The original chambering was .44 Remington with the .45 Colt and .44-40 introduced in 1879. The Remington .44 chambering must have been fairly potent; it carried a 248 grain bullet over 32 grains of blackpowder. Smith & Wesson's .44 Russian, in a shorter case, was loaded with 23 grains of blackpowder, while Colt's .45 originally packed 40 grains of blackpowder under a 255 grain bullet. This was later cut back to anywhere from 25 to 35 grains.

One other single action of note is that from Merwin, Hulbert & Co. The biggest problem with the original models is that they were of the much weaker

Note the fine target sights on these Smith & Wesson New Model #3 Target Models. Most of the target shooting records of the last century were set with the Smith & Wesson Target Model.

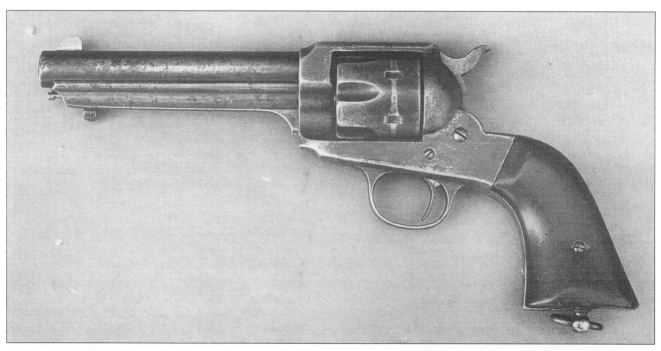

Remington Single Actions were the Model 1875 with a full web under the barrel and the Model 1890 with the cutaway web. This 1888 Remington is a transitional model between the two. Remingtons were probably better sixguns than the Colt, but they did not quite have the balance of the Model P, nor were they as fast from leather as the Peacemaker for most hands.

open-topped frame variety which hurt sales and any chance of getting government contracts. It did, however, solve the problem of the Smith & Wesson non-selective simultaneous ejection of all cases either loaded or fired. A latch was pressed on the Merwin & Hulbert that allowed both barrel and cylinder to slide forward just enough to allow spent cases to fall out the back of the cylinder while unfired cases remained. The most popular chambering was in .44-40. The double action version emerged in 1883. All Merwin & Hulberts were excellently crafted, including the final big bore model, the Pocket Army .44-40 which was a double action sixgun.

By the mid-1870s, the new double action, or self-cocking, sixgun had emerged. Colt's Lightning in .38 Long Colt and the Thunderer in .41 Long Colt were both beautiful, but quite fragile. They were used with great aplomb by Billy the Kid.

Colt's .45 Double Action Army, introduced in 1878, was a larger-framed double action sixgun. All three of Colt's self-cocking, or trigger-operated, sixguns were solid frame sixguns, loaded and unloaded through a gate exactly as the Colt Single Action Army. In 1902, the Alaskan, or Philippine, Model .45 Double Action Army emerged with a larger triggerguard for use with a gloved hand by the military.

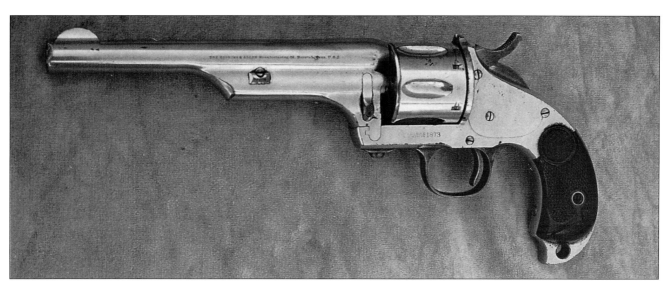

The open top Merwin & Hulbert .44-40 was a fine alternative to the Colt, Remington, or Smith & Wesson sixguns of the period.

A most ingenious design: this Merwin & Hulbert .44-40 single action allows the barrel and cylinder to rotate and move forward just far enough to eject empties while loaded rounds remain in the cylinder.

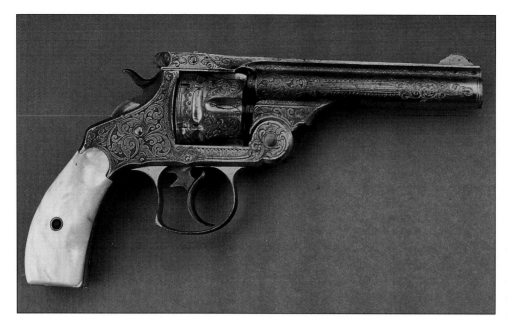

This pearl-gripped, factory-engraved Smith & Wesson DA Frontier was the forerunner of the .44 Special Triple-Lock, 1926 Model, 1950 Target Model, and today's .44 Magnum.

On the heels of the Double Action Army came Smith & Wesson's .44 Double Action, a top-break design that was basically its Single Action Russian with a self-cocking trigger. This design would last in the Smith & Wesson catalog until 1913 even though the superior 1899 Military & Police and 1908 Triple-Lock had emerged.

In 1897, Colt introduced the big New Service, the first double action with the swing-out cylinder that is so familiar today. This sixgun would stay in production until the start of World War II. There were actually more of these double actions produced than the immensely popular Single Action Army. These production figures are partly due to the fact that both the Colt New Service and the Smith & Wesson .44 Hand Ejector Second Model were used extensively in World War I as the Model 1917 chambered for the .45 ACP round.

As usual, we were not prepared for war and the government found it was impossible to produce enough of the relatively new Model 1911 semi-autos. The ingenious answer was pressing double action sixguns into service with cylinders bored for the .45 ACP semi-automatic round and used with two half-moon clips that accepted three rounds each. The half-moon clips not only provided the proper headspacing, but also provided easy ejection of the rimless rounds from a double action sixgun.

Colt's New Service was obviously designed by someone with large hands and long fingers. I have large hands with short fingers, which makes it much more difficult for me to control a New Service Double Action than a Smith & Wesson N-frame of the same caliber. The New Service would be produced in eleven chamberings including the .357 Magnum, .38-40, .44 Special, .44-40, .45 Colt, and .45 ACP.

Big bore sixguns, in general—chambered in .44 Special in particular—are my passion. My good friend Allan Jones of Speer/CCI, author of that company's latest reloading manual, has a superb 7-1/2-inch barreled .44 Special New Service Target Model that he allows me the pleasure of shooting from time to time. We have both shot this sixgun at one hundred yards offhand at paper plates. This old sixgun was really built well because it seems to have on-board radar, which makes it virtually impossible to miss if shooters even come close to doing their part.

The New Service was standardized at barrel lengths of 4-1/2, 5-1/2, and 7-1/2 inches. The Target Models carried either a 6- or 7-1/2-inch barrel and were chambered in .38 Special, .357 Magnum, .44 Special, .45 Colt, and .45 ACP. Other barrel lengths and a few other calibers were also available.

Colt had introduced a big bore double action sixgun by the turn of the century. Smith & Wesson would not bring its own forth until 1908, but when it did, it was the best double action sixgun ever offered by any factory at any time. We will pick up with twentieth century Smith & Wesson double actions in the chapter on the .44 Special.

Most of the big bore sixguns from the last part of the nineteenth century only reside in collectors' hands these days, but their influence lives on in the big bore sixguns still being produced by Colt, Freedom Arms, Ruger, Smith & Wesson, and Texas Longhorn Arms.

Special thanks to Jim Supica of Olde Towne Dispatch and co-author, along with Richard Nahas, of Standard Catalog of Smith & Wesson (Krause Publications 1996) for this chapter's pictures of antique sixguns.

CHAPTER 2

THE .44 SPECIAL—
CARTRIDGE OF THE CENTURY?

Just before the close of the last century, Smith & Wesson introduced a new sixgun and cartridge combination. The revolver was the Model 1899 Hand Ejector, chambered in a cartridge that was simply a lengthened .38 Long Colt with the blackpowder charge increased by 20 percent and the bullet weight changed from 150 to 158 grains. The .38 Smith & Wesson Special was born and housed in the Military & Police sixgun now known as the Model 10 K-frame. This was the first modern double action sixgun. The fact that it is still in production in many forms attests to its great design.

The .38 Special Smith & Wesson cartridge and the Military & Police revolver certainly comprise one of the most popular cartridge/sixgun combinations ever designed. Big bore fanciers, however, looked at the size of the little sixgun and wanted more. The .38 Spe-

cial was fine for police departments in New York and Boston, but Westerners still clung to their large caliber heritage. The little double action sixgun would not replace the Colt Single Actions in .45 and .44 caliber in the leather of many a western peace officer.

Smith & Wesson did not forget the big bore sixgunners; it just took a mite longer for the first twentieth century big bore double action Smith & Wesson to come forth. Tooling for the new sixgun was completed in 1907 and the Model 1908 in .44 caliber arrived as the New Century one year later. Once again, Smith & Wesson took an existing cartridge, the .44 Russian, lengthened it to .38 Special length, increased the blackpowder charge from 23 to 26 grains, and the .44 Special was born.

The new sixgun was more than just a larger Military & Police. Two major changes resulted in the fin-

The .44 Russian was lengthened from .097 to 1.160 inches to become the .44 Special in 1907, which was in turn lengthened to 1.285 inches and became the .44 Magnum in 1955.

est double action sixgun manufactured—ever—before or since. The ejector rod was now fully enclosed with a shroud under the barrel, and the new .44 Hand Ejector First Model's cylinder locked at the rear, at the front of the ejector rod, and also at the front of the cylinder with a beautifully machined locking mechanism at the back end of the barrel shroud and front of the yoke. This third locking feature gave the New Century .44 Special another name: The Triple-Lock.

The Triple-Lock, with its new cartridge, the .44 Special, was cataloged in both blue and nickel finishes with standard barrel lengths of 4, 5, 6-1/2, and 7-1/2 inches as a fixed-sighted duty sixgun, or an adjustable-sighted target revolver. The sixgun was

thoroughly modern, even ahead of its time, but the cartridge stayed in the nineteenth century. The ammunition companies did not significantly improve upon the .44 Special's blackpowder roots. In fact, even today the standard .44 Special loading from either Remington or Winchester is a 246 grain round-nosed bullet at around 700 feet per second muzzle velocity.

Couple the lack of ammunition, that was not even on par with the old .45 Colt, with the fact that the Smith & Wesson factory did not allow sixgunners the time to really discover the Triple-Lock, and a major sixgun tragedy loomed ahead. In 1915, after less than 16,000 New Centurys had been produced, at a selling price of $21, it was deemed to be too expensive to

Smith & Wesson .44s, all with 6-1/2-inch barrels: New Century Triple-Lock .44 Special, 1950 Target .44 Special, and .44 Magnum. The latter two have BearHug's Skeeter Skelton stocks.

manufacture and the decision was made to drop both the enclosed ejector rod housing and the third locking feature.

The .44 Second Model Hand Ejector without the enclosed ejector rod and third locking feature arrived in 1915 and sold for $19. For the sake of $2 a beautiful sixgun was dropped from production forever! The Second Model lasted until 1940 with less than 18,000 units being produced and, like the Triple-Lock, it was offered in .45 Colt, .44-40, and .38-40, in addition to the standard .44 Special. Hand Ejectors are obtainable but difficult to locate in .44 Special, and close to impossible to come by in .45 Colt, .44-40, and .38-40. I feel very fortunate to have a .44 Special Triple-Lock. Most of the early Smith & Wesson double action sixguns of this type I have encountered in my lifetime have been those originally chambered for the British .455, used by the English and Canadian military, and now rechambered to .45 Colt. These sixguns, known as the Mark II Hand Ejectors, were identical to the .44 Special First and Second Model Hand Ejectors except for the chambering and British proof marks. They were not serial numbered in the First and Second Model series, but rather carried their own serial number ranges. While less than 50,000 .44 Hand Ejector First and Second Models were manufactured, nearly 75,000 .455s were turned out.

Both the .44 Special and the Smith & Wesson sixgun, with the enclosed ejector rod that eventually became standard on most big bore Smiths, may have disappeared had it not been for the Texas firm of Wolf & Klar. Smith & Wesson had received numerous inquiries about a new .44 Special with the enclosed ejector rod housing like that on the First Model. This one feature made the Smith & Wesson .44 sixgun look better, balance better, and certainly added to its strength as compared to the Second Model. The bottom line accountants at Smith & Wesson did not feel demand warranted resurrecting the Triple-Lock. Wolf & Klar, a Fort Worth distributor, placed an order for 3,500 .44 Specials with enclosed ejector rods and the Model 1926, or .44 Hand Ejector Third Model, was born. The third locking feature was gone, but a heavy-duty .44 Special was back. It would soon become quite popular with southwest peace officers such as Texas Ranger Lone Wolf Gonzualles.

During all this time, the .44 Special cartridge was virtually ignored by ammunition factories. The stan-

Elmer Keith's idea of the perfect sixgun in 1929—his #5 .44 Special. Keith started with a Single Action Army, probably a Bisley Model. The Bisley backstrap was mated with a standard Colt Single Action Army triggerguard, and a wide hammer was fitted along with adjustable sights. Beautiful full engraving and ivory stocks, top, give a clear example of what a sixgun can be.

dard loading was identical to the 1870s .44 Russian even though the big double action sixguns were much stronger. I have to believe that none really knew what they had in the excellent .44 Special sixgun and cartridge combination. Something, however, was poised to happen to change all of that and alter the course of sixgunning forever.

About the same time that Wolf & Klar was ordering, and Smith & Wesson was producing, the Third Model .44 Specials, a hitherto unknown young cowboy entered the picture. "I started to celebrate the morning of the Fourth. Picked up an old .45 S.A. Army 5-1/2 inch loaded with 40 grains bulk by my Ideal measure and 258 grain Ideal bullet, stepped out an upstairs porch and turned the old gun up at a 45 degree angle and started shooting. When the gun rose from recoil of the first cartridge I unconsciously hooked my thumb over the hammer spur and thus cocked gun as it recovered from recoil. When I turned the next one loose I was almost deafened by the report and saw a little flash of flame. My hand automatically cocked and snapped again but no report. I stopped then knowing that something was wrong. The upper half of three chambers was gone. Also one

cartridge and half of another case. Also the top strap over the cylinder. My ears were ringing otherwise I was all O.K."

Blowing up that .45 Colt sixgun started Elmer Keith on his long career as a writer and sixgun experimenter. At this point in his life, he had never seen a .44 Special even though Smith & Wessons were available in both First and Second Models and Colt had produced a few Colt Single Actions and New Service double actions in .44 Special chambering. From what little Keith did know about the .44 Special, he deduced that this would be the platform for his big bore sixgunning.

By 1929, with the aid of Harold Croft, Neal Houchins, R.F. Sedgley, and J.D. O'Meara, Keith had what he considered the perfect sixgun. The basic gun was built under Croft's supervision. In 1927, Croft had shared four custom single actions with Keith bearing Croft's model numbers 1,2,3, and 4. When Croft and Keith worked out the details for the perfect single action it became Keith's famous #5 Single Action.

What, then, comprised this perfect single action? The caliber, of course, had to be *the* big bore cartridge of the period, the .44 Special. The basic sixgun

Three custom Single Actions, all fitted with ivory stocks, are from the collection of Elmer Keith: 7-1/2-inch .44 Special, 4-3/4-inch .45 Colt, and the famous #5, a 5-1/2-inch .44 Special.

was a Colt Single Action, probably a Bisley Model. Keith mated the high backstrap of the Bisley with a standard Single Action triggerguard for the grip frame. The hammer is the wide Bisley-style for easy cocking, the sights are a fully adjustable rear with a post front sight for long-range shooting, and the cylinder is held in place by an ingenious locking mechanism. Both the cylinder latch and the grip frame are duplicated in Texas Longhorn Arms' Improved Number Five that will be covered in a later chapter.

This sixgun's barrel is an easy shooting and packing 5-1/2 inches, the entire sixgun is fully engraved and blued, and it has carved ivory stocks. It has been my privilege to handle the Keith #5. It is a marvelous sixgun by anyone's standards, even seventy years after it was built. Using the #5, Keith would bring the .44 Special out of the nineteenth century and develop it to its full potential.

Keith first worked with 280 grain blunt-nosed bullets and #80 powder. He had the power he wanted, but the bullet was lacking in long-range accuracy. Keith went to the drawing board and designed the now famous .44 semi-wadcutter that bears his name. To be a true Keith bullet, a .44 semi-wadcutter must have three equally-sized, full-caliber driving bands and a large square-cornered grease groove to hold lots of lubrication. Cast hard, sized, and lubed, the bullet weight should be right at 250 grains. The truest Keith designs today are found from Lyman (#429421), NEI (#260.429), and RCBS (#44-250KT).

Keith developed a standard .44 Special heavy loading of his bullet, standard primers, and 18.5 grains of the then new powder, Hercules #2400, in the balloon head brass available at the time. When solid head brass arrived, case capacity was reduced and Keith dropped his load to 17 grains of #2400. Both of these loads are heavy Magnum-style loads and should only be used in heavy-framed sixguns of recent—after World War II—manufacture such as the Colt New Frontier, Single Action Army, and the Smith & Wesson Models 24 and 624, all originally chambered in .44 Special.

Keith always claimed a full 1,200 feet per second muzzle velocity with his original load. When I duplicated it in some old balloon head brass I came across and fired it in a Colt New Frontier .44 Special with a 7-1/2-inch barrel, velocity chronographed 1,233 feet per second over the Oehler skyscreens. Keith, as on most things, was right. His 17 grain load in newer brass clocks out at 1,140 feet per second in a 4-3/4-inch Colt Single Action Army .44 Special and 1,210 in a 7-1/2-inch barreled New Frontier.

Keith spent the next thirty years advocating his heavy loading of the .44 Special with a 250 grain bullet at an even 1,200 feet per second. Ammunition companies were afraid of older sixguns letting go with this load. I certainly don't blame them and I would never use this load in my Triple-Lock or New Service .44 Specials. Keith countered with "bring out a new sixgun and lengthen the brass so it will not chamber in the old sixguns." His pleas fell on deaf ears for three decades.

It was obvious to me very early on that my shooting life would be wrapped up in the .44 Special. First, I acquired a copy of Keith's 1955 book, *Sixguns*. This book arrived just before the advent of the .44 Magnum that Keith was directly responsible for. Throughout this must-read book, Keith extols the virtues of the .44 Special for long-range, game, and defensive use. I had to have a .44 Special.

I found myself in the same predicament as Keith did thirty years earlier. The .44 Special is, was, and always will be, the true sixgun connoisseur's cartridge and sixgun combination, but they have never been readily found on dealers' shelves. It was difficult to find a .44 Special before World War I, in the 1920s, during the 1950s, and it is even today. My new wife solidly entrenched herself in my heart forever on our first Christmas together when she presented me with a brand new 6-1/2-inch .44 Special Smith & Wesson Model 1950 Target. I had begun a lifelong love affair with the .44 Special.

Not only did my wife present me with my first .44 Special, but she also made it possible for me to meet another vocal proponent of the .44 Special. It has always been my regular habit to read the "640 GUNS" section every day in the morning paper's want ads; I expect to find maybe one special sixgun per year. In the early 1970s, I found one particular ad that read "Colt Single Action .44 and old belt and holster."

The address was at a trailer park just outside of town. I hustled over and found a First Generation 7-1/2-inch Colt Single Action with cartridge belt and holster. The owner explained that the .44 had belonged to his uncle, who wore it regularly as a sheriff in Colorado, and that the marks on the top strap were from his blood when he was shot—he was more concerned about having himself patched up than cleaning the Colt. As I handled the Colt, I could scarcely contain myself. Except for the minor pitting on the top strap, the old Colt .44 Single Action was mechanically in excellent shape and the case coloring had turned a beautifully aged gray. The left side of the barrel was marked "RUSSIAN AND S&W SPECIAL 44"—this was a very rare single action!

"How much?" I asked as I contemplated my budget. "Four hundred and fifty dollars." I was sorely tempted, but because we were paying for three kids

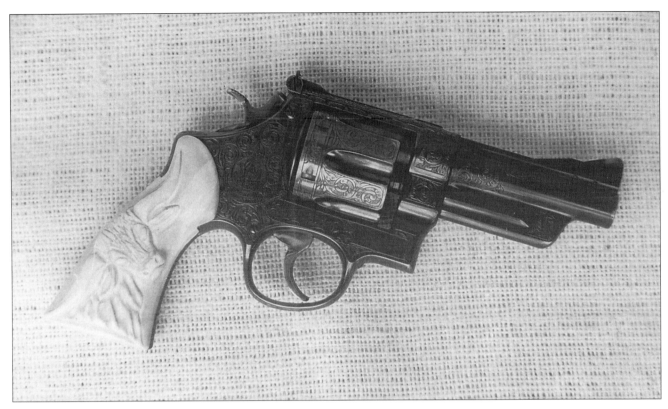

This 4-inch Smith & Wesson .44 Special, engraved and stocked by the Gun ReBlu Company, was Elmer Keith's personal and favorite double action sixgun. It was carried every day prior to the advent of the .44 Magnum.

The author's experiments led to this superbly accurate load consisting of 5.5 grains of Winchester 452AA under Bull-X's 240 grain semi-wadcutter at 850 fps in Smith & Wesson's 6-1/2-inch Model 24 .44 Special. All shots at 25 yards are in the 1-inch square orange section.

to attend private school, I felt it was out of the question. I reluctantly thanked the man for his time and left. My excitement stayed high all the way home and it was impossible to contain my disappointment as I told my wife all about the Colt .44 Special. She was more than a little surprised that I was able to resist buying that beautiful sixgun.

Later that day she headed out to do some shopping and I asked her to stop at the local boot repair shop. I had been so stirred up by the .44 Colt that I had forgotten to pick up my finished boots. When she returned home, she handed me the boots with a slight smile on her face. As I took the boots, I realized they felt a few pounds heavier than normal. The Colt was in the left boot! She had gone out on her own and purchased the .44 Special! You hold on tightly to a wife such as this one!

After doing a little research on the Colt and finding out how really rare it was, we decided it belonged to a collector, not a shooter like me. We eventually ended up trading it for the $450 we paid for it plus two shooting Colt sixguns, a Second Generation Colt

Single Action Army 5-1/2-inch .44 Special and a 7-1/2-inch New Frontier chambered in .45 Colt. That isn't the end of the story, though. This Colt .44 Special and Russian was my ticket to meeting someone very special.

Later that year I attended the NRA Show in Salt Lake City and carried pictures of the old Colt, including a close-up of the barrel inscription. I had one purpose in mind—I was looking for one particular individual. When I found him dressed in a dark suit, colored shooting glasses, and a white Stetson, I simply handed him the picture of the barrel close-up. He grabbed me by the arm and said: "Son, let's go find a place to talk." The man was Skeeter Skelton and I had found the way to his heart. Skeeter was second only to Elmer Keith in praising the virtues of the .44 Special during his writing career. Whereas Keith retired his .44 Specials after the .44 Magnum arrived, Skelton tried the .44 Magnum, found the Special better for most purposes, and went back to his first love.

No sixgun/cartridge combination has ever been so widely experimented with as the .44 Special. Keith was the first, but not the only one before World War II, to extol the virtues of the .44 Special. A group of reloaders, the .44 Associates, shared reloading information by mail and pitied those who were not smart enough to discover the .44 Special like they had. They even produced one of the first loading manuals dedicated exclusively to the .44 Special.

Even though there are many excellent .44 caliber jacketed bullets available, the .44 Special remains, first and foremost, a cast bullet sixgun. This is true for two major reasons. First, the .44 Special should not be driven to velocities that will take the greatest advantage of the expansive features of jacketed bullets. One notable exception is the Speer 225 hollowpoint and 240 grain solid jacketed bullets that consist of a full copper cup that holds a pure lead bullet. These bullets will expand at reasonable .44 Special velocities. Second, most .44 Special barrels are tight—with groove diameters of .426 inch in Colts and .428 inch in Smith & Wessons—while most jacketed .44 bullets are .430 inch in diameter. The problem is readily apparent because I do not relish driving heavy loaded .430-inch jacketed bullets down .426-inch holes. With home cast bullets, it is simply a matter of sizing bullets accordingly and bullet manufacturers such as Bull-X are now offering cast bullets in both .427-inch and .430-inch diameters.

Great loads abound for the .44 Special. In the 1950s, we did not have the abundance of powders we have today. The three standard loads I settled with can be improved upon today, but old habits are hard to break. These loads are the standard Keith load with Lyman's bullet design, the same bullet over 6 grains of Unique for a factory duplicate, and finally, 7.5 grains of Unique for 900 to 1,000 feet per second depending upon barrel length. While I keep an abundance of the heavy Keith load and the factory duplicate load on hand, my favorite load is the 950 feet per second load that delivers plenty of power for most sixgun applications and is still kind to wrists that have been ravaged by too many full-house loads for too many years from the .44 Magnum and beyond.

Truthfully, most .44 Magnum shooters settle on a loading for their everyday use that is a duplicate of the .44 Special/250 grain bullet/7.5 grains of Unique/950 feet per second combination. The .44 Magnum is a great cartridge and is, in fact, the King of the Sixgun Cartridges. In full-house loadings, though, it requires great strength and concentration for successful use.

Most of us are at our limit of comfort with the Keith .44 Special load, so why not use a .44 Special? This load shoots five-shot groups of 1 inch or less at 25 yards in both my Colt New Frontier 7-1/2-inch and my Smith & Wesson 6-1/2-inch Model. With either sixgun and the Keith load, I am certainly adequately armed for any deer or black bear that walks in Idaho.

Double Action packin' pistols: 4-inch M624 with BearHug stocks, 4-inch 1950 with ivory stocks, 4-inch .44 Magnum, round-butted and tuned by Mag-Na-Port with BearHug stocks, and 4-inch .44 Magnum, engraved by Jim Riggs with BearHug Skeeter Skelton stocks.

A "dog" becomes a prized possession: This pitted .357 Ruger Blackhawk was rechambered and rebored to .44 Special, then bead-blasted and matte-blued by Hamilton Bowen.

Forty-four Special sixguns may not be offered by Colt or Ruger, but they are easy to acquire via the custom route. Ruger brought out its .357 Magnum Blackhawk in 1955 with a promise to offer it later in .44 Special and .45 Colt, which were the reigning big bores of the day. It was not to be. By the end of 1955, the .44 Magnum was a reality. Ruger chambered three test .357 Blackhawks for the .44 Magnum and when one blew during proof testing, the company came out with the larger-framed .44 Blackhawk that would evolve into today's Super Blackhawk and New Model Blackhawk. It is a pity that the .44 Magnum came along so soon and upstaged the .44 Special and denied sixgunners a fine .44 Special sixgun from Ruger, but, alas, it was meant to be.

Not to be thwarted by an unkind fate, I decided to have a .44 Special Ruger made to my specifications after reading of such a conversion by Skeeter Skelton in the 1970s. A number of mistakes were made with my first custom Ruger. For instance, I opted for a front sight with a red insert instead of an easier to see plain black front sight. At least black is much easier

to see these days and a black post sight is the best of all.

The Ruger Old Model, or Three-Screw .357, was sent off to a gunsmith back East who rechambered the cylinder to .44 Special and relined the original barrel. The lining would have worked fine, but I believe he used a section of .444 Marlin barrel because the twist was very slow. The dream .44 Special would not shoot for the proverbial sour apples unless a full-house load of a 250 grain bullet at 1,200 feet per second was used and I did not build this gun up to shoot only Magnum-type loads. In fact, with any Ruger .44 Special conversion built on either the .357 Flat-Top or Old Model Blackhawks, I would recommend that the Keith load be used only sparingly.

The barrel was discarded and replaced with a 4-5/8-inch tube taken from my .44 Blackhawk, which made the .44 Special shoot fine with all loads. The whole gun was then finished in bright blue and fitted with ivory grips. Now this .44 Special wears a beautiful pair of Circassian walnut stocks by Roy Fishpaw. A stainless steel grip frame, like that found on the

Ruger Old Army, has also been added to give the .44 Special a little more weight. While Bob Munden was in town doing his Fast Draw show, he took the time to do an action job on this .44 Special. It is now super smooth and slick due to his spring, stone, and file work. Munden is a real genius when it comes to slickin' up single actions whether they are Colts, Rugers, or replicas.

That .44 Special Ruger was my favorite for a number of years until I met Andy Horvath. I saw his ad simply labeled ".44 SPECIAL CONVERSIONS" and contacted him at his Diagonal Rd. Gun Shop. While I talked with Horvath, I soon learned that this was a man who loved sixguns in general and, in particular, single action .44 Specials.

I wanted a very special .44 Special. I asked Horvath if he could do a round-butted, 4-inch barreled .44 built on a Ruger .357 Three-Screw, or Old Model, Blackhawk—a real .44 Special packin' pistol. The answer came back affirmative and off went a like-new 6-1/2-inch .357 Three-Screw Blackhawk, a 7-1/2-inch Super Blackhawk barrel, and some special items I had

been saving for just such a project. I pulled my last Ruger blued steel ejector rod housing and my last 1960s wide Super Blackhawk hammer from my parts box. I also sent a pair of rosewood Ruger grips that were from an over-run of .22 Single-Six Colorado Centennial stocks in the 1970s.

That .44 Special Ruger was, and is, a superb little Ruger. My article in *American Handgunner* on Horvath and his work set him on his way to becoming a nationally-known sixgunsmith. Even Hollywood actors noticed the L'il Ruger and called to ask about using it in a film. I didn't send it, because everyone knows what Hollywood actors do with a sixgun when it is empty, but Horvath was contacted and wound up making a sixgun for the movie as well as several such sixguns for actors Mickey Rourke and Don Johnson.

The bluing on the L'il Ruger .44 Special by Horvath is deep and well-matched with the round-butted grip. Horvath had polished the standard aluminum grip frame and round-butted it so it slipped into my hand perfectly. Horvath also jeweled the sides of the hammer and trigger and made a cylinder pin with a flat

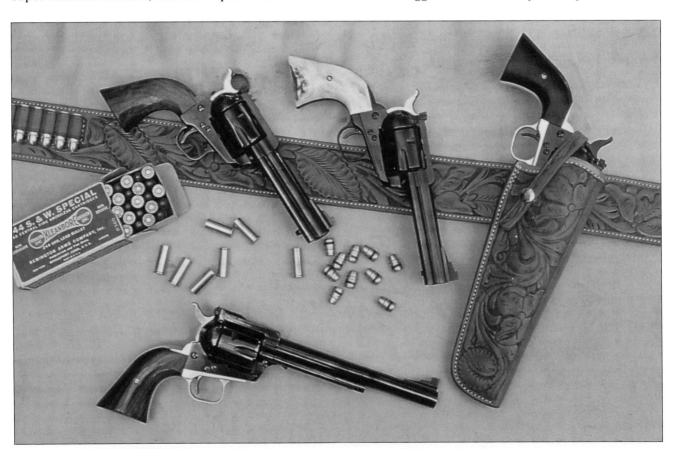

Custom .44 Specials built on Ruger .357 Blackhawks by Bill Grover and Hamilton Bowen: All feature rechambered cylinders. One-piece walnut stocks on 4-3/4-inch Flat-Top by Grover, stag stocks by Charles Able on 4-5/8-inch Flat-Top with rebored barrel by Bowen, and walnut stocks by Charles Able on 7-1/2-inch sixgun by Grover. Bowen's 7-1/2-inch sixgun has El Paso's full floral-carved Tom Threepersons leather.

face to allow maximum ejector rod travel to fully extract empties. My Horvath L'il Ruger has been engraved by grip-maker Tedd Adamovich and now wears the standard grip frame and ivory grips from my original .44 Special Ruger.

My passion for .44 Specials on Ruger .357s had been so inflamed by these two fine .44s that I began squirreling away both Flat-Top and Old Model Black-hawk .357s for later conversions to .44 Special. Old Model and the original Flat-Top Blackhawks are built on a smaller frame than the .357 New Model Black-hawks available since 1973. The latter, like all Black-hawks, are now built on the Super Blackhawk .44 frame size.

A number of years ago I saw a very special .44 Spe-cial on a Ruger Old Model. The barrel was 4-5/8 inches in length, the grip frame was brightly pol-ished, and the grips were made from bighorn sheep horns. Bart Skelton shared that it had been commis-sioned by his dad, Skeeter, before he died. Bob Baer built it and it now resides with gunwriter John Woot-ters. That sixgun made my heart pound even faster for other .44 Specials. Over the past couple of years, six .357 Magnum Rugers have been sent off to two top gunsmiths for conversion to .44 Special. Two of these went to master gunmaker and gunsmith Bill Grover of Texas Longhorn Arms and the other four went to top gunsmith Hamilton Bowen. Apparently, Bowen's fire has also been lit by the bug; he is now experimenting with Old Model Rugers in all calibers himself.

Six nearly identical Rugers went off to these mas-ter 'smiths, but they would all take different turns except for the two destined to be a matched pair. We will look at the sixguns from Bill Grover first.

Grover had been instrumental, along with friend and NRA representative Bob Baer, in building the so-called Skeeter Gun, the .44 Special sixgun that Skeeter Skelton had commissioned. Its serial number is SS1. As related earlier, John Wootters now has this sixgun. I now have SS4. The second Skeeter Gun, SS2 in the series, is now in Bart Skelton's hands, Bob Baer has SS3, Bill Grover has SS5, friend and fellow writer Terry Murbach has SS6, and Sheriff Jim Wilson, also a good friend and fellow writer, has the last gun with the serial number SS7. All of us gathered together and held a special seven gun salute and memorial service to Skelton in 1992 at the Shootists Holiday. There will be no more .44 Specials built in this special SS num-bering series.

Although all seven of us have SS sixguns, each reveals something different about the individual tastes of the owners. My particular SS4 started life as a .357 Magnum Ruger Flat-Top Blackhawk from the 1950s. It was factory-reblued and was not a collec-tor's item. None of the other .357 Blackhawks that were used for conversions to .44 Special were any-where near collector's item status, either.

Grover and I put our heads together on this one, so a double influence can be seen. The cylinder has been tightly rechambered to .44 Special to allow the use of .429-inch diameter bullets, but kept to mini-mum dimensions for long case life. The barrel/cylin-der gap was set at .0025 inches. The Ruger XR3 grip frame and steel ejector housing were not discarded, but saved for the other .44 Special Grover was build-ing. In their place, Grover fitted steel Colt parts, a Colt backstrap and triggerguard and a Colt ejector rod housing along with a Bullseye headed ejector rod.

With the installation of the Colt backstrap and trig-gerguard, it was necessary to machine a special hanger to accept the Ruger mainspring and strut. Grover also replaced the trigger return spring with a new coil spring. Grover says he made the one-piece walnut stocks "...to the likeness of Taffin. Thin, gives better control and fast handling, they make the gun point like your finger plus gives the gun better looks. Not only do you want your six-shooter to shoot good but look good also." Amen to that Brother Bill!

For sighting equipment, Grover installed a Texas Longhorn Arms Number Five bold, flat, black front sight and a Number Five base pin with a large, easy to grasp head. Now it was time for Grover to turn the gun over to the man who does the final polishing and bluing. Robert Luna did the match polishing to a mir-rored finish, which resulted in a very beautiful sixgun. Grover trained Luna himself and holds him in high esteem as one of the best in the business today. I agree wholeheartedly.

The front of the cylinder was beveled like it was on the old Colt Single Action Armys. Rod Ford engraved "SKEETER SKELTON .44 SPECIAL" on the barrel's left side and "TEXAS LONGHORN ARMS INC, RICHMOND TEXAS" on the topstrap. The serial number is marked S.S.4 in the same three places as the original Colts: on the front bottom of the backstrap, in the front of the triggerguard, and on the frame in front of the trigger-guard screw.

Grover is justly proud of his work and thinks this is one of the finest sixguns in existence, and again, I wholeheartedly agree. I expect to enjoy it the rest of my life and then pass it on to one of my grandsons. This is truly a classic single action.

For the second .44 Special-style sixgun, Grover started with a 10-inch Ruger Super Blackhawk barrel and built a 7-1/2-inch-barreled sixgun. The XR3 grip frame of SS4 now resides on this sixgun along with rosewood stocks by Charles Able. This long-range sixgun made to compliment the SS4 packin' pistol also wears a Number Five front sight and a Number Five base pin. The cylinder has also been beveled with the barrel/cylinder gap set at .0025 inches and again, Robert Luna has done his polishing and bluing magic. The top of the frame reads "TEXAS LONG-HORN ARMS, INC. RICHMOND TEXAS" and the left side of the barrel is marked "44 SPECIAL." Its serial number, JT1, is also marked in three places like the SS4 sixgun.

Both of these .44 Special sixguns shoot my every-day working load of 7.5 grains under a 240 grain Bull-X bullet superbly. Bull-X not only makes fine bullets, but is also in the leather business. My 7-1/2-inch Grover .44 Special now rides in one of its Chaparral rigs. This 1880s-style rig is one of the best I have seen. My .44 fits in it perfectly, the workmanship is superb, and the design is excellent.

Hamilton Bowen is well-known among sixgunners who appreciate really fine sixguns. He is not only a top gunsmith and past president of the American Pistolsmith's Guild, but he is also one of the handful of gunsmiths in the country, along with such men as John Linebaugh, Bob Baer, Bill Grover, Dick Casull, Bob Munden, and Andy Horvath, who really understands single action sixguns.

Three Flat-Top Ruger Blackhawks and one Old Model Blackhawk .357 have been sent off to Bowen over the past few years. Spelling my 7-1/2-inch JT1 .44 Special sixgun from Grover is a Bowen-built 7-1/2-inch .44 Special that also fits the Chaparral rig perfectly. The sixgun done by Bowen also has a post front sight, polished grip frame with black micarta grips by Charles Able, and a blued, rather than polished hammer. The left side of the barrel is marked ".44 SPECIAL CAL." The barrel is from a Ruger Super Blackhawk and the bluing is a little more subdued than the Grover sixgun because this was designed more as a working gun than a highly polished presentation sixgun. The blue finish matches quite nicely with the dull black micarta stocks.

Bowen, of course, did all his niceties on this sixgun, like he does on all others. He removed any excess endshake, smoothed out the action, and tight-

The "Skeeter Gun": This custom .44 Special was built for Skeeter Skelton by Bob Baer. Starting with an Old Model .357 Blackhawk, Baer rechambered the cylinder, fitted a .44 barrel cut to 4-5/8 inches, and installed rams horn grips from a sheep Skeeter took in Canada.

Custom .44 Special Ruger by Bill Grover: Grover started with a Flat-Top Ruger .357 Blackhawk, rechambered the cylinder, fitted a 4-3/4-inch .44 barrel, Colt ejector rod housing, one-piece grips, and used a Colt Single Action Army backstrap and triggerguard. This blued sixgun is all deeply polished steel.

ened where necessary. I really do like 7-1/2-inch single actions for long-range shooting and this one now proudly joins my Flat-Top Blackhawk .44 Magnum, Colt New Frontier .44 Special, Texas Longhorn Arms West Texas Flat-Top Target .44, and JT1 as some of the finest long-range .44s extant.into

One of the Flat-Top .357s sent to Bowen was fine mechanically, but had been ridden hard and put up wet, so to speak, and as a result, the finish was pitted. Our choice was to either do major surgery in the form of excessive polishing and filing before bluing, or take the easier and more practical route of a bead-blast finish. The latter choice made a lot of sense to me and this fine little packin' pistol wears a real working finish. The XR3 grip frame used on this sixgun was bead- blasted and nickeled by a previous owner and, along with standard Ruger walnut stocks from the 1950s, mates up fine with the subdued blue finish. This is the gun that will go in the holster when the going is likely to be anything but easy.

The final sixguns from Bowen, a matched pair, are all blue and wear perfectly executed and fitted polished staghorn stocks again from Charles Able. At first glance, they look like standard .357 Magnum 1950-ish Flat-Top Blackhawks, but close examination reveals the Texas Longhorn Arms Number Five front sight, the larger holes in the cylinder and barrel, and ".44 SPECIAL CAL." marked on the left side of the frame. Some long, cold winter I will carve a special

set of leather for these guns. I haven't quite decided if I should go totally traditional and make a double set 1880s-style with a wide belt with a double row of cartridge loops, or perhaps a 1940s-type Hollywood rig such as that worn by Tim Holt or Wild Bill Elliot, or...if the Idaho winter is long enough, perhaps I will come up with several outfits. That is part of the great pleasure of sixgunning.

Going the double action route with a custom .44 Special is not easy, but can be accomplished by rechambering a Smith & Wesson Highway Patrolman, the now discontinued Model 28 to .44 Special, and by fitting a Smith & Wesson barrel available from World Gun Parts.

I recently found such a sixgun already made up with a 4-inch barrel at a gun show. The price was only $200, so something had to be wrong with it; it is impossible to even find a Highway Patrolman for that price, let alone a customized example. The Highway Patrolman's bright, blue-finished barrel did not match the subdued, matte-finished frame, but would it shoot?

I questioned the dealer who had the table and found that the gun had been built up in Washington, but the guy who had it said it would not shoot. I could take it on the stipulation that I could bring it back for a full refund if this was the case. That was not the case. The custom .44 Special turned out to be a superb shooter. It simply did not shoot to point of aim. Apparently the

Andy Horvath built this 4-inch Ruger .44 Special with a rounded butt and wide hammer.

previous owner was unaware of the fact that the sights could be adjusted. With a couple of turns of both the windage and elevation screws, I was popping spent shotgun shells at 35 yards with my favorite 900 foot per second .44 Special load.

So what does one do with a matte-finished sixgun with a bright blue barrel? This Model 28 .44 Special was sent off to Hamilton Bowen, who bead-blasted the entire sixgun before placing it in the bluing tank. The result is a perfect double action mate to the previously mentioned matte blue-finished Ruger single action .44 Special. I now have a pair of real workin' sixguns with no worries as to whether the finish will be hurt in bad weather or adverse conditions.

I have also built up a couple of .44 Specials on Colt Bisleys. The .44 Special was never a factory chambering in the Bisley Colt, but a few years ago it was possible to find well-worn Bisleys at very good prices and also to pick up Second Generation .44 Special barrels and cylinders, but alas, those days are gone forever. Both the 4-3/4-inch and 7-1/2-inch Bisleys I had built up are excellent shooters.

As far as American manufacturers are concerned, the .44 Special sixgun has fallen on hard times. There are many .44 Magnum-chambered sixguns available, but no manufacturer offers a full-sized .44 Special. This is not a total loss, though, because .44 Magnum sixguns make easy shooting sixguns when fired with .44 Special loads. This is especially true when pressing a .44 Magnum into service as a defensive sixgun. A short-barreled Colt, Ruger, or Smith & Wesson double action sixgun is very easy to control with .44 Special factory loads.

The big advantage of a .44 Special sixgun over the same in .44 Magnum chambering is the fact that .44 Special sixguns are much lighter and easier to pack. Simply compare a Colt Single Action to a Ruger Super Blackhawk, or a Smith &Wesson 1950 Target to a Model 29 .44 Magnum and one can easily see the difference. A half pound of weight makes a big difference during a long day.

One problem could surface if many .44 Special loads are used in a .44 Magnum on a regular basis. All sixgun cartridges deposit a ring around the inside of the cylinder chamber at the mouth of the fired case.

The Colt Single Action Bisley Model was never factory-chambered in .44 Special. These have been converted to .44 Special. Hamilton Bowen completely restored the top gun.

The .44 Special, which is shorter than the .44 Magnum, will leave a ring that could interfere with the chambering and firing of the longer .44 Magnum case. If the build-up is such that it interferes with the chambering, it will also interfere with the release of the bullet as the cartridge is fired, which results in much higher pressures. This is the same problem that can occur if the .38 Special is used in a .357 Magnum and definitely will occur when the .45 Colt is used in a .454 Casull.

The .44 Special was the first new sixgun cartridge of the twentieth century. It paved the way for the .357 Magnum, the .44 Magnum, and all the other Magnum sixgun cartridges. Without the experiments of men like Keith and the .44 Associates with the .44 Special, the potential of Magnum cartridges would never have been realized. It is truly more than a trailblazer to be relegated to the museum display, though. For most of us it is the only sixgun and cartridge we will ever need for 99 percent of our big bore shooting.

CHAPTER 3

THE .45 COLT—
125 YEARS OF SERVICE

The .45 Colt is as old as the sixguns carried by Custer's 7th Cavalry at Little Big Horn and as new as the custom .45 Abilene I used to take a ten-point whitetail this past fall, with a whole lot of grand history in between. The Colt company was caught napping in the 1860s as Smith & Wesson hired Rollin White, who held the patent for bored-through cylinders that accepted fixed-ammunition. As a result, Smith & Wesson introduced the first big bore sixgun firing cartridges rather than round balls loaded over blackpowder through the front of the cylinder. That first big bore sixgun was the .44 Smith & Wesson American.

Colt may have been asleep after the Civil War, while it rested on its laurels and fat bank account from Army contracts for 1860 cap-n-ball sixguns, but immediately woke up and prepared for the ending of the White patent. Three years after Smith & Wesson's introduction of the first big bore sixgun to fire fixed-ammunition, Colt did it bigger and better. In 1873, the Colt Single Action Army chambered for the .45 Colt arrived on the sixgunning scene. After more than a century, the same basic sixgun is still available, both from Colt and as a replica from various importers, and the cartridge is more popular than ever. This speaks extremely well of the Colt Single Action Army and the .45 Colt.

My first big bore sixgun was a 4-3/4-inch Colt Single Action Army, now referred to by collectors as the Pre-war, or First Generation Single Actions. Chambered in .38-40, or .38 Winchester Centerfire, that Single Action started my lifelong love affair with the Colt. Shortly after purchasing this fine old sixgun, the Second Generation Colt Single Action Army arrived after a fifteen year absence from Colt's production schedule. This brand new 7-1/2-inch Single Action Army purchased in 1957 was in .45 and I've never been without at least one .45 Colt sixgun over the past four decades.

The .45 Colt is such a grand cartridge and the Single Action Army, with a history so thoroughly entwined with the cartridge, is such a beautiful piece of the sixgunner's art that I am almost willing to say both were not invented, but in reality, like electricity and atomic energy, were discovered. They are both that good!

The .45 Colt cartridge is the only centerfire sixgun cartridge that spans the time from the blackpowder era to the heaviest big bores available today. It is perfectly at home with 255 grain flat-point bullets, properly lubed and loaded with 35 grains of Triple F at 800 feet per second in duplicated 1875-style blackpowder loads for Cowboy Action Shooting or, in the proper sixgun, with 300 grain Keith or LBT bullets at 1,550 feet per second—it can run with any sixgun now in existence and also takes the toughest game animals in the world.

The .45 Colt has been hampered by bad press and the myth of weak brass for many years. Somehow the idea got started that .45 Colt brass was weaker than other brass. This is very strange when one realizes that Dick Casull began the experiments with .45 Colt brass that lead to the .454 Casull simply because .45 Colt brass was the strongest available in 1954. Casull's work should have ended the myth of weak brass forever. Unfortunately, it did not.

Perhaps the myth of weak brass started with Elmer Keith's first article in 1925 that described the destruction of a .45 Colt Single Action. Everyone remembered the event, yet few remembered the cause: oversized bullets over blackpowder crushed to the consistency of flour and fired in a decrepit old blackpowder single action. The brass Keith used was the old style balloon head or folded head brass. This brass did not have the solid head that all modern brass is composed of and the rims of .45 Colt brass, that are the same diameter as .44 Special or .44 Magnum brass, do not match up well with the fatter case. The .45 Colt cartridge measures .480 inch above the base compared to the .44 Magnum's .455 inch, while they both have the same diameter rim, .505 inch. Couple the minuscule rim of the .45 Colt with a poorly fitted shellholder and, especially with the old style brass, and case heads often would pull off when the cartridge case was run through the sizing die and back out again.

The truth is that .45 Colt brass is as strong as the sixgun it is contained in. Colt Single Actions have almost paper-thin cylinder walls and should only be used with standard loads. Also, their cylinders'

length precludes the use of heavyweight Keith-style 300 and 325 grain cast bullets crimped in the crimping groove.

Most modern .45 Colt sixguns have groove diameters of .451 to .452 inch and one should be careful to see that the loading dies employed are made for these smaller bullets rather than pre-war .454-inch bullets. My first set of dies for the .45 Colt did not size the brass down enough to prevent .452-inch bullets from sliding down into the case. Dies of modern manufacture are made for .452-inch bullets. Poor dies will add to the second myth of the .45 Colt.

Five strength levels of the .45 Colt: 1. Colt SAA, use with 260 grain cast bullets at 900 to 1,000 fps; 2. Colt New Frontier, suitable with 260 grain bulleted loads at 1,000 to 1,150 fps; 3. Ruger Blackhawk, 300 grain cast bullets at 1,200 fps; 4. custom five-shot cylindered .45 on Ruger frame by Jim Stroh, 300 grain bullets at 1,500 fps; 5. Freedom Arms Casull, 300 grain bullets at 1,700 to 1,800 fps.

A longtime bad rap for the .45 Colt has been poor accuracy. This is again, a myth. The problem has mainly been one of excessive case capacity for the available powders or the strength of the guns that the .45 Colt has been chambered for. The use of heavy-weight cast bullets reduces this voluminous case capacity and makes the .45 Colt extremely efficient. Newer powders such as Winchester's WW231, Hodgdon's Universal, or Accurate Arms' N-100, perform exceptionally well when used in small doses in the large .45 Colt cases. Proper dies also give a tight friction fit on the loaded bullet and as a result, the powder burns efficiently. I have fired 300 grain bullets in the .45 Colt at 1,100 to 1,200 feet per second to a full 800 yards and can attest to the accuracy of the old .45 Colt.

There are really five levels of .45 Colt sixguns available to sixgunners now. All will be discussed in depth, some in this chapter and others in later chapters such as the one concerning custom sixguns. The .45 Colt Single Action and the Smith & Wesson Model 25-5 .45 Colt are great for 260 grain wadcutters in the 900 to 1,000 feet per second range and are perfect for self-

defense and are certainly adequate for deer and black bear at reasonable ranges.

Moving up the line, we encounter the .45 Colt New Frontier that has an adjustable-sighted heavy top strap, which gives added strength to the frame of the .45 Colt Single Action for loads of 1,000 to 1,150 feet per second with the 260 grain Keith semi-wadcutter bullet such as Lyman's original #454424. Again, these loads are perfect for defense or deer-sized game.

Since 1971, .45 fanciers have had the advantage of the heavy-framed Ruger .45 Colt, first the Old Model Blackhawk, then the New Model Blackhawk, and now the excellent Bisley Model. These guns are perfect for 300 grain cast bullets at 1,200 feet per second. Now, add the latest Colt, the Anaconda, and Dan Wesson's .45 to this list and we stretch the range of the .45 Colt and make the possibility of taking an elk with a .45 a little more plausible. It may not be the best gun for the job, but it would certainly do the job should the opportunity present itself.

The .45 Colt gets a lot of attention from custom gunsmiths. For instance, both Hamilton Bowen and

The .45 Colt Abilene and .45 Colt New Frontier are easy packin' sixguns: John Linebaugh converted both of these sixguns. The Abilene was originally a .44 Magnum and the Colt was a .357 Magnum. Linebaugh chambered both cylinders to minimum dimensions and fitted a Douglas barrel on the Abilene and a Colt barrel on the New Frontier. Both sixguns will shoot!

John Linebaugh specialize in the .45 Colt. I am fortunate enough to know these gentlemen and to have shot their guns extensively. Many years ago, they certainly opened my eyes to the real potential of the .45 Colt in a proper sixgun. I am talking .45 Colt revolvers that will easily handle 260 grain cast bullets at 1,600 to 1,700 feet per second and 300 grain cast bullets at 1,500 to 1,600 feet per second—not bad for a 125 year old cartridge.

There is so much versatility and we still have one .45 level left, the .454 Casull. As mentioned, all of Dick Casull's work developing the .454 was done with standard .45 Colt brass. When the Casull finally reached the production stage, the brass was lengthened by 1/10 inch to preclude the possibility of it being fired in a .45 that could not handle its pressures. I have an extra cylinder in .45 Colt for my 4-3/4-inch .454 Casull for using the much more reasonably priced .45 Colt brass; its use is limited to how much recoil I want. I will give out before the brass will. I have gone as high as 1,400 plus feet per second with 400 grain—yes I did say 400 grain—bullets. Yes, the recoil is horrendous, and, no, I won't publish the load. My normal

everyday load in the short-barreled Casull packin' pistol now is a 300 grain gas-checked flat-nose from BRP Bullets, or NEI's 310 grain cast Keith-style semi-wadcutter #310.451 at 1,100 to 1,200 feet per second. With this load, that pressure tests at around 24,000 pounds, the sixgun, the brass, and I will all last forever. At least the gun and brass will.

Forty-five Colt brass is to the .454 Casull as .38 Special and .44 Special are to the .357 Magnum and .44 Magnum, respectively. Freedom Arms, however, does not recommend the use of .45 Colt brass in its .454 cylinders for one simple reason. When the shorter brass is used in the .357, .44, or .454 cylinder, powder and lead residue build up in the cylinder chamber at the mouth of the case as it is fired. Enough of this build-up changing the diameter of the cylinder at this point, coupled with a .454 Casull load in the 50,000 to 60,000 pound pressure level, could result in real trouble. Don't do it unless the cylinder is **thoroughly** cleaned after every use with .45 Colt brass! For most of us, that shortens to **don't do it**.

The Colt Single Action Army and the .45 Colt cartridge began life together as the Colt Single Action

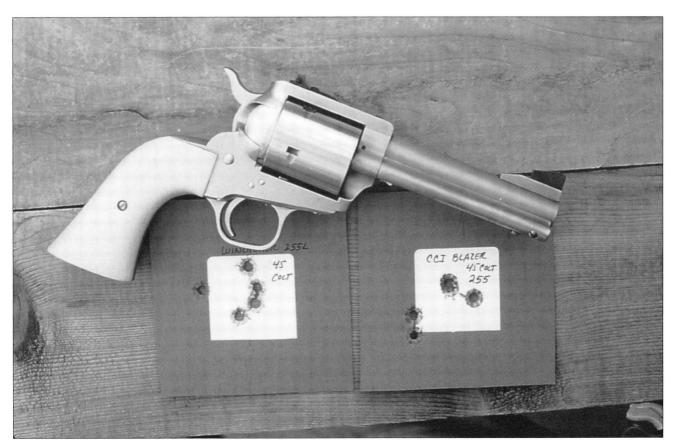

This accurate-shooting .45 Colt is a Freedom Arms .454 fitted with an auxiliary .45 Colt cylinder. White squares are 2-inch wide and groups were fired at 25 yards.

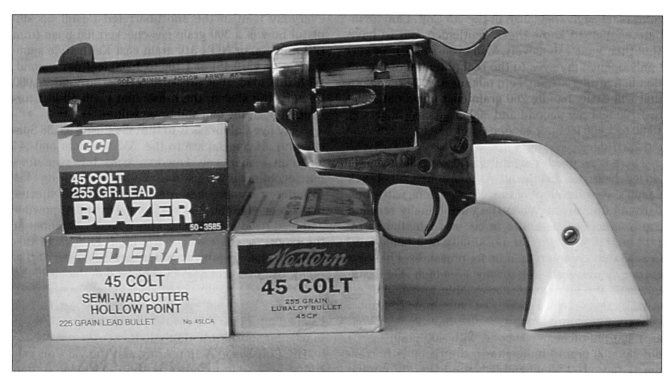

The Classic Colt Single Action Army: This Second Generation .45 x 4-3/4 inch wears ivories by Charles Able.

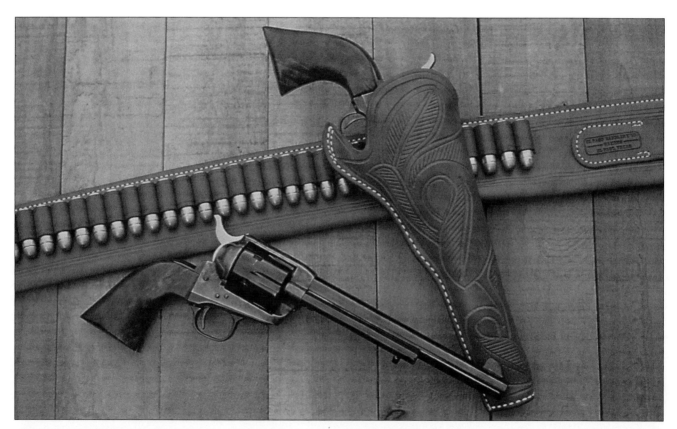

Third Generation Colt Single Actions: .45 Colt x 7-1/2 inch, Jesse James rig by El Paso, one-piece stocks by Tedd Adamovich, and tuned by Bob Munden.

Army Serial Number 1, a 7-1/2-inch-barreled sixgun, blued, with a case-hardened main frame, and one-piece walnut grips, appeared in 1873 destined for the U.S. Army. Some would say the superb balance of the Peacemaker—never an official name as it was known at the factory as the Model P—was an accident, or the long-barreled 7-1/2-inch Cavalry Model .45 would never have been offered. The 5-1/2-inch Artillery Model and the 4-3/4-inch Civilian Model are easier to pack and have been much favored by Fast Draw enthusiasts over the past forty years, however, I am particularly fond of the long-barreled 7-1/2-inch Peacemaker for general use. It balances, shoots, and sights easier for me. Let's look at the .45 Colt sixguns of recent manufacture including those we have just briefly touched upon.

COLT'S .45 COLTS: Without hesitation I will say that the Colt Single Action is the best looking, best feeling, easiest shooting big bore sixgun ever. The fine natural grip of the Model P is shaped so that a .45 Colt (or .44-40 or .44 Special) Single Action just seems to hang in the hand with everything in the proper place resulting in a natural pointability that cannot be duplicated by any other sixgun. Cock the hammer and listen carefully. You will hear C-O-L-T as the hammer makes its arc from rest to full cock. Fire the grand old sixgun and you will immediately find your throat going dry from the dust of a great herd of cattle on the long drive from Texas to Kansas, your nostrils will flair as you smell bacon and beans cookin'

over a campfire, and your ears will perk up as they hear the tinkling of a piano from a saloon on Main Street in Dodge. No other sixgun has this effect.

In 1941, Colt ended production of both the Single Action Army and Double Action New Service. Both had been chambered in .45 Colt since their inceptions. Together, they represent a total production of three-quarters of a million big bore sixguns. Whether this is true or not is hard to determine, but the story is that the machinery was moved to the parking lot (!) for storage as the Colt plant switched over to wartime production. Of course, when the war ended in 1945, horror of horrors, the machinery was in rusted ruins. It is probably closer to the truth, at least in the case of the Single Actions, that the machinery was already worn out and sales of the Model P had been continually dropping for years.

Colt had no intentions of bringing the Single Action Army back. It was a dead issue. Two things changed the minds of the powers that be. First came the tremendous effect of television and, more specifically, old Western movies on TV, coupled with an upstart gunmaker in Connecticut who was actually making money selling single actions. The man was Bill Ruger and the sixgun was the .22 Single-Six. By 1956, Colt was back in the Single Action Army business, first with the .45 Colt and .38 Special, soon to be followed by the .357 Magnum and .44 Special.

It was about this same time that the sport of Fast Draw arrived and the number one sixgun in use was the Colt Single Action in what else, but .45 Colt. By

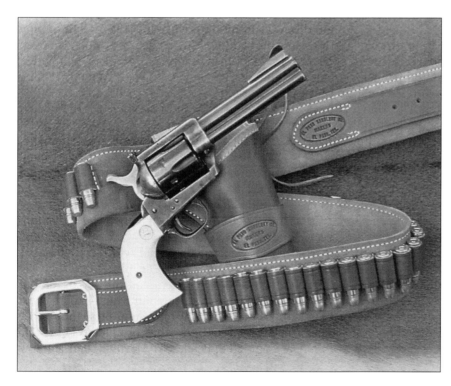

Colt New Frontier: Factory ivories, tightly rechambered from .357 Magnum by John Linebaugh, and fitted with a 4-3/4-inch Colt barrel. El Paso's Duke Rig leather is patterned after John Wayne's outfit.

Taffin long-range shooting with the 5-1/2-inch New Frontier.

the mid-1970s, the machinery had worn out again and the production of the Colt Single Action Army was halted, but Colt promised to bring it back with new machinery. By the end of the 1970s, the Third Generation of Single Action Armys were in full production. They would last well into the 1980s and the .45 Colt was number one again. It was joined by the .44-40, .44 Special, and .357 Magnum.

The Colt Single Action was dropped from production—again—for the third time. The Model P is a survivor, though, and now the .45 Single Action is back, sometimes labeled as a Custom Shop proposition, and other times as a standard catalog item. This time, in addition to the standard .45 Colt chambering, the Single Action is also available in .44-40, and for the first time since the late 1930s, also in .38-40.

Meanwhile, Colt was also producing a sixgun that I consider a modern classic, the New Frontier. In late 1961 (only two were made in this year), Colt introduced the New Frontier. Like Ruger did seven years earlier, Colt flat-topped the frame of an existing model and added an adjustable rear sight and a radically sloping ramp-style front sight and created one of the most beautiful sixguns ever. The New Frontier, just like the Colt Single Action Army that gave birth to it, carried a deep blue finish on its barrel, cylinder, and grip frame topped off with beautifully mottled colors on its case-hardened main frame.

During the production of the First Generation Colt Single Action Army sixguns from 1873 to 1941, a few target models, both Single Action Army and Bisley, were produced with a slightly flat-topped frame, a rear sight adjustable for windage by drifting and locking in place, and a front sight that could be adjusted up and down. During the 1920s, Elmer Keith tried to interest Colt in modernizing the Colt by flat-topping the frame and adding fully adjustable sights. He even offered to loan his custom sixguns, including his famous Number Five and custom 7-1/2-inch that King Gun Works worked over to perfection, to Colt, but it would not listen. Had Colt been open-minded, Ruger may never have materialized.

In 1962, a Colt Single Action Army .45 Colt cost—gulp—$125. The .45 New Frontier was priced even higher at an unreachable $140. This came at the same time that .357 and .44 Magnum Ruger Blackhawks were going for less than $100 and the superbly crafted and blued Super Blackhawk in .44 Magnum was selling for $116.

The Colt New Frontier began with serial number 3000NF, which stayed in the Colt plant. The last Second Generation New Frontiers had the serial number 7288NF or 7289F, depending upon which expert is listened to. From 1961 to 1974, a total of slightly more than 4,000 New Frontiers were produced. Four calibers, .45 Colt, .38 Special, .357 Magnum, and .44 Spe-

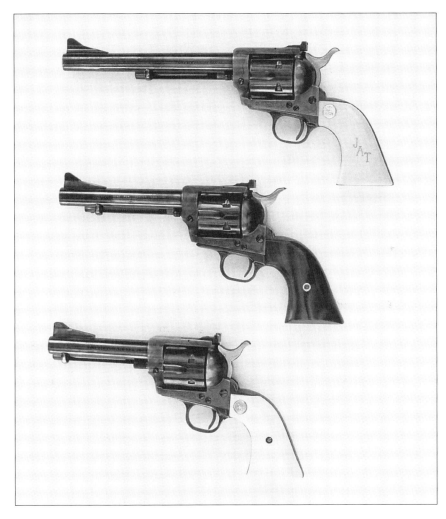

Colt's Classic .45 New Frontiers: 2nd Generation 7-1/2 inch with Leskovec stocks; Third Generation 5-1/2 inch with Able stocks; 2nd Generation 4-3/4 inch with factory ivories.

cial, were made in this first run of Colt Flat-Top Target sixguns. In 1978, the New Frontier went back into production with the Third Generation Colt Single Action Army. The serial numbers began at 01001NF, with five digits instead of four. In the last and, according to Colt, final run of New Frontiers, the calibers were .45 Colt, .357 Magnum, .44 Special, and .44-40. The Colt New Frontiers maintain the beautiful look, feel, and balance of the Colt Single Action Army with the added advantage of adjustable sights. It is a rare fixed-sighted sixgun that shoots to point of aim, and when it does, it is normally for only one load. The New Frontier's sights allow any reasonable load to be dialed in.

Until the advent of the Colt Anaconda in .45 Colt, the New Frontier remained the finest hunting sixgun in .45 Colt Hartford ever offered. A short-barreled New Frontier in .45 Colt caliber makes an excellent packin' pistol that is easy to carry and relatively lightweight when compared to .454 Casulls and Ruger .44 Magnums. With heavy .45 Colt loads, one can handle any American critter up close except the big bears. Loading for the .45 Colt New Frontier for this sixgun-

ner is pretty traditional. It literally begs for cast bullets and is at its best with hard cast, Keith-style or semi-wadcutter bullets.

I can only think of two improvements for the New Frontier. First, like almost all sixguns, they cry for custom grips. All New Frontiers were equipped with the plainest unfinished walnut grips in existence. Second, I would use a flat, black post front sight instead of the glare-gathering, sloping ramp front sight. Colt's factory front sight does go well with one of my favorite sixgun shooting pastimes, long-range shooting at small rocks on yonder hill. The secret to this style of long-range shooting is not holding over as one does with a scope-sighted rifle or pistol, but simply holding up enough front sight with the intended target perched on top. <u>This is only for shooting at inanimate objects, not for hunting.</u> Misses don't count on the former, but they can be really messy on the latter.

New Frontiers are gone from production, but seem to be readily available at gun shows. The really good news is that they are not regarded as highly by collec-

The accuracy of the Colt New Frontier .45 Colt with Lyman's #454424 over 20 grains of H4227; distance is 25 yards.

Colt 4-3/4-inch SAA, ivory-gripped by Charles Able, and 7-1/2-inch New Frontier with stocks by Bob Leskovec, both in .45 Colt chambering, make great companion sixguns to Winchester's Trapper .45. Leather is El Paso's Duke rig.

Colt's Anaconda—finally, after fifty years, the New Service is replaced.

tors as the Single Action Army, so prices are usually quite a bit lower.

After nearly fifty years without a .45 Colt double action from Hartford, Colt finally came forth with the Anaconda in its biggest bore. It is big and strong and good enough to make one forget all about the Prewar .45 New Service. The .45 Colt Anaconda weighs 51 ounces in the 6-inch barreled, stainless steel double action sixgun I enjoy. Colt's largest snake has the best features of Colt's two .357 Magnums, the King Cobra and the Python. It has rugged, good looks, and this sixgunner would classify it as even better looking than either the Python or King Cobra. But then again, I am probably prejudiced by the size of the holes in the barrel and cylinder. The entire gun is nicely polished stainless, except for the flattened-off top of the frame and barrel— which is highly appreciated—and the hammer and trigger are both finished in a non-reflecting dull gray, which detracts heavily from the generally great look of the .45 Colt Anaconda. Sights are strictly King Cobra-style: the adjustable rear sight is white outline-style and the ramp-style front sight has a pale red insert.

Premier gunsmith Teddy Jacobsen brought my personal Anaconda .45 Colt to double action sixgun perfection. Jacobsen brought the double action pull down to a smooth 9 pounds, and the single action pull is now at 3-1/4 pounds. To dress up the stainless Anaconda, Jacobsen polished the cylinder's flutes, and then to really upgrade the looks of the big .45, he polished and jeweled both the hammer and trigger. The factory-furnished grips on the .45 Colt Anaconda are finger groove rubber and are too small for my fat fingers. There is a touch of sadness associated with the big .45; my good friend Deacon Deason of Bear-Hug grips made one of the last pair of Skeeter Skelton grips for this sixgun before his untimely death.

The Anaconda is a grand shooting .45 Colt and has the ability to group both cast bullets and jacketed bullets, in both standard and heavy weight persuasion, all in tight little groups. We finally have an easy packin' Colt double action .45 sixgun for hunting, self-defense, or just plain woods bumming.

SMITH & WESSON'S .45 COLTS: Colt and Smith & Wesson seemed to have had an unwritten pact for the first three-fourths of this century. Colt offered a very small number of its sixguns chambered for the .44 Smith & Wesson Special, while Smith & Wesson reciprocated with a minuscule number of its sixguns chambered in .45 Colt. Now, any of either manufacturer's sixgun in the other's caliber is a collector's

Smith & Wesson's .45 Colts: 8-3/8-inch M25-5 with BearHug stocks and 4-inch Mountain Gun with Herrett's stocks.

item. Of the more than 350,000 Colt Single Actions manufactured between 1873 and 1941, less than 1-1/2 percent were in .44 Special. Smith & Wesson offered the .45 Colt in four models in its .44 Hand Ejector series—Triple-Lock, Second Model, Model 1926, and 1950 Target—but its ratio was probably even smaller than Colt's.

Finally, in the 1970s, Smith & Wesson came forth with an honest-to-goodness, genuine Smith & Wesson double action .45 Colt in the Model 25-5. Yes, it is nothing more than a Model 29 .44 Magnum with larger holes in barrel and cylinder, however, it handles .45 Colts just fine, at least after Smith & Wesson got cooking and stopped supplying oversized cylinder mouths like it did on the early examples. The 4-inch-barreled Model 25-5 in .45 Colt is an easy packin' and easy shootin' defensive sixgun and is certainly one of the best sixguns available for this purpose. There are a number of excellent factory loads offered for use in the .45 Colt Smith & Wesson for duty carry or defensive purposes, including Speer's 200 grain "Flying Ashtray" hollowpoint, Winchester's 225 grain Silver-Tip hollowpoint, and Federal's 225 grain lead semi-wadcutter.

The same sixgun has also been available in both 6- and 8-3/8-inch barrel lengths for the outdoor buff and hunter. While I usually would not recommend the same loads I use in my .45 Blackhawks for the Smith & Wesson .45 Colt, in either barrel length it makes a fine hunting handgun for close-range use on deer-sized critters.

Recently Smith & Wesson dropped the Model 25-5 .45 Colt from production, like it has with virtually all of the traditional square butt, blue finish, standard barrel sixguns, but it has been supplanted by the Model 625-5, a stainless .45 Colt with a round-butted grip frame and heavy underlug barrel.

A few years back I ran an exhaustive test as I looked for what I call pleasure loads. These are superbly accurate loads with 250 to 260 grain bullets under 1,000 feet per second muzzle velocity for the .44 Special, .44 Magnum, .45 Auto Rim, and .45 Colt in Smith & Wesson sixguns. Surprise of surprises, the .45 Colt Model 25-5 proved to be the most accurate Smith & Wesson sixgun overall of all sixguns tested, which also included Models 29, 24, and 25-2.

Smith & Wesson is presently offering one of the finest .45s ever in the .45 Colt Mountain Gun. This is a round-butted, 4-inch barreled, stainless steel sixgun that makes a most excellent packin' pistol. Previously, the Model 25-5 carried the heavyweight bull barrel as found on the Model 29, while the Model 625-5 .45 Colt Smith & Wesson has a heavy underlug barrel. The Mountain Gun in .45 Colt is a very trim sixgun with the old tapered slim barrel like those found on previous Smith & Wesson sixguns going back to the .357 Magnum from 1935 and the .44 Special from 1908. It fills a niche in the 1990s and looks thoroughly up-to-date to this sixgunner.

RUGER'S .45 COLTS: When Ruger completely modernized the single action revolver in 1953 and then went to the beautiful .357 Blackhawk with flat-top frame and completely adjustable sights, sixgunners were teased with promises of the same sixgun chambered in .44 Special and .45 Colt as soon as the factory caught up with orders for the .357 Magnum version. Alas, it did not happen, for only one year later, the .44 Magnum arrived.

Ruger chambered three of its Colt Single Action frame-sized .357 Blackhawks for the new .44 Magnum and Elmer Keith, the reigning sixgun writer of the day, warned that the frame was too small for the new .44 Magnum, but he wanted to have one of the prototypes to use as a .44 Special. Keith was correct as usual, and when the factory blew one of the prototypes, the Blackhawk was given a larger frame and cylinder to house the .44 Magnum. That was in 1956. Fifteen years later Ruger finally offered the .45 Colt on not the original .357 Blackhawk frame, but the larger .44 frame. It turned out to be a grand decision.

While I was attending graduate school and living in Missoula, Montana, one mundane day was totally brightened when I found the newest Ruger in the local gun shop. Not only was it chambered in the highly desirable .45 Colt, but it had a 7-1/2-inch barrel, which I prefer for most single action sixgun applications, and an auxiliary cylinder for using .45 ACP loads. I was in sixgunner heaven!

From 1873 until approximately one hundred years later, all factory-produced sixguns in .45 Colt were designed to be used with standard .45 Colt loads. The cylinder walls were very thin and had little margin of safety for anyone foolish enough to try to hot rod the cartridge. The advent of the Ruger Blackhawk in .45 Colt changed this. The Ruger .45 can be safely used with loads that are substantially above standard .45 Colt loads. The .44 Magnum has a working pressure (Copper Units of Pressure—CUPS) of 40,000 pounds plus. The .45 Colt can be held to less than 30,000 pounds (CUPS) and still give powerful, game-getting muzzle velocities and energies.

For example, a 260 grain Keith cast .45 bullet at 1,400 feet per second from a 7-1/2-inch barrel goes 28,000 pounds, a 300 grain cast bullet at 1,300 feet per second goes 30,000 pounds, and a 325 grain cast bullet at 1,200 feet per second goes 26,000 pounds. All loads use either H110 or WW296. Fast burning powders should never be used to build high-performance .45 Colt loads. These loads are all well within the capabilities of the Ruger Blackhawk in .45 Colt. It is extremely interesting that a 260 grain .45 cast bullet at 1,450 feet per second is slightly over 30,000 CUPS, while a 250 grain .44 Magnum requires just slightly under 40,000 CUPS to give 1,500 feet per second. That is nearly 10,000 pounds more pressure for 50 feet per second more!

The Ruger Blackhawk in .45 , offered in both 4-5/8-inch and 7-1/2-inch barreled versions, with or without auxiliary cylinders in .45 ACP, is a relatively rare six-

Ruger's first .45 Colt, the Old Model Blackhawk: This sixgun, dating from 1970, was the first factory-offered .45 Colt that was capable of such heavy .45 Colt loads as 300 grain bullets at 1,200 fps.

gun because its production run lasted only about two years. In 1973, Ruger dropped what is now referred to as the Old Model Rugers in deference to the New Model with a transfer bar safety. For the first time a single action was safe to carry with a loaded round under the hammer. <u>ALL TRADITIONAL SINGLE ACTIONS WITHOUT TRANSFER BAR SAFETIES SHOULD ALWAYS BE CARRIED WITH AN EMPTY CHAMBER UNDER THE HAMMER.</u> Let me repeat that. <u>ALWAYS.</u>

Old-timers often carried rolled-up paper money in that extra chamber. They also knew the easy way to load a traditional single action: Open the loading gate, pull the hammer back to half-cock, load one round, skip the next chamber, load four more rounds, pull the hammer to full cock and lower it gently on the empty chamber which has now rotated under the firing pin. Load one. Skip one. Load four. Cock hammer. Lower gently.

The New Model Blackhawk in .45 Colt, in both the blued and stainless model, is still in production. Ruger's tremendously popular Super Blackhawk .44 Magnum, with the old square-backed grip frame like that found on the 1848 Colt Dragoon, had been in production since 1959. All other calibers on the New Model frame used the modified Colt Single Action-style grip frame known as XR3-RED as opposed to the original Single-Six and Blackhawk's grip frame known as XR3. The latter was a deadringer in shape for the Colt Single Action grip frame. In 1963, it was modified to allow more room for the fingers behind the trigger-

guard. Sometime after Ruger had the New Model Blackhawk design, the decision was made to offer a different grip frame.

The April 1929 issue of *The American Rifleman* carried one of the earliest articles by a then young cowpoke, Elmer Keith. The title of the article was "The Last Word" and described, in detail, Keith's idea of a perfect sixgun. The Single Action sixgun that was pictured, and also later in Keith's monumental work *Sixguns*, is a fully engraved 5-1/2-inch .44 Special with adjustable sights, a modified post front, and the rear set in a flat-top frame. The grips are ivory, but there is something strange about their shape.

Keith relates: "My good friend, S.H. Croft, put in a lot of time, thought, and money improving the S.A. Colt. He was working to obtain a light-weight weapon for self-defense purposes. However a combination of some of his improvements added to the regular-weight sixgun makes the last word in a fine S.A. for target or game shooting. Mr. Croft has designed the changes necessary to convert an ordinary S.A. Colt into the finest single action imaginable, either in the Featherweight model, or at my suggestion, in a heavy, all around sixgun."

"Mr. Croft had four models of Featherweight guns made up from S.A. Army and Bisley Colts, which I described in a previous issue of *The Rifleman*. He worked out and had made his No. 3 grip, which is perfect. At about the same time, or a little later, J.D. O'Meara finished up his pet sixgun grip. Both he and Croft used the Bisley backstrap and S.A.A. guard and

Ruger's .45 Colts—the 7-1/2-inch Vaquero and Bisley. Stocks by Tedd Adamovich and Charles Able.

Ruger's first fixed-sighted centerfire—the Vaquero. This particular sixgun is a 7-1/2-inch .45 Colt. The Vaquero is very popular in Cowboy Action matches.

frontstrap. The Bisley backstrap is bent to the same angle as the S.A.A. When O'Meara had finished, I found that his grip and Croft's No. 3 were almost identical. This No. 3 is the latest and best grip ever put on a sixgun."

"The S.A.A. is one of the best-balanced and easiest handled of sixguns. The regular S.A.A. backstrap, while by far the best shaped of any on the market, does not come up high in the back as it should to completely fill the hand. By bending and welding the Bisley backstrap to the same general contour as the S.A.A. and combining with the S.A.A. guard and frontstrap, we have the No .3 grip."

Keith often bemoaned the fact that Colt never incorporated many of the improvements that various gunsmiths of the period made on the Colt Single Action including adjustable sights and even coil springs to replace the breakage prone flat springs of the Colt. Ruger did pay attention, though, and vastly improved the Colt design by replacing all flat springs with coil springs and placing adjustable sights on all Blackhawk and Super Blackhawk models.

Sixty years after Keith, Croft, and O'Meara worked out what they considered the perfect grip shape for single actions, Ruger introduced the Bisley Model Blackhawk in .357 Magnum, .41 Magnum, .44 Magnum, and—praise the Lord—in .45 Colt.

The Ruger Bisley is basically a Super Blackhawk with a new trigger, hammer, and grip frame. The hammer's shape is similar to that found on the original Colt Bisley, the trigger is radically curved, and the steel grip frame is very close to that found on Keith's

#5 Single Action. I have handled the original #5 and it is slightly smaller than the Ruger Bisley grip frame. The original Colt Bisley had a radically curved frontstrap that allowed the sixgun to seat deep in the hand. The Ruger Bisley frontstrap is almost straight with even less of an angle than the Colt Single Action frontstrap. Is it an improvement or a drawback? It has been greeted with widely differing reactions. One friend and fellow gunwriter called it "the solution to a problem that never existed." Another tagged it as "the best single action grip ever devised and the only one to use for heavy recoiling sixguns."

In an effort to judge for myself, I used three 7-1/2-inch Rugers all with steel grip frames to get them as near as possible to the same weight and then fired them with the same heavy load to see how each one transmitted recoil. Three sixguns used were: An Old Model or Three-Screw .45 Blackhawk fitted with a stainless steel grip frame from a Ruger Old Army, a New Model .45 Ruger equipped with a Super Blackhawk steel grip frame, and of course, the .45 Bisley Blackhawk. All carried thin, smooth wood, factory-style custom grips. The load used was Lyman's #454424 Keith 260 grain semi-wadcutter over 21.5 grains of #2400, CCI Magnum Pistol Primers, and Federal .45 Colt brass. This load is not for any other .45 Colt sixguns and should be approached carefully. The Three-Screw Blackhawk clocked out at 1,430 feet per second, and the top of trigger finger was rapped solidly as the gun came back in recoil. With the New Model, the muzzle velocity dropped slightly to 1,398 feet per second, and as expected, the Super Blackhawk grip frame rapped me soundly both in the palm and on the knuckle. The Bisley Model saw further reduction in muzzle velocity to 1,380 feet per second, while the recoil was a heavy push in the palm of the hand. For me at least, the Bisley Model is definitely the best Ruger single action sixgun ever produced to handle heavy recoiling loads.

With the rise of Cowboy Action Shooting, Ruger produced a third .45 Colt Blackhawk and now offers its first fixed-sighted centerfire single action. The Ruger Vaquero has been made to look as much like a nineteenth century single action as possible and still use the Ruger platform. The Vaquero is a classic-looking single action sixgun, but its profile is different from other Blackhawks due to its fixed rather than adjustable sights. Now, Cowboy Action Shooting is big and the nineteenth century aficionados can now have an authentic looking single action sixgun with virtually unbreakable lockwork. As an extra added bonus, it has the standard Ruger transfer bar which makes it perfectly safe to carry loaded with six rounds.

Because these are fixed-sighted guns, it is sometimes a real problem to get a gun that shoots to point of aim. Ruger has allowed for this with plenty of front sight blade so individual sixgunners can adjust the sights by filing for the particular load and hold preferred. My 7-1/2-inch .45 Vaquero shot 3 inches low with 300 grain bullets and even lower with 260 grain bullets. It is now filed in and dead on with 255 grain bullets at 800 feet per second for Cowboy Action Shooting.

The stainless steel version of the Vaquero fits the need perfectly for an outdoor devotee's sixgun, especially for a packer or guide or woods bum who wants a strong, dependable sixgun that will shoot one load to the preferred point of aim and distance with no worries about adjustable sights getting out of whack.

My choice for this would be an easy packin' 4-5/8-inch .45 Colt, home gunsmith-adjusted to hit point of aim with 300 grain bullets at 1,100 feet per second.

How well do Vaqueros sell? As one of my undercover peace officer friends who looked at a Vaquero said: "Just look at the price tag! $1,200 for the Colt and under $400 for the Vaquero. Guess which one I will buy?"

DAN WESSON'S .45 COLT: The Dan Wesson .45 carries the same excellent characteristics as all other medium- and large-framed sixguns from the Wesson factory, including a cylinder that locks at the front and the rear, interchangeable front sights, interchangeable barrels in various lengths, a one-piece frame, and stocks that wrap around a grip frame stud, not bolted to a grip frame. That is the good news. The bad news is that after years of struggle to keep afloat, it looks like Dan Wesson, which became Wesson Firearms when it reverted back to the Wesson family in its later years, is gone forever. All is not lost, though, for us big bore sixgunners, because Dan Wessons are readily available on the used gun market and they have yet to acquire collector status. I do not believe many .45 Colt Dan Wessons were ever manufactured, so they will be much harder to find than .357 or .44 Magnums.

Dan Wesson .45 Colt sixguns were available in both blue and stainless models in the standard barrel lengths of 4, 6, 8, and possibly 10 inches. Weighing in at just 3 ounces under 4 pounds with the heavy weight 8-inch barrel, the Dan Wesson .45 Colt is an exceptionally pleasant big bore to shoot even when used with heavyweight bullets of 300 grains or more. If one doesn't mind packin' the nearly 4 pounds of steel that comprises a Dan Wesson .45, it is an excellent hunting handgun. It is about 1 pound above what this shooter considers maximum for waist belt or car-

The fine natural grip of the Dan Wesson .45 Colt.

Ruger's gunfighter-length Vaquero, the 4-3/4-inch .45 Colt with stocks by Tedd Adamovich.

Superb accuracy from Dan Wesson's .45 Colt: This group was fired at 25 yards with a load consisting of SSK's 340 grain cast bullet at 1,200 fps.

Taffin's favorite packin' .45 Colt Single Actions: Three six-shot sixguns, a 4-3/4-inch Colt SAA, a 4-5/8-inch Ruger Blackhawk, and a 5-1/2-inch Abilene, plus a custom .45 built on a Ruger Super Blackhawk frame by Jim Stroh. The latter has a five-shot cylinder that allows added safety with the use of heavy .45 Colt loads.

tridge belt carry. Fatigue sets in quickly once handguns get over the 3 pound weight limit and they are carried at waist level, so I prefer to carry them in a top quality shoulder holster that evenly distributes the weight between shoulders and the waist belt. Such a rig is used to carry the Dan Wesson .45 Colt perfectly. Idaho Leather offers its #41 Deluxe Shoulder Rig for Dan Wesson as well as other revolvers. This outfit consists of a spring clip pouch and is made of top grain leather, with wide shoulder straps to distribute the weight, plus most importantly, it fastens on the waist belt both with a strap on the back of the holster and a 24-capacity cartridge carrier on the off-side. The complete outfit is secure, carries comfortably, and provides plenty of ammunition space for the handgun hunter.

The Dan Wesson large frame revolver is the only double action sixgun of recent memory that came with useable factory grips. There is no checkering to punish the hands through long strings of fire and was

obviously shaped by someone who understands shooters' needs, but there is always room for improvement. I found that improvement when I ran into Rod Herrett at the NRA Show in St. Louis a few years back. Herrett reached into his briefcase and came out with his latest offering, a smooth two-piece grip for the large frame Dan Wesson. I have been using this grip on the Dan Wesson .45 Colt ever since.

The .45 Colt is, for lack of a better term, a survivor. It was "replaced" at various times in its long history by the .38 Special (in 1899), the .45 ACP (in 1911), the .357 Magnum (in 1935), and the .44 Magnum (in 1956). At times it has gone down, but it always comes back. Even with the sixguns that have been dropped from production in recent years, there are still more models of Colt .45 sixguns available than at any time in history and the .45 Colt cartridge has enjoyed a grand resurgence the past few years. Once in awhile I run into a sixgunner who doesn't own a .45 Colt. I am always amazed one can survive under such a handicap.

CHAPTER 4

THE .357 MAGNUM—
THE FIRST MAGNUM

It is 1930. The depression has set in and the age of the gangster has arrived. Local police officers find themselves armed with the .38 Special in a Smith & Wesson Military & Police or Colt Official Police sixgun as they go against criminals who are armed with 1911 .45 semi-automatics and Thompson submachine guns and wear bulletproof vests. Members of the police force feeling undergunned against the criminal element is definitely not something relative only to the 1990s.

The two great handgun manufacturers of the time, Colt and Smith & Wesson, both decided to come up with better armament for our nation's peace officers. Both companies had the same goal in mind, but they took entirely different paths. The 1930s were not that far removed from World War I and the most popular Colt at the time was the 1911 .45 that so many soldiers had been introduced to in 1917. Colt decided to use the 1911 platform to come up with a handgun that would have more firepower, greater penetration, and could also be used successfully against automobiles.

The result was the .38 Super, a new cartridge that was simply the old .38 Automatic Colt Pistol cartridge with an increased powder charge that gave its 130 grain full metal jacketed bullet a muzzle velocity of 1,300 feet per second. Chambered in the 1911, the new .38 offered peace officers a handgun with a capacity of ten rounds. Colt really had something here, however, it went to the threshold and did not cross over. The .38 Super is a semi-rimmed case that headspaced not on the case mouth as all other semi-automatics, but rather used the very slight rim to hold the loaded round in place as the gun was fired. The result was terrible accuracy.

My personal .38 Super, a Colt Commander, was good for 12-inch groups until Bill Wilson rebarreled it with a barrel that properly headspaced the .38 brass on the mouth of the case and brought the groups down to 2 inches. It would take Colt fifty years to properly barrel its .38 Supers. Today's Colt .38 Supers are correctly set up and quite popular in Action Shooting.

Smith & Wesson took a different direction and stayed with the tried and true sixgun. At the time, it had two double action platforms with which to experiment, the medium-framed Military & Police offered in both .38 Special and .32-20, and the .44 Third Model Hand Ejector, or Model 1926 .44 Special. The latter was a large-framed sixgun with an enclosed ejector round housing—a true heavy-duty sixgun that was quite popular with peace officers, especially those in the southwestern part of the country.

Smith & Wesson chambered the large-framed 1926 Model in .38 Special and the .38/44 Heavy Duty was born. The rather anemic .38 Special loading of the time was a 158 grain round-nosed bullet at 775 feet per second. For use only in the .38/44 Smith & Wesson, Remington introduced a 158 grain full metal jacketed bullet at over 1,100 feet per second.

Peace officers took to the new sixgun and load very quickly. The .38/44 Heavy Duty had the old Pre-war long double action from Smith & Wesson that was incredibly smooth in double action fire. The heavy frame dampened recoil and allowed for quick recovery between shots even with the more powerful ammunition. Unlike Colt, Smith & Wesson did cross over the threshold and realized what it had in the .38/44 Heavy Duty.

With fixed sights and a barrel length of either 4 or 5 inches, the .38/44 Heavy Duty was the best sixgun that had ever been offered to the police officer. Smith & Wesson saw other applications as well and added adjustable sights to a 6-1/2-inch-barreled Heavy Duty and offered shooters the .38/44 Outdoorsman.

Major D.B. Wesson of Smith & Wesson realized the potential of the .38/44 and its use as a hunting handgun. He enlisted the aid of two of the top sixgun experimenters of the time, Elmer Keith and Phil Sharpe, to see just what could really be accomplished with the heavy-framed .38. Keith used #80 powder (Hercules #2400 was not yet available to him) and his 173 grain bullet (Lyman's #358429) to develop loads at a muzzle velocity of over 1,150 feet per second. He reported that the .38/44 Smith & Wesson sixgun handled the heavy loads perfectly.

Early on, Phil Sharpe urged Smith & Wesson and Winchester to bring out an even more powerful cartridge and sixgun combination, and was probably most influential in bringing about the new cartridge based on the .38/44 in 1935. Winchester increased the case length of the .38 Special to 1.285 inches and loaded Sharpe's 158 grain bullet over #2400 ignited by large primers and the result was the .357 Magnum, "The World's Most Powerful Handgun." In those pre-Model number days, the Smith & Wesson .357 Magnum was known simply as the .357 Magnum.

Like the .38/44 Heavy Duty, the new .357 Magnum was offered in both a peace officer's sixgun and an outdoorsman's handgun. The first .357 Magnums carried 8-3/4-inch barrels that gave a muzzle velocity of

1,550 feet per second! The Magnum era had definitely arrived. Keith's 173 grain bullet was too long to use in the new .357 Magnum brass when crimped in the crimping groove as it protruded through the front of the cylinder. Sharpe's 158 grain bullet had a shorter nose and worked perfectly in the new cartridge.

The Sharpe bullet was beautifully shaped with its semi-wadcutter profile, found today in RCBS's #38-150KT, however, there was a fly in the ointment; the original factory bullets were too soft and leaded quickly and badly. Keith used his heavier hard cast bullets in .38 Special brass in the new sixgun and developed a standard loading of 13.5 grains of #2400 with this combination. This is definitely a heavy loading and for use only in large-framed .357 Magnums or .38 Specials such as the Colt Single Action and Smith & Wesson Outdoorsman and Heavy Duty.

The .357 Magnum, while not strictly fitting the definition, earned its niche in the big bore category when it developed a muzzle velocity that was nearly double that of the .44 and .45 caliber sixguns of the time. Today we take the .357 Magnum rather matter of factly, but it was definitely a giant step forward in 1935. Phil Sharpe, the leading reloading expert of the time, offered the fol-

Phil Sharpe used the 4-inch .38/44 Heavy Duty and the 6-1/2-inch .38/44 Outdoorsman in the early 1930s for developing the .357 Magnum.

lowing advice for reloading the .357 Magnum in 1937: "Developing the full-charge load is a major problem. Essentially the factories use a special non-canister grade of Hercules #2400, not available to handloaders. The obvious step then is Standard #2400. Charges must be weighed carefully, and if this powder is used, it must not be varied beyond recommended charges. The powder will not work well at low pressures and is inclined to be erratic if the load is increased even slightly beyond the recommended limit. The writer does not recommend the handloading of full charges by the average person and desires to make this known. You are loading far more power than has ever been crammed into a revolver cartridge before, and in doing so you load at your own risk. The Hercules Powder Company and Smith & Wesson refuse to recommend the reloading of this particular number because of these strings. It can be done by one who is very careful, however. But if care was ever needed in the reloading of a revolver cartridge, it most certainly applies to this particular number. The handloader will do much better to use these cases and load standard .38 Special charges."

Doug Wesson promoted the new Smith & Wesson .357 Magnum by heading West for a handgun hunting trip. At Cody, Wyoming, Wesson took his first shot at game with a 50 yard shot at an antelope. Call it buck fever or whatever, but Wesson's shot only wounded the antelope and the quarry immediately ran off. When Wesson caught up with the pronghorn, he made a shot that proved to be 232 paces and dropped the antelope. The next animal was an elk taken at 150 yards and this was then followed by the taking of a large bull moose at 100 yards. In both cases the .357 bullet penetrated all the way to the skin on the opposite side. By now, Wesson had great confidence in the .357 Magnum and decided to go for bigger game—grizzly. Wesson traveled to British Columbia and continued to enjoy incredible good fortune and took a 700 pound grizzly at over 100 yards.

With no place to go but up, Wesson decided to go for the ultimate, an Alaskan brown bear!—with a .357 Magnum! Wesson made the trip, never saw a bear, and finally realized how lucky he had been with the grizzly and also not seeing a brown bear. "For this trip I carried two revolvers for added power. We never did get to see a brownie, for which, in my older and more intelligent days I feel sincerely thankful."

Through the words of Phil Sharpe and the hunting exploits of Doug Wesson, we get a very precise picture of how the .357 Magnum was viewed when it arrived upon the sixgunning scene. Sixty years later, everyone loads for the .357 Magnum and I cannot believe anyone would pursue elk, moose, or grizzly bear with a .357 Magnum sixgun!

Ed McGivern, known best as one of the fastest, if not the fastest double action sixgunner that ever lived, took to the .357 Magnum early as a long-range sixgun. Using an 8-3/4-inch .357 Magnum equipped with a special rear peep sight, McGivern and his followers shot the .357 Magnum on man-sized silhouettes out to a full 600 yards. They had no trouble keeping half or more of their shots on the silhouette target all the way out to 600 yards and fired one target that put four out of five shots in the chest area. This was long before the proliferation of long-eye relief pistol scopes and accomplished with iron sights!

For police use, the .357 Magnum was offered in a 3-1/2-inch sixgun. The first production .357 Magnum with an 8-3/4-inch barrel was presented to the FBI's J. Edgar Hoover and the short-barreled version of the .357 Magnum soon became a favorite with FBI agents. A young Army lieutenant purchased one of the 3-1/2-inch .357 sixguns in Hawaii in 1935. It had ivory grips, was carried in an S.D. Myres holster, and on the hip of General George Patton in World War II, it became a symbol of his great leadership. Patton actually carried two different sixguns with ivory grips and the .357 Magnum was spelled from time to time by a Colt Single Action .45 that was purchased just before Patton accompanied Black Jack Pershing into Mexico before World War I. The Colt had several notches on the grip from Mexico and Europe, however Patton referred to his Smith & Wesson .357 Magnum as his "killing gun."

Smith & Wesson's .357 Magnum was a beautifully crafted sixgun that sold for $60 in the midst of a depression. The first guns carried special registration numbers and certificates outlining the features of each sixgun as they were virtually custom made. In spite of the economic times, Smith & Wesson was unable to keep up with the demand.

The top of the ribbed barrel and frame as well as the rear sight rib on the .357 Magnum were checkered, and still were when the .357 Magnum, known as the Model 27, was recently dropped from production. The adjustable rear sight could be mated up with a variety of front sights including a gold bead. Each gun was individually sighted in at the factory for the distance requested by the purchaser.

Colt soon took up the .357 Magnum and chambered both the New Service and Single Action Army in the powerful new cartridge. When war broke out in Europe and the disarmed British populace called for arms to protect itself from invasion, many Colt Single Actions chambered in .357 Magnum went across the Atlantic.

Both Colt and Smith & Wesson turned their facilities to wartime production in 1942, and stopped the manufacture of the .357 Magnum. After the war, Smith & Wesson slowly resumed producing the large-framed .357 Magnum, while Colt found itself without machinery to produce either the New Service or Single Action Army. For nearly ten years after World War II, the Smith & Wesson .357 Magnum was the only Magnum sixgun offered and there were more buyers than there were sixguns available.

In the mid-1950s, .357 Magnum sixguns finally became at least semi-readily available to shooters twenty years after the cartridge's introduction. In 1954, both Colt and Smith & Wesson brought forth new models of the .357 Magnum. Colt's .357 Magnum was on the .41 frame that had been used with the .38 Official Police, while Smith & Wesson introduced a less finely finished .357 Magnum, the Highway Patrolman. The latter, with its subdued matte blue finish with a 4-inch barrel, quickly became popular with peace officers, while the longer barreled 6-inch Highway Patrolman became a favorite of outdoorsmen. Both guns were rugged, dependable, and carried no frills whatsoever.

Colt had been working on a quality .38 Special target sixgun with a silky smooth action and heavy underlugged barrel with ventilated rib. It was originally offered in .357 Magnum, instead of .38 Special, with a 6-inch barrel. The Python was, and is, regarded

as the Cadillac of .357 Magnums by its many proponents.

While Colt was unveiling a heavy target-style .357 Magnum, Smith was going the other direction. Bill Jordan, then of the Border Patrol, looked at the medium-framed .38 Special Military & Police with adjustable sights known as the Combat Masterpiece and thought why not? Why not the same basic sixgun in .357 Magnum? The original Smith & Wesson .357 Magnum became very heavy during a long day or night of duty. Jordan was correct in his thinking: a medium-framed .357 with less weight and a smaller cylinder would be the ideal peace officer's sixgun. Smith & Wesson listened to Jordan, made up a medium-framed Magnum cylinder that completely filled the K-frame cylinder window, added a heavy weight barrel with enclosed ejector rod, and specially heat-treated the whole package and the Combat Magnum was born.

The new kid on the block, Bill Ruger, had successfully introduced his .22 Single-Six in 1953. Patterned after the Colt Single Action Army, the Ruger was scaled down in size for the .22 cartridge, but carried a full Colt-sized grip frame and virtually unbreakable coil springs powered the action. Two years later, the Single-Six went full size, picked up fully adjustable sights, and the magnificent .357 Blackhawk had arrived. I would not want to count the number of shooters that started with a Ruger .22 and then

The excellent accuracy of the 8-inch Colt Python .357 Magnum: This group, shot at 25 yards, measures less than 1 inch. The load consisted of Lyman's #358156 Thompson Gas Check bullet over 15 grains of #2400.

Blue and nickel 8-3/8-inch Smith & Wesson M27 .357 Magnums (BearHug stocks), 3-1/2-inch .357 Magnum (Fishpaw stocks), and 5-1/2-inch Colt New Frontier .357 (stocks by Tedd Adamovich).

moved up to a Ruger .357 Magnum. Both sixguns have Outdoorsman written all over them. Most of the .357 Blackhawks purchased forty years ago are still perfectly serviceable even though used routinely by outdoor enthusiasts and those who farm, fish, hunt, ...well, you get the picture.

Add in the soon to arrive Second Generation Colt Single Action Army in .357 Magnum, and the Great Western Single Action Army also in .357 Magnum and its own version, the .357 Atomic, which was simply a 158 grain bullet in standard .357 brass over 16 grains of #2400, and sixgunners in the 1950s suddenly had a choice of .357s from a field of three single actions and five double actions.

This was almost overwhelming after two decades of an acute shortage of .357 sixguns. Now, forty years later, only two of the above mentioned .357 Magnums remain, the Python and the Combat Magnum. Yes, Ruger still has the .357 Blackhawk, but it is built on a different frame and is much larger and heavier than the original.

A lump comes to the throat when one realizes the original .357 Magnum, the Smith & Wesson known as the Model 27 for so many years, is no longer cataloged by Smith & Wesson after sixty years of great service.

It may be gone, but even today the Smith & Wesson .357 Magnum is the Magnum by which all other .357s are judged. The original barrel length of 8-3/4 inches was soon changed to a standard 8-3/8 inches to comply with sight radius restrictions under target shooting rules. It was a superb long-range sixgun in the 1930s and remains so today. At the other end of the spectrum, we have the short-barreled 3-1/2-inch .357 Magnum that is absolutely the most business-like looking sixgun ever made available. Dirty Harry did not originate "Make my day!," the 3-1/2-inch .357 Smith & Wesson Magnum did!

In between the long-range .357 Magnum and the easy packin' 3-1/2-inch sixgun, we find the most practical 5-inch barreled Model 27, that is perfect for holster use. This sixgun would be hard to ignore should

Ruger's Single Actions progressed from the 5-1/2-inch Single-Six (1953) to the 4-5/8-inch .357 Blackhawk (1955) to the 6-1/2-inch .44 Blackhawk (1956).

one be restricted to only one .357 Magnum—for me its only real competition would be the easier packin' 4-inch Combat Magnum. Carried high on the belt in a Tom Threepersons-style holster, it is out of the way, quick into action, and much easier to shoot than either the long or short Smith & Wesson .357 Magnums.

I was a kid fresh out of high school in 1957 and already had a passion for big bore sixguns. I started a charge account to buy my first sixguns and I do not believe it was ever completely cleared! In those days a teenager could legally purchase a handgun and even get credit at the local sporting goods store decades before the abundance of plastic money.

My first .357 sixgun was a single action 4-5/8-inch Ruger Blackhawk that was soon followed by a 4-inch Highway Patrolman. I would like to tell you that I listed all the .357 Magnums available and weighed all of their personal virtues, however, my choice was much simpler than that. I simply purchased the first two .357 Magnums I ever saw. As I recall, the Ruger sold for $87.50 and the Smith was an even $85. My neighbor had a genuine Smith & Wesson .357 Mag-

num with a 6-1/2-inch barrel that I lusted after many times, but it was the only such sixgun I saw for many years. It would take awhile for all models of the .357 Magnum to hit my area.

My early years with the .357 Magnum did not last very long because I quickly switched to the .44 Special and .44 Magnum. Brass for the .357 Magnum was hard to come by, so most of us made do with .38 Special brass. It was mainly a case of economics because .38 Special brass was available and cheap. I used Keith's heavy .38 Special load with his bullet and also Ray Thompson's gas-checked 158 grain bullet which is cataloged by Lyman as #358156GC. Thompson was a real genius when it came to bullet design and I consider his gas check bullet for the .357 Magnum the best standard weight bullet available. It has two crimp grooves so it can be seated deep or in the bottom groove as the reloader wishes. Both of these bullets, over Keith's recommended charge in .38 Special brass, will give 1,400 feet per second plus in long-barreled .357 Magnum sixguns.

When we could get, or afford, .357 Magnum brass, we assembled most loads with Thompson's gas

Taffin's .357 Magnums from the 1950s: 5-1/2-inch Great Western .357 Atomic with staghorn stocks, Ruger 4-5/8-inch Flat-Top Blackhawk with Charles Able stag stocks, and 4-inch Smith & Wesson Combat Magnum with BearHug Skeeter Skelton rosewood stocks.

Smith & Wesson's 4-inch Combat Magnum Model 19 and 5-inch .357 Magnum Model 27 with BearHug stocks, and 6-1/2-inch Ruger .357 Blackhawk with stocks by Charles Able in leather built by the author.

The long, 8-3/8 inches, and short, 3-1/2 inches, of Smith & Wesson's .357 Magnum. Stocks by BearHug.

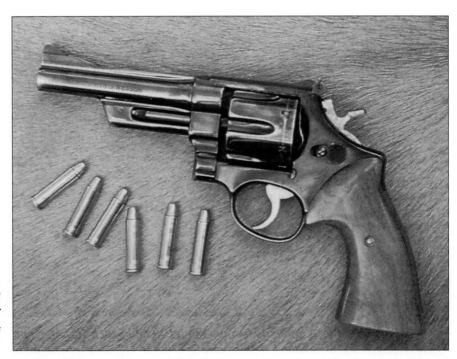

Skeeter Skelton's favorite barrel length in the Smith & Wesson .357 Magnum was 5 inches. BearHug Skeeter Skelton stocks.

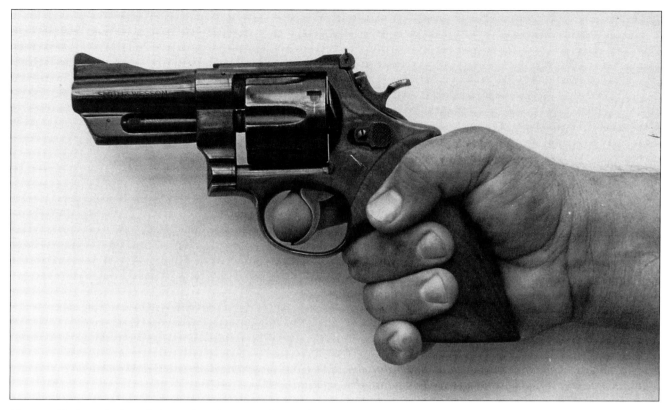

Skeeter Skelton designed these double action Smith & Wesson stocks. He started with Walter Roper's design for double action stocks, curved them more smoothly behind triggerguard, and widened them at the base to perfectly fit the hand for fast double action shooting.

check bullet over 14.5 to 15.5 grains of Hercules #2400. Some older manuals even go as high as the load used by Great Western in its .357 Atomic, 16 grains of #2400, but I do believe #2400 is hotter than it was forty years ago or maybe it is just that the primers are so much better. In either case, charges of 14.5 grains are plenty warm enough now.

I found myself in a real quandary with the Highway Patrolman .357. Its matte blue finish and standard walnut Magna grips made it look very plain. I saw a beautiful pair of white pearl, really pearlite, synthetic grips that really improved the looks of the .357 sixgun in the gun shop. Lawman Tom Threepersons carried a .45 Colt Single Action Army with real pearl grips. General George Patton became quite livid when someone mistakenly called his ivory grips pearl and uttered his famous quotation relegating pearl grips to New Orleans pimps.

Should I follow Patton or Threepersons? Threepersons won, but only briefly. The first time my new bride fired my Highway Patrolman, the pearl grips cracked and came apart in her hand and that was the end of that. A check for $12 went off to Herrett's Stocks and the Highway Patrolman was soon wearing a pair of walnut Trooper stocks that filled in behind

the triggerguard and the back of the backstrap. The Highway Patrolman was eventually sold to a cousin. I still have my wife and the Herrett's stocks. The stocks would come in mighty handy when I purchased my first Smith & Wesson .44 Magnum.

The .357 Magnum Model 27 cannot be replaced, but Smith & Wesson still offers some excellent .357 sixguns. The Combat Magnum, now Model 19, remains along with its stainless steel counterpart the Model 66. As .357 Magnum factory ammo became hotter with lightweight jacketed bullets, the Combat Magnum started developing problems with the forcing cone especially. Bill Jordan envisioned it as a .38 Special for most shooting with the capability to handle .357 Magnum loads for duty use. When it was used heavily with .357 Magnums, it was found wanting.

Smith & Wesson beefed-up the forcing cone area and enlarged the cylinder, but kept the K-frame sized grip frame. The result was the L-frame available in blue as the Model 586 and the stainless 686. Both guns carry full underlug barrels and have proven to be very accurate and rugged .357 Magnums. The latest Model is the 686 Plus with a seven-shot cylinder.

Meanwhile, Colt and Ruger were not just sitting around watching Smith & Wesson build .357 Mag-

The first modern centerfire single action: Ruger introduced this .357 Magnum 4-5/8-inch Blackhawk with a virtually indestructible coil spring action and excellent adjustable sights in 1955.

Ruger's three models of the .357 Blackhawk: The Flat-Top introduced in 1955, Old Model or Three-Screw brought forth in 1963, and New Model with transfer bar safety in 1973. The latter is in stainless steel.

Ruger's original Blackhawk has a smaller frame—Colt Single Action Army-size—than the stainless New Model Blackhawk, which is built on the Super Blackhawk-sized frame. The cylinder of the New Model is 9 percent longer than the original.

nums. The Colt Python is a superb sixgun to be sure. I have always been partial to the double action feel of Smith & Wesson sixguns, however, a dear friend recently went Home and it was his wish that I have his prize Python, an older 6-inch .357 that Fred Sadowski tuned to perfection. My friend's family concurred and I now have a Python with a double action pull that is as fine as ever found on any slicked-up Smith & Wesson. It is all in knowing how and Sadowski certainly knew how.

The Colt Python is based on an old design that has become quite expensive to produce. If Colt was to have a good share of the .357 Magnum market, it had to come up with a sixgun that could be sold for a lot less than the $800 price tag on a Python. The first answer was the Trooper series, a serviceable sixgun to be sure, but a long way from being awe-inspiring. Then Colt hit paydirt with the King Cobra series. These Colt .357 Magnums are good looking, accurate, rugged, owner proud, and most importantly, they have served as the platform from which Colt has offered the first .44 and .45 caliber double actions since before World War II. That sixgun, of course, is the large-framed Anaconda now offered in both .44 Magnum and .45 Colt.

Ruger had been producing single action sixguns for two decades and now entered the double action market in a big way with the Security-Six series of .38 Specials and .357 Magnums. After producing more than a million Security-Sixes, Ruger dropped the

design in favor of the more modern GP-100 which was then used to launch the first double action Ruger chambered in .44 Magnum, the Redhawk and Super Redhawk series. A few Redhawks were available in .357 Magnum chambering, but they are very difficult to find. Ruger also chambers its Bisley in .357 Magnum, and was one of the first manufacturers to offer a five-shot .357 Magnum with the SP-101, a most excellent .357 Magnum for concealment.

Dan Wesson entered the .357 Magnum field in the 1970s with the ugliest double action sixgun since the double action Smith & Wessons of the nineteenth century. The aesthetics were soon improved upon and with the coming of long-range silhouetting, the Dan Wesson really found its niche. We will cover the Dan Wessons in depth in later chapters on Silhouetting and SuperMags.

Taurus is the new kid on the block in big bore sixguns and offers quality .357 Magnums at prices below most of those produced in the USA. Diversity is definitely alive and well at Taurus, and it is now offering both seven- and eight-shot large-framed .357 Magnums.

After sixty years of straight forward .357 Magnums, manufacturers have started to take side roads and offer a new look for the .357 Magnum. First came Freedom Arms and the .357 Magnum-chambered Casull revolver that is barrel-marked not .357 Magnum, but 353 Casull. The Silhouette Model has a 9-inch barrel instead of the 10-inch barrels available on the .454

Ruger's GP-100 has proven to be a rugged .357 Magnum. These 6-inch guns have factory stocks (top) and BearHug stocks (bottom).

and .44 Magnum because it will not make the 4 pound competition weight limit with a longer barrel. The 353 Casull is a natural follow-up to the .454 Casull and 252. Don't let the name fool you; it handles all .38 Special and .357 Magnum brass and loadings and there is no 353 Casull ammunition except for custom specialty .357 Magnum ammunition from Cor-Bon with 180 grain bullets for hunting contained in a box labeled for use in the 353 Casull only.

The 353 Casull is a standard Freedom Arms revolver built the same as the .454 Casull. The technicians at Freedom Arms pre-drill the cylinders, fit them to the frame, and then line-bore them to the barrel, all in an effort to ensure perfect alignment with barrel and cylinder at the time the bullet is transferred to the barrel upon firing. That is, each cylinder is chambered as it is fitted to the frame. Cylinders are not chambered in mass quantities and then simply fitted to a frame. Each barrel, frame, and cylinder is a precisely fitted unit.

With the .357 Magnum chambering in the 353 Casull, amazing things happen. We are talking 160 grain bullets at 1,750 feet per second, 180 grain bullets at 1,650 feet per second, and 200 grain bullets at 1,500 feet per second. To put that into perspective, one needs only to look at some standard .357 Magnum loadings. These same jacketed bullets custom

loaded for my pet 8-3/8-inch .357 Magnum, the original .357 from Smith & Wesson, will safely do 1,350, 1,250, and 1,050 feet per second respectively. That is, to say the least, a dramatic difference.

Most of my shooting of the 353 Casull has been with a standard production Silhouette Model with 9-inch barrel and Iron Sight Gun Works rear sight and sharply undercut black Patridge front sight. The factory gun has a groove diameter of .357 inch and 1:14 twist barrel designed to stabilize the heavier 180 grain and 200 grain .357 bullets used for silhouetting and hunting.

The argument continues over whether or not the .357 Magnum is a hunting handgun. My friend Bill Ripple of Ohio, a thoroughly experienced Eastern deer hunter, says that the standard .357 Magnum is adequate for everything east of the Mississippi River. If the standard .357 Magnum is adequate for Eastern deer hunting, the .357/353 Casull combination will be superb. For the first time we have a .357 Magnum that will utilize Hornady 158 grain XTPs at 1,750 feet per second and both 180 grain XTPs and Cor-Bons will do 1,600 plus feet per second. Bob Baker of Freedom Arms took the first game with the 353 Casull, a black buck antelope at over 100 yards on the Y.O. Ranch with a 180 Cor-Bon at 1,600 feet per second.

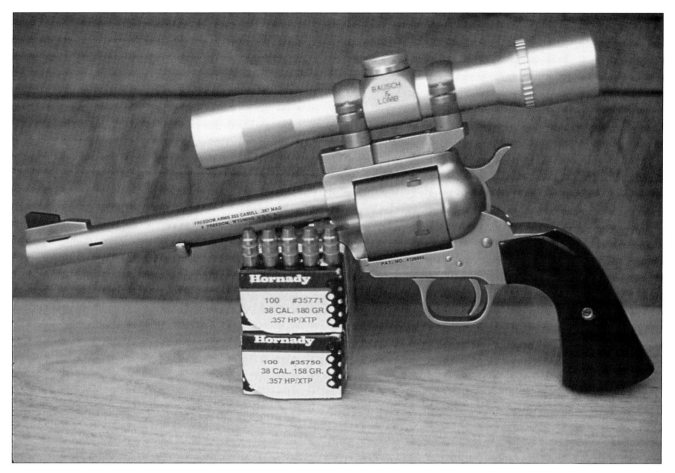

The Freedom Arms .353 Casull and Hornady's XTP bullets are an excellent combination. For the first time in a .357 Magnum we can drive 158 grain and 180 grain hunting bullets at 1,700 fps!

The 353 Casull can be loaded far above the performance of any other .357 Magnum or .357 Maximum/SuperMag revolver, but that is not its only claim to fame. It makes a perfectly superb .357 Magnum when used with standard loads that gave an average 25-yard five-shot group of 1.08 inches and an average 50-yard five-shot group of 1.25 inches. Those averages are miles above average for .357 Magnum revolvers! A direct result of the precision fit of the Casull revolvers.

Smith & Wesson, the first to produce a .357 Magnum more than sixty years ago, has taken a completely different path than that taken by Freedom Arms which produced the largest and most powerful .357 Magnum. Smith & Wesson is now offering its smallest .357 Magnum ever. Interestingly enough, both of these relatively new .357 Magnums are five-shooters, but the similarity ends there.

The first successful stainless steel revolver was Smith & Wesson's Chief's Special .38 in its stainless steel counterpart known as the Model 60. Smith's new Model 60 .357 Magnum weighs in at 22 ounces

unloaded. The barrel length is 2-1/8 inches, but the frame and cylinder are 1/4 inch longer than the original Model 60 .38 Special which makes the entire little J-frame .357 3/8 inch longer than the original.

The stainless steel Model 60 .357 Magnum has a carbon steel trigger and hammer with a smooth-faced trigger. The firing pin, unlike most Smith & Wesson revolvers, is frame-mounted rather than hammer face-mounted. The sights are a square rear, milled into the top of the frame and mated up with a black ramp front pinned into place. This combination gives an excellent sight picture. The factory grips are Uncle Mike's large finger groove-style that are out of place on a pocket pistol. They are much too large for ease of concealment and were quickly replaced with Uncle Mike's Boot Grip design. This is the smallest possible grip that I am aware of available for a J-frame round butt as this Model 60 is.

As one might expect, muzzle velocities with the Model 60 are nowhere near what one would obtain with a 6-inch sixgun, but the Speer Gold Dot 125 grain jacketed hollowpoints, for example, do break 1,200

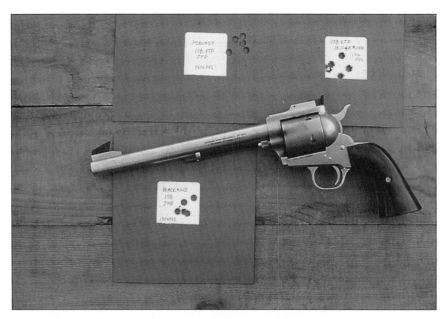

The superb accuracy of the .353 Casull: These groups, shot with Hornady and Black Hills factory ammunition at 25 yards, are all less than 1 inch in size.

Smith & Wesson's latest: A five-shot 2-1/8-inch Model 60 in .357 Magnum! Uncle Mike's Boot grips help to conceal this little powerhouse.

All the bases are covered .357 Magnum-style with these BearHug-stocked Smith & Wessons: A 3-1/2 inch for duty use, a general purpose 5 inch, and an 8-3/8 inch for long-range shooting.

feet per second from the short barrel of the Model 60 .357 Magnum. That is a lot of punch from such a small package. The same load does 1,500 plus feet per second from a 6-inch barrel which results in a loss of 300 feet per second when going from a 6-inch to a 2-inch barrel.

I receive many inquiries from those who are ready to move up from a .22 to a centerfire sixgun, and the question is always about caliber. In return, I ask them exactly what they want the new sixgun to do for them. Most people want a gun that will serve for protection, for informal target shooting, for packing when camping or fishing, and for providing a general feeling of security. If big game hunting is not mentioned, I do not hesitate to recommend the .357 Magnum.

Every .357 Magnum also accepts .38 Special ammunition, and the .38 Special and .357 Magnum loading offerings are tremendously varied and travel from easy shootin' 148 grain target loads in .38 Special to full-house 180 grain jacketed loads for the

.357 Magnum. The purpose of any defensive sixgun is to stop the fight and 125 grain jacketed hollow-point loads in the .357 Magnum have the best stopping power record of any of the calibers normally used for defensive purposes. If these provide more power than is comfortable for all members of the family to handle—all members of the family should be familiar with the use of any defensive sixguns—it is an easy shift to the same bullet in an easier shooting .38 Special round.

The .357 Magnum has now been serving the six-gunning population for more than six decades. It not only does its job with minimum recoil, but is also extremely versatile. It can be loaded for small game and varmints as well as silhouettes and it does each job very well. As a defensive proposition, it can be handled by most shooters competently at least in full-sized sixguns that do not have the nasty recoil of the pocket .357s as offered by Ruger, Smith & Wesson, and Taurus. It is not the best choice for big game hunting, but can be pressed into service by a very

More than sixty years of great shootin' sixguns from Smith & Wesson are represented by the 4-inch .38/44 (1930), the 3-1/2-inch .357 Magnum (1935), the 4-inch Combat Magnum (1956), and the 3-inch M65 (1992).

Ruger made a small number of .357 Blackhawks with 10-inch barrels.

careful sixgunner. Most of my hunting with the .357 Magnum has been of small game and varmints, however, I have taken two deer-sized critters with it and neither one took a step after being hit. On the other hand, a friend shot a black bear with his .357 Magnum and he now carries a Ruger Blackhawk in .45 Colt loaded with 300 grain bullets.

The .357 Magnum, the first Magnum, still remains the most popular Magnum because it offers the most in power for the least in recoil. I do not expect that to change in my lifetime.

CHAPTER 5

THE .44 MAGNUM— KING OF THE SIXGUNS

In 1871, the .44 Russian cartridge, adapted from the .44 Smith & Wesson American at the request of the Russian government—which subsequently ordered 20,000 of the new Smith & Wesson sixguns—arrived on the sixgunning scene. As the twentieth century dawned and everyone was looking to the future, Smith & Wesson lengthened the Russian case and introduced the .44 Special. The .44 American had carried an outside lubricated bullet, the Russian moved the lube grooves inside the case, and the advent of the Special increased brass length from .970 inch to 1.160 inches.

The .44 Special first saw the light of day in what is probably the finest double-action sixgun ever produced, the New Century Hand Ejector First Model, more lovingly known as the Triple-Lock. The name comes from the fact that the first N-frame Smith & Wesson locked the cylinder at the rear, the front, and also at the end of the ejector rod. The New Century rivaled a fine watch in its craftsmanship.

The .44 Special cartridge, in spite of its capabilities in the new large-framed Smith & Wesson .44, was only loaded to its mid-range .44 Russian velocities, however it gathered a small, but knowledgeable following of reloaders and experimenters around it. Like its older brother, the .44 Russian, the .44 Special was a superbly accurate cartridge. I have run tests with blackpowder and Pyrodex loads in both the old .44 Russian brass, all of which were balloon head-style as opposed to the more modern solid head brass we have had in most handgun cartridges since the 1950s, and balloon head .44 Special brass. Both were capable of 1-inch groups at 25 yards from handguns of the period.

Although it would be twenty years after the Triple-Lock was introduced, one of those to discover the .44 Special was, of course, Elmer Keith. Keith found that he could load both Colts and Smith & Wessons to

speeds more than 50 percent above the factory loading of the .44 Special. Keith used a 250 grain semi-wadcutter bullet of his design, and first used #80 powder, now long gone, and as it became available, #2400 to achieve speeds of 1,200 feet per second with the .44 Special.

Keith used the old balloon head .44 Special brass and settled on 18.5 grains of #2400 for his powerful load that he considered far and above any sixgun load including the .357 Magnum that came along in 1935. Keith tested the new .357 Magnum from Smith & Wesson and wrote it up in *The American Rifleman*. His conclusion was that the .44 Special with his loads was superior.

Our local gun shop, Shapel's, always seems to come up with the most interesting guns as well as many accessories that go with them. A few years back, they purchased an estate that included a good supply of balloon head brass in .45 Colt, .44-40, .38-40, .44 Russian, and thankfully, .44 Special. I was most happy to take this link to the past off their hands. I duplicated Keith's .44 Special load in a 7-1/2-inch Colt New Frontier .44 Special. It gave me a reading on the Oehler M35P chronograph of 1,246 feet per second. When solid head brass became available, Keith dropped his standard loading to 17 grains of #2400 for slightly over 1,200 feet per second.

Handgun hunting today is a most popular pastime with dedicated sixgunners as well as those who espouse the long-range capabilities of single-shots such as the superbly accurate and deadly efficient Thompson/Center Contender. Keith, who wrote much about hunting with a handgun, was not a handgun hunter in the strictest sense; he instead preferred to carry a powerful rifle afield. He did, however, kill a lot of game with first the .45 Colt, and then his beloved .44 Special, simply because he always carried a sixgun and viewed it as a weapon of convenience with

Elmer Keith was the number one person responsible for Smith & Wesson's decision to introduce a .44 Magnum.

his heavy handloads in Colt Single Actions and Smith & Wesson Triple-Locks, as well as Model 1926 and Model 1950 .44 Specials.

For nearly thirty years Keith urged ammunition companies to bring out his load. They were afraid that the load was too powerful for some of the older sixguns, so Keith urged that they do the same thing that they did in 1908: increase the length of the existing .44 case, thus allowing it to only chamber in new revolvers specifically chambered for the new ".44 Special Magnum."

While Keith was urging adoption of a powerful .44 Special load, another writer was taking a different route. John Lachuk, like Elmer Keith, was also a member of the .44 Associates. In the 1940s he had discovered a real fondness for Colt Single Actions, in general, and the .44 Special chambering in particular, especially in its most powerful loadings. He wanted more, though. After experimenting with several bullet designs, he decided to go the wildcat route. This was

at a time when .44 Special brass was only available in balloon head-style and Lachuk felt that a solid head case would give him more strength and higher velocities with safety. Using three Colt Single Action sixguns, two with 7-1/2-inch barrels and the other with a 5-1/2 inch, Lachuk set about to go the .44 Special one better.

For brass, Lachuk shortened .405 Winchester and .30-40 Krag rifle brass to .44 Special length. This diminished case capacity, however, due to the thickness of the rifle brass resulted in the need to lengthen the case as long as possible and still use 240 grain bullets in the Colt cylinders. Lachuk cut the rifle brass to length to allow a capacity of 34 grains of #2400. This is case capacity not a suggested load!

Lachuk chambered three .38 Special cylinders to accept the wildcat .44 round. Each of the three Single Actions that received these custom cylinders were also fitted up very tightly with minimum barrel/cylinder gaps, oversized base pins, and locking bolts. Tol-

Elmer Keith's everyday .44 Magnum with carved ivory stocks. Keith designed the knife.

erances are extremely important when using high pressure sixgun loads.

In 1949, Lachuk submitted an article on his wildcat .44. It was rejected. He tried to get Hercules to pressure test his round, but its equipment would only handle .44 Special length brass. He tried to interest Colt in chambering for his new round. This idea was also rejected.

At the same time, Keith was still trying to get Smith & Wesson interested enough in his .44 Special load to build a new sixgun around it. Finally in 1953, Keith got Remington and Smith & Wesson talking together and both said they would do their part. Smith would build the sixgun if Remington would supply the ammunition; Remington would build the ammunition if Smith & Wesson would supply the sixgun. Keith had the promise, but he didn't think it would really go anywhere.

Elmer Keith did not invent the .44 Magnum as some have mistakenly said. He and his kind, such as the other members of the .44 Associates that loaded the .44 Special to its capacity (some would say over-capacity) and freely swapped information, were

directly responsible for the .44 Magnum. Keith did not invent the .44 Magnum, but he certainly was the major force behind the .44 Magnum becoming a reality, because he touted his .44 Special loads in both magazine articles and books for three decades.

Keith and Lachuk had taken different routes to the .44 Magnum. Both were at the point that neither expected anything to happen with the major firearms and ammunition companies so Keith was as surprised as anyone when he received a call from Smith & Wesson in January of 1956— it was sending him the first .44 Magnum. Actually, Keith received the third one out of the factory. Number one went to Remington, developer of the ammunition, and the second went to Major Julian Hatcher of *The American Rifleman* staff.

Keith had spent thirty years asking for a 250 grain bullet at 1,200 feet per second; he got even more with a 240 grain bullet at 1,450 feet per second. Actually, the original loads were even hotter. He was tremendously pleased about the new gun and caliber. He retired his .44 Specials and carried a 4-inch Smith & Wesson .44 Magnum daily until his incapacitating

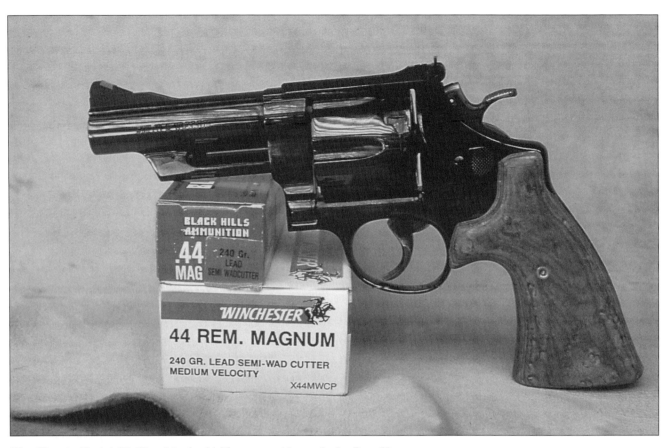

The Classic Model 29: The 4-inch .44 Magnum with stocks by BearHug.

Smith & Wesson produced 2,500 Elmer Keith Commemorative 4-inch .44 Magnums in 1985.

stroke in 1981. He would spend the last three decades of his life promoting the .44 Magnum, in general, and the Smith & Wesson sixgun in particular. He sold more Smith & Wessons through his writings than any salesman ever dreamed of.

Keith did not spend years searching for the perfect load for the .44 Magnum. He did not build endless pages of loading data. He simply found one .44 Magnum load and used it exclusively. The load was his .44 caliber 250 grain bullet over 22 grains of #2400, and as with all of his sixgun loads, he used standard primers only. This is a very powerful load and recoil in a 4-inch .44 Magnum is noticeable, to say the least.

Remington worked on the cartridge and Smith & Wesson worked on the sixgun, and together they developed the .44 Magnum. The first four factory prototype .44 Magnums were Smith & Wesson 1950 Target .44 Specials with specially heat-treated cylinders and frames. Anyone with much experience shooting

heavy loads in the .44 Special realizes that recoil is right up there. Those engineers worked with a .44 Special sixgun and loads that were 350 feet per second faster than the Keith load in a .44 Special. They certainly paid their dues! With the 39 ounce weight of the 1950 Target giving such excessive recoil, weight had to be added. A bull barrel and a full length cylinder were added, bringing the weight of the final 6-1/2-inch .44 Magnum up to an even 3 pounds. The change was made for weight, however, it resulted in one of the best looking sixguns ever.

The early Smith & Wesson .44 Magnums came very close to the precision fitting of the 1908 Triple-Lock, albeit without the third locking feature, and carried a beautiful finish known then as S&W Bright Blue. Keith was so pleased with the new gun and cartridge that he immediately had one cut to a barrel length of 4-1/2 inches and had it completely engraved and ivory-stocked by the old Gun Re-Blu Company. It became

The recoil of Smith & Wesson's 8-3/8-inch .44 Magnum with Keith load of 250 grain hard cast bullet over 22 grains of #2400 is stout, but not punishing.

The first .44 Magnums—Smith & Wesson's .44 Magnum and Ruger's Blackhawk. Both have 6-1/2-inch barrels, the Smith & Wesson has BearHug stocks, and the Ruger has Charles Able stocks.

one of his everyday .44 Magnum packin' pistols, even before 4-inch guns were available from the factory. Prior to the advent of the .44 Magnum, he carried a 4-inch .44 Special, also stocked and engraved by Gun Re-Blu. After the mid-1950s, he actually had at least three short-barreled .44 Magnum sixguns that he carried regularly, including the custom sixgun from Gun Re-Blu, a factory 4-inch gun completely engraved, and a plain vanilla 4-inch blue sixgun. All three carried ivory stocks.

The Smith & Wesson .44 Magnum came with hand-filling grips that had previously been supplied on its sixguns destined for target shooting. They seemed somewhat out of place on the 4-inch .44 Magnum and I tried smaller stocks. Ouch! I often wondered how Keith could shoot his heavy loads in the 4-inch Smith & Wesson .44 Magnum because the recoil is brutal, especially with the standard Smith & Wesson Magna-style stocks that Keith preferred. He called them plainclothes stocks because they could be carried under a jacket easier than the full target stocks that came standard on the new .44.

The smaller stocks neither filled in behind the triggerguard nor at the hump of the backstrap. I discov-

ered the secret of recoil control when I had the privilege of unloading and examining his sixguns after his death. Each of his sixguns was equipped with meticulously carved ivory stocks. As I held them in my hand, I discovered that each stock was carved on the right side so that it naturally filled in the palm of the shooting hand and helped control felt recoil—a wise man indeed! I have since had gripmaker Bob Leskovec make me a set of carved stocks for a 4-inch sixgun. It seemed apropos to put them on a 4-inch Smith & Wesson Elmer Keith Commemorative .44 Magnum. I wish I had known this secret of good stocks thirty years ago.

When Keith reported on the .44 Magnum in *The Gun Digest* one year later, he showed once again how smart he really was. He reported that he had fired the new sixgun 600 times during the year. That averages to twelve rounds per week, and creates a shooting schedule that is guaranteed to allow both shooter and sixgun to last for a long time!

When Lachuk received his first batch of the new .44 Magnum ammunition, he found it to be a deadringer for his wildcat round and that it also fit the chambers of his wildcat Single Action Army sixguns perfectly. He removed the wildcat cylinders, replaced them with .44 Special cylinders, and took up the Smith & Wesson .44 Magnum. A very wise move as far as .44 Magnums in the Colt Single Action are concerned!

While Keith settled in with one load in the .44 Magnum, Lachuk, ever the experimenter, tried every bullet and load combination he could and shared his knowledge through magazine articles and *The Gun Digest*. It has been my privilege to meet John Lachuk in recent years. I've enjoyed his writing immensely over the years and have found him to be just as enjoyable in person. The fact that we both love Single Action Armys, Smith & Wessons, .44 Specials, and .44 Magnums, probably does not hurt our relationship in the least.

It was previously stated that Lachuk's wildcat round had a capacity of 34 grains of #2400. Balloon head .44 Special brass went 36 grains, solid head brass filled up to the mouth of the case held 32

grains, and the new .44 Magnum brass would accept 35 grains. Again, this is capacity, not recommended loads. He also found that his wildcat load of 22.5 grains of #2400 with a 235 grain bullet was close enough to the factory .44 Magnum to be a virtual deadringer, both as to bullet weight and muzzle velocity.

While Remington and Smith & Wesson were experimenting with and introducing the new .44 Magnum ammunition and a beautiful new sixgun, what about the new kid on the block? Sturm, Ruger & Co., which introduced the .22 semi-automatic in 1949, the .22 Single-Six in 1953, and the .357 Blackhawk in 1955, had only been around for seven years.

Somehow, someway, someone at Ruger received word of a new cartridge's development. The story goes that a Ruger employee found a piece of brass in the trash at Remington—one has to wonder what he was doing there—but it at least makes a good story. Ruger went to work rechambering its .357 Blackhawk

The original Ruger Blackhawk .44 Magnum, the Flat-Top, came with a 6-1/2-inch standard barrel length; only about 1,000 were made in each the 7-1/2 and 10 inch lengths.

to the new ".44 Special Magnum." The .357 Blackhawk of the 1950s was built with a smaller frame and cylinder than the present .357 New Model and Keith told the Company that the gun was too small, but he would like to have one to use as a .44 Special.

Before he was given the first .44 Ruger, factory testing proved he was right when the .357 Magnum converted to .44 Magnum blew. This also points to how close to the edge Lachuk may have been with its wildcat .44 in the Colt Single Action frames and cylinders that are the same size as the original Ruger Blackhawk. I have fired a Colt Single Action .44 Magnum that Dick Casull built up, however, it has a specially heat-treated frame; Casull did not use a rechambered factory cylinder, but rather built up a custom cylinder made as large as possible to completely fill the frame window. He also chambered it himself for the .44 Magnum. Tolerances are as close as we would see later on the Freedom Arms line of Casull revolvers. Ruger went back to the drawing board and the result was the larger-framed .44 Blackhawk now known to collectors as the Flat-Top.

In some parts of the country, the Ruger .44 was actually seen before the Smith & Wesson .44 Magnum. That was 1956 and the Smith & Wesson, beautifully finished with magnificently smooth action and trigger pull, sold for $140. I was a teenager, just finishing high school, making $15 a week with a paper route at the time. The Ruger, not quite as nicely finished, sold for $96.

A local gun store/outdoor shooting range rented out the first Smith & Wesson .44 Magnum to hit my part of the country to all who wanted to try the big .44 Magnum. The recoil was absolutely awful, though few would admit it at the time. After I graduated from high school, I bought the first Ruger Blackhawk in the area for the full $96 at a time when I had now progressed to a regular job and made ninety cents an hour. I had yet to see a Smith & Wesson for sale. This would soon change.

The first Smith & Wesson .44 Magnums, residing in their fitted wooden cases, were absolutely beautiful. They were purchased by guides and outfitters and handgun hunters who were ahead of their time. Many gun stores soon had used .44 Magnums, both Smith & Wessons and Rugers, for sale with a box of cartridges with six empties and forty-four .44s still intact. One cylinderful was all it usually took for many shooters to realize that this was more pain than they wanted. In the report in *The American Rifleman*, Major Hatcher said firing the big sixgun was not unlike getting hit in the palm of the hand with a baseball bat! Keith said it wouldn't bother a "seasoned sixgun

man." The truth was somewhere in between the two statements—at least for shooters in the 1950s.

I have a like-new .44 Ruger I purchased from a widow. It came with a box of original Remington ammunition with twelve empty cases and thirty-eight loaded rounds. Its previous owner was braver than most. He fired *two* cylindersful before he put it away.

Ruger wisely decided that its .44 Magnum was too light for the cartridge and in 1959 introduced the now classic Super Blackhawk. To increase weight, a non-fluted cylinder was used and the grip frame was increased in size from the Colt Single Action-style to the Colt Dragoon- style and it was made of steel rather than a lightweight alloy as on the Flat-Top. It still kicked like the proverbial mule.

The .44 Magnum was not a great selling sixgun in those early days because many were afraid of the recoil. It was so far ahead of anything ever offered that it would take some learning time for those of us used to the recoil generated by standard .45 Colts, .44 Specials, and .357 Magnums to be able to handle a .44 Magnum. Time and experience solved the problem immensely.

The .44 Magnum could easily have remained a very slow-selling specialty sixgun, but along came Dirty Harry. Clint Eastwood's famous character, whose exploits with the Smith & Wesson .44 Magnum began in the early 1970s, created a huge demand for the .44 Magnum mainly from people who had never shot a .44 Magnum. Some had never even shot a handgun, for that matter, but were caught up in the movie-style "Make my day" nonsense.

The demand could not be satisfied no matter how much Smith & Wesson increased production. Suddenly, .44 Magnums which had been selling at less than retail were going for double-retail and more. Those who could not get Smith & Wessons turned to the Ruger Super Blackhawk, and it then became nearly impossible to find a Ruger .44.

Two positive things came out of this situation, though. First, shooters who could not get a .44 Magnum looked to that other big bore Magnum, the .41, and found they had discovered another fine sixgun. Second, other companies began to look at the possibility of producing a double action .44 Magnum.

The rise of handgun hunting and silhouetting created a real rather than a phoney demand for .44 Magnum sixguns in the mid-1970s. Now there was a genuine need for .44 Magnums and the Ruger Super Blackhawk and the Smith & Wesson Model 29 .44 Magnums would soon be joined by the new wave of larger and heavier .44 Magnums. With the rise of handgun hunting and heavier sixguns chambered for the .44 Magnum, the reloading of the .44 Magnum would also

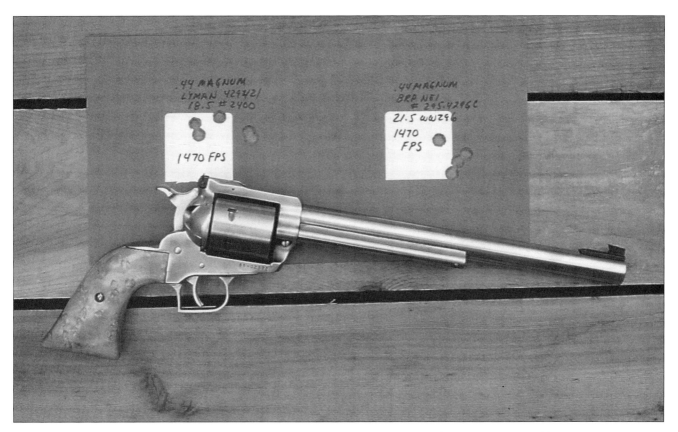

Ruger's current long-barreled .44 Magnum is the superbly accurate Stainless Super Blackhawk. These loads, Keith/Lyman #429421 over 18.5 grains of #2400 and BRP 310 grain Keith over 21.5 grains of WW296, both clocked-out at 1,470 fps and are in the 1-inch category.

change dramatically. The old standard Keith load had been his 250 grain hard cast semi-wadcutter bullet over 22 grains of #2400. This was, and still remains, an excellent hunting load for many applications, but as bigger and bigger game, including elephant and Cape buffalo were hunted with the .44 Magnum, the standard hunting load became a hard cast 290 to 320 grain bullet at 1,300 to 1,400 feet per second.

The forty year history of the .44 Magnum is basically a Smith & Wesson and Ruger story with some input from Colt, Dan Wesson, Freedom Arms, Texas Longhorn Arms, Taurus, and a few other foreign imports.

The first Ruger .44 Magnum Blackhawk carried a 6-1/2-inch barrel and a single action grip configuration identical to the Colt Single Action. I've never been able to figure out why Ruger used the 6-1/2-inch instead of the standard Colt 7-1/2-inch barrel. Later it would add 7-1/2-inch barrels, but they are very rare and usually reside in Ruger collectors' hands. The .357 Magnum Blackhawk and the later .41 Magnum Blackhawk have never been offered in a 7-1/2-inch length, which to me is very close to a crime. The .45 Colt and .30 Carbine, however, come standard with 7-

1/2-inch barrels and all the centerfire Bisleys, the .357, .41, .44, and .45 Colt, are all offered only with 7-1/2-inch barrels. Who can figure?

The fine-feeling Colt-style grip was perfect for the Blackhawk until the trigger was pulled! Up to this point in time, the Colt-style grip had never experienced anything hotter than a full-house .44 Special. The natural roll of the single action grip did not handle the recoil of the full-house .44 Magnums loads very well at all. In fact, one of my acquaintances who insisted upon firing a full-house .44 Magnum load in the Blackhawk, allowed it to roll right out of her hand and down, down, down, into the mud. I learned a lot from that experience and to this day never, ever, let anyone begin with full-house loadings of any of the big bore Magnums.

The first time I fired the .44 Blackhawk, it removed a substantial chunk of skin from the back of my hand as the big .44 recoiled and the hammer dug in. It would be a number of years before I realized that the .44 Magnum had to be approached differently than other sixgun cartridges and required sixguns fitted with custom grips and, more importantly, a completely new mental attitude.

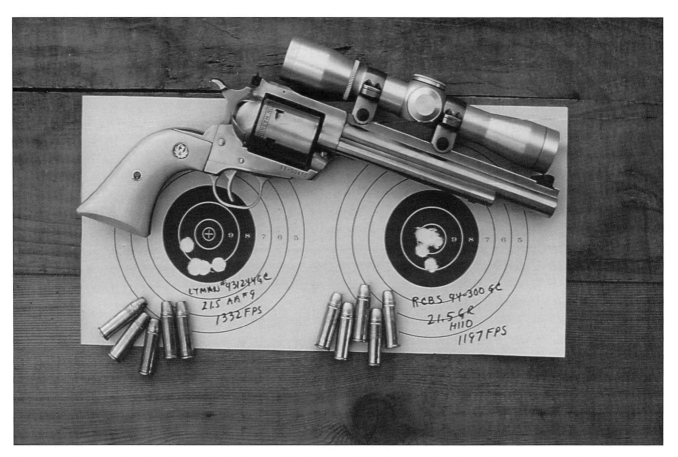

Ruger produced only a few Hunter Model Super Blackhawks: This fine hunting sixgun has a stainless finish, rounded-off triggerguard, and a 7-1/2-inch heavy barrel set up for Ruger rings for easy scope mounting. These groups were shot at 50 yards. The black bullseye is 3 inches.

It didn't make sense not to use full-house loads at least occasionally in a sixgun that could handle them, so the Blackhawk was eventually fitted with a wide Super Blackhawk trigger and hammer, the barrel was cut to an easy packin' 4-5/8 inches and, most importantly, was fitted with stocks that did not have the recoil accentuating taper of the factory's offering. I also learned that the Good Lord had given us two hands for a good reason and the .44 Magnum was definitely a two-handed proposition. It was carried many miles for many years on many trips into the Idaho hills as a favorite packin' pistol.

The .357 Blackhawk of 1955 was immediately followed by the .44 Blackhawk of 1956. By 1963, the .44 Blackhawk was dropped in favor of the Super Blackhawk which had been introduced in 1959 and still exists as the New Model Super Blackhawk. All Ruger Single Actions, except the Old Army, became New Models in 1973 with the addition of a transfer bar safety.

The Super Blackhawk has been one of the real workhorses of the handgunning world. Ruger, early in the silhouetting game, introduced a long-barreled .44, a 10-1/2-inch barreled silhouette model. My wife and I used a pair of these New Model Blackhawks for silhouetting and found them to be exceptionally accurate sixguns. We added a third long-barreled stainless .44 Super Blackhawk to our working collection later for hunting and it has proven to be even better at punching small groups than the two blued models. The two original silhouette sixguns? They are both now doing great service as packin' pistols. One is now a 5-1/2-inch sixgun with custom brass grip frame of the standard-style from Qualite Pistol & Revolver, and the other has been converted to a 5-1/2-inch five-shot .45 Colt by Jim Stroh. I expect to pass them both on to grandkids when my time is done.

My experience with long-barreled .44 Blackhawks started even before the New Models arrived. Less than 1,000 of the original .44 Blackhawks had been made with 10-inch barrels and my wife presented me with one of these to celebrate my finishing graduate school. Had I known what awaited me at the end of that experience, I would have enjoyed it more! That

Flat-Top .44 Magnum became a favorite hunting six-gun and I carried for years in a Goerg shoulder holster. Al Goerg was a real pioneer of handgun hunting and developed a real working shoulder holster. Unfortunately, he was killed on a hunting trip in Alaska in the late 1960s.

The Super Blackhawk remains the number one bargain in a .44 Magnum sixgun to date. Consider the fact that it sells, as of this writing, for only $3 more than an Italian Colt Single Action replica .44 Magnum that is without adjustable sights and coil springs. In spite of all its virtues, I am one who has never liked the square-backed Dragoon-style triggerguard on the Super Blackhawk grip frame and have either replaced it with an Old Model or New Model standard grip frame, or have had the grip altered to a rounded triggerguard. As mentioned in the chapter on the .45 Colt, I was very happy to see the introduction of the Bisley Ruger because the grip frame is perfect for my hand; it feels a lot like the Freedom Arms single action grip and the original Keith #5SA grip now found on Texas Longhorn Arms Improved Number Five. The Bisley in .44 Magnum is nothing more than a Super Blackhawk fitted with a superior grip shape and a hammer spur that rides lower. Everything good we can say about the Blackhawk applies in spades to the Bisley.

In addition to the Bisley, available only in blue finish with a 7-1/2-inch barrel, and the Super Blackhawk, available in 7-1/2- and 10-1/2-inch lengths and in blue or stainless finishes, Ruger also offers a 5-1/2-inch Super Blackhawk in blue or stainless with a standard Blackhawk grip frame of steel rather than lightweight alloy as on the other Blackhawks. As expected, this rather lightweight .44 Magnum is a superb packin' pistol, but kicks like a mule.

Not only does Ruger have the single action .44 Magnum bases thoroughly covered by the Super Blackhawk, but it also has a real one-two punch with what is probably the strongest double action .44 Magnum available. The unreal demand for double action .44 Magnums Dirty Harry created was not broken until Ruger introduced its first double action, the Redhawk. This is a big, tough .44 Magnum—actually

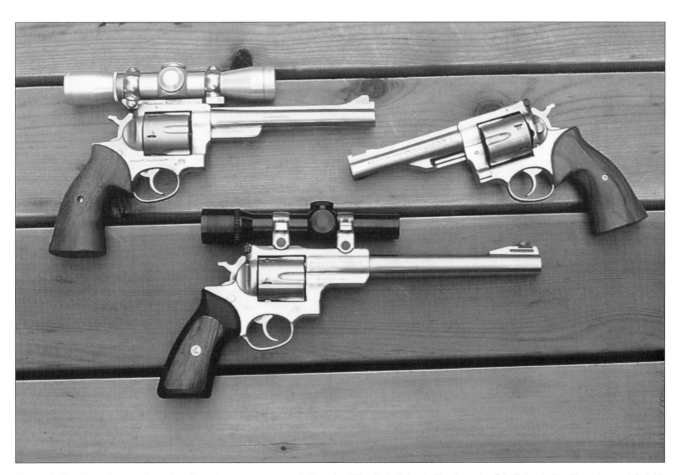

Ruger's Redhawks are hunting handguns, pure and simple: The 7-1/2-inch Redhawk, 5-1/2-inch Redhawk, and 9-1/2-inch Super Redhawk will all easily handle the heaviest .44 loads.

larger and probably stronger than the Super Black-hawk—and has become a real favorite of handgun hunters who use a lot of 300 grain hard cast bullets over heavy doses of WW296 or H110. The first Redhawk was a 7-1/2-inch stainless sixgun, and models are now also available in a 5-1/2-inch length and in either a blue or stainless finish.

The Redhawk is also available scope-ready with scalloped barrel and Ruger rings. A 10-inch barrel was promised early, but has never materialized. What has come about, though, is an even larger double action .44 Magnum, the Super Redhawk with a 9-1/2-inch barrel. Everything that can be said about the strength of the Redhawk can be increased when one talks about the Super Redhawk.

The Redhawk .44 represented the .44 Magnum of the '80s. It was big and tough and was able to withstand the recoil of not only standard .44 Magnums, but also of the new heavyweight bullet loads that handgun hunters soon demanded. Smith & Wesson had built its .44 Magnum around the basic design of the 1908 New Century Triple-Lock. Ruger started from scratch with new technology and came up with a sixgun of superior strength. Handloaders found that the durable Redhawk was capable of delivering 300 grain cast bullets at 1,500 feet per second from its 7-1/2-inch barrel, a load that gives maximum .44 Magnum penetration on large game.

Once the Redhawk was solidly entrenched and Ruger caught up with the demand, it introduced the Super Redhawk. The Super Redhawk is not simply a larger Redhawk as one would expect. Instead of just changing the Redhawk, Ruger used the GP-100 as the basis for its latest .44 Magnum. The Super Redhawk is actually the result of the blend between the GP-100's and the standard Redhawk's best features.

Three major changes are found in the newest Redhawk. First, the Super Redhawk has separate springs for the trigger and hammer, reminiscent of the hammer spring and strut used in its single action revolvers. The result is a much smoother from-the-box trigger pull. The second major change is found in the grip area. The GP-100 stud that accepts the rubberized GP-100 grip panels, or better yet, custom grips has replaced the Redhawk grip frame. The third change is by far the most radical. The Ruger Super

Recoil of the Ruger Super Redhawk with 300 grain .44 Magnum hunting loads.

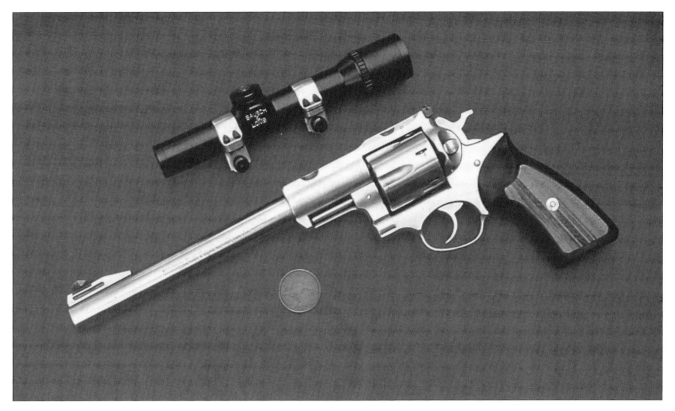

Ruger's Super Redhawk is easily scope-mounted with Ruger Rings and scallops on frame.

Redhawk has a distinctive profile not found on any other revolver. The frame itself has been extended forward of the cylinder so that the frame actually encloses the first 2-1/2 inches of the barrel. This feature accomplishes two things. First, the frame is made heavier and stronger, and second, an integral scope mounting system may be used on the frame rather than the barrel.

The Super Redhawk, like some Redhawks, comes with stainless scope rings that mount solidly on the frame using one large screw for each and semi-circular recesses on each side of the frame. The rings install easily, and once the scope is zeroed-in, it will come back very close when the scope is removed and replaced again. This easy on-again, off-again feature allows almost instant use of scope or iron sights, and makes the Super Redhawk very popular as a foul weather hunting sixgun.

With four .44 Magnum models offered to sixgunners, including the Super Blackhawk, the Bisley, the Redhawk, and the Super Redhawk, it would be difficult to find a .44 situation that could not be covered by at least one of the Ruger .44s.

The Smith & Wesson .44 Magnum has now been in production for more than four decades. In 1957, the .44 Magnum became the Model 29 as Smith & Wesson switched from such soul stirring names as the Heavy Duty, the Outdoorsman, and the Combat Magnum, to a system of model numbers. The whole world began a process of depersonalizing about the same time and I, for one, long for the days of names rather than numbers.

Shortly after going to the numbering system, the Model 29 was available in a new look. The first of the long-barreled .44 Magnums arrived as the Model 29 joined the Model 27 .357 Magnum with an 8-3/8-inch barrel length. These quickly became quite popular with hunters and long-range shooters. At this same time in 1958, the H.H. Harris Co., a Chicago distributor, placed an order for 500 5-inch barreled Model 29s. These sixguns are now very rare and quite valuable. I've never seen one.

Smith & Wesson fell on hard times in the 1980s because it was under the control of those who seemingly cared nothing about providing quality sixguns. Two special features of the now classic Model 29 were dropped: the pinned barrel and counter-bored cylinder both disappeared. From time immemorial, all double action Smith & Wesson sixguns had barrels that were held tightly in place not just by thread pressure, but also by a pin that fit into the frame through a slot in the top of the barrel threads. All Magnums carried recessed cylinders, or cylinders that completely enclosed the rim of the cartridge case. Both

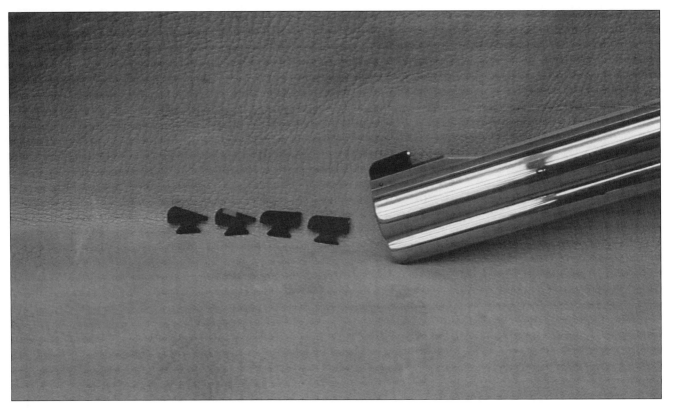

Smith & Wesson's Classic line-up features interchangeable sight blades including, from left to right, black ramp, red insert ramp, black post, black post with white bead, and on the sixgun, black post with gold bead.

are a sign of manufacturing quality and both are gone. Like bad legislation, once a change occurs, it is extremely difficult to go back.

With the coming of long-range silhouetting, shooters started pounding hundreds of rounds of full-house loads down range in a single day. Remember Keith had fired his .44 Magnum only 600 rounds per year! Trouble started almost immediately. When a cartridge was fired, the cylinder would unlock and rotate backwards and when the hammer was cocked for the next shot, the fired round would be back under the firing pin. About the same time silhouetters were shooting huge amounts of 240 grain bullets, and handgun hunters discovered 300 grain bullets, which put a further strain on the mechanism whose basic design went back to 1899.

Smith & Wesson could have led the way in correcting the problem. Instead it refused to publicly acknowledge that anything was amiss and instead brought forth a "Silhouette Model" in 1983. This was a beautiful sixgun that featured a 10-5/8-inch heavy bull barrel and sights with a standard adjustable rear sight with a higher blade and also a four-position adjustable front sight. The front sight was to be set for the four distances addressed in long-range silhouetting, BUT the mechanical problem remained. Of all the .44 Magnum

Smith & Wesson sixguns I have shot over the past four decades, this one, Smith & Wesson's first answer to the unlocking cylinder problem, is the only one that I have ever encountered in which the cylinder unlocked and rotated backwards on a regular basis! Silhouetters did not embrace the .44 Magnum Silhouette Model and Smith & Wesson lost that lucrative market. I traded mine for a 4-inch standard Model 29.

Finally, with a change of management, Smith & Wesson began to address some of the problems associated with the .44 Magnum Model 29. By now, both Ruger and Dan Wesson had heavy-duty .44 Magnum sixguns on the market that were designed around heavy usage. Smith engineers went to work. The retention system on the yoke, or cylinder crane, was strengthened, and studs within the frame were radiused to help remove metal stress. Cylinder notches were made longer to prevent the bolt from jumping out of the notch upon recoil. At the same time, the bolt was changed and the innards of the Model 29 were changed to provide a method of holding everything tightly together when the .44 was fired to prevent battering under recoil. The result is a sixgun that is probably a mite stronger and tougher, but remember, the cylinder and the frame are still the same size as found on the Triple-Lock of 1908.

The latest .44 from Smith & Wesson's Performance Center features a 6-inch ported barrel. Stocks by Hogues and Leupold scope in Weigand mount.

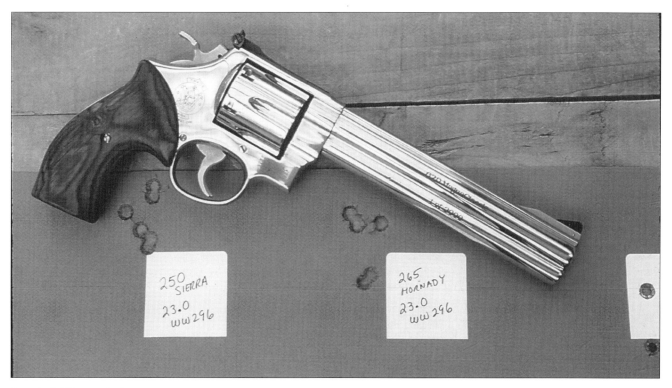

Smith & Wesson's finest .44 since the Triple-Lock and the original .44 Magnum—the Magna Classic. These groups were shot at 25 yards through the 7-1/2-inch-barreled Magna Classic.

Smith & Wesson .44 Magnums 1956 to 1990: 6-1/2-inch M29, 6-inch M629, and 5-inch M629, all have BearHug stocks, while 6-inch Classic 629 has Herrett stocks.

For thirty-five years, the .44 Magnum Model 29 maintained its beautiful classic shape. The arrival of a sixgun with the non-classic shape is now called the Classic. Now .44 Magnums from Smith & Wesson are also available with a full underlug barrel, non-fluted cylinder, drilled and tapped for scope mounts, plus the upgraded mechanical package offered in the standard Model 29. The Classic .44 also ushered in the round-butted grip frame on the N-frame series of Smith & Wesson sixguns.

The present Model 29 sixguns are somewhat stronger and, in many cases, are better shooting sixguns than the originals, but they are not nearly as finely polished and blued and, of course, do not have the same classic outline as the original .44 Magnum. Sadly, the 4-inch sixgun has been quietly removed from production. The 4-inch .44 Magnum, when loaded properly, is one of the best choices in a fighting handgun. It stands as an equal with the same basic sixgun chambered in .44 Special, .41 Magnum, and .45 Colt. Again, properly loaded with defensive loads in the 750 to 900 feet per second muzzle velocity category. The only better sixgun I can think of

would be a 4-inch Smith & Wesson N-frame Model 25-2 which accepts .45 ACP rounds with half- or full-moon clips that allow the fastest possible reload with a sixgun. Unfortunately, all of these sixguns are noticeably absent from the latest Smith & Wesson catalog.

In addition to the standard blued Model 29s—all nickeled sixguns are gone as well—the Model 629, a stainless steel .44 Magnum introduced in 1978, is offered in 4-, 6-, and 8-3/8-inch barrel lengths. Like the blued Model 29, the stainless Model 629 is also available as the Classic with a full underlug barrel. A most pleasing Model 629 is the Magna-Classic. These highly polished, heavy-underlugged, 7-1/2-inch barreled .44 Magnums with interchangeable front sights and marked on the barrel "1 of 3000" have been proven to be superbly accurate sixguns. Mine is sighted in for 100 yards using the gold bead front sight insert and 300 grain cast bullets over 21.5 grains of WW296 or H110.

After all of the heavy-underlugged barrel treatment, the most sought after Model 629 remains the Mountain Gun. These are round-butted, slim-bar-

Freedom Arms .44 Magnum with Leupold scope is an excellent hunting sixgun. These 300 grain jacketed bullet loads, Speer 300 and Ballard Built 300, were shot at 50 yards.

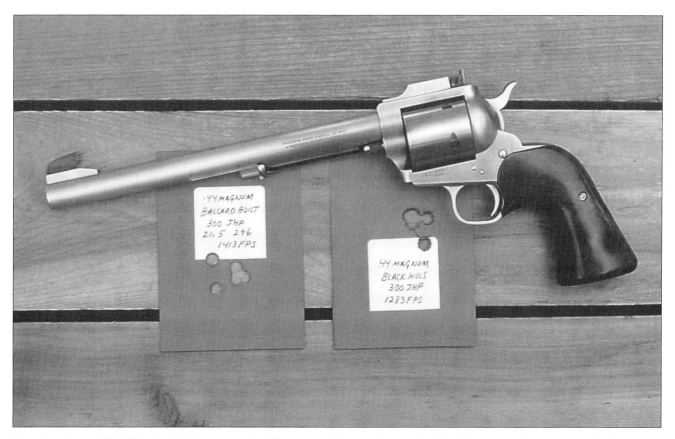

Freedom Arms 10-1/2-inch .44 Magnum with silhouette sights and stocks by Tedd Adamovich— sixguns don't get any better than this. These 25-yard groups measure less than 1 inch.

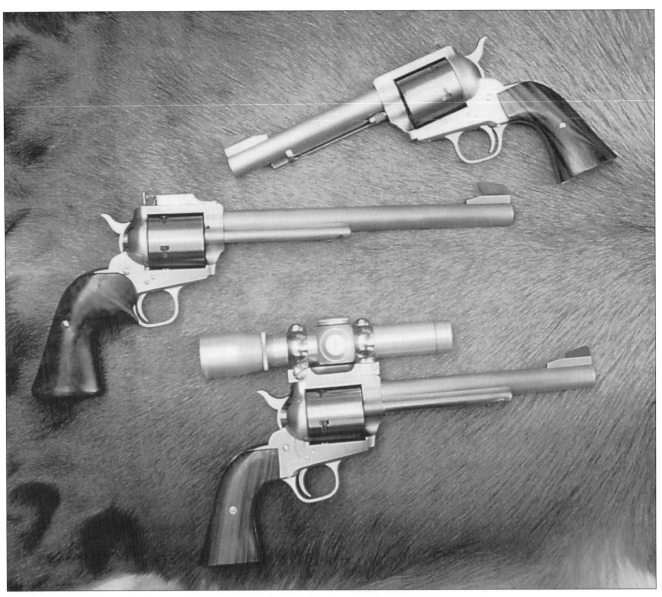

Taffin's .44 Magnums from Freedom Arms are set up for easy packin' and close-range with a 6-inch barrel, silhouetting with a 10-1/2-inch barrel, and hunting with a 7-1/2-inch barrel and Leupold scope.

reled, 4-inch packin' pistols. The barrel profile is neither the heavy underlug-style, nor the heavyweight bull barrel of the original Model 29, but rather the tapered barrel like that found on the original 4-inch 1950 Target .44 Specials. This is a superb defensive sixgun especially when loaded with .44 Specials.

One of the latest Model 629s available from Smith & Wesson is the Performance Center's Model 629-4 with PowerPort. This is a 6-inch heavy underlug barreled .44 Magnum with a special recoil-reducing port in front of the front sight. Like all recently manufactured big bore sixguns from Smith & Wesson, the PowerPort is already drilled and tapped for scope mounts. With a 4X Leupold scope on Weigand mounts

in place, this .44 Magnum of the 1990s is quite manageable and an excellent choice for hunting.

The Model 29 is one of my favorite sixguns. It is such a favorite, especially in the 4-inch length, that it is the first sixgun I ever stocked with ivory and also the first sixgun I ever had engraved. It is right up there in my heart and runs a very close second to the Colt Single Action Army. To love something is to also understand it. When it comes to the Model 29, I understand it and, as such, I treat it right. There was a time in my younger, more foolish days that I would not think of shooting any load except the Keith load in a Smith & Wesson. Today I know better. Any of the early Model 29s, before the strengthening package

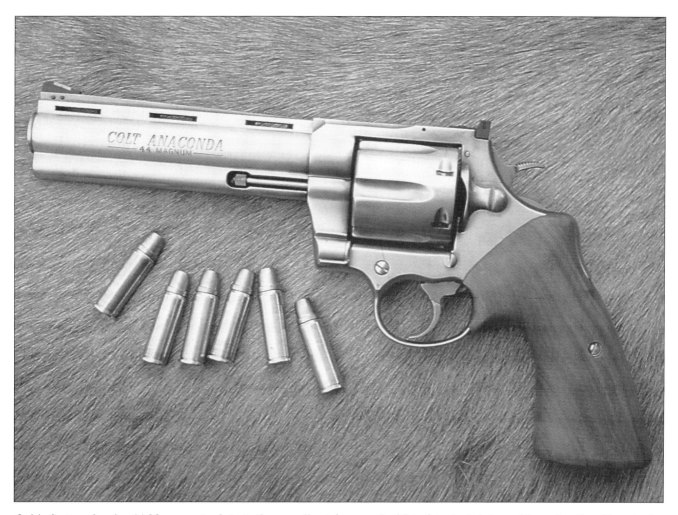

Colt's first and only .44 Magnum to date is the excellent Anaconda. This 6-inch stainless .44 carries BearHug stocks.

was added, are treated gently. I still use the heavy loads, but only infrequently. My standard loads are either a 250 grain or 300 grain hard cast bullet over 10 grains of Unique for 1,150 feet per second. This load is close to the original heavy .44 Special load and serves me just fine for most uses.

Ruger was not the only company that noticed the great demand for double action .44 Magnums in the 1970s. I talked with Dan Wesson in 1978, just before his untimely death, and he told me of the work that was being done on the Dan Wesson .44 Magnum. It took a few years to get it off the ground, but Dan Wesson's .44 Magnum became a reality in the early '80s.

When the Dan Wesson .44 Magnum was introduced, silhouetters very early took to the 8-inch 44VH, or Heavy Barrel Model, and the 10-inch barreled 44V version with a standard shroud that came in under the 4 pound weight limit. This gave shooters maximum sight radius plus maximum weight to help reduce felt recoil of the .44 Magnum.

There are a number of features that contribute to the long-range accuracy of the Dan Wesson .44 Magnums. The barrel system is such that the barrels are interchangeable, that is, barrels of different lengths, normally 6, 8, and 10 inches, are available for each particular caliber and the shooter can exchange barrels at will. Because these said barrels are locked at the front with a barrel nut, and each barrel is installed without being torqued up tightly at the factory, there is no problem with the forcing cone end of the barrel being squeezed to the point of being tighter than the muzzle end. Another feature that contributes to its accuracy is the cylinder that locks at the front on the frame, like the old Smith & Wesson Triple-Lock, but not at the end of the ejector rod. The frame is a solid one-piece-style instead of fitted with a sideplate.

Firing the Dan Wesson .44 Magnum is about as good as it gets when firing the big .44. With a weight of nearly 4 pounds even without a scope, felt recoil is

The Anaconda easily handles standard weight 240 grain bullets such as the loads from Federal. This group, with five of the six shots in one hole, was shot from 25 yards.

reduced considerably. By felt recoil, we refer to the amount of recoil that the individual shooter actually perceives when the handgun is fired. Both the heavy weight and excellent factory stocks help minimize this felt recoil.

All of the foregoing is, of course, the good news. The bad news is that the Dan Wesson .44 is strictly found in the used gun market. Dan Wesson, which became Wesson Firearms when it reverted back to the Wesson family, is now out of business—probably forever. It is a great loss to sixgunners because the big bore Dan Wessons were both accurate and comfortable to shoot. We will look at them in depth in the chapter on silhouetting.

With all of the available .44 Magnums from Ruger and Smith & Wesson, as well as the Dan Wessons at the time, why would Freedom Arms, well-known for the World's Most Powerful Revolver, take a step backwards and also offer a .44 Magnum when it already has the .454 Casull chambering? The reasoning is simple. Many shooters are already set up to reload and cast bullets for the .44 Magnum and hesitate to add more reloading dies, bullet moulds, etc. These same shooters, however, are willing to invest in what is simply the finest built and strongest .44 Magnum ever offered to the shooting public. At a price well in excess of $1,200, it better be!

The .44 Magnum from Freedom Arms is not a sixgun, but a five-shooter just like the .454 Casull. The .44 Magnum is made with the same exacting care that is used in its bigger brother. For instance, the cylinder is line-bored, which means the cylinder chambers are reamed after the cylinder has been fitted to the frame and locked up under the same torque that is present when the revolver is fired. This results in as-near-as-possible perfect barrel/cylinder/frame alignment.

The Freedom Arms .454 is the strongest handgun made and will handle loads far above conventional revolvers. The .44 Magnum is the same gun with smaller holes in the barrel and cylinder and made of the same material, strength, and quality. An added bonus to .44 Magnum shooters is the fact that .44 Magnum loads in the .44 Freedom Arms revolver seem much lighter in recoil than they do in conventional revolvers. This is attributed to the specially designed grip of the Casull line of revolvers which minimize felt recoil as much as possible.

With full-house .44 Magnum loads, the .44 Casull is much more pleasant to shoot than the full-house .454s and this is also a drawing card for many shooters who simply do not need the power that is possible with the .454 Casull. The .44 Magnum Casull, which is as strong as the .454, is handicapped only by the capacity of the .44 Magnum brass itself. Handloaders will run out of cases before they achieve the pressures that this .44 Magnum is engineered to function with. My full-house hunting load in the .44 Freedom Arms is a 240 grain bullet at 1,700 feet per second. I will not share the load because I do not want anyone to think it is safe in another manufacturer's sixgun. I have used the .44 Magnum Freedom

Arms revolver for hunting, taking both mountain lion and white-tailed deer.

In the past there has only been one .44 Magnum revolver that could be dubbed as "comfortable to shoot." That revolver is the 4 pound class Dan Wesson .44 Magnums with 8- and 10-inch barrels. We are talking about full-house .44 Magnum loads, of course. Now the Freedom Arms .44 Magnum joins the ranks of the "comfortable" .44 Magnum revolvers and does it with one-third less weight and the ability to handle even hotter loads. This is no reflection on the fine Dan Wesson .44 Magnum, after all, added bonuses should be expected in a revolver that does cost more than twice as much as any other .44 Magnum revolver.

The .44 Magnum Freedom Arms revolver is also offered to competition shooters as a first class silhouette revolver with competition sights, which are probably the finest sights ever offered on a revolver, and a tuned action with a 2-1/2- to 3-pound trigger pull.

The Freedom Arms Premier Grade .44 Magnum is available with either adjustable sights or fixed sights in barrel lengths of 4-3/4, 6, 7-1/2, and 10 inches. All custom options, such as custom grips, tuned action,

scope mounts, and so forth, that are available on the .454 are also available on the .44 Magnum.

Colt finally was convinced that the .44 Magnum was here to stay and introduced the Anaconda after not offering a .44 or .45 caliber double action since before World War II. Colt's biggest snake is available in 4-, 6-, and 8-inch barrel lengths. This is a fairly large gun weighing 52 ounces in a 6-inch barreled stainless steel double action sixgun, 5 ounces heavier than the original .44, the 6-1/2-inch Smith & Wesson .44 Magnum.

The Anaconda, available in stainless only, should also be offered in a blue model, especially even the old Colt Royal Blue, but, alas, I'm afraid those days are gone forever. It looks like the healthy offspring of the marriage between a stainless Python and a King Cobra with the barrel being pure Python, albeit larger in diameter and the rest of the gun, definitely descended from the King Cobra. Except for the King Cobra-shaped triggerguard, it is a strikingly handsome sixgun, and is even better looking than either of its parents.

I have tested the Anaconda extensively. Factory loads from 180 grain jacketed hollowpoints to 330 grain cast-bulleted heavy hunting loads, handloads

Taurus's .44 Magnum is a superb shooting sixgun, especially with Black Hills factory ammo. Groups under 3 inches at 100 yards are commonplace.

with both jacketed bullets from 240 to 300 grains and cast bullets from 240 grains through 300 grains have all been fed to the biggest snake. It thrives on all of them. The Anaconda does it all. It can't tell the difference between a cast bullet and a jacketed bullet. It can't discern if it is being fed lightweight bullets or heavyweight bullets. Give it anything and it spits out nice, tight little groups consisting of .44 caliber holes closely spaced together. Colt did it right even though it did take nearly fifty years to bring back a .44 double action.

Two other sixguns chambered in .44 Magnum deserve to be mentioned. One is the "right-handed single action" from Texas Longhorn Arms. It will be covered in a subsequent chapter. Basically this book is about America's best offerings in the big bore line-up of sixguns, however, there is one foreign made double action .44 Magnum of note, namely the Brazilian made Taurus.

Taurus has long been known for high quality, relatively low priced handguns. The Model 44 .44 Magnum is available in both stainless and blue steel versions and in barrel lengths of 4, 6-1/2, and 8-3/8 inches, all with the smooth action that Taurus is well-known for and the trigger is as all triggers were meant to be, smooth-faced with no serrations. Both hammer and trigger are of the wide target-type.

Sights on all Model 44 .44s are fully adjustable, with a white outline rear sight and a red ramp front sight. An unusual touch on the Taurus is the presence of serrations that run from the rear sight's front to the front sight's back. These are not just placed on the top of frame and barrel, but are inside a milled slot. This gives the Model 44 a custom look, to say the least.

Alongside the front sight on both sides one finds four holes, or ports. This integral compensator system is designed to give the shooter valuable help in controlling felt recoil. The ports are aided in their task by the heavy full underlug barrel that brings the weight of the long-barreled Model 44 up to 56 ounces or 3 pounds, 8 ounces on my postal scale.

Accuracy with the Taurus Model 44s I have tested has been exceptional. Firing at 100 yards revealed that it was not at all unusual to keep five shots within 3 inches. This, of course, is with the use of a scope using the Weigand base and rings.

I consider the .44 Special tremendously important not only for its own capabilities, but also for leading the way to the .357 Magnum and .44 Magnum. The .44 Magnum, however, is definitely the King of all Sixgun Cartridges. It is the first chambering most people think of connected with awesome power. In capable hands, it has taken all species of large game up to and including elephants, it has proven to be a superb long-range cartridge on the silhouette range, with proper loads it can also be a top rate defensive sixgun, and it is chambered in some of the best sixguns ever offered. Versatility? Definitely rate it an A+. The King is alive. Long live the King!

CHAPTER 6

THE .41 MAGNUM—THE ALMOST FORGOTTEN MAGNUM

Both the .357 Magnum and the .44 Magnum are genealogically correct. That is, they both took straight paths to their final destinations. In 1899, the .38 Long Colt was lengthened and became the .38 Special. In the 1930s, D.B. Wesson and arms expert Phil Sharpe worked together to hot load the .38 Special in the .38/44 Heavy Duty. In 1935, the .38 Special was lengthened and the result was the .357 Magnum—a straight path from .38 Long Colt to .38 Special to heavy loading of the .38 Special to the .357 Magnum.

The .44 Magnum's roots go back even further. In 1870, Smith & Wesson introduced the first big bore centerfire Single Action sixgun, the .44 American. The Russians liked the Smith & Wesson and changed the .44 American cartridge from a cartridge case that accepted an outside lubricated bullet with a heel only that was inserted inside the case to an inside lubricated bullet that was smaller in diameter than the cartridge case—the .44 Russian had arrived. By 1907, Smith & Wesson had lengthened the Russian case and we had the .44 Special. For more than thirty years, experimenters heavy loaded the .44 Special and finally in 1955, the result was the .44 Magnum. This traces another straight path from .44 American to .44 Russian to .44 Special to heavy loads for the .44 Special to the .44 Magnum.

On the contrary, the .41 Magnum's path is not so straight forward. Its roots go back to the .38-40, or .38-40 Winchester Centerfire, and the .41 Long Colt with wildcatters coming up with new brass to use in Colt Single Actions with barrels marked .38 WCF or .41 LC. It is a story of a major firearms company dropping the ball before the advent of the .357 Magnum and also a sad story of a cartridge that was born twenty years too late and is out of synch with the natural scheme of things. The .357 and .44 Magnums had parents; the .41 Magnum had aunts and uncles.

The .38-40 began life, not as a sixgun chambering, but as a rifle cartridge. In 1873, Winchester introduced its legendary levergun chambered for the .44-40. This slightly bottle-necked cartridge, which was basically a .45 caliber necked to .44, employed a 200 grain bullet of .427-inch diameter over 40 grains of blackpowder for 1,300 plus feet per second from a rifle. Its name came from the caliber, .44, and powder charge of 40 grains.

By 1878, Colt had chambered the Single Action Army for the .44-40 and two years later Winchester introduced another big bore chambering for the 1873 Winchester. This time the .44-40 case was necked-down to accept a .40 caliber bullet of 180 grains over 40 grains of blackpowder. It should have been named the .40-40. Instead it somehow came out labeled as the .38-40. Consequently, we have two .38 caliber sixguns, neither one of which is a .38! The .38-40 is a .40 and the .38 Special is a .36, or more correctly, a .357. The Magnum that grew from the .38 Special corrected the error by being named the .357 Magnum.

Colt soon chambered its Peacemaker for the .38-40 and also had a chambering known as the .41 Long Colt. Strangely enough, even though the bullet diameters are quite different, .400 inch for the .38-40 and .386 inch for the .41 Long Colt, Colt used the same groove diameter barrels for both. Only the markings on the outside were different.

How could this be? The .386 is called a .41, while the .400 is called a .38 and they both use the same barrel? At first the .41 Long Colt bullet, as the .44 Smith & Wesson American, was the same diameter as the cartridge case with an outside lubricated bullet and a heel that fit inside the cartridge case. When the bullet was changed to an inside lubricated-style, rather than change the barrel groove diameter, the .41 Long Colt was henceforth loaded with a soft lead bullet with a hollow base. When the sixgun was fired,

Colt has resurrected the first .40, the .38-40. This Third Generation .38 WCF Single Action is an excellent shooter as testified by this 1-inch group shot at 25 yards.

pressure would cause the heel of the .41 Long Colt bullet to swell up and seal the bore.

While the .38-40 was a powerful sixgun load—it approached 1,000 feet per second in the old factory blackpowder loading—the .41 lagged far behind, but it was nonetheless fairly popular, especially in the Colt double action sixgun, the Thunderer. It was said that a man would rather be shot with a .45 than the old outside lubricated .41 Long Colt that picked up dirt and crud and carried it with the bullet as it entered the body of the unfortunate soul that was shot. Infection was a terrible problem with the .41 while the .45 was "clean."

Even before Elmer Keith started heavy loading the .44 Special and Phil Sharpe looked to the same type of loads in the .38 Special, the .38-40 was being wildcatted. The .38-40 brass does not lend itself to heavy sixgun loads because it is bottle-necked and is consequently very thin in the neck area. Cyril Eimer, better known as "Pop," who wished to use the Colt Single Action and keep the .38-40 bullet, looked for a better way. Eimer kept the .38-40 barrel intact, but special cylinders were built, chambered for the .40 Eimer Colt Special. This was in 1924.

Eimer cut off .401 Winchester brass to a 1.25-inch length and loaded 200 grain bullets. He reported in the October 1926 issue of *The American Rifleman* that he achieved velocities significantly higher than those from the same sixgun chambered for the .38-40. Eimer

tried to interest Colt, through its well-known representative J. H. "Fitz" Fitzgerald, in the new cartridge for use in the Single Action Army and New Service.

Colt must have been somewhat interested because in 1932, Remington ran some special loads for Colt. The boxes were marked .41 Special. Fred Moore was the factory superintendent at Colt and was interested in producing a new sixgun cartridge with a 210 grain bullet at 900 feet per second. Again, this was in 1932. Three different variations on this theme were tried, with the final version, chambered in a New Service, achieving 1,150 feet per second.

In those pre-Magnum days, Colt had the cartridge and the sixgun to go forward and it shelved the project. The .41 Colt Special had a case length of 1.260 inches, or 1/10 inch longer than the .38 Special or .44 Special case. When the .357 Magnum arrived three years later it would utilize a cartridge case length of 1.290 inches. Colt could have chambered the Colt Single Action Army and the big New Service double action in a powerful .41 three years before the .357 Magnum brought us into the Magnum era. Colt had the ball and fumbled!

In the 1920s Eimer had his .40, Colt experimented with the .41 Special in the 1930s, and now we enter into the 1940s. Another well-known experimenter and gunsmith turned to the .40 caliber after working with the .357 Magnum, .38-40, .44 Special, and .45 Colt. He was looking for a flat shooting powerful cartridge to

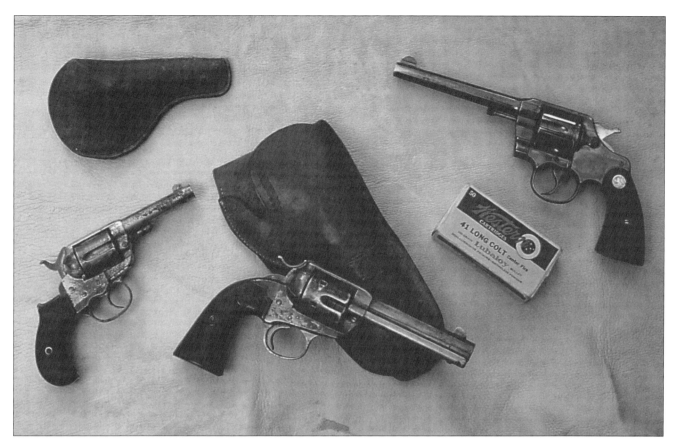

In addition to the Single Action Army, Colt chambered the .41 Long Colt in the double action Thunderer, the Bisley, and the Army Special.

use in his Colt Single Actions—something better than any of these four sixgun chamberings.

Gordon Boser used a 5-1/2-inch Colt Single Action Army and trimmed .401 Winchester brass to 1.218 inches, loaded .38-40 bullets, and chambered cylinders to .401 Special. Eimer did not have Hercules #2400 powder in the 1920s; Boser did. He used 18.5 grains of #2400 with .38-40 bullets and a 200 grain bullet of his design, Lyman's #401452. Boser, like Colt and Eimer before him, had a .40 Magnum decades before the .44 and .41 Magnums emerged and did not know it.

How good were the Pop Eimer and Gordon Boser's wildcats? Ray Thompson, another sixgun experimenter and designer of the excellent Lyman gas check bullets #358156 (156 grain) for the .38 Special and .357 Magnum, #429215 (215 grain) and # 431244 (255 grain) for the .44 Special, and #452490 (255 grain) for the .45 Auto Rim, reported that 18.5 grains of #2400 with the Boser bullet in the .401 brass gave a full 25 percent more tissue destruction on live targets than did the .357 Magnum.

Boser also made a number of significant improvements in the Colt Single Action more than ten years

before Ruger redesigned the old action and powered it with coil springs in the Single-Six and Blackhawk. In addition to a special tool steel cylinder bushing, Boser also made a two-piece bolt with a coil spring, a hinged hand and a trigger that also used coil springs, and a V-shaped main spring. Today custom gunsmiths such as Jim Stroh and Hamilton Bowen install blocks in single actions to hold the bolt tightly in place as the sixgun is fired. Gordon Boser was doing it fifty years ago.

While Colt was toying with the .41 Colt Special and Boser was shooting the .401 Special in his Colt Single Action, Elmer Keith continued to use his heavy loaded .44 Specials in both Colt and Smith & Wesson sixguns. Keith had one goal in mind, and that was to get his heavy .44 Special load made available from the ammunition companies and chambered in a new sixgun. He was not interested in the smaller .40 caliber.

Once the .44 Magnum was firmly established, however, Keith, along with Bill Jordan, met with firearms and ammunition company executives and received a promise that they would look at the possibility of a .41 Magnum as a duty weapon and cartridge combination to replace the .38 Special. The .357 Magnum

The .41 Family: From left to right, 38-40, .41 Long Colt, .401 Power-Mag, .41 Magnum, and .41 Special.

had not yet established itself as the number one duty revolver for peace officers use, for this was long before the widespread use of the 125 grain jacketed hollowpoint .357 ammunition available today.

The main idea behind the .41 Magnum was to present a new load for police use at around 900 to 1,000 feet per second with a 200 grain bullet plus a loading in the 1,400 to 1,500 feet per second bracket for the hunter and outdoor buff. As it turns out, it was a mistake to try to accomplish both with one cartridge. It did not take Remington long to bring forth two loadings once Smith & Wesson and Ruger promised to chamber their sixguns for the load.

To preclude its use in any of the old .40 calibered sixguns, the .41 Magnum is a true .410 caliber. The cartridge case is the same length as the .357 and .44 Magnums. Smith & Wesson used its .44 Magnum as the platform for the new sixgun and introduced the Model 57 .41 Magnum with a 6-inch barrel. Ruger immediately responded with the Blackhawk in both 4-5/8- and 6-1/2-inch barrel lengths.

Remington supplied two loads: a 210 grain jacketed bullet at 1,500 feet per second and a 210 grain lead bullet for police use at 950 feet per second. Smith added a third sixgun to the .41 Magnum line-up, the Model 58. This sixgun was a deadringer for the .38 Military & Police with fixed sights and it lacked the shrouded ejector rod housing of the Smith Magnums; however, it had the same frame size as the .44 and .41 Magnum Models 29 and 57.

Keith and Jordan originally pushed the .41 Magnum as a cartridge for police use. They had the right goal in mind, but somehow the idea traveled down the wrong path. A few police departments went to the .41 Model 58 and the Police loading, but it never achieved popular status with peace officers for a couple of reasons. The double action sixguns that housed it, the Smith & Wesson Models 57 and 58, were both bigger and heavier than most police officers wanted to carry all day. It had been ten years since the advent of the easily carried medium-framed .357 Magnums; packing a heavier sixgun would have definitely seemed like a step backwards.

Of even greater importance is the fact that most police officers, though dedicated, hard-working individuals, are not shooters. Their guns are badges of authority, not tools that are practiced with on a regular basis; the vast majority of them never fire their duty weapons from one qualification time to the next. This past month I ran into two men who, from the guns they were shooting and the equipment they had with them, were obviously police officers. We struck up a conversation and I found out that they were in fact deputy sheriffs and were out on their own time spending their own money practicing because the budget had been cut for qualification times and they wanted to be sure that they were proficient with their duty handguns, rifles, and shotguns. These men are definitely the exception, not the rule.

In 1964, the medium-framed .38 Special was the number one duty gun. Compared to the .38 Special, the .41 Police loading kicked enough to lower qualification scores of those who, unlike the two deputy sheriffs, did not spend time on their own shooting their duty guns and were not used to anything above .38 Special target loads.

The .41 Magnum has never quite known what its status really is. Was it to be a police sixgun or an outdoor enthusiast's sixgun? As the latter it is superb, but as a police sixgun it was ill-conceived. Had it been delivered as a medium-framed .41 Special the same size as the Smith & Wesson Model 19 Combat Magnum or Ruger GP-100, it would still probably be the number one duty weapon today.

Before Smith & Wesson joined forces with Remington to produce the .41 Magnum, one company had already legitimized the .401 Special. It was the greatest sixgun cartridge before or since—at least if one believes the advertising. "The fabulous .401 Power-Mag caliber has the power of the .44 PowerMag with less recoil. This is the ideal large caliber revolver cartridge. Will kill any animal on the face of the earth or shoot through the cylinder block of any automobile. It will flatten a human no matter where you hit him." Thus read the less than subdued account of the .401 PowerMag cartridge as found in Herter's catalog from the 1960s.

"With this revolver you can hunt all North American and African game." The .401 was chambered in the "Herter's Famous Custom Grade Super .401 PowerMag Revolver" and boasted such amenities as "advanced design hammer spur, man sized grips for more accurate shooting, built in rear sight protectors, frame strengtheners, holster slippers [?], heavy-duty triggerguard, and custom hand finished and polished, individually custom blued....the finest quality all steel single action revolvers in all respects humanly possible to make."

The original Herter's .401 PowerMag ammunition was absolutely awful. Apparently, nothing had been learned since the introduction of the .357 Magnum with soft lead bullets in 1935 because factory ammunition for the .401 was made up of soft swaged bullets that leaded terribly.

This did little or nothing to enhance the .401's reputation. Handloading changes all of this, and with proper bullets, the .401 is the full equivalent of the .41 Magnum.

This 4-inch .41 Magnum Smith & Wesson has been tuned to double action perfection by Teddy Jacobsen who slimmed the hammer and rounded and smoothed the trigger. With the proper loads, it would be hard to equal as a duty or defensive sixgun for those used to recoil and weight.

Herter's PowerMags: Top, original 6-1/2-inch .401 PowerMag; bottom, .401 converted to .38-40 by Hamilton Bowen. The Herter's PowerMags were made in Germany in the 1960s and became a victim of the Gun Control Act of 1968.

The .401 PowerMag was chambered in only one revolver, the very stout Herter's PowerMag sixgun made by Germany's Sauer and Sohn. It was killed off by the introduction of the .41 Magnum coupled with the Gun Control Act of 1968, which stopped all mail sales of firearms to individuals.

If Colt had brought out the .41 Special in the 1920s or 1930s, as it seemingly should have happened, then the natural turn of events would have been the introduction of the .41 Magnum in the 1950s or 1960s. Instead, the .41 Magnum came on the scene without the customary Special cartridge first. What the factories failed to do, custom sixgunsmith Hamilton Bowen did. I first shot the .41 Special in a Bowen Ruger Security Six at The Shootists Holiday in 1987. I liked the concept, so much so that I handed over a Colt Single Action to be made into a 5-1/2-inch barreled .41 Special. My idea was a sixgun that would handle 220 grain bullets at 900 to 1,200 feet per sec-

ond or about the same as heavy loaded .44 Specials with 250 grain bullets.

Bowen returned my Colt with a 5-1/2-inch Douglas barrel and custom .41 Special cylinder. Except for the non-fluted cylinder, it looks like an ordinary Colt Single Action Army, but ordinary it is not. It is one of the finest shooting single actions I have ever come across in a forty year love affair with the Peacemaker.

Brass for the .41 Special for this mild wildcat is easily made. Using an RCBS case trimmer set to .44 Special length and hooked up to a quarter-inch drill for power is all that is necessary for the .41 Special.

My first loadings for the .41 Special were all accomplished with Bull-X 215 grain semi-wadcutters. These are machine cast commercial bullets, but the first five shots over 12.5 grains of #2400 cut one ragged hole at 25 yards! This is from a standard, fixed-sighted Colt Single Action Army sixgun. Standard except for the Bowen cylinder and Douglas barrel.

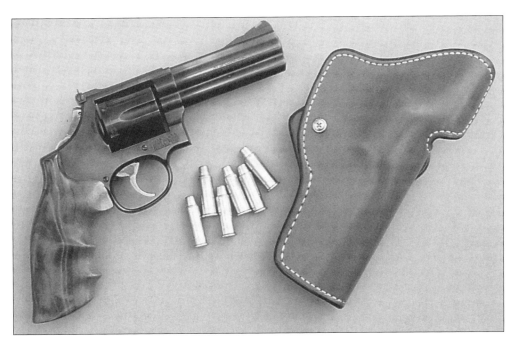

Taffin's custom .41 Special on a Smith & Wesson 586 by Hamilton Bowen has Hogue stocks and leather by Milt Sparks. Is this the sixgun that should have been? The answer is in the text.

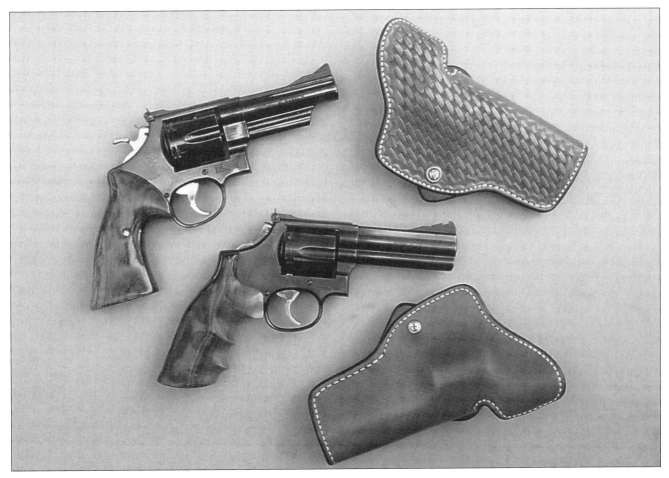

Taffin's .41s: Top, Model 57 Smith & Wesson .41 Magnum with BearHug stocks; bottom, Hamilton Bowen-built .41 Special with stocks by Hogue. Leather by Milt Sparks.

One of Taffin's favorite shooting single action six-guns is this .41 Special. Hamilton Bowen made the six-shot .41 Special cylinder and installed a new 5-1/2-inch .41 caliber barrel. With the right load, it will cut one-hole groups at 25 yards.

Muzzle velocity is 1,063 feet per second and it is very mild and pleasant to shoot. Increasing the load to 13.5 and 14.5 grains of #2400 gave velocities of 1,167 and 1,227 feet per second and both of these loads will stay well within 1-1/2 inches at 25 yards. Had these loads and sixgun surfaced in the 1940s, and then been followed by the .41 Magnum before the advent of the .44 Magnum, the .41 Magnum would have been properly hailed as a grand design, been given its rightful place in the scheme of things, and would have been the perfect lead-in to the .44 Magnum. Alas, it was not, and the .41 Magnum has been destined from day one to be ever in its bigger brother's shadow. It deserves better treatment.

Most peace officers deemed the Model 58 .41 Magnum to be too large for duty use, however, I have had Hamilton Bowen build what I believe is the peace officer's .41 sixgun that should have been. It started as a Smith & Wesson L-frame .357 Magnum Model 586 with a heavy underlugged 4-inch barrel, and the cylinder has been rechambered to .41 Special, the barrel rebored to .410, the hammer bobbed, and the action changed to double action only operation. The result is a near perfect defensive sixgun.

When a 200 to 220 grain jacketed or cast bullet is used, the .41 Magnum is a flat-shooting, accurate long-range sixgun that will handle all but the biggest of big game. For most of us, in fact, it is a better choice for hunting in most instances than either the .357 Magnum or .44 Magnum. The .357 is at its best for varmints, small game, and close-range shots at small deer. The .44 Magnum, loaded with 300 grain bullets delivers the penetration needed for the big deer, elk and moose, and even the big bears if one is so inclined. The .41 Magnum is perfect for everything in between which just happens to be the natural pursuit for most handgun hunters. It delivers more energy on target than the .357 Magnum with less recoil than the .44 Magnum.

Boser used 18.5 grains of #2400 with his 200 grain bullet in the .401 Special; I go with 19 grains under Lyman's 220 grain #410459 for right at 1,400 feet per second from a long-barreled sixgun. This is certainly adequate for deer and black bear-sized critters. Recoil, though stout, is less than the .44 Magnum affords.

Not only did the .41 Magnum follow a zigzag path to its birth, it has also been on a rocky road ever since. In Smith & Wesson persuasion, the .41 Magnum has been offered in both blue and nickel finishes and in standard barrel lengths of 4, 6, and 8-3/8 inches. In the Police Model 58, both blue and nickel have also been offered with one barrel length only, 4 inches.

In the mid-1980s, Smith & Wesson's .41 Magnum went stainless with the Model 657 and the same standard barrels lengths as the Model 57. The Model 657

Taffin's .41 single action sixguns: Custom 5-1/2-inch .41 Special Colt SAA built by Hamilton Bowen, Ruger 4-5/8-inch Old Model Blackhawk .41 Magnum, Ruger 7-1/2-inch Bisley .41 Magnum, and Herter's 6-1/2-inch .401 PowerMag.

These two Model 57s by Smith & Wesson are now both out of production: An 8-3/8-inch is great for hunting and long-range shooting, while an easy packin' 4-inch is ideal for self defense. Both wear BearHug stocks.

has also been available in all barrel lengths in the heavy underlugged style. That makes a grand total of at least fourteen .41 Magnum variations from Smith & Wesson since 1964. How hard is the road the .41 Magnum travels now? Smith & Wesson offers exactly one .41 Magnum, the Model 657 with a 6-inch barrel—call it Smith & Wesson's token .41 Magnum.

Meanwhile, over at Ruger, the .41 Magnum has been available to those that appreciate this fine cartridge in both the Old and New Model Blackhawks with barrels lengths of 4-5/8 and 6-1/2 inches, the Redhawk in stainless and blue with barrel lengths of 5-1/2 and 7-1/2 inches, and the Bisley only with a 7-1/2-inch tube. The latter model is one of the finest shooting long-range sixguns I have ever encountered. It is also as difficult to find as a truthful politician. The Old Models, of course, are gone, and the Redhawk is now in .44 Magnum only, but the others remain for three .41 Magnums from Ruger.

Colt? It only took Colt thirty-five years to accept the .44 Magnum! And never a .41 Magnum from Hartford. Dan Wesson provided .41 Magnums in both its beautiful high-polish blue and stainless and in barrel lengths of 4, 6, 8, and 10 inches, most with both standard and heavy barrel options. There have been other .41 Magnums too, including the Seville, the Abilene, and even a couple of imports. The list keeps shrinking. I hope and pray that it doesn't get any smaller.

My good friend Jack Pender was a real .41 Magnum aficionado and had Hamilton Bowen build up what is probably the finest .41 Magnum in existence. It started with a Ruger Super Blackhawk fitted with a non-fluted custom cylinder; Hamilton did all the tightening and tuning that only he can do. One of Bowen's ovate, ribbed, heavy barrels, 7-1/2 inches in length, was then installed. It is a superb sixgun, to say the least. Jack has now gone Home, but the Bowen-built .41 lives on in the hands of our mutual friend, the pistol packin' pastor, Jim Taylor. Neither Jack nor I could wish it a better home.

There are two sixguns I would most definitely like to see in .41 Magnum. First, Colt should resurrect the New Frontier, redesign the action to use coil springs, build it the same way Freedom Arms builds its revolver, and chamber it in .41 Magnum with a 7-1/2-inch barrel. Unfortunately, this is not likely to ever happen. The Second sixgun could easily come to pass; that is simply to see Freedom Arms chamber its superb five-shot revolver for the .41 Magnum. This excellent cartridge could find no better home. With the life it has led, it deserves it.

While I have had the good fortune to experience dozens of sixguns on each of the other Magnums, the .44 and the .357, as well as the .44 Special and .45 Colt, my contact with the .41 Magnum has been limited to two Smith & Wessons, a 4-inch and an 8-3/8-inch, two Rugers, a 4-5/8-inch and a 7-1/2-inch, and last, but certainly not least, the Dan Wesson. I am one who prefers to buy sixguns at bargain prices. While such sixguns are easily found in both .357 Magnum and .44 Magnum chamberings, the same in .41 Magnum is not so easily found. The above mentioned 4-5/8-inch Ruger, an Old Model, was found a few years back in unfired condition

Dan Wesson's 6-inch heavyweight, and most comfortable shooting, .41 Magnum.

Custom .41 Specials by Hamilton Bowen: 5-1/2-inch Colt SAA with non-fluted cylinder and .410 inch barrel, and Smith & Wesson 4-inch M586 with rechambered cylinder and rebored barrel. Grips by Charles Able and Hogue.

at a local gun show for only $200. A situation such as this doesn't occur very often.

Our local gun shop, Shapel's, has a number of excellent new and used .357 Magnum and .44 Magnum sixguns in stock. Even though the store has scores of handguns on hand, not one is a .41 Magnum. Those who buy .41s tend to hold on to them.

The .41 Magnum is certainly a more suitable chambering for the Smith & Wesson N-frame than the .44 Magnum, because .41s never experienced the Smith & Wesson .44 Magnum syndrome. Some Model 29s, when fired, would result in the cylinder bolt unlocking, which allowed the cylinder to rotate backwards before the internal strengthening package was added in the 1980s. I have not heard of this being a problem with the softer recoiling .41 Magnums.

The short-barreled .41 Magnums make excellent packin' pistols. I must admit, however, that I see very little difference in recoil when using full-house loads in either a 4-inch Model 29 .44 Magnum or a 4-inch Model 57 .41 Magnum. They both get your immediate attention. The 4-5/8-inch Ruger Old Model Blackhawk is a real ripsnorter of a hard kickin' sixgun when loaded with SSK's 295 grain bullet at 1,300 feet per second.

The long-barreled .41 Magnums are easier shootin', powerful sixguns. I do notice a difference in recoil when it comes to the 8-3/8-inch Smith & Wessons, and the .41 is definitely the tamest of the two. Ruger's .41 Bisley is exceptionally accurate and flat shooting for long-range games. It is, in fact, one of my best sixguns for relaxed long-range shooting at inanimate objects.

With the far reaching shortage of .44 Magnum sixguns during the Dirty Harry days, many sixgunners discovered the .41 Magnum. Unless something of the same ilk happens again, I don't see a lot of hope for a bright future for the .41 Magnum. It will be a serious loss to sixgunnin' should it disappear from manufacturers' catalogs. Shooter's likes and dislikes take strange turns. The .44-40 was dead and all but buried as a sixgun cartridge, but is now alive and well due to tens of thousands of shooters discovering Cowboy Action Shooting. If the .44-40 can be made whole and healthy again, perhaps there even exists hope eternal for the .41 Magnum.

We need someone of the stature of Elmer Keith to tout the .41 Magnum like he did the .44 Special and then the .44 Magnum for more than fifty years. Unfortunately there will never be another time like his nor will there ever be another like him.

CHAPTER 7

THE .454 CASULL—RIFLE POWER AND PRECISION IN A SIXGUN

The 1950s were a great time for anyone interested in single action sixguns. Non-collectible, well-worn, but repairable Colt Single Actions, the Pre-war Colts, were available in abundance with the price tag often in the reachable range of $40-50. A young, virtually unknown gunsmith had already established a love affair with the Colt Single Action as he rode the Utah hills he called home with a .45 Colt Peacemaker as his cherished companion. Dick Casull was about to embark on the path that would lead to today's .454 Casull.

Casull joined a select group of men, all sixgunners, who wanted more. They simply were not satisfied with the available factory offerings in their revolvers.

Elmer Keith started with the .45 Colt, but after blowing one apart on the Fourth of July in 1925, he then switched calibers and spent thirty years shooting, reloading, and writing about his heavy loads in the .44 Special. Such notables as Gordon Boser and "Pop" Eimer went to a smaller bore using cut down .401 Winchester brass for the .40 wildcats they preferred in the Colt Single Action. Nearly three decades before the dawn of the .41 Magnum, it had already been wildcatted.

Casull preferred the .45 Colt chambering in the Colt Single Action because he had found the old, slow moving .45 Colt, dating back to 1873, to be a much better killer on game than the modern high-stepping

Dick Casull, creator of the .454 Casull.

100

.357 Magnum, the only Magnum available at the time. In his experiments, Casull played with numerous calibers in Colt Single Action sixguns from the diminutive .22 Hornet up through the .44s, but he always returned to his first love, the .45 Colt.

While Elmer Keith was using the .44 for his experiments, Casull did not feel that the .44 Special brass was stout enough for his goal. The favorite sixgunner's big bore of the time, the .44 Special, was only available with folded head, or balloon head, brass while Winchester had just introduced solid head cases for the .45 Colt. This resulted in much stronger brass which would be needed for the experimenting that lie ahead.

The Colt Single Action was a marvelous handgun and even today still holds a soft spot in the heart of many a sixgunner, but Colt Single Action cylinders are thin, almost paper thin, in the .45 Colt chambering with little or no margin of safety built in because the design goes back to blackpowder days when pressures were relatively low. The early experiments in pursuit of a more powerful .45 saw Casull bulge many cylinders. The cartridge was willing, but the sixgun was weak. Along the way, frame-mounted firing pins were used along with special barrels and heat-treated frames—all to no avail—cylinders burst and top straps blew.

Ignition problems also developed, so primer pockets were reamed to accept rifle primers. This helped some, but not enough. The "Magnum .45" experiments were far ahead of the powder capability as nothing was yet available to deliver the velocities that Casull was looking for. The problem was solved, for the time being at least, by going to duplex and triplex loadings. The best powder available at the time was Hercules #2400, but it did not ignite satisfactorily, and gave erratic results and unburned powder granules. A triplex loading, consisting of three Hercules powders, Unique, #2400, and Bullseye, was developed. The powders were loaded in sequence and were held in place by compression. Winchester's 296 and Hodgdon's H110 had not yet been developed and their entrance onto the scene removes all need for duplex and triplex loads. All modern .454 loads are assembled without mixing powders.

The goal was to get a 230 grain bullet to a muzzle velocity of 1,800 feet per second—in a .45 Colt! The brass could do it; the specially loaded ammunition could do it; the guns could not. Note very well what has just been said. For years, even to this day, the myth has been circulated and re-circulated that .45 Colt brass is "weak," whatever that means. It almost seems as if we are to believe that .45 Colt is made in a special section relegated to producing weaker brass.

Dick Casull's experiments should have laid the .45 Colt brass myth to rest for all time because all of his experiments were carried on with standard Winchester .45 Colt brass. If he was to succeed, it would be with this as his vehicle.

Whatever the strength level of the brass, a conventional six-shot cylinder was just not strong enough to contain the pressures that would be generated. The answer seemed to be a five-shot cylinder that would give greater strength because there would be more metal between chambers. Dick Casull saw the need for the extra strength and five-shot cylinders were designed and made as large as possible to still be able to fit the frame window of the Colt Single Action. Muzzle velocities of 1,300 feet per second were obtained when 4140 steel and five-shot cylinders were used. This was 100 feet per second faster than Keith's heavy loaded .44 Special, but was still a long way from the desired 1,800 feet per second.

By now Casull, still in his early twenties, became interested in heat-treating and metallurgy and discovered a way to heat-treat frames to 40 Rockwell without warping them in the process. This was 1954, and with a Colt Single Action .45 with a special five-shot cylinder, he obtained results of 1,550 feet per second with 250 grain bullets! This was more than the soon to be unveiled .44 Magnum was to deliver.

The power was there, but there was little margin of safety. In all of his experimenting, Casull was concerned with two things: ultimate power in a portable package, and along with this power, the technology to make the guns completely safe. Without this safety factor, the sixguns would be worthless. It had to be a combination of power plus a large margin of safety.

Casull turned to P.O. Ackley for special barrels using a 1:24 twist instead of the conventional .45 Colt twist of 1:16. The accuracy increased significantly with the change of barrel twist. Casull had been using specially heat-treated Colt Single Actions and Bisleys fitted with his five-shot cylinders and Ackley's barrels, however, in pursuit of his goal of power plus safety, he decided to go a step further and build his own single action frame. This was 1957. Casull was now at the point that he could engineer parts as needed and, using 4140 steel for the frame and 4150 steel for the cylinder, the first ".454 Magnum" was created. The .454 had progressed from modified Colt Single Actions, to five-shot cylindered Colts to a custom-built, five-shot single action. The .454 Casull had arrived.

Up to this point, all work with his .454 was accomplished with standard .45 Colt brass. It is very easy to see the problem that was waiting to rear its ugly head. Casull's load could not be offered; it would be

Dick Casull's personal 12-inch .454 (top), a 7-1/2-inch experimental model (middle), and a converted Colt Single Action with muzzle brake (bottom).

a disaster if such a load were dropped into a Prewar .45 Colt Single Action Army. Through the 1960s and 1970s, Casull built a number of custom .454s and, at one time, was even converting Ruger Super Blackhawks to his .45 Magnum on the .45 Colt case. These, of course, required special reloading on the part of the owner. In 1979, after a number of false starts, Casull and Wayne Baker came together and the result was Freedom Arms. Casull provided the engineering know-how while Baker met all the obstacles head on that always seem to surface with a new firearms business. Without Baker, the .454 Casull would never have become a factory sixgun and cartridge combination, nor would it have survived once it did. It had been a long, hard process that had taken thirty years, but finally in 1983, the first factory-built .454 Casull revolver from the new Freedom Arms factory on the Wyoming/Idaho border was delivered in the beautiful Star Valley area of Freedom, Wyoming.

With the new revolver came .454 Casull brass and factory ammunition. This brass carried large primer pockets for large rifle primers, but for added strength, this was soon changed to small primer pockets, which allowed more metal in the head of the brass case. It is a minor change, but one that points

to Casull's desire for complete safety for a load that operated at 55,000 pounds pressure—or more.

With other big bore sixgun calibers, one has numerous revolvers to choose from. This is not so with the .454. The Freedom Arms revolver is the only factory sixgun available chambered in .454 Casull. The revolver and the cartridge are inseparable. To talk about one is to talk about the other. From time to time other revolvers surface that are chambered in the .454. At the present time, an Italian import is at least advertised as available in .454. I would have none of it. I know what safety margins are built into the Freedom Arms .454. I do not know about any others.

Simply put, the .454 Casull is the finest and strongest factory-built revolver ever assembled. This is not meant to detract from other assembly line sixguns, such as those offered by Colt, Ruger, or Smith & Wesson, but the .454 Casull is an expensive—and well worth it!—factory-built, custom revolver. From the very beginning, both Dick Casull and Wayne Baker insisted that every .454 that bears the Freedom Arms and Casull names be as close to perfection as it is humanly possible to build a single action revolver. Nothing less is acceptable.

The .454 Casull, which is constructed of 17-4PH stainless steel, speaks quality from its near-perfect

In addition to the easy packin' 4-3/4-inch barrel length, .454s are also available in 10, 7-1/2, and 6 inches and the new 3-inch Packer length.

cylinder/barrel alignment to the precise fitting of the special designed grips to the 1:24 twist barrel that has proven to be the best for the pressures and velocities that the .454 attains.

The .454 Casull is a traditionally-styled, but completely modern, single action revolver. Dick Casull's love and appreciation for the Colt Single Action can immediately be seen in the Freedom Arms .454 Casull. It is made of the most modern materials available, but looks and feels like a single action out of the Old West. Of course, the cylinder is a five-shot affair that allows a lot of steel between the chambers. The cylinder does not have the "play" that is common to most factory produced revolvers. The reason is simple. Although they are factory-made, .454 Casulls are, in reality, custom-built—no long assembly lines here. All .454s are carefully, even meticulously, made by employees who care about turning out a quality revolver.

Everything about the .454 Casull speaks of tremendous strength, and yet it is only slightly larger than other single action revolvers. One very important feature is the locking arrangement on the cylinder base pin. Ever chase a base pin from a regular single action across the landscape because it let loose under recoil? That cannot happen with the Casull. A screw is threaded through the base pin and fits into a recess under the barrel. The base pin will not move under recoil. All custom sixgunsmiths use this same

arrangement now when building quality single action sixguns.

Because it is a single action, grip frame screws on the Freedom Arms .454 can loosen under recoil. A little Loc-Tite will take care of this. I am not one that enjoys cleaning sixguns, however, the Casull is such a precisely made piece of shooting machinery, that it must be cleaned regularly. There is simply no room for the dirt and crud that some of us allow to build up on the cylinder pin. Cylinder chambers that are recessed to accept the case heads of the .454 ammunition must also be kept clean.

The Casull grip is not the traditional single action grip that rolls up in the hand on recoil. If it were, it would probably roll right out of the hands with some of the heavy loads that are possible. The grip is much straighter than on either the Colt Single Action or Ruger Super Blackhawk. It definitely did take some getting used to for a hand that has been curled around a standard single action grip almost daily for more than thirty years. The .454 Casull grip is an achievement in human engineering that actually makes felt recoil in the .454 Casull manageable, and with some loads, it actually feels less than that of .44 Magnums and heavily loaded .45 Colts in other single action revolvers.

A traditional sixgunner will find himself right at home with the .454 Casull because it loads exactly

Taffin shooting and en-joying(?) the recoil of the 10-inch .454 Casull. Load is 300 grain factory offering at 1,700+ fps.

like the old style Colt Single Action revolver does. The hammer must be brought back to half-cock, the loading gate opened, and the cylinder rotated to either load or unload. Traditional but also modern, the .454 is fitted with a safety bar that is put into operation by drawing the hammer back about 1/8 inch. The hammer is then held away from the frame-mounted firing pin. The safety is independent of the trigger, so a smooth trigger pull can be had on the .454 Casull. Because I am traditional, spelled old-fashioned, I still carry all single action sixguns, with or without safeties, with an empty chamber under the hammer. That makes the .454 sixgun, which is really a fivegun, a fourgun for me. The Freedom Arms .454 action's design is such that once the first shot is fired, the loading gate can be flipped open, and an empty chamber awaits another loaded round without rotating the cylinder.

Whether it is fed hard cast or Freedom Arms jacketed 260 grain bullets at 2,000 feet per second, or 300 grainers of the same persuasion at 1,700 feet per second, or even standard .45 Colt loads at 850 feet per second, the excellent accuracy of the .454 Casull is readily apparent. My first trip to the Freedom Arms factory allowed me the pleasure of test-firing a ran-

domly picked .454 Casull; all .454s are test fired before leaving the Freedom Arms plant. With the .454 Casull locked into the specially designed rest, I carefully placed the big revolver and its carrier forward, shot, and then returned it back into battery for each succeeding shot. The target came back from its abiding place 35 yards down range. The result? One ragged hole made with five shots. That speaks highly of the precision that is built into the Freedom Arms .454 Casull revolver.

Premier Grade and Field Grade, which is simply a less finely-finished Freedom Arms revolver, .454 Casulls are available in standard barrel lengths of 4-3/4, 6, 7-1/2, and 10 inches. The shooter also has the option of choosing either fixed or adjustable sights and other barrel lengths are available upon special order. My first .454, purchased in 1986, was a 10-inch gun with special silhouette sights. In fact, I do believe that this was the first .454 set up for silhouetting. It was used quite successfully with Speer's 260 grain .45 Colt bullet and now long gone Winchester's W680 powder with Remington's # 7-1/2 Bench Rest Rifle Primers for 1,600 feet per second, flat shooting, ram bustin' loads.

Each .454 Casull is treated by the skilled craftsmen at Freedom Arms as a custom-built sporting arm that

Custom President's Pair of .454 Casulls with fixed sights, 5-1/2-inch barrels, black micarta stocks, and full engraving.

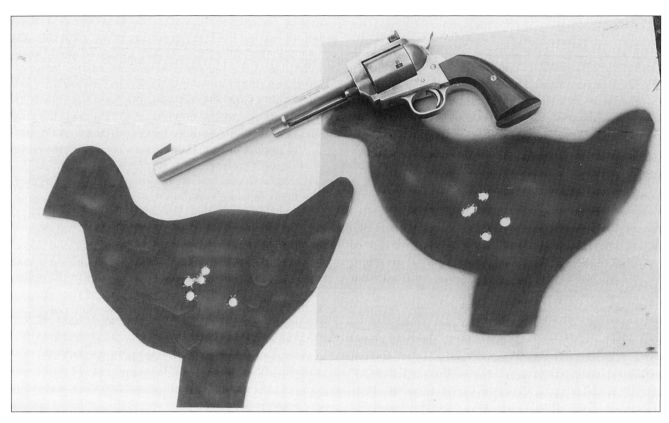

Fifty-yard accuracy from Creedmore position with the .454 Casull: Load is author's silhouette load of 260 grain Speer at 1,600 fps using Winchester's now obsolete WW680 powder.

is destined to give years, even a lifetime or several lifetimes, of trouble-free service. This does not mean that they are indestructible, though. Guns do come back to the factory for minor repairs and some come back that look like the owners tried to deliberately destroy them. It is, however, impossible to get into trouble with handloads in the .454 using conventional Magnum powders, quality bullets, and even a lick of common sense. My personal 10-inch .454 Casull has been pounded unmercilessly for years and is still as tight as the day it left Star Valley. No longer used for silhouetting, it has been fitted with a Mag-Na-Brake from Mag-Na-Port, and a scope, and now serves as a hunting sixgun.

The first time I met Dick Casull, I showed him a condition that I called a Casull Knuckle. The .454 kicks with full power loads and it kicks HARD. The knuckle on the middle finger of my shooting hand had become very hard and calloused from constantly being rapped. Casull had the same malady.

Once I had made all the payments on my first .454 Casull, I had to have another. The second .454 I selected was at the other end of the spectrum; I chose a real packin' pistol, a 4-3/4- inch barreled version. Freedom Arms' Bob Baker did a superb trigger

job and Charles Able made the ivory micarta grips that complete this perfect packin' pistol. My heavy load in the 10-inch .454 consisted of an SSK 340 grain hard cast flat-nosed bullet at 1,800 feet per second. Firing those loads in the short-barreled .454 was exhilarating to say the least. I feel that this load can handle any critter that walks, crawls, flies, or swims. My short-barreled .454 is now one of the most versatile sixguns extant. It has been returned to the factory three times to have new cylinders retro-fitted as they became available in .45 Colt, .45 ACP, and .45 Winchester Magnum.

Anyone who has experience loading the other Magnum revolver cartridges, .357 Magnum, .41 Magnum, and/or .44 Magnum, should have no trouble reloading for the .454 Casull because the .454 is a straight-walled revolver cartridge that is 1/10 inch longer than standard .45 Colt brass. There are, however, procedures with the reloading of the .454 Casull that must be followed for complete success. Many other revolvers will accept casually assembled reloads—the .454 Casull will not! Reloads must be specifically tailored to fit the tight chambers of the .454 Casull, or the result will be a large quantity of ammunition that will not chamber.

Freedom Arms .454 becomes four-guns-in-one with factory-offered auxiliary cylinders in .45 Colt, .45 ACP, and .45 WinMag.

The Freedom Arms .454 Casull is built to exacting and minimum tolerances; reloaded ammunition must be assembled the same way. Three areas in particular are critical: 1) the resizing of fired brass; 2) the selection and seating of primers; 3) the selection of bullets, and in the case of cast bullets, the sizing thereof.

First the resizing of brass. Standard .45 Colt dies are generally not satisfactory. Reloading dies for the .454 Casull available from Freedom Arms are designed to full length size the brass to fit the tight chambers of the .454 Casull. Because of the pressures involved with full-house loads, cylinder chambers are reamed to minimum tolerances to contain the brass as much as possible when loads are fired. Thus, fired brass must be brought back to a size that will enter the chambers freely. It is also recommended that all new brass be full length sized before the first loading. Sizing dies made for the .45 Colt will not, in all probability, full length size .454 brass small enough to either allow the sized brass to enter the chamber, or provide a tight friction pull on the reloaded bullet. Freedom Arms .454 dies are also designed to provide a crimp that will hold under heavy recoil.

Second, primers must be seated flush, or even below the top of the primer pocket on the head of .454 Casull brass. Failure to do so will result in a high primer that will bind the cylinder, at best, and prevent rotation, at worst. Do not use loads with high primers in the .454 Casull or any other sixgun for that matter because it is possible for a high primer to result in detonation of a loaded round when it is not lined up with the barrel. A precision primer seating tool separate from the reloading press, such as RCBS's bench mounted or hand held priming tool, is recommended for the seating of primers. All .454 brass of current manufacture is designed to accept small rifle primers to handle the pressures of top loadings in the .454 Casull. Pistol primers may be used for lighter loadings.

Finally, bullet selection for the .454 Casull is critical. Jacketed bullets designed for the .45 Colt may be used in the .454 Casull with complete success IF they are used properly. None of these bullets are designed for the velocities possible in the .454 Casull and there is the possibility of jacketed .45 Colt bullets coming apart under high pressures. Jacketed bullets for the .45 Colt that are used in the .454 Casull should be kept at velocities of 1,600 feet per second or less.

Freedom Arms offers three jacketed bullets that have been designed to withstand the pressures of full-house loads in the .454 Casull. These bullets are offered in a 240 grain hollowpoint, and 260 and 300 grain soft points. All of these bullets have jackets that are a full .032 inch in thickness, plus a hard alloy core that allows the developing of .454 loads to their highest potential.

These Freedom Arms jacketed bullets are designed to prevent base deformation at the time of firing and

The superb accuracy of the .454 Casull: This one-hole group was shot at 35 yards with factory 260 grain ammunition.

allow the bullet to enter the forcing cone intact, thus reducing wear and producing the highest possible velocities. These same bullets, due to their inherent strength, will hold together and give the deepest penetration on big game.

The Freedom Arms .454 Casull, with its 1:24 twist barrel, is a natural with heavyweight cast bullets. Again, however, caution is in order when selecting cast bullets. Bullets designed for the .45 Colt may be used, but some of these suffer accuracy problems with high velocity loadings because they were simply not designed with enough bearing surface to allow them to be shot at velocities approaching, and often surpassing, 2,000 feet per second in a revolver. It is a matter of experimenting with .45 Colt cast bullets to ascertain at which velocity levels they will perform accurately in the .454 Casull.

A good case in point is the Lyman #454424 Keith bullet. This is an excellent bullet and a favorite of .45 Colt shooters. My standard loadings for various .45 Colt sixguns varies from 8.5 to 10 grains of Unique for 800 to 1,100 feet per second. When used in the .454 Casull, the best results will be obtained with muzzle velocities from standard .45 Colt loadings up to around 1,400 feet per second . After this, the 260 grain Keith bullet behaves erratically.

Freedom Arms offers Lyman mould #454628 exclusively. Designed by Dick Casull for use in his revolver,

this mould gives a 255 grain flat-point, gas-checked bullet that is specifically designed to function with the operating pressures of the .454 Casull and should be used when a 255 grain cast bullet is desired in full-house loads for the .454. I have fired this bullet in Casull's personal 12-inch .454 with loads surpassing 2,000 feet per second and they will penetrate a 3/8-inch steel plate and surpass the .30-06 in muzzle energy.

Chambers of the .454 Casull are T-I-G-H-T. Bullets must be sized accordingly. Most resizing dies are tapered, which allows bullets to be sized larger at the shoulder end of the bullet than at the base. Cast bullets for the .454 must be completely sized their entire length or they will not allow the loaded round to be chambered as the bullet will not enter the chamber throat. Some bullets, such as NEI's 310 grain and 325 grain Keith semi-wadcutters have large, full caliber shoulders and will not enter the .454 chambers unless they are loaded with the brass crimped over the front of the driving band. They can, however, be used if chambers are kept clean in .45 Colt brass in the .454 Casull.

Freedom Arms also provides a second Casull-designed Lyman mould #454629 that drops a 300 grain flat-point, gas-checked bullet that is engineered specifically for the .454 Casull. This mould is only available from Freedom Arms. Because of its bearing surface design and gas check feature, this 300 grainer can be used in the .454 Casull to a full 1,800 feet per second with excellent accuracy. It also provides excellent performance in the Colt Anaconda .45 Colt or Ruger Blackhawk .45 Colt at 1,100 feet per second. The 300 grain Casull bullet is available expertly cast, sized, lubed, and gas-checked from BRP Bullets. This latter load is quite pleasant to shoot and has been fired at a full 700 yards using my short-barreled .454 Casull. Both accuracy and penetration are excellent. We have managed to hit 2-foot square targets, not regularly mind you, but more than once out of a box of cartridges. Shooting at an old log cabin in the mountains of Wyoming at 700 yards resulted in penetration of both walls in the heavy timbered structure.

The .454 Casull is a reloader's dream come true with its ability to deliver outstanding accuracy with both cast and jacketed bullets at velocities from mild 800 feet per second loads up to full-house 2,000 feet per second loads and beyond. A wide range of powders are applicable to the .454 <u>BUT</u> only H110 and WW296 should be used in assembling full-house loads. The use of faster powders in trying to achieve top velocities will result in very high pressures and possibly ruined brass—or worse. Save other powders for the lighter loads.

At the other extreme, <u>DO NOT</u> try to use H110 and WW296 for light loads. The result can be squib loads in certain weather situations, such as extreme heat or cold, and even dangerously high pressures. <u>Use these two powders only for full Magnum loadings of the .454 Casull.</u> I have settled on two standard full-house loadings for the .454 and have used either H110 or Winchester 296 powder. With the 255 grain bullet, the charge is 34 grains for 1,800 feet per second muzzle velocity in the 10-inch .454 and 32 grains with the 300 grain bullet for 1,,750 feet per second in the same sixgun.

The .454 Casull will last a lifetime of reloading and give excellent results if reloads are assembled carefully with attention given to the above details. Because of the minimum tolerances in the .454 Casull, as mentioned earlier, it must be kept clean. Powder residue and bullet lube will build up on the cylinder pin, hindering rotation and also preventing loaded rounds from chambering if the recesses that accept the rims of the cases are not kept clean. A cylinder full of factory .45 Colt loads with soft swaged bullets used in the .454 Casull will often result in the cylinder becoming bound up tightly as pieces of lead work their way between the front of the cylinder and the back of the barrel.

The Freedom Arms .454 Casull is first and foremost a hunting handgun, and as such is the first factory revolver to offer both rifle-type energy and rifle-type accuracy to the handgun hunter. Anything the .44 Magnum can do, the .454 can do quicker, further, and surer! While the .44 Magnum has less energy at the

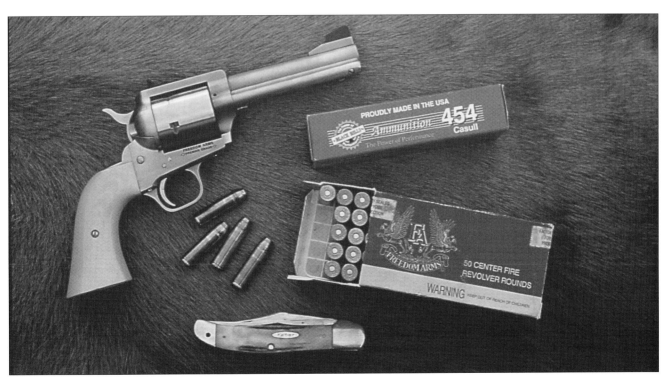

Both Freedom Arms and Black Hills offer 300 grain factory ammunition for the .454. Freedom's offering is full-house, while Black Hills loading is in between factory .454 and full-house .44 Magnum.

Excellent accuracy of the .454 Casull with full-house 300 grain bulleted loads: This group was shot at 25 yards.

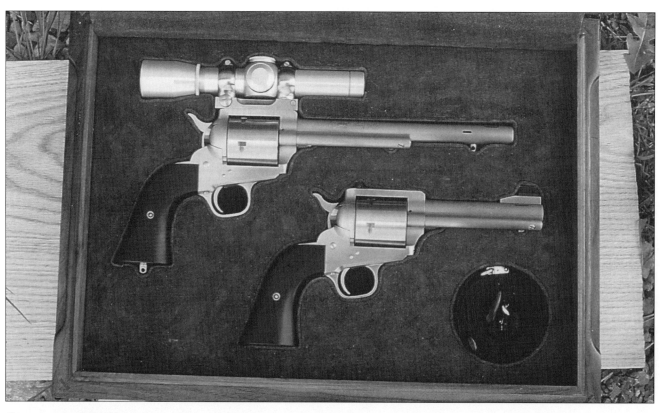

Custom-cased Freedom Arms .454 with black micarta stocks. Scoped 7-1/2-inch is for hunting and 4-3/4-inch size is the perfect packin' pistol.

The 3-inch .454 is one of the toughest sixguns to shoot. Its heavy recoil, coupled with relatively light weight, requires intense concentration for successful shooting.

muzzle than a .30-30 at 100 yards does, the .454 Casull can be loaded 20 percent above the muzzle energy of one of the most popular hunting rifle calibers, the .30-06! That makes the .454 a first-class hunting handgun by anyone's definition.

Not only does Freedom Arms offer the .454 Casull as a premium hunting handgun, but it also offers both factory ammunition and jacketed bullets with the hunter in mind. Factory rounds can be obtained with 240 grain jacketed hollowpoints at 1,875 feet per second, 260 grain jacketed flat-points at 1,800 feet per second, and 300 grain jacketed flat-points at 1,600 feet per second. The latter is designed for maximum penetration on really large game. All three bullets are available for hunters who prefer to roll their own.

Factory loaded .454 Casull rounds are also available full-house-style from Cor-Bon with either a 260 grain or 320 grain bonded core bullet designed for maximum penetration or from Black Hills in a loading that utilizes Hornady's 300 grain XTP bullet at a muzzle velocity that falls midway in between full-house .44 Magnums and .454 Casull levels.

The .454 Casull is a true mouse-to-moose handgun with the accuracy to take the smallest game and the power to down the largest. It has been used successfully on Alaskan brown bear, African lion, Cape buffalo, and the largest of the game animals, the African elephant. In addition, it has been used on all American game from pronghorn to mulies to whitetail to black bear to elk to everything with complete success.

A number of sight options are available for the adjustable-sighted .454 Casull Single Action revolver. In addition to the standard sights consisting of an adjust-able rear and ramp front sight, various ramp front sight heights are available in both plain black and with orange inserts. The available heights are .280, .330, .380, and .430 inch. Front sights fit into a slot on the ramp base and are easily interchangeable by loosening a socket head screw at the front of the base itself. With four sight heights available, any Casull revolver can be sighted in with any load/bullet weight combination from 185 grain target loads to full-house 340 grain hunting handloads without having to raise the rear sight excessively.

Also available, and especially popular with hunters, are express sights for the Freedom Arms revolver. Consisting of a shallow V-notch rear and brass bead front, express sights are very fast for game shooting, and the front sights are also available in various heights for precision sighting in of each revolver and load combination.

The .454 Casull is one revolver that will definitely outshoot its iron sights and thus is designed to be easily fitted with a scope. Many big game hunters prefer scopes to allow as little sighting error as possible. Due to the recoil that is involved with any large bore Magnum handgun, the .454 Casull revolver requires a special scope mount base and Freedom Arms can supply the extremely strong SSK T'SOB scope mount base with three rings for extra holding power. Silver Finish Leupold Scopes in either 2X or 4X can be precisely mounted at the factory. Scope mount bases are available only for adjustable-sighted Freedom Arms revolvers.

For those who prefer a more compact scope mount base, stainless steel bases are available that fit

The .454 x 7-1/2-inch Hunting Handgun Supreme has now been joined by the same revolver, from left to right, in .44 Magnum, .353 Casull, and .50AE.

the rear sight channel. The Freedom Arms revolver is the only revolver that is designed so the scope mount base is in, as well as on, the revolver. This is accomplished by a projection on the bottom of the scope base that fits into the rear sight channel on the top strap. This results in a very strong mounting system.

Barrel lengths of 4-3/4, 6, 7-1/2, and 10 inches are available—7-1/2 inches is the most popular and most practical for hunting. My third .454 Casull is a 7-1/2-inch barreled Field Grade fitted with black micarta stocks, a Freedom Arms trigger job, and a Leupold scope.

Many hunters are going to the 4-3/4-inch .454 Casull as a true back-up gun simply because it has the power that can be delivered immediately in a touchy situation. Carried high on the hip in a proper holster, or better yet tucked up under the arm in a shoulder holster, it is always there and always ready.

The range at which game can be taken and the type of game to be taken with the .454 Casull will be limited only by the hunter's ability and desire. The .454 will deliver. With a scope-sighted .44 Magnum sixgun, I confine myself to shots out to 100 yards.

With the .454, I am confident to 150 yards. In both cases we are talking about thin-skinned, non-dangerous game shot while standing from a solid rest. It is one thing to shoot long-range at inanimate objects; it is quite another when the quarry is a living creature.

In 1935, Smith & Wesson introduced the first sixgun to be known as "The World's Most Powerful Revolver," the .357 Magnum. We could not go any further. We had arrived. We had reached the ultimate. There were a number of reloaders, especially those that favored the .44 Special who questioned the claim, but by and large, the handgun shooting world accepted the proclamation. When the new "Most Powerful Revolver," the .44 Magnum came upon the scene in 1956, everyone knew that this was really the ultimate. There was simply no way that a handgun could ever be made that would be more powerful than the big .44 Magnum. Everyone knew that we had reached the apex. Well, almost everyone.

Wayne Baker and Dick Casull believed more, much more was possible. The result is a superb revolver firing a superb cartridge. Maybe this time we really have reached the ultimate.

CHAPTER 8

THE .44-40— REDISCOVERED IN THE '90s

Miracles really do happen! In the 1990s we have been witnesses to a modern miracle of sorts with the resurrection of the .44 Winchester Centerfire, or .44-40. No cartridge has ever been so dead, buried so deep, forgotten so long, and still brought back to life. No cartridge has ever been so written off by the modernists and still return back to life. This miraculous life-giving resuscitation of a century old cartridge is a result of two things. As Colt prepared to shut down production of the Single Action Army for the third and last time, it looked for sales in every possible way and the Third Generation

Single Action Army and the New Frontier were chambered in .44-40 in the early 1980s. Prior to this, Colt had also offered two .44-40 Commemoratives, a blued and case-colored 7-1/2-inch Skeeter Skelton Commemorative—this sixgun was at least announced. If it exists at all, it is very rare, and I've never seen one—and a 7-1/2-inch nickeled .44-40 Frontier Six-Shooter.

The second, and major reason, for the return of the .44-40 is Cowboy Action Shooting. This new game, requiring the use of pre-1898 sixguns, leverguns, and shotguns, or replicas thereof, will be covered in a separate chapter. It is sufficient to say here that

The Classic "Frontier Sixshooter," a 4-3/4-inch Colt Single Action Army .44-40 with eagle grips.

thanks to Cowboy Action Shooting, the cartridges of the nineteenth century are finding great new popularity as we prepare to enter the twenty-first century.

The Winchester '73, "The Gun That Won The West" had as its first and finest chambering, the .44 Winchester centerfire. The 1860 Henry .44 Rimfire brought forth the first really successful levergun that could "be loaded on Sunday and fired all week." The 1866 Yellow Boy changed the system of loading from a .22-style tube under the barrel to a loading gate on the side, and the 1873 Winchester gave us a centerfire .44 cartridge. With a 200 grain bullet over 40 grains of blackpowder, the .44 Winchester centerfire became known as the .44-40. The year 1873 was certainly a banner year for firearms as the Winchester 1873 was joined by the Colt Peacemaker .45 Colt and the 1873 Springfield .45-70. One hundred and twenty-five years later, all three cartridges are among the most popular available. Shooters are willing to wait for up to four years to get a copy of the Sharps rifle in .45-70. The .45 Colt, never available in leverguns on the frontier, is now offered by Marlin and Winchester in levergun form. Finally, the .44-40 is not only a standard Colt Single Action chambering, it is soon to be offered by Marlin in a levergun. Both the .45 Colt and .44-40 are available in replica single actions as well as replica leverguns Model 1866, 1873, and 1892-style.

Introduced independently of the .45 Colt and for a levergun rather than a sixgun, the .44-40 looks a lot like a .45 that has been necked-down to .44 which gives a slightly bottlenecked cartridge for ease of feeding in the lever action Winchester. In these days of belted Magnums and super long-range varmint rifles, it is hard to conceive of the .44-40 as a serious rifle cartridge, but it was a tremendous step forward in 1873. It may not have been a long-range rifle as we think of the concept today, but the .44-40 1873 Winchester was the "assault rifle" of its day, with a large magazine capacity and, in the right hands, capable of fending off the enemy way out yonder and then some. It was definitely The Gun That Won The West.

It had to happen early in the 1870s. Certainly some frontiersman looked at his Colt Single Action Army and Winchester 1873 and said "Why not?" It was inconvenient for the two-gun man to buy two different cartridges for his sixgun and carbine, and since the .44-40 and .45 Colt were both loaded with 40 grains of blackpowder over 200 and 255 grain bullets, respectively, and because the .44-40 brass was only .020 inch longer than .45 Colt, it made a lot of sense to chamber the Model P sixgun for the .44-40. This was finally done in 1878.

All was not perfect, however. Jefferson Davis Milton, an early Texas lawman, noted the convenience of having his carbine and sixgun both chambered in the same cartridge and made the switch to the .44-40 Colt Single Action in 1880. At the first shot from his new sixgun, Milton reported that the primer flowed back into the firing pin hole, binding the hammer-mounted firing pin. This prevented the cocking of the hammer for the next shot and this, of course, immediately locked the sixgun, which took it out of action. Many modern sixguns, especially Magnums, carry frame-mounted firing pins to prevent this flowing of fired primers from heavy loaded cartridges into a hole in the frame. It is doubtful that the .44-40 cartridges loaded with blackpowder were so hot as to cause this. Perhaps the Colt Single Action Army had an enlarged firing pin hole, but whatever the case, Milton swore off the .44-40 and carried a .45 Colt the rest of his life.

Milton's predicament could not have been a common problem because the .44-40 was second only to the .45 Colt in popularity in cartridges chambered in the Colt Single Action followed by the .38-40 (.38WCF) and .32-20 (.32WCF), both of which were also chambered in the Model 1873 Winchester. All three WCF cartridges were later chambered in the grandest of all lever action saddle guns, the Model 1892 Winchester carbine. All were, however, totally eclipsed with the coming of smokeless powder and the ultra-modern .30-30 in 1894.

Colt produced more than 150,000 .44-40 Colt Single Action Armys prior to World War II. All of these .44-40s were barrel marked "FRONTIER SIXSHOOTER". In 1888, Colt introduced its Flat-Top Target Model. These were simply Single Action Armys with the top of the frame flattened and the installation of a rear sight moveable for windage, as furnished on the original Ruger Single-Sixes in 1953. Elevation was accomplished by a movable blade in the front sight held in place by a screw. It was very crude by today's standards, but was a start towards modern target-sighted revolvers. Less than 1,000 Flat-Top Target Models were made, with only 21 in .44 Winchester centerfire.

Colt also chambered the big New Service double action revolver in .44-40, and Smith & Wesson made a few Frontier Models in both single action and double action for the .44-40; a few Triple-Locks also saw chambering in .44WCF. By 1941, the Colt Single Action was removed from production and the .44-40 was dead and buried and looked like it would stay that way. In fact, with the coming of the .357 Magnum in 1935, it appeared that the .44-40, .44 Special, and .45 Colt would all become history. After all, we had the .357 Magnum in a fine double action sixgun, and the .45 Automatic in the 1911 Colt. What more could anyone ask for?

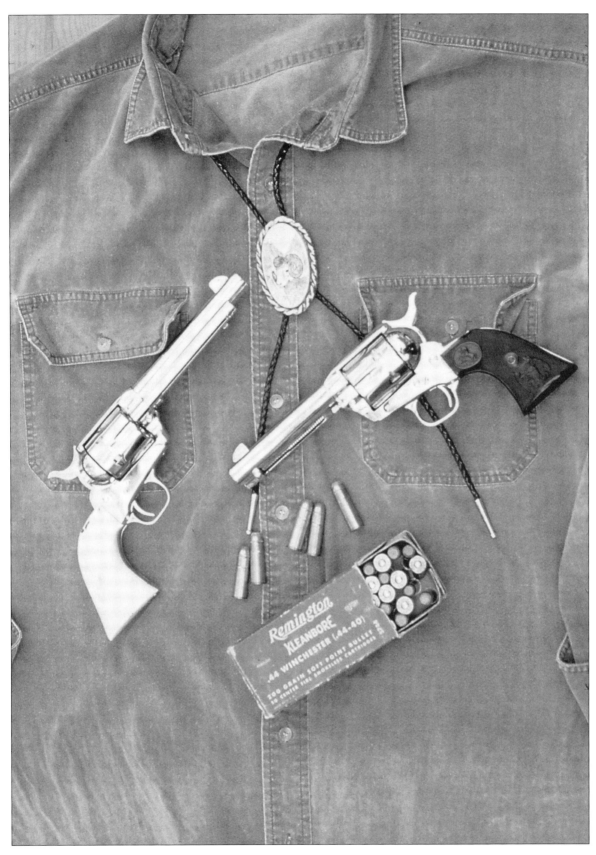

Two beautiful examples of Colt Custom Shop nickeled .44-40s: 5-1/2 inch with stag stocks by Charles Able, and 4-3/4 inch with factory eagle grips.

After more than six decades, the .45 Colt and .44-40 are both offered by Colt. These 5-1/2-inch nickeled examples carry stag stocks by Charles Able and one-piece maple stocks by Tedd Adamovich.

When Colt resumed production of the Colt Single Action in 1955, followed by the modernized version of the Flat-Top Target, the New Frontier in 1962, the calibers were .45 Colt, .357 Magnum, .38 Special, and .44 Special. None were produced in .44-40. The Colt died again in 1974, only to be resurrected in 1978. This time, before it was removed from production for the third time in the early 1980s, it was once again chambered in .44-40 in both Single Action and New Frontier versions with a few Sheriff's Models being made with both .44-40 and .44 Special cylinders.

Until very recently, the only way to get a .44-40 was to have one custom made. Actually, all it took was an extra cylinder for an existing sixgun. For best results, one had to start with a .44 Special, not a .44 Magnum. The reasoning is simple. Factory .44-40 cartridges measure .443-inch outside diameter at the case mouth and carry a bullet with a diameter of .426 inch, while .44 Magnums are normally loaded with bullets of .430 to .431 inch and mike out at .455-inch outside diameter. Rechamber a .44 Magnum cylinder to .44-40 and one already has a chamber that is .455 inch minus .443 inch, or .012 inch oversize. Add a properly chambered .44-40 cylinder to a .44 Magnum sixgun and an undersized bullet literally wobbles down the

barrel. The best compromise when using a .44-40 cylinder with a .44 Magnum sixgun is to cut the cylinder to accept .430-inch bullets in .44-40 brass.

Post-World War II Colt Single Action .44 Specials carry tight barrels with groove diameters of around .426 to .428 inch. This makes them perfect candidates for adding a .44-40 cylinder. For the best results and the least expense, Third Generation Colt sixguns can be fitted with factory .44-40 cylinders. It is best to start with a .357 Magnum or .44 Special cylinder and rechamber to .44-40 if one intends to fit a Second Generation or Prewar Colt Single Action with a .44 Winchester centerfire cylinder. Third Generation Colt Single Action Armys carry a different ratchet/hand/cylinder bushing set-up than the First and Second Generation-styles. Actually with Prewar, or First Generation sixguns, it is much easier to find a .44-40 sixgun than a rare .44 Special because 300 .44-40s were manufactured for every single .44 Special. Fitting a .44-40 with a .44 Special cylinder for the sixgunner that desires both options is the easiest way to go—sometimes.

In order to obtain a good-shooting .44-40, we have to go a different direction and install a proper barrel. Many years ago, for $160, I purchased a Colt Single

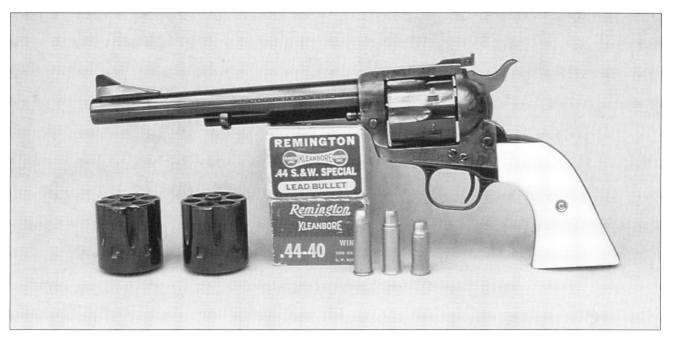

Colt's Third Generation 7-1/2-inch New Frontier .44 Special with ivory stocks by Charles Able has been fitted with two extra Third Generation cylinders by Hamilton Bowen. One is a factory .44-40 and the other is a .357 Magnum rechambered to .44 Russian.

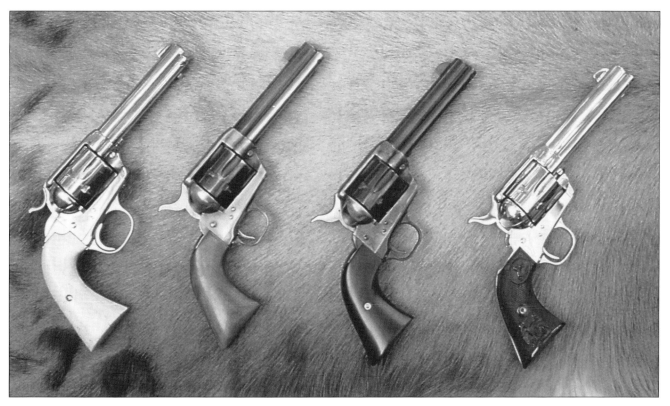

Four generations of 4-3/4-inch .44 Colts: Prewar Bisley .44-40 with maple stocks by Tedd Adamovich, Second Generation .44 Special with one-piece Pau Ferro stocks by Tony Kojis, Third Generation .44 Special with black micarta stocks by Charles Able, and Colt Custom Shop .44-40 with factory eagle grips.

Ballistically equivalent to the defensive cartridge of the 1990s—the .40 Smith & Wesson—the Colt Single Action .38-40 carries well under a sport coat in a Milt Sparks holster. Stag grips by Charles Able.

A favorite rig for plain woods bummin' is this 4-3/4-inch-nickeled .44-40 Colt Single Action Army mated with an El Paso basket weave belt and #1920 Tom Threepersons holster.

Action Army Bisley Model which was marked with the .44-40 inscription "FRONTIER SIXSHOOTER (BISLEY MODEL)" on its 4-3/4-inch barrel. In spite of its lack of finish, it proved to be in good mechanical condition, but the bore slugged out at a well-oversized .432 inch and the cylinders would not accept bullets larger than .428 inch. The old barrel came off, was replaced by a 7-1/2-inch .44 Special barrel of .426-inch groove diameter and that old Bisley has given 25 yard groups of 1/2 inch using 9 grains of Unique and the Lyman #42798 .44-40 flat-point bullet. Consequently, there seems to be no real standard for barrel groove diameter with old sixguns chambered for the .44-40, with specimens running from .426 inch all the way up to .432 inch—or more. Sixguns in .44-40 chambering must be measured as to groove diameter and treated accordingly.

As stated above, if a .44 Magnum cylinder is rechambered to .44-40, one winds up with a chamber mouth that is greatly oversized. Couple this with the natural thinness of the .44-40 brass and one has a situation in which the brass is heavily worked and expands a great deal when fired and then is contracted when resized. The result is a very short life for reloaded brass. Ruger recently began offering its Vaquero in .44-40. The engineers designed a beautiful .44-40 cylinder with tight chamber mouths and then mated it with a .44 Magnum barrel. The result is poor accuracy, to say the least. The best solution for those that have these sixguns is to fit a tight barrel; the easier solution is to open the chamber mouths to accept .430-inch bullets for use in the .44-40 cylinder.

Presently, I have three prized sixguns that carry auxiliary .44-40 cylinders. One is a Third Generation 7-1/2-inch .44 Special Colt New Frontier with adjustable sights that is fitted with a Third Generation .44-40 cylinder. Adjustable sights are really necessary to get the best out of a .44 Special/.44-40 combination as the .44 Special is normally loaded with 250 grain bullets while the .44-40 utilizes 200 grain bullets. They will usually not hit to the same point of aim and adjustable sights allow one to dial in the desired load as far as point of aim is concerned.

The second combination sixgun is the Colt Bisley Model, mentioned above, that has the original .44-40 cylinder as well as a .44 Special cylinder and a .44 Special 7-1/2-inch Colt Second Generation barrel. This sixgun with fixed sights is sighted in for .44 Special 250 grain bullets at 950 feet per second, so loads with 200 grain bullets from the .44-40 do shoot lower.

The third combination sixgun is a Texas Longhorn Arms Flat-Top Target .44 Special. Bill Grover, of Texas Longhorn Arms, fitted this special sixgun with extra cylinders in both .44 Magnum and .44-40, that are all designed to carry .430-inch bullets. I especially prefer Speer's 225 grain jacketed hollowpoint semi-wadcutter bullet in both the Special and .44-40 brass in this sixgun. This particular sixgun and bullet, with its copper cup jacket and pure lead core, allow for successful use of the .44 Special and .44-40 at around 1,100 to 1,200 feet per second muzzle velocity for hunting of deer-sized game.

For best results, all three of these .44 Special/.44-40 sixguns require custom reloading to mate the proper bullet with the barrel/cylinder combination. For most situations I use .428-inch hard cast bullets in the two Colts and .430-inch jacketed bullets in the Texas Longhorn Arms sixgun.

Another way to come up with a dandy .44-40 is the one chosen by my good friend, Terry Murbach. Murbach started with a Smith & Wesson .44 Special double action sixgun, in his case a 6-1/2-inch Model

Friend Terry Murbach's Smith & Wesson 6-1/2-inch Model 24 .44 Special fitted with Herrett's stocks does double-duty with the extra fitted .44-40 Smith & Wesson cylinder and extractor rod.

These .44s all become .44-40s with auxiliary cylinders: Top, 7-1/2-inch Colt Bisley .44 Special with stag grips; middle, 7-1/2-inch .44 Magnum Texas Longhorn Arms with one-piece factory stocks; bottom, Colt 7-1/2-inch New Frontier with one-piece stocks by Tedd Adamovich.

Ruger now chambers its Vaquero for .44-40. This 4-5/8-inch blue and case-colored example has had the chamber throats opened to allow the use of .430-inch bullets in .44-40 brass mated with the .44 Magnum-sized cylinder.

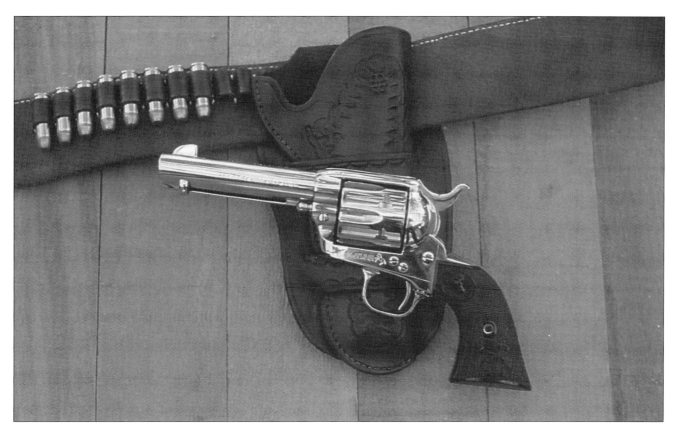

This 4-3/4-inch .44-40, paired with leather by TrailRider, is for Cowboy Action Shooting.

24. He then fitted a .44-40 cylinder and extractor rod from the special run of Commemorative .44-40 sixguns offered by Smith & Wesson a few years back. The .44-40 was never a major chambering with Smith & Wesson, but for some reason it chose this caliber for its 1986-issued Texas Wagon Train Commemorative. The .44-40 cylinder was greater in length than the .44 Special frame allowed, so it was necessary to machine quite a bit of metal from the front of the cylinder to fit the Model 24 frame. The result is a double action sixgun that handles both cartridges very well.

As previously mentioned, Cowboy Action Shooting has really brought new life to the .44-40. Colt paid attention, did not allow the Third Generation Single Action Army to languish, and instead made it a Colt Custom Shop option. Call it Third Generation Part Two, or Fourth Generation, whatever, the Colt Single Action is back with Colt now offering both blue/case-colored and nickeled Single Action Armys in barrel lengths of 4-3/4 and 5-1/2 inches. They are terribly pricey, but we just grit our teeth and pay the freight for a genuine Colt Single Action. Replicas also abound in .44-40 chambering with not only Single Action Army copies available, but also Remington 1875s and Smith & Wesson Schofields.

All of these mate well with levergun replicas also available in .44-40 in 1873, 1892, or even 1866 Yellow Boy copies. For Cowboy Action Shooting, I personally cannot think of a better combination than a pair of single actions, Colt, Remington, or Smith & Wesson Schofield types, mated with a replica 1873 Winchester, all chambered in .44-40.

Like the .45 Colt, the .44-40 has also been saddled with the "weak brass" syndrome, and as in the case of the .45 Colt, the problem is not brass, but the sixguns that these cartridges have been chambered for dating back more than 100 years. Do not, however, take this to mean that every sixgun chambered for the .44-40 can handle maximum loads. With modern sixguns chambered for the .44-40, a long-time standard load with the 200 grain Lyman #42798 bullet has been 18.5 grains of #2400. This load has been published in numerous books and magazines. It is a warm load that has been used with success in both Colt Single Actions and replicas. I would expect the New Frontier to thrive on this load. It has proven, however, to be too hot in my 7-1/2-inch New Frontier, and gives cratered primers and sticky extraction of fired cases. For this particular .44-40, I have settled on 17.5 grains of #2400 as a maximum load. Every sixgun is a law unto itself and carries its own personality. Do not take any-

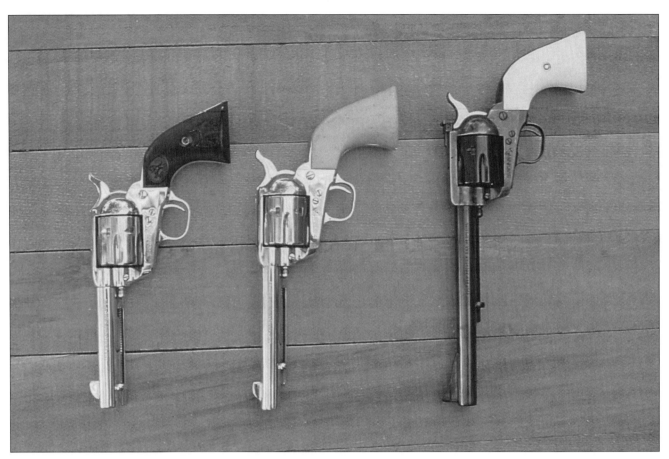

Three Colt .44-40s: 4-3/4 inch nickeled with factory eagle grips, nickeled 5-1/2-inch with one-piece maple stocks by Tedd Adamovich, and 7-1/2-inch New Frontier with ivory stocks by Charles Able.

thing for granted when it comes to working with maximum loads!

All older, and many recent, reloading manuals have separate sections for reloading the .44-40 for the Model 1892 Winchester listing loads that use nine grains <u>more</u> #2400 than my maximum sixgun load and eight grains <u>more</u> than my maximum H4227 load. So much for the weakness of .44-40 brass. **WARNING!!** **<u>Such rifle-type loads would be like hand grenades in many sixguns!</u>** When using reloading manuals, especially some of the older ones, please make sure the .44-40 section is for sixguns.

The original loading of 40 grains of blackpowder cannot be duplicated in modern solid head .44-40 brass. The most I can get into a case and seat the #42798 bullet properly is 35 grains of FFFg which gives slightly over 900 feet per second. The same volume of Pyrodex P raises the muzzle velocity to 1,000 feet per second and both loads will group in 2 inches at 25 yards.

Target shooting with the .44-40? Although not thought of as a target load, my tests over the past two decades have shown the .44-40 to be capable of target accuracy even in single action sixguns with long hammer falls, lacking the refinements of target double action sixguns and semi-automatics. With proper loads in the right sixgun, the .44-40 will shoot right along side, or better than, any other cartridge.

Hunting? Probably more deer, and even larger game, than anyone could count have fallen to the .44-40, but it is certainly not a top choice for hunting. It is, nonetheless, an excellent small game and varmint load. Two-hundred grain flat-nosed cast bullets and my Remington .44-40 Model 1875 is a favorite combination for large varmints and I have taken many a big Idaho jack with mine.

Even with full-house blackpowder loads for Cowboy Action Shooting, or just plain enjoyment, the .44-40 is one of those relaxing cartridges that I find myself appreciating more and more. When the wrist has taken all the punishment it can stand from full-house .44 Magnum and .454 loads, out comes a truly easy shootin' big bore, the .44-40.

The miracle of resurrection experienced by the .44-40 has been so encompassing that it pulled another dead cartridge out of the grave as it came forth with

Colt made a special run of 3-inch-barreled Sheriff's Models with .44 Special and .44-40 cylinders in the early 1980s.

The Winchester centerfire Colt Single Action Armys: Top, nickeled 4-3/4-inch .44-40; bottom, 4- 3/4-inch .38-40 with one-piece stocks by Tedd Adamovich. Leather is by TrailRider.

The excellent accuracy of the Third Generation Colt Single Action Army .38-40 with 4-3/4-inch barrel: The range was 25 yards with Lyman's #401043 cast bullet over 8 grains of Unique. A few strokes of the file will bring the point of impact up where it should be.

great new life. In 1880, the Winchester 1873 was chambered for a new cartridge as the .44-40 was necked-down to .40 caliber. The powder charge remained the same, the bullet weight was reduced to 180 grains, and the .38-40 or .38 Winchester Centerfire was born. The caliber was .40, but the name given to the new offering was .38. Maybe .40-40 just didn't sound right.

A few years later, the Colt Single Action Army was chambered for the new round and it found great acceptance among sixgunners. It not only shot flatter and faster, it also shot easier recoil-wise than either the .44-40 or .45 Colt. In 1990, the ultimate defensive handgun round was offered in the .40 Smith &Wesson, which turns out to be a deadringer ballistically to the old .38-40. In fact, the .40 Smith & Wesson began life as a wildcat cartridge chambered in the Browning Hi-Power using factory .38-40 bullets.

The .38-40 was a favorite sixgun chambering of early Western star Tom Mix, and John Wayne used a .38-40 Colt Single Action in his early "B" Westerns. By the late 1930s, the .38-40 was, for all intents and purposes, a gone goose and was dropped from produc-

tion by Colt prior to World War II. In its sixty year history, it had been chambered in the Colt New Service as well as the Single Action Army and Bisley and also by Smith & Wesson in its New Model Number Three, the double action Frontier Model, and very rarely in the Triple-Lock.

Personally, I will always have a soft spot in my heart for the .38-40 because it was the chambering of my first centerfire sixgun, a 4-3/4-inch Colt Single Action Army. That gun cost me two weeks pay in 1957, but it was beautiful with its case-hardened frame that had turned gray over nearly sixty years, its thinning but well cared for blue finish, and the smoothly worn black gutta-percha factory stocks.

I foolishly allowed that sixgun to get away from me and spent decades trying to find a replacement for it. I even had Hamilton Bowen build a custom 4-3/4-inch .38-40 using a Herter's PowerMag with the .401 cylinder rechambered to .38-40. PowerMag .401-inch barrels are perfect for the .38-40. It was not enough. With the advent of the 10mm, Ruger made a small number of Blackhawks with two cylinders chambered in .38-40 and 10mm. I acquired one of these and had the

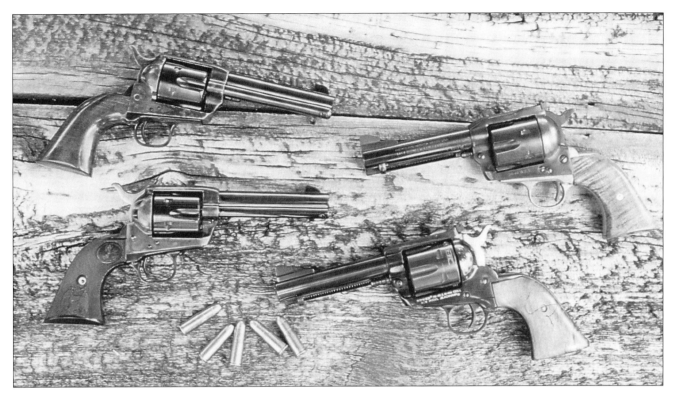

Modern .38-40s, from top left: EMF Hartford 38-40 x 4-3/4 inch, Bowen Custom .38-40 built on Herter's .401 PowerMag with grips by Charles Able, Ruger's .38-40 Blackhawk cut to 4-3/4 inches, and Colt's finest .38-40 ever, the Third Generation Single Action Army.

barrel cut to 4-3/4 inches, but it was still not enough to soothe my longing for a 4-3/4-inch Colt Single Action Army.

Finally, after nearly sixty years of being out of production, the .38-40 is back, chambered in the Colt Single Action Army. Colt now offers .45 Colt, .44-40, and .38-40 in both blue and nickel finished 4-3/4-inch and 5-1/2-inch barrel lengths. Ain't progress wonderful?

Realistically speaking, all of us, myself included, could certainly survive quite well without a .44-40 or .38-40 sixgun. Practically speaking, both have been hopelessly outclassed by other sixgun chamberings. Traditionally speaking, I am terribly pleased to have these two sixgun chamberings back among the living. They are perfect for Cowboy Action Shooting and add immensely to the Spirit of the Game. There is something about touching off a blackpowder round in one of these original chamberings that stirs the heart, soul, and spirit. It is the best thing I know of short of consuming an elixir from the elusive Fountain of Youth.

As sixgunners, we don't always have to be realistic or practical. A great deal of, and in fact, the vast majority of sixgunnin' should just be plain, pure enjoyment. The .38-40 and .44-40 fill this important need quite well.

CHAPTER 9

THE SUPERMAGS— .357, .375, AND .445

The length of sixgun cartridges has always pretty much been determined by the sixgun itself. The first centerfire big bore cartridges, .44 American for Smith & Wesson, and .45 Colt for Colt Patent Firearms, were designed to fit revolvers whose cylinder length was adopted from cap-n-ball revolvers of the 1850s and 1860s. Had they stayed with the old and much larger Walker Colt and its cylinder, sixgun history might have been written differently.

Winchester introduced its 1873 levergun chambered for a cartridge, the .44 Winchester centerfire, that was destined to become a sixgun cartridge just five years later. Smith & Wesson's .44 American soon became the .44 Russian with a case length standardized at .955 inch, the Colt's .45 measured in at 1.285 inches lengthwise, and the Winchester offering, the .44-40, came in at an easy-to-feed-through-leverguns length of 1.305 inches.

When Smith & Wesson decided to chamber its New Model No. 3 Single Action for the .44-40, it increased the frame and cylinder length of its single action sixgun by .125 inch, bringing it up to Colt Single Action Army size. Smith & Wesson presented the first centerfire sixgun cartridge of this century with the .44 Special with a case length of 1.160 inches. Smith & Wesson's cylinder length in the 1907 New Century Triple-Lock was just slightly shorter than that found in Colt's Single Action Army.

As we entered the Magnum era with the .357 Magnum in 1935, and continuing with the .44 Magnum in 1955, both new cartridges came in right at the same length as the old .45 Colt, requiring nothing new in cylinder or frame length. Smith & Wesson simply rechambered existing models, the .38/44 Outdoorsman in the case of the .357 Magnum, and the 1950 Target .44 Special became the .44 Magnum. The latter received a cylinder that completely filled out the

frame window, along with a bull barrel, to add 9 ounces in weight to help tame the ferocious recoil of the .44 Magnum. Later .44 Magnums, the Dan Wesson Model 44 and Ruger Redhawk in particular, would be built with larger and longer cylinders to add more weight and also allow the use of longer, heavier bullets, which were becoming quite popular. Ruger's and Dan Wesson's double action .44 Magnum offerings both had a great advantage over Smith & Wesson's. The good folks from Springfield used an existing platform that dated back to 1907 to build the .44 Magnum in 1955; Dan Wesson and Ruger had twenty-five years of .44 Magnum history behind them when they set out to construct a .44 Magnum sixgun to handle the .44 Magnum ammunition of the 1980s.

Silhouetters were putting great demands on .44 Magnums to handle full-house loads over and over. And over. And over again. At the same time hunters were using 300 grain bullets in their .44 Magnum loadings at 240 grain velocities. Ruger and Dan Wesson both took special note of these two sixgun happenings and produced bull-strong sixguns. Cylinder length, however, was not greatly affected. Case length for sixgun cartridges was to be held right at approximately 1.300 inches. All the great modern cartridges, .357 Magnum, .44 Magnum, .41 Magnum, and the old workhorse .45 Colt, set the standard that it appeared would never change.

One man felt there was a need for improvement, or at least a change in attitude. Elgin Gates, who was then president of IHMSA (International Handgun Metallic Silhouette Association) attended a trade show with a number of new wildcat cartridge samples in his pocket. All the new cartridges were dubbed SuperMags by Gates and were 1.610 inches in length, or about 3/10 inch longer than standard Magnum cartridges. That made all of them rifle cartridges by most standards because they were too long to fit the cylinder of any existing revolver. Gates had Super-Mag cartridges made up in .357, .375, .44, .45, .50, and .60 caliber. The .357 SuperMag brass was made by welding two .357 Magnum cases together, the .375, .44, .45, and .50 SuperMags came from cut down, and, in some cases, blown-out rifle brass in calibers .375 Winchester, .444 Marlin, .45-70, and .50-70, respectively. The .60 must have been made from some African Rifle cartridge because Gates had been a worldwide hunter. One of the company engineers, upon seeing a .357 SuperMag cartridge, told Gates "...the .44 Magnum was the most powerful cartridge that could ever be used in a revolver."

Gates later shared that "He stalked away, shaking his head at the thought of having to talk to nuts that came out of the woodwork at the trade shows. It's probably a good thing I did not show him the prints and prototypes of the .375, .445, .455, .505, and .610 I had in my pocket. It really would have blown his mind."

Gates was not dissuaded, and the SuperMag series of cartridges became a reality in the 1980s. Gates, who sold many silhouette guns through IHMSA, and Dan Wesson Arms, which also sold a lot of sixguns through Gates and IHMSA, combined to introduce the first maximum length cartridge, the .357 SuperMag. The SuperMags would never have been brought forth had it not been for the rapid rise of silhouette shooting in the early 1980s, coupled with the good working relationship between IHMSA and Dan Wesson.

The SuperMags in general, and the .357 SuperMag in particular, were advanced as a way to flatten trajectory of sixgun cartridges. To do this, it was deemed necessary to provide adequate case capacity to achieve higher velocity with heavy bullets that were needed to increase knockdown power espe-

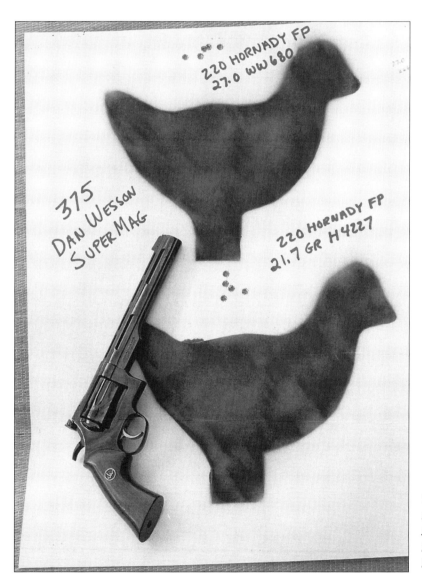

These two 50-meter targets show the importance of front sight height. The accuracy is superb, but the point of impact is 8 inches too high. Changing the front sight brought the loads down to the chicken body.

Dan Wesson SuperMag revolvers came in four of the stretched Magnum calibers, the .357 SuperMag, the .375 SuperMag, the very rare .414 SuperMag, and the .445 SuperMag.

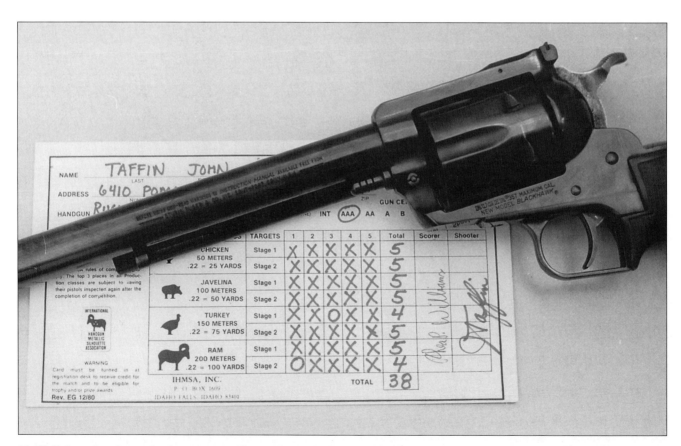

Taffin's favorite sixgun for long-range silhouetting—the Ruger .357 Maximum. This match was shot with Speer's 180 grain silhouette bullet and handloads at 1,450 fps.

cially on 200 meter 60 pound steel rams. The .357 SuperMag would be able to accomplish with a 180 to 200 grain bullet the muzzle velocity achieved by a .357 Magnum with a 158 grain bullet. And then some.

The SuperMag series of cartridges allows case capacity to be used to the ultimate and, in the .357 SuperMag, 200 grain bullets can be safely driven at speeds of 30 to 40 percent over the same weight bullet in a .357 Magnum. This flattens out the trajectory and cuts down on the sight adjustment that is needed going from 50 meter chickens to 100 meter pigs to 150 meter turkeys to 200 meter rams *plus* gives the power necessary to send bent and wind-supported targets tumbling from their stubborn perches.

My early .357 Magnum load in a 10-inch Contender consisted of a 200 grain cast bullet at 1,400 plus feet per second. Beautifully accurate, flat-shooting, and adequately powerful, it could not be duplicated in a .357 Magnum revolver. I could use 200 grain bullets at 1,100 feet per second, or I could choose 158 grain bullets at 1,400 plus feet per second. I could not have both. Until the .357 SuperMag arrived.

While Dan Wesson stretched the frame and cylinder of its .44 Magnum revolver to accept the 3/10 inch longer SuperMag ammunition, Ruger began to really get interested in the silhouette game and also decided to enter the stretched frame/cylinder market. The Ruger Super Blackhawk was fitted with a longer cylinder and a 10-1/2-inch .357 barrel and the Ruger New Model .357 Maximum arrived. The .357 SuperMag and the .357 Maximum are the same cartridges. Dan Wesson called its sixgun a SuperMag while Ruger chose to stay with .357 Maximum and all its guns are so marked. Ammunition is interchangeable, however, I have found that rounds loaded for the Dan Wesson with one set of dies will not enter the tighter, smoother chambers of my Ruger Maximum.

We constantly hear charges of media bias to which the media always pleads not guilty. This is ridiculous, of course, because we are all biased, and some are much more than others. Bias certainly was present in the hearts of some gunwriters as they approached the .357 Maximum/SuperMag. I will give them the benefit of the doubt and chalk it up to ignorance. They simply did not understand the purpose of the .357 SuperMag, assigned to it a different purpose, and when this did not prove possible, did their best to kill the cartridge. The .357 SuperMag has the distinction of being the one new sixgun cartridge in my memory that many gunwriters tried to kill off before it had a chance to prove itself with proper use.

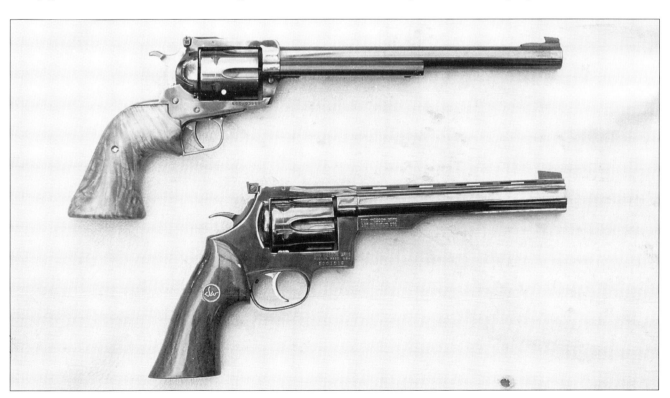

Two of the best sixguns ever produced for long-range silhouetting: Top, Ruger's 10-1/2-inch .357 Maximum with stocks by Tedd Adamovich; bottom, Dan Wesson's 8-inch .357 SuperMag with factory stocks. Wesson's revolver is marked "SuperMag" on the barrel and ".357 Maximum" on the frame.

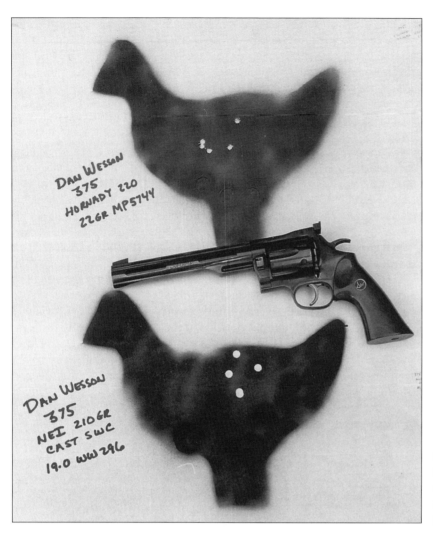

Dan Wesson
375
HORNADY 220
220GR MP5744

DAN WESSON
375
NEI 210GR
CAST SWC
19.0 WW 296

The .375 SuperMag performed whether used with jacketed bullets or cast and, in this case, the Hornady 220 flat-point (top) and NEI 210 grain cast gas check (bottom). Range was 50 meters with these silhouette chickens.

Early reloading attempts to make it into a hyper velocity .357 Magnum resulted in poor accuracy and worse. Bullets designed for .357 Magnums, mainly 110, 125, 140, and 158 grain versions, were not up to the pressure that was being applied to them in the new .357 SuperMag Dan Wesson or .357 Maximum Ruger Blackhawk, and often came apart in mid-air after leaving the barrel. At least in theory, some bullets would actually bulge out as they passed from cylinder to barrel.

This is not why the .357 SuperMag was advanced. Shooters had found that standard .357 Magnums loads were not adequate for silhouetting before the topple point rule was established. A problem had developed especially with "hard set" targets, targets that were too far forward on the rail to topple as easy as they should when hit solidly, or targets that were bent and would not react properly when hit. This new ruling allowed targets to be set farther backwards and, in some cases, narrow the width of the bases of the targets in order to change the point of balance and allow them to fall easier.

Even after the rule allowed targets to be set back for easier knockdown, .357 Magnum shooters often found pigs and rams remained stubborn when supported by a strong wind coming from behind the targets, just like they did in cold, wet weather which seemed to anchor the targets even more solidly. The .357 SuperMag/Maximum was designed to give .357 Magnum velocities to heavyweight bullets, not to see how fast a standard weight bullet could be driven. This was accomplished by stretching both cartridge case and cylinders by 3/10 inch.

Those early misunderstood loads with high velocity, combined with light bullets, resulted in fast throat erosion, top strap cutting, and complaints from shooters. "We don't need this cartridge!" became the cry of the unknowing. Dan Wesson bowed to pressure and packed an extra barrel with its .357 SuperMags to use when the first one experienced excessive throat erosion. I never unpacked mine. During all of my silhouette days the original barrel, used only with proper loads, worked just fine.

While pundits called the .357 SuperMag a bad mistake, silhouetters were setting all kinds of long-range records with it. Serious shooters were interested only in accurate heavyweight bullet loads at Magnum velocities. That is, bullets in the 180 to 200 grain weight range that would shoot with silhouette accuracy at 1,300 to 1,500 feet per second.

Until the advent of the Freedom Arms line-up of revolvers, the finest long-range revolver shooting I had ever accomplished in more than thirty years of shooting was with a 10-1/2-inch Ruger .357 Maximum using 180 grain bullets at 1,400 feet per second. The Ruger Maximum is certainly one of the finest long-range revolvers to ever come out of a gun factory. The fact that my shooting hand is basically single action-shaped could have something to do with this feeling on my part.

One would think that such a fine sixgun would have a great future. The .357 Ruger Maximum would continue, other maximum cartridges would be developed, and sixgunners would reap the benefits. It was not to be. The Ruger .357 Maximum began to develop gas cutting under the top strap above the barrel/cylinder junction. It only went so deep and then stopped. It meant nothing. Any Magnum sixgun that has been shot a lot will exhibit the same markings.

Something, other than the top strap erosion, happened to cause Ruger to pull the .357 Maximum from production. I do believe that something was uttered in print by some silhouette writer(s) that annoyed Ruger to no end and had a lot to do with the demise of a really fine sixgun. Ruger blamed the cartridge for top strap erosion while some in the upper echelon of IHMSA blamed Ruger for making the cylinder "too short." The battle was on, Ruger's attitude was we don't need this, and the Ruger Maximum disappeared. It has never been brought back into production and is fast approaching collector status.

One only has to look at the results each year from the Internationals, IHMSA's championship matches, to see the status of the .357 SuperMag today. Matches are no longer won with SuperMags, they are won with standard length cartridges, most often in Freedom Arms revolvers. The old SuperMag shooters have gone on to other things, Dan Wesson may or may not be producing sixguns as this is written, and top shooters have discovered the excellent accuracy of the Freedom Arms offerings.

We had .357 SuperMag sixguns before brass was available and most of us did our early shooting with .357 Magnum brass used in the longer-cylindered SuperMag. I simply took my standard .357 Magnum silhouette load consisting of an RCBS 200 grain cast gas-checked .35 Remington bullet #35-200FN loaded

in .38 Special brass at 1,100 feet per second, switched to .357 Magnum brass, increased the powder charge sufficiently to achieve 1,300 feet per second, and I was in the SuperMag business.

The favorite jacketed bullet loads for the .357 Maximum/SuperMag are assembled with 19 to 20 grains of H4227 with either the 180 grain Hornady or Speer Silhouette bullet, and 19 grains of H4227 with the 200 grain Speer FMJ. I have also had good results using 19 grains of WW296 and 180 grain full metal-jacketed bullets. These 180 grain-bulleted loads are in the 1,250 to 1,300 feet per second range in the 8-inch Dan Wesson .357 SuperMag and will do over 1,400 feet per second muzzle velocity in the 10-1/2-inch Ruger .357 Maximum.

Once the .357 SuperMag was established, Gates decided it was time for a second SuperMag chamber-

The hardest long-range silhouette target is the 150 meter turkey. The .375 Dan Wesson put these five shots on the turkey target with Hornady's 220 grain .375 flat-nose bullet at 1,350 fps muzzle velocity.

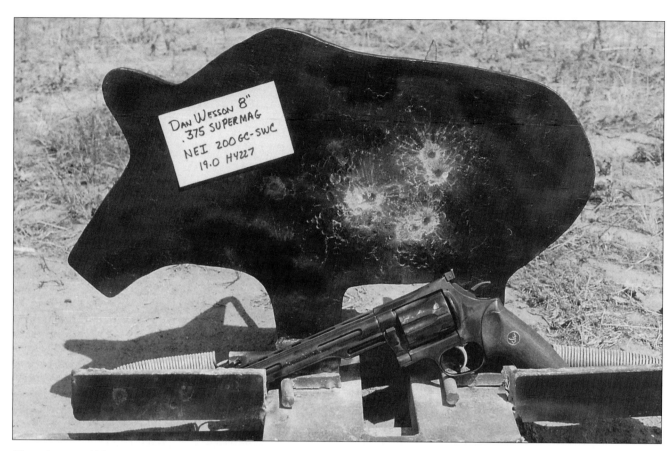

Five shots at 100 meters using Dan Wesson's 8-inch .375 SuperMag and cast bullets.

ing. If ever a sixgun cartridge was received with less enthusiasm than the .375 SuperMag, I certainly do not know which one it would be. The .357 SuperMag brought shouts of joy or derision—the .375 SuperMag barely evoked a yawn.

The .375 SuperMag, like its smaller and only slightly older brother the .357 SuperMag, is 1.610 inches in length. Brass is made from .375 Winchester or .30-30 Winchester brass, cut slightly over length, and then filed to final length in a trim die. The result is a tapered case, rather than a straight-walled case such as the .357 Magnum or .357 SuperMag. When Elgin Gates first talked to me about this new cartridge, I wanted to wait for the production of a straight-walled case, while he wanted to get it on the market as quickly as possible by using formed rifle brass. In retrospect, seeing the reception it received, one has to wonder what the rush was, but then it is always easier to quarterback on Monday morning.

Dan Wesson simply chambered its .357 SuperMag to .375 SuperMag, fitted a .375 barrel, and the .375 SuperMag unfolded. Ruger was never tempted and the .357 Maximum was never offered in .375 Maximum.

The .375 SuperMag never quite reached legitimate status. It could not be reloaded with standard carbide dies because it was a tapered case. It was only very briefly offered as a factory round and if I recall correctly, only through IHMSA. At the present time, no one is offering a .375 SuperMag sixgun, nor is any factory ammunition available. In its short life, it was offered in sixguns by both Dan Wesson and Seville.

The Seville was a single action sixgun that enjoyed success as a silhouette revolver in the early 1980s. U.S. Arms offered both blue El Dorado and stainless Seville sixguns that were basically a Ruger Super Blackhawk copy with slightly different action and a rounded triggerguard. First chambered in .357 Magnum, .41 Magnum, .44 Magnum, and .45 Colt, both the cylinder and frame of the Seville were stretched to accept the .357 and .375 SuperMags when they appeared on the scene. A split in the company found one faction going West and the other distributing the basic El Dorado/Seville sixgun as the Abilene through Mossberg.

As a silhouette cartridge, the .375 SuperMag, properly loaded and used especially in a long-barreled single action sixgun such as the 10-1/2-inch Seville, was as good as, and perhaps even better than the .357

Five shots from the Dan Wesson 8-inch .375 SuperMag at 200 meters using Hornady's 220 grain flat-point and Winchester's 680 powder.

SuperMag. It certainly spoke with greater authority, coupled with relatively low felt recoil.

The first time I shot the .375 SuperMag in the then new Seville revolver, I experienced a sensation I had never before achieved from a sixgun. Gates lent me his personal Seville .375 SuperMag before other sixguns chambered in .375 SuperMag were available. Very few of these sixguns must have ever seen the light of day because production ceased shortly after this time. When the Seville surfaced again, I acquired the first one through IHMSA. The serial number was one digit higher than Gates' .375 Seville.

Shooting the Seville on rams was definitely a new experience. Normally, when rams are shot with a revolver, there is an instant, that sometimes seems like an eternity, from the time the trigger is pulled until the bullet either strikes the dirt in a miss, or the target slowly changes color in the sun as it begins to topple. With all revolvers I had previously shot, .357 Magnum, .41 Magnum, .44 Magnum, and .357 SuperMag, there was time to recover from recoil and watch for the hit—not so with the .375 SuperMag in the Seville. With the new .375 SuperMag, it seemed that the target went down almost instantly. In fact, for the first time ever, I did not have time to see the ram topple.

The reason for this rapid reaction was simply that the .375 SuperMag allowed the use of Hornady's .375 220 grain rifle bullet at a muzzle velocity of 1,700 feet per second in the 10-1/2-inch Seville revolver. That load, my favorite in the .375 SuperMag, was assembled with Winchester's WW680 powder, the same powder used with favored silhouette loads in .357 Magnum, .44 Magnum, and .454 Casull. Unfortunately, WW680, as the .375 SuperMag is long out of production.

The Dan Wesson 8-inch .375 SuperMag, which would only do around 1,350 feet per second with the same loading, never achieved anywhere near the popularity of Wesson's .357 SuperMag. Only the advent of the .454 Casull made such speeds like those found with the .375 Seville commonplace with heavy bullets in a sixgun.

In 1981, I made the acquaintance of a dedicated handgunner and wildcatter, one Lew Schafer. Schafer had wanted more power than offered in any factory chamberings in the Thompson/Center Contender and came forth with his .444 Schafer Magnum, chambered in a Super Fourteen Contender. The .444 Schafer Magnum was nothing more than the .444 Marlin case-swaged and then turned on a lathe to give the same

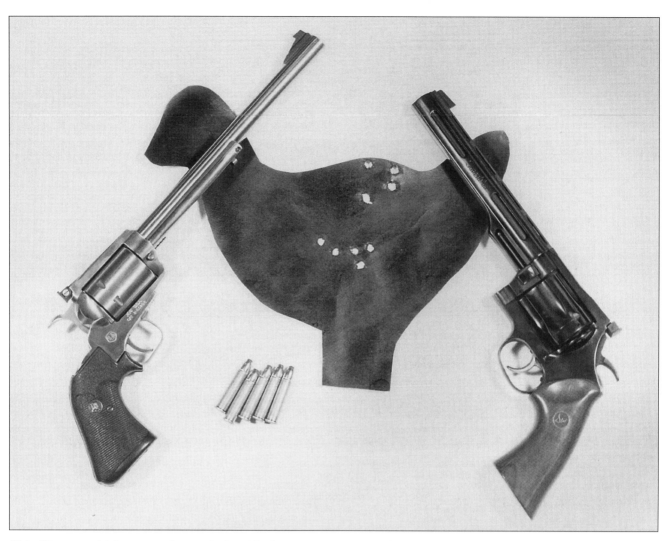

This 50-meter chicken was shot with the U.S. Arms 10-1/2-inch .375 Seville and the Dan Wesson 8-inch SuperMag. Both used the Hornady 220 grain flat-point and WW680 powder.

outside dimensions as the .44 Magnum. The .44 Magnum measures a straight .456 inch in diameter from above the rim to the case mouth while the heavier .444 Marlin brass tapers from .470 inch to .453 inch.

Schafer wanted to come up with a sixgun cartridge that rivaled his single-shot wildcat, but no sixgun was available to house it. As soon as I heard rumors of the .357 SuperMag, I informed Schafer. He immediately began to make plans to convert one of the first .357 SuperMags to what he would call the .44 Schafer UltraMag. I do not know if Schafer made the first .44 SuperMag or not, but we were experimenting in 1981 using .44 Magnum Contenders rechambered to a l.610-inch "SuperMag .44."

We used a l0-inch Contender chambered for the .44 UltraMag, and went to 2,200 feet per second with Hornady 200 grain jacketed hollowpoints, and 2,000 feet per second with both the Sierra 220 grain full metal

jackets and the Hornady 240 grain full metal jackets. All velocities were obtained safely with no dangerous pressure signs; accuracy was excellent.

Schafer was chafing at the bit, to say the least. He now had the cartridge, dies, chambering reamers, and test results, but no revolver. We tried to be patient. Finally, Dan Wesson announced the .357 SuperMag and the first .357 SuperMag Dan Wesson revolver to arrive locally never fired a shot until it was rechambered to .44 UltraMag and fitted with a shortened and rethreaded 10-inch .44 Dan Wesson barrel and a .44 Magnum shroud. The resulting 6-inch barreled Dan Wesson rechambered to .44 UltraMag digested Schafer's handloads consisting of the 200 grain Hornady jacketed hollowpoint at a muzzle velocity of 2,000 feet per second, Sierra's 220 grain silhouette bullet at 1,900 feet per second, the 240 grain Hornady jacketed truncated cone bullet at 1,800 feet per second, and Hornady's offering

Lew Schafer's first .44 UltraMag: This 6-inch sixgun, built on a rechambered and rebarreled .357 SuperMag, used 1.610-inch long brass made from the .444 Marlin.

The .445 SuperMag has proven to be exceptionally accurate when used with 300 grain bullets such as the NEI 295 grain Keith gas check, SSK's 310 grain flat-point, and Sierra's 300 grain jacketed flat-point.

for the .444 Marlin, the 265 grain jacketed flat-point did 1,650 feet per second, or 300 feet per second faster than my .44 Magnum loads with the same bullet in a 10-1/2-inch sixgun.

Schafer thought of the .44 UltraMag as simply a faster .44 Magnum. I wanted him to forget the standard .44 Magnum bullets and try it with heavyweight cast bullets. He even had a 305 grain cast gas-checked bullet that he had designed for the .444

Schafer Magnum. It took awhile, but I finally convinced him to try his heavyweight cast bullet in his UltraMag. Test loads were assembled and we sat down at the bench on a very cold morning.

We went to work—while I shot, Schafer recorded the results. The first shot over the Oehler 33 chronograph registered just under 1,600 feet per second! As I fired the second shot at 25 yards, Schafer said "No hole in the paper. You must have missed." At 25

Taffin's 8-inch Big Bore Dan Wessons: .44 Magnum, .445 SuperMag, and .45 Colt. Note that the SuperMag is not that much larger than the others even though it is much more powerful.

yards, I thought, no way. As I fired the third shot, he said still only one hole and then he realized what was happening. All the shots were going in one hole.

At the time, Schafer spent considerable time trying to interest Dan Wesson in bringing out a .44 Super-Mag. It, of course, was just getting the .357 SuperMag off the ground and was not really interested. I wrote up Schafer's wildcat for the IHMSA paper, *The Silhouette*, and the editor at the time sent my article back saying this was a dangerous idea. A few years later, IHMSA would be selling .445 SuperMag Dan Wessons through *The Silhouette*.

Schafer did first-class conversions, but they were expensive because the .44 Magnum Dan Wesson barrels did not have the same thread as the .357 SuperMag barrels, so it was more than a matter of simply rechambering a .357 SuperMag cylinder and screwing on a .44 barrel. The cost was double the price of the gun alone. The .44 SuperMag has been a fairly popular wildcat chambering as done by Schafer and other gunsmiths.

In 1988, the .44 SuperMag became a reality. Gates again worked with the engineers at Dan Wesson in bringing out the third of the SuperMag cartridges, behind the .357 and .375 SuperMags. At the time, Gates was still president of IHMSA and offered the new long .44 and .445 brass through *The Silhouette*.

After discussing the new sixgun with both Gates and Bob Talbot, chief engineer at Dan Wesson, I was

scheduled to receive one of the prototype Dan Wesson .445s, a small lot of the first brass, and a set of Redding .445 SuperMag dies. Upon the arrival of the .445 SuperMag from Dan Wesson, I was very pleased to find not only a blued 10-inch Dan Wesson .445 with zebrawood grips, but also an extra 8-inch barrel in the Heavy Barrel configuration, and a pair of the newest Dan Wesson "gripper" style one-piece wood grips.

My .445 SuperMag bears Serial Number 003, which makes it the third gun out of Dan Wesson; the first two were those sent to IHMSA. I had a big advantage in the beginning when it came to reloading for the .445 SuperMag, for I had all the data collected with Schafer's UltraMag. As a starting point for loading for the .445 SuperMag, I went back to the loading data for the .44 UltraMag and also compared the capacity of the .445 SuperMag brass with the wildcat .44 Ultra-Mag brass. Factory .445 SuperMag brass is not as heavy as the wildcat brass made up from either .444 Marlin or .30-40 Krag brass, based on the .44 Magnum case rather than heavier rifle brass used in wildcatting of the long .44.

To be legal for IHMSA silhouetting, the .445 Super-Mag has to meet a required weight limit of 4 pounds and both models, the 10-inch regular barrel and the 8-inch heavy barrel weigh in just about 1 ounce under the legal weight. Actually, the weight limit is really a moot point as this sixgun is too big and produces too

Dan Wesson's .445 SuperMag, designed to be suitable for both hunting and silhouetting, is represented by these 8-inch heavy-barreled and 10-inch standard-barreled .445s with factory stocks.

much recoil to be a first choice silhouette sixgun. Its niche, if there is to be one, will be in the hunting field.

Early .445 brass was too soft and resulted in sticky extraction with higher loads. When I loaded the .445 brass for the first time, I followed my normal procedure of full length resizing all brass, in this case with the .445 carbide full length resizing die provided by Dan Wesson. The brass came out with a nice, burnished look, ready to be neck-expanded, primed, and loaded. The trouble came when I tried to resize the fired brass. The sizing die raised a very sharp belt at the bottom of the brass. As the brass was being resized, some brass was seemingly being pushed ahead of the tight carbide sizer and winding up as a ridge that prevented the sized brass from entering the chamber of the Dan Wesson .445.

My first thought was that the die had just been made too tight, so I went to some .44 Magnum dies I had on hand. The same thing happened with both Redding and RCBS .44 Magnum carbide sizing dies. Now what? I had a batch of fired brass I could not resize, which meant that they could not be reloaded.

Rescue came in the form of my old set of standard RCBS .44 Magnum dies. I did not relish the idea of having to lube all the cases, but the .445 brass was rolled on the lube pad, run through a twenty year old .44 Magnum sizing die and the cases dropped easily into the chambers of the .445.

The mystery was solved when it was learned that Dan Wesson, rather than slow down the project by waiting for the .445 reamers, had chambered the prototype .445 with standard .44 Magnum reamers that were simply moved deeper into the chambers. The result was a chamber that was oversized just enough at the back end to allow the tight .445 SuperMag dies to push excess brass ahead of the carbide sizing ring. Dan Wesson replaced the cylinder on my sixgun and all later .445s came with properly chambered cylinders.

I decided early to feed the .445 SuperMag a steady diet of 300 grain cast bullets. With NEI's 295 grain Keith-style gas-checked bullet, I settled on 33-36 grains of WW680 giving 1,450 to 1,550 feet per second muzzle velocity from the 10-inch barrel. My load of 29

Dan Wesson's two big bore boomers: Top, the 10-inch .445 SuperMag with factory zebrawood stocks; bottom, the 10-inch Model 44 .44 Magnum with Pachmayr grips for ease of control.

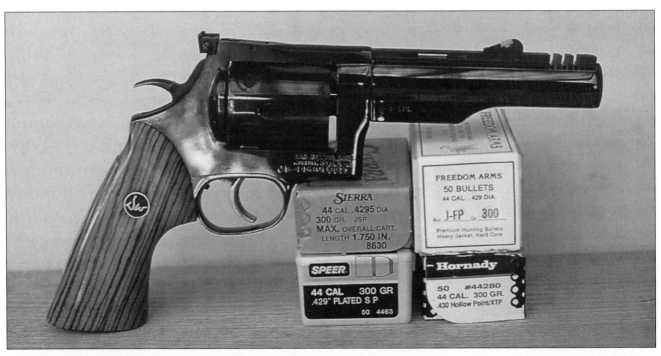

Dan Wesson's 4-inch .445 SuperMag with factory compensator helps control the recoil when used with full-house loads using 300 grain bullets from Speer, Sierra, Hornady, and Freedom Arms.

grains of H110 turned out to be the published maximum load in Hodgdon's manual for use with a 300 grain bullet and the .445 SuperMag.

As a hunting handgun, the .445 is at its best with bullets in the 300 grain range and delivers excellent accuracy with both cast and jacketed bullets in this weight range. Recoil, while heavy, is not going to hurt anyone, especially with the well-designed Dan Wesson factory stocks, particularly the finger groove-style.

The Dan Wesson family lost control of the business, got it back again and changed it to Wesson Firearms. It lost control again and the doors were finally closed. The Wesson family, made up of Seth, Carol, Seth Jr., and Eric, are fine people. Eric was a top competitor in long-range silhouetting. I hated to see them lose the company.

Before this all happened, a fourth SuperMag was issued in very limited quantities. The .414 SuperMag was a stretched .41 Magnum, as the .357 and .44 SuperMags were longer .357 and .44 Magnums, respectively. I was promised a test gun in .414 SuperMag, but the company folded before this gun was delivered. At the present time, all parts inventory has been purchased and the word is that Wesson is once again producing sixguns. I have not, as of this writing, seen any of the current production.

The SuperMags are probably a dead issue even if the company is able to come back. Introduced as the best solution for the sixgunner shooting silhouettes, they have all but been completely buried by the Freedom Arms Silhouette Revolver in .353 Casull and .44 Magnum chamberings. It would be John Linebaugh who would carry on the SuperMag idea with his .475 and .500 Linebaugh Longs on the Ruger Maximum frame.

CHAPTER 10

THE BIG BORE SIXGUNS OF JOHN LINEBAUGH

I've been a .45 Colt man for more years than I would care to count. Just at the time in my life when I was really getting into sixguns, Colt made the wonderful decision to bring back the Colt Single Action Army and I started a charge account—they trusted teenagers in those days!—at the local gun shop to purchase the first 7-1/2-inch .45 Colt to arrive in my area. The first of what would be called the Second Generation Colt Single Action, it was put together every bit as well as the pre-World War II sixguns.

I learned to reload using that sixgun and a Lyman #310 hand tool. Bullets were cast over my mother's kitchen stove, then lubed by setting them base down in a pie pan and pouring melted lube around them, and then sized by running them through a die inserted into the Lyman tool. She was a tidy housekeeper, but my mother never once complained of the mess and smell in her kitchen, nor the spattered lead drops on the side of her refrigerator.

While attending graduate school in Missoula, Montana, I found the first Ruger .45 Colt, again a 7-1/2-inch barreled sixgun, and I was soon introduced to the beginnings of the real possibilities with the old .45 Colt cartridge. The Colt handled 260 grain bullets at 900 to 1,000 feet per second muzzle velocity; the Ruger easily accepted 300 grain bullets at 1,200 feet per second. For ten years or so, I wrongly assumed that the .45 Colt loads I was using were all that could be expected from the then century year old cartridge. I was about to have my eyes opened and the man to do it was John Linebaugh.

Linebaugh had read some of my articles in the early issues of *The Sixgunner*, the official paper of Handgun Hunters International, and knew I loved the big bore sixgun cartridges, which in those days were the .44 Special, .44 Magnum, and his passion, the .45 Colt. He contacted me because he wanted me to know of the custom .45 Colt sixguns he was building and he also

wanted to send along a test gun, if I was willing to step out on faith—faith in him and his sixguns. Linebaugh made some unbelievable claims, and even insisted his .45 Colt sixguns would carry a heavier payload than the .44 Magnum and also do it faster. "John, our guns are capable of shooting 260 grain bullets at 1,700 feet per second." That got my attention very quickly. I had been doing extensive testing with the .44 Magnum with all bullet weights and I could no way get anywhere near this kind of performance.

That was in 1983, and everything he said then, and since, about sixguns has turned out to be true. I learned long ago to believe John Linebaugh when it comes to sixgun performance. Linebaugh sent one of his custom .45 Colts built on an El Dorado frame. This sixgun, as well as the Seville, were virtually deadringers for the Super Blackhawk and were made in the early 1980s by U.S. Arms in New York. They were later slightly modified and distributed through Mossberg as the Abilene. These are very strong sixguns. Linebaugh had fitted the El Dorado with a custom slow-twist barrel and an oversized cylinder. The cylinder was made oversized by utilizing all of the frame window possible and also made as long as possible with no excess gap between the front of the cylinder and the frame.

In those first Linebaugh custom revolver testings, I used .45 Winchester-Western brass, 260 grain bullets, both cast and jacketed, at 1,700 feet per second; 310 grain cast bullets at 1,565 feet per second; 325 grain bullets at 1,600 feet per second; and 385 grain bullets at 1,300 feet per second. This young gunsmith had something!

If one examines fired brass from most factory .45 Colt cylinders, either the eye or the fingers will reveal that the case is bulged slightly. This is simply due to the fact that so many .45 Colt chambers are cut large. Factory .45 Colt loads expand .004 inch in both the 7-

These five custom sixguns represent some of John Linebaugh's early five-shot conversions on the Ruger Bisley. Note the variations in barrel length.

John Linebaugh uses the full frame window opening to fit an over-sized cylinder. Compare this Ruger .44 Magnum cylinder with a .500 Linebaugh cylinder on the right.

1/2-inch Second Generation Colt Single Action and 7-1/2-inch Ruger Blackhawk mentioned above. The key to safely using heavy loads in a sixgun is tight tolerances. Linebaugh's custom .45 Colt, even with heavy loads, allowed brass to expand only .001 inch in diameter above the base of the cartridge. The pressure is contained by the tight cylinder and consequently brass lasts a long time.

John Linebaugh will meet you straight on and does not hesitate to tell you what he really thinks about sixguns in general, and his sixguns in particular. I've never heard him run down another custom maker. In fact, he does just the opposite. He has nothing but praise for the top sixgunsmiths in the country and will not hesitate to tell you that he has learned from them. He simply, and very bluntly, states his ideas about what a sixgun should and should not be. He is, as he calls it, "old school" when it comes to sixguns, or in the case of most of his really big bore conversions, fiveguns. He believes in what he and I both define as packin' pistols, sixguns that can be carried comfortably all day in a hip holster and then slipped under a bedroll or pillow at night. These handguns that are always available, always ready. Linebaugh's sixguns are to this century what the Colt Single Action Army was to the cowboys and adventurers of the last century.

You won't find any scopes, oversized rubber grips, long barrels, or muzzle brakes on a Linebaugh handgun. Linebaugh is a 100 percent believer in the thoughts and theories of Elmer Keith when it comes to sixguns. Linebaugh's philosophy of handguns is found in the following quote from one of his brochures:

We are a custom sixgun shop dedicated to the old school sixgunner. We follow the theories of Elmer Keith and John (Pondoro) Taylor. Their's was one of big bullets, so is ours. Bullet weight and caliber are constants in external ballistics; velocity is a constantly diminishing variable. I believe high velocity to be a superb killer if placed with exact precision, and if it reaches the inside of the animal. But without exact placement, it lacks the penetrating qualities and thus it wastes its energy in flesh wounds. The big bullet does not have these shortcomings. It will penetrate fully from any angle, thus letting the hunter take shots with confidence that he would otherwise pass up with a 'little gun.' I for one do not like big guns, just big bullets. With this in mind we offer models and ideas to the old school sixgunner. Remember, old school to us is powerful, practical, and packable.

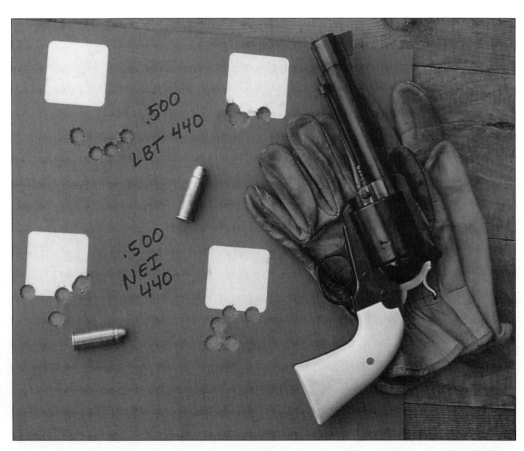

Targets shot at 25 yards by Taffin with 440 grain bullets in the 5-1/2-inch .500 Linebaugh. White squares are 2 inches on side.

The last three words describe exactly every sixgun built by John Linebaugh. It must be powerful. The .45 Colt is not the largest sixgun that Linebaugh builds, but the smallest. His world begins with the old .45 Colt and goes upwards. Why the .45 Colt? Simply stated, the .45 Colt will drive a 260 grain bullet with greater diameter than a 240 grain .44 Magnum bullet faster and with less chamber pressure. This does not mean one should go forth and start loading his factory .45 Colt to exceed .44 Magnum performance. It could be disastrous. It only works in a properly chambered and built .45 sixgun.

It must be practical. The main purpose of every Linebaugh sixgun is to be able to hunt anything that walks in the area the user is likely to find himself. It must be packable. Linebaugh builds the most powerful sixguns ever devised, but they are all about the same size as a Super Blackhawk. Every sixgun from Linebaugh Custom Guns wears easy on the hip and packs easily in a traditional holster.

How strongly is John Linebaugh influenced by Elmer Keith? In the 1920s, Keith built the perfect sixgun by his standards. It was a Colt Single Action Army with a modified Bisley grip frame, 5-1/2-inch barrel, adjustable sights, and in the best chambering available at the time, the .44 Special. Today, all of Linebaugh's serious hunting handguns are single actions with Ruger Bisley grip frames, 5-1/2 to 6-inch barrels, adjustable sights, and chambered in the most powerful cartridges available.

A basic Linebaugh conversion is the rechambering of smaller calibers such as the .357, .41, and .44 Magnums to .45 Colt. The first sixgun that Linebaugh did for me was a Second Generation .357 New Frontier that was sent along to him accompanied by a 4-3/4-inch .45 New Frontier barrel. Linebaugh rechambered the .357 cylinder to a minimum-dimensioned .45 Colt, installed the Colt barrel, tightened everything up, and the result is a .45 New Frontier that shoots one hole groups at 25 yards—powerful, practical, and packable.

For this type of conversion, Linebaugh prefers to rechamber Ruger New Model single actions to .45 Colt. Starting with a Ruger of .357, .41, or .44 caliber, the cylinder is rechambered to .45 Colt, the gun is tightened up, and a special slow-twist Douglas barrel is installed. With this .45 Colt conversion, the sixgunner can expect 260 grain cast bullets to achieve 1,400 feet per second, and 310 Keith cast bullets will go 1,300 feet per second. I chose not a Ruger, but a .44 Magnum Abilene for this custom conversion. With its .45 Colt chambering and 5-1/2-inch barrel, it is also powerful, practical, and packable, even more so than

the .45 New Frontier. It is one of the most accurate sixguns I own and is used for hunting, its last target being a ten-point whitetail.

For those who want the ultimate in .45 Colt performance, Linebaugh offers his five-shot .45 Colt. This sixgun is built on a Ruger Single Action and, rather than rechambering the Ruger cylinder, the frame is fitted with an oversized cylinder, one that completely fills in the frame cylinder window. A slow-twist Douglas barrel is installed, and the gun is rebuilt throughout, tightening and minimizing tolerances in the process. With this .45 Colt conversion, sixgunners can expect 1,700 feet per second with 260 grain Keith bullets, and 1,500 feet per second with 310 Keith bullets.

The old Colt Single Action grip frame like that found, though slightly modified, on the Ruger Blackhawk, is perfect for standard loads, but Linebaugh's .45 Colt sixguns are capable of more power which results in more recoil than the standard Blackhawk grip frame can comfortably handle. Fortunately, Ruger vastly improved the single action grip frame in the mid-1980s with the introduction of the Bisley Model Blackhawk.

When the Bisley was introduced, comments such as "If the grip was so good why did Colt drop it?" and "The Bisley grip is the answer to a problem that doesn't exist!" were heard. In reality, the Bisley grip frame is the most comfortable grip frame for shooting heavy loads ever offered by either Colt or Ruger. A vast improvement over the original Bisley, it is not the same as that found on the old Colt because it does not come up as high behind the triggerguard. Ruger's original answer to handle heavy recoil, the Super Blackhawk grip frame, is especially punishing to me with heavy loads as it solidly, and painfully, raps my knuckle and the top of my trigger finger.

Linebaugh prefers the Ruger Bisley Model for his five-shot conversions, however, they are not always available as they are run according to Ruger's production schedule. To avoid the non-availability problem, Linebaugh simply installs the main Bisley components, grip frame, trigger, and hammer to Ruger Blackhawks and Super Blackhawks. This also became a problem when these parts were not available. So rather than be at the mercy of Ruger's parts supply to be able to continue to offer his big guns, Linebaugh now has his own castings made of Bisley-style grip frames in blued steel, stainless steel, and brass, as well as triggers and hammers. Linebaugh calls the Bisley grip frame "superior for accuracy and comfort." His big guns would be unmanageable without it.

Linebaugh's first custom offering caliber-wise was the .50 caliber. He freely admits that this was not his original idea, but one learned from others, and then brought to perfection. Two Utah gunsmiths, Neil Wheeler and Bill Topping, came up with the .50WT Super quite some time ago and Elmer Keith shot their gun and cartridge, though I don't recall ever seeing a report from the Grand Old Man on this big gun. Wheeler and Topping also built at least one five-shot .45-70 on a Ruger Super Blackhawk by cutting and welding two main frames together end-to-end-to get a frame with sufficient length.

Linebaugh used the .348 Winchester case to arrive at his .50 caliber. The .500 Linebaugh is at the outer limits of caliber size in a packable pistol. To get the .500 into a packin'-sized gun, it is necessary to discard the standard-sized Ruger Bisley cylinder and go with an oversized five-shot cylinder for two reasons: 1) six .50 caliber holes will not fit in a standard-sized cylinder and allow enough metal between chambers for safety, and 2) five-shots allow the bolt cut to be placed between, rather than under, cylinder chambers. Many .45 caliber sixguns can be found with bolt cuts that are literally paper thin.

Linebaugh's first .500 was made on a Seville frame with its Super Blackhawk-style grip frame with a rounded triggerguard rather than the distinctive square back found on the Ruger. At 1,300 feet per second with a 450 grain bullet, the gun was sufficiently strong, but the recoil was more than the grip frame

could handle and the gun would twist in the hand tremendously.

It was about this time in 1986 that Ruger's Bisley Model became available and Linebaugh built his second 6-inch .500 on a Ruger Bisley. That gun went to Ross Seyfried, appeared on the cover of *Guns & Ammo*, and John Linebaugh was about to be recognized as a top sixgunsmith.

John's Big Fifty, the .500 Linebaugh, thrives on 400 to 450 grain bullets and large doses of slow burning pistol powders such as H110, H4227, and WW296. Cartridge cases for the .500 must be made by trimming .348 Winchester brass to 1.400 inches, forming it in special RCBS dies, and then loading with RCBS dies.

As stated above, Linebaugh believes in big bullets, not big guns. His .500 revolver, with a five-shot cylinder and a 5-1/2-inch barrel built on a Ruger Bisley Model weighs 47 ounces, or about the same weight as a Smith & Wesson Model 29 .44 Magnum. The unfluted, oversized cylinder is full length, the barrel is now much heavier, and the geometry has been changed to make this sixgun into a fivegun. Open the loading gate and the new cylinder spins freely like the beautifully crafted part that it is. Literally no end play and the barrel/cylinder gap is set at .003 inch or less. Mine will not accept a .002 inch gapping tool blade.

.500 Linebaughs: Top, high-grade case-colored example; bottom, Taffin's standard blued 5-1/2-inch sixgun. Cartridge slide is by Von Ringler.

These ivory-stocked 4-inch .44s—three .44 Magnums and one .44 Special—were Elmer Keith's personal sixguns. Note the strategic carving of the stocks for minimizing recoil.

EMF's nickel-plated Hartford Model 7-1/2-inch .44-40s with leather by Mario Hanel.

In Texas this is called a Bar-B-Que Sixgun—this 4-inch .44 Magnum, engraved by Jim Riggs, is all dressed up for special occasions. Stocks by BearHug and leather by El Paso.

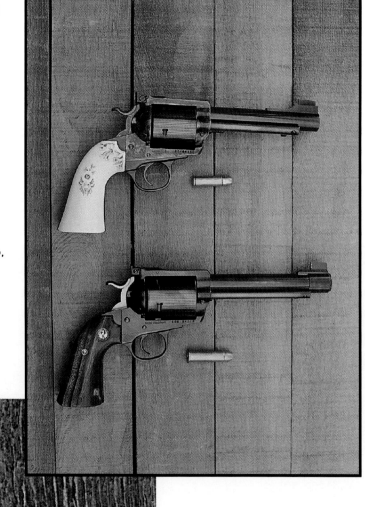

Wayne Lucas's personal sixguns: Top, .45 Colt with ivory micarta stocks by Dustin Linebaugh, case-colored frame, and Patridge front sight, and bottom, .475 Linebaugh Long with Bowen rear sight and Patridge front sight.

Texas Longhorn Arms 4-inch .44 Magnum Border Special with bird's head-style grip frame, black micarta stocks, and "barb wire" factory engraving.

Ivory and ivory micarta take scrimshaw well as evidenced by these stocks from the Freedom Arms Custom Shop.

Above: Featherweight .50 AE on a Ruger Blackhawk by Hamilton Bowen features a five-shot cylinder, ivory micarta grips, and a weight saving alloy grip frame and ejector tube as well as a dished out recoil shield.

Above: Border-stamped, double weight leather Buscadero by John Bianchi's Frontier Gunleather carries a pair of Colt Single Action .45s.

Right: Smith & Wesson now offers laminated stocks for its sixguns—ebony on 4-inch .45 Colt, and round butt finger groove rosewood on 3-inch M65 and 2-inch M60 .357 Magnums.

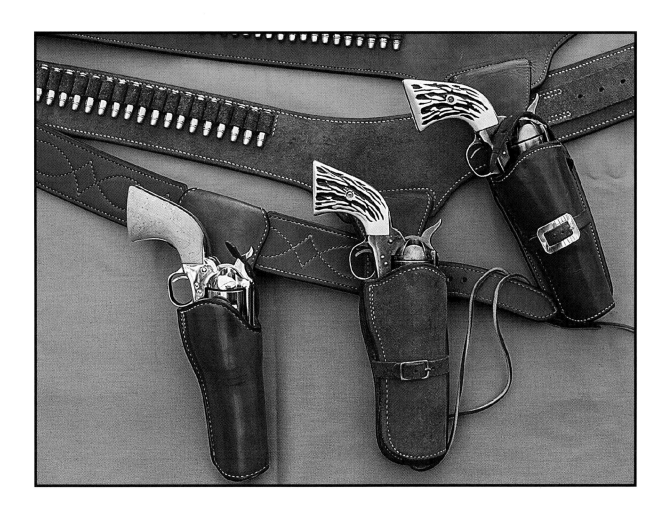

Above: Fast Draw holsters from the 1960s from the left: Andy Anderson Gunfighter with Colt Single Action .45, Arvo Ojala Rough Out rig with Great Western Single Action .357, and Bohlin Rig with Great Western Single Action.

Right: Presentation grade carved Buscadero by John Bianchi's Frontier Gunleather with silver conchos, carved buckle, and engraved, black micarta-stocked Freedom Arms .454 Casull.

This 1903 vintage .45 Colt Single Action was totally rebuilt and remarked with proper vintage markings by Peacemaker Specialists, and was fitted with a new barrel, cylinder, and one-piece ivory grips. Charlie Baker engraved it. Topped off with a deluxe action job, this personalized sixgun reflects total pride of ownership on the part of its owner, Eddie Janis.

Ivory-stocked custom Rugers by Hamilton Bowen: Top, .44 Special with top strap made into fixed sighted version, and bottom, .38-40 with full-length rib and post front sight.

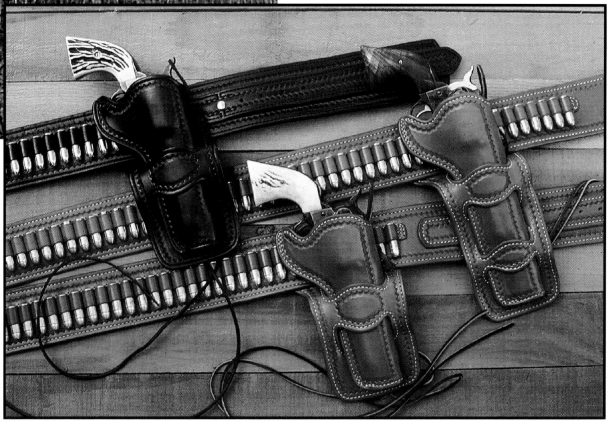

The Leather Arsenal now offers the Cowboy Action Shooter high quality double weight leather in black or tan, with a border-stamped design. These examples carry .45 Colts, Great Western Single Actions with 4-3/4-inch and 5-1/2-inch barrels, and a 7-1/2-inch Ruger Vaquero.

Milt Morrison of Qualite Pistol &
Revolver built the Special
Shootists 10th Anniversary Sixgun.
This .45 Colt New Model Ruger
Blackhawk features tuned action,
high lustre blue finish, gold bead
front sight, gold embellishments,
and custom walnut stocks by
Dave Wayland.

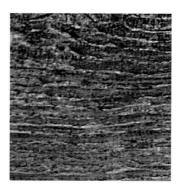

Straight from the silver
screen—Legends in
Leather duplicated the
rigs Hopalong Cassidy
and Roy Rogers wore.

These ivory polymer grips by Bob Leskovec are copies of
the ivory grips Elmer Keith favored. The top sixgun is a Colt
New Frontier 7-1/2-inch .45 Colt, and the bottom sixgun is a
Smith & Wesson Elmer Keith Commemorative 4-inch .44
Magnum.

Custom round-butted 4-inch-barreled Little Rugers by Andy Horvath. Clockwise from top right: David Dworsky's Old Model .357 converted to .41 Magnum with ivory micarta grips and New Model stainless .44 Magnum rechambered and rebarreled to .45 Colt, Taffin's Old Model .357 Magnum turned into a .44 Special with round-butted factory grips, Jerry Danuser's Old Model converted to .44 Special with ivory micarta grips, and New Model .45 Colt with ebony grips.

Custom sixguns from Bill Grover are unique in that they are mirror images of each other. Note the loading gate and ejector rod are on the left side of the top gun and the right side of the bottom gun. Everything else, including the engraving, is reversed on the bottom sixgun. Engraving by Dan Love and ivory inlaid ebony grips by Dennis Holland.

Above: The Colt Single Action Army's triggerguard and the Colt Bisley's backstrap were combined to become Elmer Keith's #5SA grip frame as supplied today on the Texas Longhorn Arms Improved Number Five.

Above: Authentic replica leather from Mario Hanel with Cimarron-engraved 7-1/2-inch .44-40, Great Western 5-1/2-inch .357 Atomic, and Navy Arms in holster. Bottom holster carries an 1861 Colt Navy.

Mag-Na-Port builds some beautiful sixguns—this outstanding example is the company's 25th Anniversary Model with dual trapezoidal porting and custom pinstriping. Photo courtesy of <u>Guns</u> magazine.

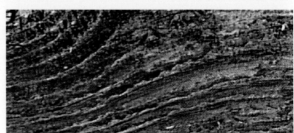

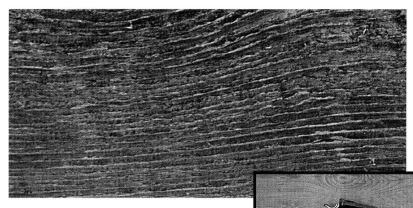

Right: These 7-1/2-inch Ruger Magnums—Flat-Tops, Super Black-hawk, and Bisley—are in leather by El Paso and stocks by Charles Able. Each one is a superb hunting sixgun.

Below: Master engraver Lynton McKenzie engraved this Freedom Arms .454 Casull in 1987. This revolver is fitted with a 7-1/2-inch barrel and has a polished stainless steel finish with AAA fancy French walnut grips. It was built for Wayne Baker, President of Freedom Arms. Photo courtesy of Freedom Arms.

Full floral-carved leather from El Paso: Tom Threepersons with Custom Colt 4-3/4-inch .45 Colt with ivory stocks, and Border Patrol with 4-inch Smith & Wesson M29 .44 Magnum engraved by Jim Riggs and stocked with ivory micarta by BearHug.

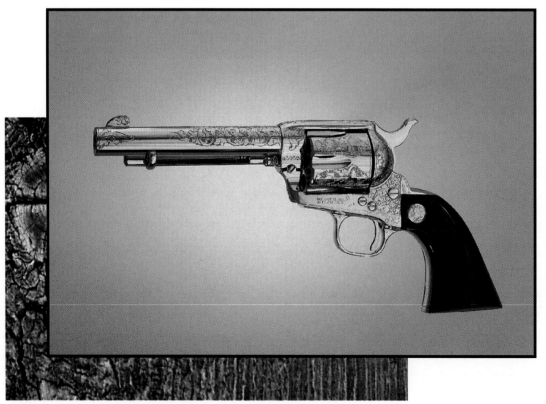

This current production 3rd Generation Colt Single Army was engraved in Colt's Custom Shop. The pattern is known as the Engravers Sampler, because it features different types of engraving styles on the same revolver. Photo courtesy of Colt Manufacturing.

Nothing personalizes a sixgun like good engraving. Jim Riggs did this pair of sixguns: The Smith & Wesson has a 4-inch barrel with ivory micarta Skeeter Skelton grips by BearHug, while the 4-3/4-inch Colt Single Action is fitted with real ivory grips. Both guns have the same pattern and are finished in antique nickel to highlight the engraving.

Stainless New Model .357 Ruger Blackhawk rechambered and rebarreled to .45 Colt with a 4-inch barrel, round-butted grip frame, and ebony grips. All by Andy Horvath.

An engraved nickel trio from the Cimarron Firearms Custom Shop. It is in this shop that contemporary American master engravers reproduce the historical styles of nineteenth century master artisans such as Gustave Young, C. Helfricht, George Ulrich, and Louis Nimschke. These three sixguns are modern-day masterpieces. Photo courtesy of Cimarron Firearms.

Taffin shooting the .500 Linebaugh.

Two hands are better than one when shooting any Linebaugh sixguns. This one is in .500 Linebaugh with 440 grain bullets at 1,200 fps.

Recoil? Of course, the .500 recoils—heavy! With loads of 400 grain bullets up to 1,200 feet per second and 440 grain bullets to 1,100 feet per second, the felt recoil is no worse, perhaps even less than standard .44 Magnum loads. Hit the pedal on 440 grain bullets at 1,300 feet per second and one knows that he has exceptional power in his hands. Power to take anything that walks. Anywhere.

Linebaugh's maximum recommendations for the .500 use Hodgdon's H110 or Winchester's 296 under 400 and 440 grain bullets. In my 5-1/2-inch barreled .500, these loads clock out at 1,300 and 1,200 feet per second, respectively. Bullets for the .500 are available from several sources. For those who cast their own, LBT and NEI offer several excellent designs. Cast bullets are available from BRP, and jacketed bullets, that Linebaugh helped design, can be purchased from Golden Bear Bullets. Golden Bear also offers formed brass. Ben Forkin also offers brass for all of the Linebaugh cartridges as well as cast bullets.

Linebaugh's Custom .500 is expensive, but I've never heard any owner say it wasn't worth the price. It is a masterpiece of workmanship and design, giving real rifle-type power in a 3 pound sixgun that is easily packed all day in a shoulder or hip holster. It is designed for one thing, hunting the world's biggest game. It cannot be surpassed as a close-range sixgun for elk, moose, even big bears. It is not a gun for beginners, but for seasoned sixgunners who have much experience with heavy loaded .45 Colt and/or .44 Magnum and/or .454 Casull. Used the wrong way, it can hurt one physically. This is not a gun for pounding hundreds of rounds through at a session. It must be approached with good common sense.

Just about the time the .500 was really going well, a monkey wrench hit the machinery. Linebaugh received word that Winchester was going to drop .348 brass. Without this brass, .500 Linebaugh brass could not be made. Without .500 brass, there would be no demand for .500 Linebaugh sixguns. Fortunately, .348 brass was not dropped from production, but the scare did force Linebaugh to look for another possibility for chambering in his fiveguns.

Linebaugh used a Marlin 1895 .45-70 as a saddle gun, so he had plenty of .45-70 brass on hand. That set him to thinking. There will always be a good supply of .45-70 brass because it is one of our most popular rifle cartridges. He cut .45-70 brass to .500 length, expanded it to take .475 bullets, and began to look for the suppliers he would need for bullets and barrels. LBT cut bullet moulds for flat-nosed .475 bullets at 385 and 420 grain cast weights, and Linebaugh found

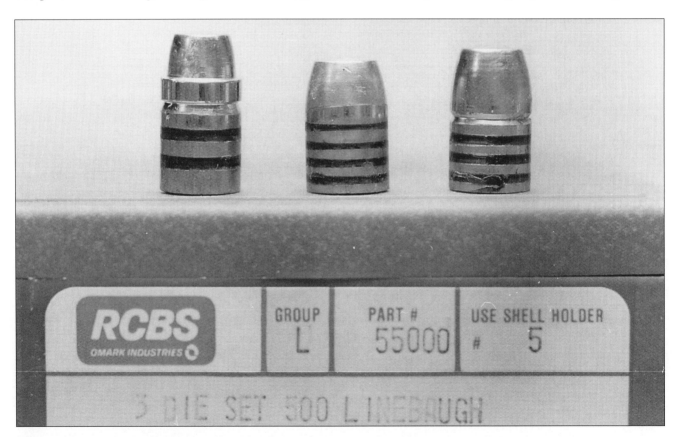

NEI's 440 grain .500 bullet, LBT's 400 and 440 grain bullets, and RCBS dies for the .500 Linebaugh.

Taffin's 5-1/2-inch .500 Linebaugh with Charles Able micarta grips.

a source for .476-inch barrels. The .475 Linebaugh was a reality.

The .475 did not replace the .500 by any means. It simply gives the sixgunner another option; one can use slightly lighter bullets at slightly faster muzzle velocity for slightly better penetration. Choose the .500 for weight and caliber; go with the .475 for speed and more penetration, although it is doubtful that one would ever need more penetration than the .500 affords. Optimum bullet weight for the .475 seems to be in the 350 to 400 grain weight category, while the .500 is at its best with 400 to 440 grain bullets. Using bullets of the same weight, 400 grains, the .475 picks up 100 to 150 feet per second over the .500.

The .475 is made by trimming the afore-mentioned .45-70 brass to 1.400 inches and reloading with RCBS Custom .475 dies. Neither the .475 nor the .500 can be loaded without the use of special custom dies from RCBS. When loading the .475 Linebaugh, trim Winchester Western .45-70 brass to the proper length, run the trimmed brass through the RCBS full length sizer die and expander die in sequence, prime, charge with powder, and seat and crimp the bullet. LBT offers at least three designs for the .475 to be cast from its excellent double cavity moulds, #476.370LFN (350 grain), #476.420LFN (395 grain), and #476.440LFN (405 grain); NEI also offers a flat-nosed 380 grain .475 bullet, #390.477. All .475 bullets are sized to .476 inch.

What can one expect in performance from the .475? With 400 grain bullets, the .475 will deliver muz-zle velocities comparable to a .44 Magnum with a 240 grain bullet! This is from a sixgun that is the same size, or even smaller than, the .44 Magnum revolver.

Anyone with a great deal of experience with heavy recoiling single action sixguns knows keeping the ejector rod housing intact is a real problem. Ruger went from a steel ejector tube to a lighter weight alloy one to cut down on the inertia of the tube as the gun is fired and recoils. Linebaugh now builds all of his five-shot revolvers with a 5-1/2-inch barrel with a machined-on barrel band that holds the front sight and also gives support to the ejector rod housing, preventing it from flying forward under the tremendous recoil generated by these five-shot guns.

Linebaugh is an expert when it comes to fitting, timing, etc. of single action revolvers, and is in fact, one of a handful of sixgunsmiths in the country who really understands the single action sixgun. One is not likely to find a single action anywhere any smoother in operation than a Linebaugh-built Custom Single Action. He is a fanatic on tolerances and his guns are built to minimum dimensions and the tightest possible tolerances. No sloppy cylinder chambers, large barrel cylinder gaps, or cylinders that rock side to side or back and forth are ever found on his custom guns.

Linebaugh now had his five-shot revolvers built to perfection in .45 Colt, .475 Linebaugh, and .500 Linebaugh. What would be next? Linebaugh was about to go Long. The Maximum idea started with the .357 SuperMag Dan Wesson and Ruger .357 Maximum

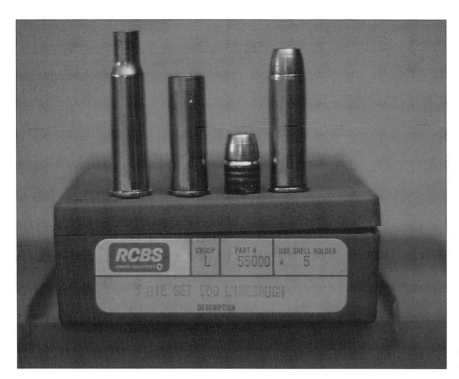

The .500 Linebaugh is made from .348 Winchester brass, trimmed to length, and formed with RCBS dies.

The .475 Linebaugh begins with .45-70 brass, trimmed and formed with RCBS dies.

revolvers that were created with the perfect long-range silhouette revolver in mind. The frames and cylinders of existing .44 Magnum revolvers, the Ruger Super Blackhawk and the Dan Wesson Model 44, were stretched to accept a new cartridge that was made by also stretching .357 Magnum brass. The new cartridge, the .357 SuperMag, was about .3 inch longer than the standard Magnum.

The .357 SuperMag was followed by the .375 Super-Mag with brass being made by cutting .375 Winchester brass to 1.610 inches, and this was followed by the .445 SuperMag which used .44 caliber brass at 1.610 inches in length. Long before the advent of the .445 SuperMag, my friend Lew Schafer was experimenting with .357 SuperMag Dan Wessons rechambered to his .44 UltraMag and fitted with Dan Wesson

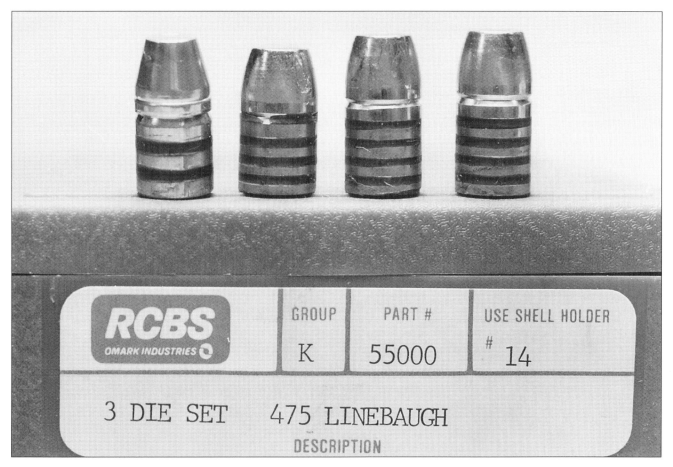

RCBS dies and heavyweight bullets are necessary to load the .475 Linebaugh. These cast bullets are by NEI and LBT and range in weight from 350 to 410 grains.

Linebaugh's favorite sixgun chamberings, the .45 Colt, .475 Linebaugh, and the .500 Linebaugh, all loaded with jacketed heavyweight bullets of 330, 365, and 400 grains by Golden Bear.

Size comparison of .44 Magnum with .475 Linebaugh, .475 Linebaugh Long, .500 Linebaugh, and .500 Linebaugh Long.

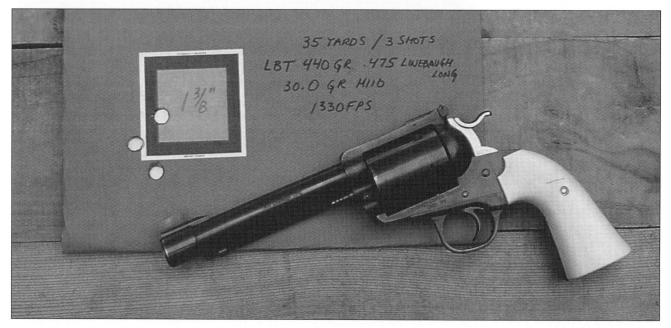

Accuracy of the .475 Linebaugh Long using 440 grain bullets at 1,330 fps: The range was 35 yards and the group is 1-3/8 inch.

.44 Magnum barrels. Schafer's UltraMag brass was made from .444 Marlin brass cut to length, swaged, and turned on a lathe.

Linebaugh uses the only single action sixgun generally available for conversions to Linebaugh Long calibers and that sixgun is the out-of-production Ruger .357 stretched frame Maximum. One can immediately see the problem here. If Ruger Bisleys are an on again-off again situation production-wise, imagine how difficult it is to find a Ruger Maximum. One usually has to pay at least $500 to get one to use as a platform for conversion. Then virtually everything except the main frame is discarded. The conversion requires a new five-shot cylinder, a new barrel, Bisley parts, namely grip frame, hammer, and trigger. With-

out even beginning the custom work, we are well above $1,000 in parts alone!

Linebaugh simply stretched his two calibers, the .475 Linebaugh and the .500 Linebaugh, each to 1.600 inches, and the Linebaugh Longs were born. One might expect the "Long" conversion to result in a poorly-balanced, awkward-looking and handling single action. This is not the case. The big guns balance well, pack easily, and one has to look twice to even notice that the cylinders are made to handle brass that is 1/3 inch longer than the normal .357 or .44 Magnum.

These Linebaugh Long-chambered sixguns KICK—HARD! Recoil with the .475 Linebaugh Long is probably at least three times heavier than a full-house .44 Magnum. Recoil is such a factor that I have never

Taffin experiencing the recoil of the .500 Linebaugh. Note use of heavy gloves to help lessen felt recoil.

Standard 7-1/2-inch .45 Colt Ruger Vaquero compared to Plainsman sixguns by Linebaugh Custom Sixguns: Six-shot .45 Colt with lengthened grip frame and micarta grips by Dustin Linebaugh, John Linebaugh's personal .500 stainless Plainsman with micarta grips by Dustin Linebaugh, and round-butted 4-inch .45 Colt. All Plainsman feature free-wheeling cylinders.

shot more than thirty-five to forty rounds at a session and even that is pushing it. If I were smarter, a couple of full cylinders at a time would be plenty.

Loads for both Linebaugh Long cartridges are assembled with the same bullets, brass, dies, and powder as the standard Linebaugh chamberings. The only difference is that brass is trimmed to 1.600 inches rather than 1.400 inches.

Maximum loads for the .475 Linebaugh Long are a 380 grain cast bullet at 1,600 feet per second, a 410 grain cast bullet at 1,500 to 1,550 feet per second, and a 430 grain cast bullet at 1,400 to 1,450 feet per second. These are serious loads and should be approached very seriously. To do otherwise could result in injury.

If the recoil with the .475 Linebaugh Long is serious, then call the recoil with the .500 Linebaugh Long in full-house loadings super serious. We are talking 400 to 450 grain bullets at 1,500 to 1,600 feet per second. In a 3 pound sixgun! It takes a tremendous amount of concentration and strength to fire thirty to forty rounds of this biggest of all revolver cartridges that will still fit in a portable package. I have fired thousands upon thousands of the heaviest revolver cartridges from .44 Magnum to .445 SuperMag to .454 Casull to .475 Linebaugh and .500 Linebaugh. With the Linebaugh Longs, I have met my match and then some! As stated, the .475 Linebaugh Long revolver generates at least three times the recoil of a .44 Magnum and the .500 Linebaugh Long almost puts the .475 Linebaugh Long in the mild class.

We have reached the ultimate top, the apex of sixgun power. Perhaps we have gone over. There is simply no way to combine more power with portability. Both of these sixgun chamberings require tremendous concentration and strength and are only for those revolver shooters with vast experience shooting big bores. Very few handgunners are able to handle the recoil of these biggest of all big bores.

Even John Linebaugh freely admits that the Linebaugh Long conversions cost twice as much as his regular conversions. For the same money, I would be happier and better served with a .475 and a .500 rather than just one of either of these calibers in the Long version. The Linebaugh Longs also increase recoil significantly, and only deliver 5 percent more penetration. In fact, John and I have often discussed the fact that 1,200 to 1,400 feet per second *with heavy bullets* is the optimum muzzle velocity needed for maximum penetration in a sixgun. Anything more may flatten out the trajectory for long shots but long shots should never be taken with a sixgun on live targets.

How do the various big bore sixgun chamberings compare? A lot is published about muzzle energies that are derived by a formula that gives the advantage to the lighter, faster bullets. A better formula, at least for comparison purposes, is that worked out by John "Pondoro" Taylor, a long time elephant hunter of days past. Taylor's Knockout Theory, or TKO, takes into consideration the caliber being used and assigns a number to each load found by multiplying the caliber times the bullet weight times the muzzle velocity, all divided by 7,000. All this does is assign a ranking to various big bore loadings. The number means nothing else. For comparison purposes here are some TKOs of the big ones:

.44 Magnum	240 grain bullet @ 1,400 fps	21 TKO
.44 Magnum	300 grain bullet @ 1,300 fps	25 TKO
.45 Colt	300 grain bullet @ 1,300 fps	25 TKO
.454 Casull	260 grain bullet @ 1,800 fps	30 TKO
.454 Casull	300 grain bullet @ 1,600 fps	31 TKO
.475 Linebaugh	385 grain bullet @ 1,480 fps	39 TKO
.500 Linebaugh	440 grain bullet @ 1,200 fps	38 TKO
.475 Linebaugh Long	380 grain bullet @ 1,600 fps	41 TKO
.500 Linebaugh Long	425 grain bullet @ 1,550 fps	47 TKO

Again, these figures only give us a comparison from cartridge to cartridge, but note well that the 300 grain bullets in either .45 Colt or .44 Magnum, both proven to be exceptional game getters have a TKO of 25, while the .500 Linebaugh Long is nearly double that at a TKO of 47. And it is definitely felt on both ends.

The .475 and .500 Linebaugh Long chamberings are to the revolver what the .458 Winchester and .460 Weatherby are to rifles. Most of us, at least in this

Linebaugh has now standardized his five-shot conversions on the Ruger Blackhawks. All of these sixguns carry 5-1/2-inch barrels with a barrel band that holds the front sight and ejector rod housing, and have Bisley grip frames, and Bisley hammers. Left to right: Harry Lunt's stainless .45 Colt, Manfred Schneider's stainless .475 with micarta grips by Dustin Linebaugh, and Vince Donzi's .500 with case-colored frame.

country, are better served with the .338 Winchester and .375 H&H of sixguns, the .475 and .500 Linebaugh. If one wants the ultimate in sixgun power, though, these big Linebaugh Long five-shot sixguns are the most powerful revolvers one can have when dealing with really nasty four-legged beasts that have a bad habit of chewing or stomping on shooters that don't put them down immediately.

The advent of Ruger's latest sixgun, the Vaquero, has opened up totally new avenues of custom work for Linebaugh Custom Sixguns. Coupled with the Vaquero's arrival, John Linebaugh is now joined by his son, Dustin, who does the metal work as well as grip work for Linebaugh Custom Sixguns.

The Vaquero is not only for Cowboy Action Shooters, but is also a very practical, portable, powerful packin' pistol. Linebaugh calls his Vaquero conversions Plainsman. All feature short barrels of 4 to 5 inches and can be had in the original Ruger .45 Colt and barrel or fitted with either an oversized six-shot cylinder in .45 Colt or five-shot cylinders and custom barrels in .45 Colt, .475 Linebaugh, or .500 Linebaugh.

Yes, the Vaquero will handle both the Linebaugh chamberings. Recoil, however, is severe. To combat this problem, Linebaugh installs Bisley-style grip frames, hammers, and triggers. He can also extend the standard Blackhawk grip frame to allow a more solid grip to help handle felt recoil. One of Linebaugh's Vaquero conversions fitted with a 4-inch barrel and a round-butted Bisley grip frame makes into a very practical "pocket" pistol.

One problem that Cowboy Action Shooters have found with the Vaquero is that unlike the Colt Single Action, when one hears the click as the cylinder is rotated, it is already too late. That is, the empty chamber has rotated just far enough that a new cartridge cannot be inserted. With Linebaugh's Plainsman Vaqueros, all cylinders are free-wheeling, meaning they will spin either direction. If the cylinder is rotated too far forward, one simply brings it back to allow the empty chamber to line up with the loading gate.

If one is looking for a reasonable-sized big bore sixgun that shoots big, heavy bullets accurately, Linebaugh Custom Sixguns could very well be the answer whether the question demands the power level of the .45 Colt or the heavier and larger big bores. They are not for everyone, but for those who need more than the .44 Magnum can deliver, look to Linebaugh.

CHAPTER 11

SIXGUNS AND SILHOUETTING

During the first half of this century, at least back to the days of Pancho Villa prior to World War I, live chicken shooting was quite popular in Mexico. Chickens would be tied to a stake and shooters would back off a hundred meters or more and the one who hit the chicken won it for his dinner. As long as military-style bullets were used, little meat damage occurred to either the chickens, pigs, or turkeys that were offered as live targets. With the advent of modern ammunition, a chicken or turkey especially, was heavily meat damaged and the "sport" became more of a bloody fiasco.

Sometime in the late 1940s, silhouettes, or metal cutouts of animals, were substituted for the real thing. The first organized rifle match using metal targets of animals was held in Tucson in 1969. By the early 1970s, rifle silhouette shooting was well-established with four types of targets, chickens, javelinas, turkeys, and rams. The farthest target, the ram, was shot at 500 meters—offhand.

As the popularity of rifle silhouetting grew, it would only be a matter of time until some enterprising individuals adapted the sport to handguns. Lee Jurras proposed the first handgun silhouette match to be held on the ranch of Skeeter Skelton's friend, Evan Quiros, in early 1975. Jurras was also deeply involved during this time as the founder of the Outstanding American Handgunner Awards Foundation, president of Club de Auto Mag, and also the head of his own company, Super Vel. The spring match never got off the ground, but Jurras, Dutch Snow, and Dale Miller were able to put a match together in September 1975 in Tucson.

Fifty men signed up for that first match, with forty-six actually competing. Targets were chickens at 50 meters, javelinas at 100 meters, turkeys at 150 meters, and rams at a full 200 meters. Any handgun of .357 Magnum or larger was allowed. Scopes or artifi-cial rests were not allowed, however, the shooter could fire from a standing, sitting, kneeling, or prone position. Jurras, Snow, and Miller were match directors, aided by Jeff Cooper and George Nonte. Two men who have since become my very close friends, J.D. Jones and Hal Swiggett, were the only gunwriters to take part in the actual shooting.

Of the forty-six competitors who fired at the first handgun silhouette course, fifteen used semi-automatics, fourteen selected Auto Mags, and one stayed with the venerable 1911 Government Model; one single-shot shooter used a Thompson/Center Contender—the gun that would eventually be the number one choice of silhouette shooters—and thirty went with the traditional sixgun. Those thirty sixguns broke down as follows: twelve Smith & Wesson Model 29 .44 Magnums, eight Ruger Super Blackhawk .44 Magnums, seven Colt Python .357 Magnums, and one each of the Ruger .357 Blackhawk, the Smith & Wesson Model 57 .41 Magnum, and a Smith & Wesson Model 25 chambered in .45 Auto Rim. I find it quite interesting to look at this list of sixguns and then compare it to what one would find a few years later at a silhouette match. As we shall see, the sixgun line-up changed drastically in a very short time.

That first match really started something, to say the least. One year later, the International Handgun Metallic Silhouette Association, or IHMSA, would be formed and long-range silhouetting would become the fastest growing shooting sport throughout the 1980s.

Silhouetting was a natural. Everyone that owned a handgun, at least every serious shooter, had to try his hand at long-range shooting. Rocks had been a favorite target for decades, and now we had an organized sport that would utilize our long-range skills. We were also soon to find that a close hit on a far rock equaled a miss on a metal silhouette target. But we would learn very quickly.

Three basic types of handguns are used in silhouetting. The single-shot factory Production gun as exemplified by the Thompson/Center Contender, the Unlimited handgun such as the custom-built XP-100s, and the Revolver. Originally, Production Class lumped the single-shots and sixguns together, but eventually a separate Revolver Class was established.

A basic silhouette match consists of forty targets, ten each of chickens, javelinas, turkeys, and rams. Targets are shot in banks of five each with two minutes allowed to fire five shots. My first match, in the late 1970s, was fired with a favorite hunting sixgun, a 7-1/2-inch Ruger .44 Magnum Flat-Top Blackhawk. I hit seven targets and I was hooked. The first time one hears the metal CLANG! and sees the target go down is all that it takes to become a dedicated competitor.

My first score was disappointing, but my enthusiasm was not. I had fired my first match using the old standard long-range sixgunner's position of sitting back with one knee drawn up and the sixgun rested against the outside of that knee. Other shooters were more than happy to instruct me in the Creedmore position. This strange looking, and feeling, shooting position put one down completely on one's back with both feet flat on the ground and the knees drawn up

and placed together to form a triangle. The sixgun is then laid along one knee with the elbow of the shooting hand rested on the ground—a rock steady position, to say the least.

All during my silhouette shooting days, I found an almost universal attribute among most silhouetters: the willingness to help newcomers to the game even though it meant that they might eventually be beaten by that same newcomer. Silhouetting, for the vast majority of competitors was, and remains, a family atmosphere, with helping one another being a major part of the sport. Yes, there are a few whose only goal is to win and the rest of the shooters do not matter, but this type of individual is only the rare exception rather than the rule. It is not unusual to see the two top competitors spotting for each other, that is one serves as a spotter to tell the other where the shots are hitting.

Silhouetting is highly competitive. Not so much from shooter to shooter, but between the shooter and the targets. How many times have I missed a target simply because I shot it in my mind before I shot in actuality? How many times has every competitor sworn that the turkey moved just as we shot?

Two minutes is a long time to shoot only five targets, especially with a sixgun that does not require

Shooting the 10-inch Dan Wesson .357 Magnum from the Creedmore position—blast shield protects leg from injury due to gases and lead that escapes from the barrel/cylinder gap.

working the action and loading each cartridge individually during the actual shooting time. Even so, I have often had two shots left when the microphone blares "THIRTY SECONDS." The sights line up on turkey number four. Don't hurry. Slowly squeeze the trigger. BANG! CLANG! Only one target to go. How much time is left? Don't hurry the shot. Take your time. Align the sights. Squeeze the trigger. BANG! CLANG! BUZZ! You made it. All the turkeys are down.

As silhouetting grew and spread across the country, it began to have a tremendous effect on handgun developments. It did not take long for the course to be conquered by both Production and Unlimited single-shot handguns. The real challenge was in the Revolver Class. In 1975, the longest barreled sixgun available for silhouetting was the Smith & Wesson line of 8-3/8-inch sixguns in .357 Magnum, .41 Magnum, and .44 Magnum. Ruger's 7-1/2-inch Super Blackhawk .44 Magnum and Colt's 8-inch .357 Python were also used by early competitors. In a very short period of time these sixguns would only be seen very rarely on the firing line. A new power in sixgunning, at least silhouette-style, was about to emerge.

Dan Wesson, great grandson of Daniel Baird Wesson, co-founder of Smith & Wesson, was born in Massachusetts in 1916. At the age of 22 he had joined the family company as a machine operator and was named Assistant Superintendent three years later in 1941, at a time when Smith & Wesson was very close to bankruptcy. Dan Wesson worked with President Carl Hellstrom through those hard times to save Smith & Wesson.

In 1963, Dan Wesson was named Plant Superintendent, but trouble was immediately ahead. It came in 1966 with the acquisition of Smith & Wesson by Bangor Punta; Dan Wesson tried to avoid the takeover by buying enough shares of stock. When he failed, he resigned from the company. History would prove this was unfortunate because the Bangor Punta days at Smith & Wesson saw a decline in quality that took years to bring back.

After the War years, Dan Wesson had formed his own side company in 1948. D.B. Wesson, Inc. began as a tool and die company, however, in 1968, after leaving Bangor Punta's Smith & Wesson, Dan Wesson changed D.B. Wesson, Inc. to Dan Wesson Arms. One year later the new Dan Wesson .357 Magnum was being shown and in 1970, the public was able to purchase the first .357 Magnum from a new company since the Great Western and Ruger Blackhawk .357s of the mid-1950s.

The Dan Wesson .357 Model 12 was a radical new design incorporating interchangeable barrels, interchangeable grips, and interchangeable front sights. Until the Dan Wesson arrived, all sixguns of the time wore fixed barrels, fixed front sights, and two-piece stocks. Everything about the Dan Wesson was modern. Instead of two pieces of wood that bolted to two sides of the grip frame, the Dan Wesson stocks were a solid one-piece. Instead of a grip frame, the Dan Wesson sixgun had a stud that accepted the one-piece grip that in turn bolted on from the bot-

Dan Wesson's sixguns can be changed from iron sight to scope sight by simply removing the nut at the end of the barrel and changing the shroud.

Shooting the 10-1/2-inch .44 Magnum Super Blackhawk in Standing Class—most silhouetters use single shots for this class.

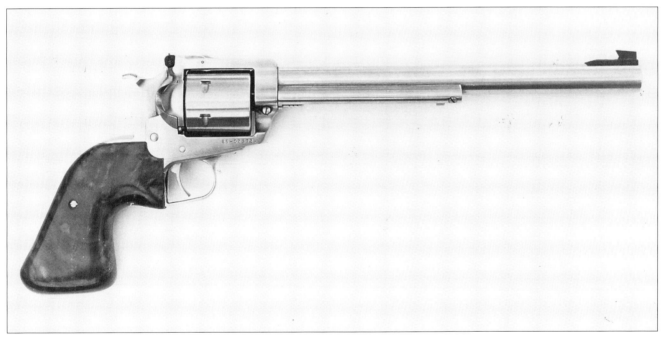

Ruger's 10-1/2-inch .44 Magnum with undercut front sight and grips by Tedd Adamovich—an excellent set up for silhouetting.

tom. To this day, the Dan Wesson revolvers are the only big bore double action sixguns in recent memory to come from the factory with truly usable wooden grips.

What really made the Dan Wesson unique, though, was the interchangeable barrel system. The original idea was simply to offer multiple barrel lengths. To be able to offer interchangeable barrels, it was necessary to have a system that allowed the shooter to easily change barrels. With the devised system, the shooter received an extra bonus of excellent accuracy.

Changing barrels on conventional revolvers requires a barrel vise and a good bit of leverage. Dan Wesson abandoned the idea of a traditional barrel and instead provided a barrel of minimum diameter, that can be hand-tightened and removed without using a vise. The barrel is screwed into the frame until it bears against a feeler gauge of .002 inch to .006 inch, depending upon the caliber. Then a heavy shroud is placed over the barrel and a hole in the back of the shroud matches with an aligning pin on the frame. A barrel nut is then screwed on the muzzle end of the barrel and, using a special wrench pro-

The Smith & Wesson .44 Magnum set up for silhouetting with inner endurance package (radius stud package that rounded all sharp studs and pins within the action to relieve stress and a new cylinder yoke retention system), BearHug stocks, and Smith & Wesson silhouette sights, with results shooting Creedmore at 100 and 200 meters. This sixgun was ten years too late to become a vital part of the silhouetting scene.

vided with each gun, is tightened against the shroud. In addition to a barrel that was locked at the front of the muzzle, the Dan Wesson cylinder latch was located, not at the rear, but at the front of the cylinder. This, along with the front locking barrel, also contributed to accuracy.

As long-range metallic silhouetting soared in the early 1980s, the Dan Wesson revolver was upgraded with an improved barrel locking nut that resided inside the shroud rather than at the end of it, a heavy barrel was added, and the Dan Wesson Model 15 .357 Magnum became *the* silhouette sixgun. A marriage began between IHMSA and Dan Wesson, and Dan Wesson sixguns were sold to club members, and likewise, silhouetters embraced the Dan Wesson tightly and almost unanimously.

I was first introduced to the real capability of the Dan Wesson .357 sixgun when I watched a local shooter in the early 1980s beat everyone handily using a Dan Wesson .357 Magnum with a heavy 8-inch barrel. By this time, Dan Wesson was offering four styles of barrels: standard, heavy, standard ribbed, and heavy ribbed. When loaded with heavyweight bullets at moderate velocities, the heavyweight-barreled Dan Wesson .357 competed on an equal footing with the 10-inch barreled Ruger Super Blackhawk .44 Magnum—probably more than equal; less recoil gave the .357 Dan Wesson a decided advantage.

After winning the state shoot in 1981 with a Ruger .44 Magnum, I soon switched to the Dan Wesson .357 Magnum with the 10-inch heavy barrel. Dan Wesson and Ruger were the only major revolver manufacturers to listen to silhouette shooters at the time. Ruger had seen the importance of silhouetting early and introduced the Ruger Super Blackhawk with a 10-1/2-inch barrel. My wife and I used a pair of these for silhouetting with fine success. Later, Ruger would stretch the frame of the Super Blackhawk and give sixgunners the excellent shooting .357 Maximum. The Ruger .357 Maximum was my favorite silhouette sixgun for many years.

United States Arms produced a Super Blackhawk clone in the Seville. It would also find favor with silhouette shooters both in standard and stretched frame versions. All of these single action sixguns, Ruger Super Blackhawk .44 Magnum, Ruger .357 Maximum, and Seville, were superb shooting sixguns for silhouetting, but Dan Wesson definitely ruled the firing line at silhouette matches all over the country during the 1980s.

The Dan Wesson .357 Magnum was a natural for cast bullets, and I developed a load using .38 Special brass and RCBS's 200 grain gas-checked flat-point bullet originally designed to be used in the .35 Reming-

ton lever action rifle. It was necessary to use .38 Special brass instead of .357 Magnum brass to be able to crimp the long 200 grain bullets and still allow them to fit the relatively short cylinder of the Dan Wesson. At 1,100 feet per second, that load was extremely accurate and I never lost a target, that is, I never had a target fail to go down when hit. In silhouetting, only targets that actually topple are counted for score.

Once the .357 Magnum was a proven success, Dan Wesson began experimenting to build a large-framed revolver in .44 Magnum. In my file I have a copy of a letter received from Dan Wesson in April 1977. I had written asking for a larger sixgun in .44 Magnum and .45 Colt and was told that "...the .44 Magnum is on the drawing board." Unlike Smith & Wesson, which was able to use its .357 Magnum-sized frame for its .44 Magnum, Dan Wesson had to go back to square one and build a new gun. Smith & Wesson had built its .357 Magnum in 1935 on the .44 Special frame of 1907. Dan Wesson's Model 15 .357 Magnum was too small to handle the .44 Magnum.

When the .44 Magnum Dan Wesson came along, it weighed in at over 4 pounds with the 8-inch heavy barrel. The new silhouette sixgun was too heavy to make the 4 pound weight limit, and many early .44 Wesson sixguns were weighed in the balance at local matches and found not wanting, but overabundant. By slightly reshaping the heavy shroud, the factory was able to get the new .44 Magnum to make weight and to also offer a 10-inch standard barreled model, my particular favorite, that also made it just under the 4 pound weight ceiling.

Dan Wesson's Model 15 .357 disappeared from the firing line to be replaced by Model 44s. Although the long-barreled .357 Magnum *properly loaded* with heavyweight bullets was entirely adequate, especially after the topple point rule went into effect, the switch to the bigger, heavier recoiling .44 Magnum was made. It was not to last very long.

The topple point rule allowed targets to be set back further to make them fall easier. A problem had developed with competitors overloading their .357 Magnums to get more knockdown power. Instead of using heavyweight bullets at moderate velocities, they were seeing how fast they could drive 158 grain bullets. Some went too fast and I had the unfortunate experience of a shooter next to me blowing his .357 Magnum apart with over maximum loads. It was not a pleasant experience, and he was so embarrassed that he never came back to a local silhouette match. Simply put, the new rule was a good one.

The Dan Wesson .44 Magnum is the easiest shooting of all factory .44 Magnums ever offered, and I

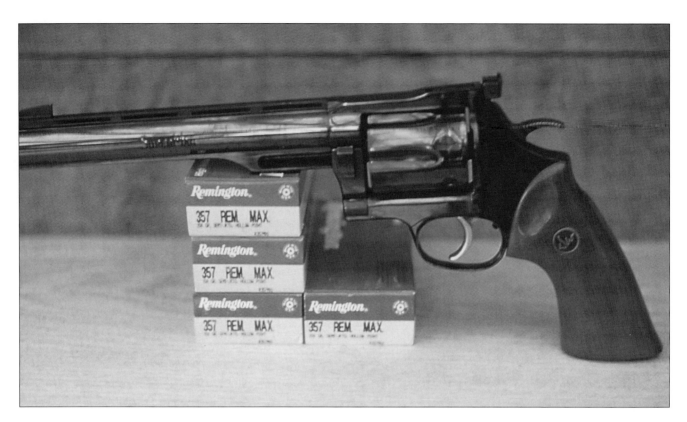

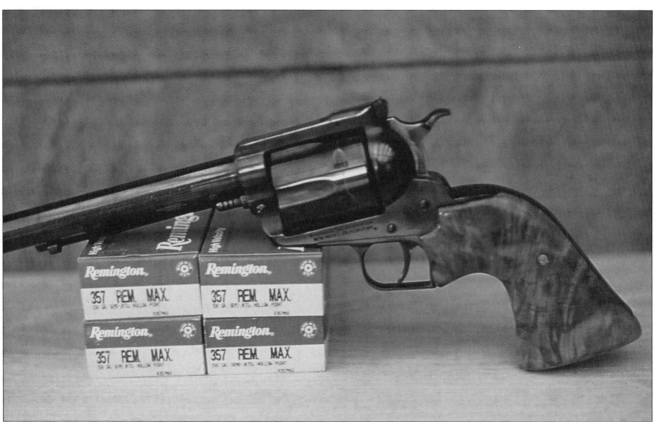

Two of the best sixguns for silhouetting are the 8-inch Dan Wesson .357 SuperMag with factory stocks and the Ruger 10-1/2-inch .357 Maximum with stocks by Tedd Adamovich.

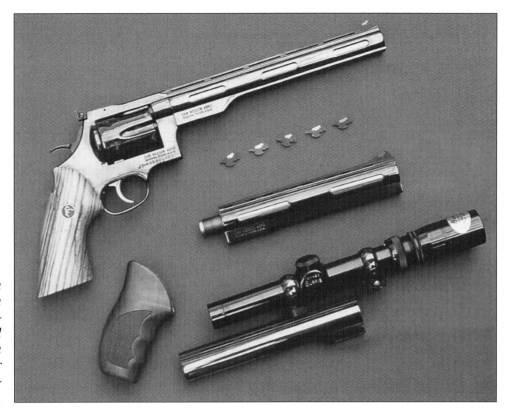

The versatility of the Dan Wesson: This .44 Magnum has a 10-inch barrel for silhouetting, an 8-inch barrel for general use, and a scoped 8-inch barrel for hunting, plus interchangeable stocks and front sights.

cherish my mismatched pair of Dan Wesson .44s, one with a heavy 8-inch barrel with extra shroud that carries a scope, and the 10-inch standard barrel model. When other .44 Magnums have beaten me into submission, I simply pull out the Dan Wesson .44 pair and enjoy life once again. The only other .44 Magnums that I have ever found that shoot easier than the Dan Wesson .44s are custom sixguns like those Jimmy Clark builds on the Smith & Wesson Model 29 and Ron Power likewise on the Ruger Super Redhawk. Both of these savvy sixgunners use heavy barrels for weight and expansion chambers to reduce felt recoil.

Both the Dan Wesson Model 15 .357 Magnum and Model 44 .44 Magnum offered the silhouette shooter a choice of front sight options. The standard red ramp insert was offered as well as yellow and white, but more importantly, a flat black post, or Patridge-style front sight that showed up well for silhouetting applications. Wesson was first to offer interchangeable front sights, and now Smith & Wesson, Ruger, and Freedom Arms all offer sixgunners a choice.

The third and final phase of the Dan Wesson/Silhouette marriage came shortly after the emergence of the .44 Magnum Model 44. Dan Wesson had enlarged the frame of the Model 15, changed the engineering, and came up with a great big bore sixgun, the Model 44 .44 Magnum. Within just a few short years, the Model 44 was also altered. The frame and

cylinder were stretched to accept 1.610-inch brass instead of the standard Magnum brass length of 1.300 inches and the SuperMag was born.

The .357 SuperMag would become the winningest revolver in silhouetting history—for awhile. It seemed that every top competitor used a .357 SuperMag Dan Wesson. When a sixgun arrived that would challenge the Wesson, IHMSA adopted a price ceiling rule that mandated a handgun could not be used in Production or Revolver Class if its manufacturer's suggested retail price exceeded a certain limit. For a few years, this rule would protect the Dan Wesson and keep it King of the Silhouetting Sixguns, but with a change in leadership at IHMSA, the price ceiling rule was dropped and a new silhouette sixgun was about to emerge.

In 1985, I contacted a relatively new company at the time, Freedom Arms. Wayne Baker and Dick Casull had formed the company just a few years earlier and were producing the finest revolver of all time, the .454 Casull. I asked Baker to set a 10-1/2-inch .454 up for silhouetting with special sights consisting of a Bomar rear sight matched up with a radically undercut front post sight. In addition to the first Freedom Arms silhouette sixgun, I also received dies, brass, bullets, and some loading information. The barrel cylinder gap was set at .002 inch and the trigger pull was under 3 pounds.

Taffin shooting the 8-inch Dan Wesson .44 Magnum from the standing postion.

More than 140 loads were worked up for that sixgun and my article on The Perfect Silhouette Sixgun was published in the March 1986 issue of *The Silhouette*, the official IHMSA paper. I settled on a silhouette load for myself consisting of Speer's 260 grain bullet with Winchester's WW680 powder at a muzzle velocity of 1,600 feet per second.

It was also at this time that Freedom Arms hosted what was to become the first annual meeting of The Shootists. The Shootists began as a group of like-minded sixgunners I invited to gather together to exchange ideas and knowledge. As we met in Freedom, a couple of us who were silhouetters gave a demonstration of sixgun silhouetting on the range that Freedom Arms had set up. It was Freedom Arms first exposure to the game and immediately the company realized that this was a sport that was perfectly suited for its revolver.

Jim Morey, who was Freedom Arms sales manager at the time, and I met together and discussed a silhouette sixgun in .44 Magnum chambering and also who should get the first guns. I suggested a .44 Freedom

Arms Silhouette revolver be sent David Bradshaw, a top competitor at the time. I shot beside Bradshaw at the 1986 Internationals using my .454 as he used the first .44 Freedom Arms sixgun set up for silhouetting. Later that same year I would travel to Raton, New Mexico, with Morey to shoot in the NRA Nationals. Jim Rock of RPM was shooting a .44 Freedom Arms by now and, as far as I know, the three of us were the first to use Freedom Arms revolvers in competition.

At the 1986 International matches, I discussed the price ceiling rule with Elgin Gates. He was going to propose a limit on the cost of guns to be used in Production or Revolver Class. The price mentioned was above the cost of either the Freedom Arms revolver or the Colt Python, and no current guns would have been effected. When it became a reality, the price ceiling rule barred both Colt's Python and Freedom Arms' Casull from competition.

A total change of leadership at IHMSA resulted in the price ceiling rule being dropped and a new chapter was about to be written in sixgun silhouetting. Freedom Arms began offering silhouette sixguns in both .454 and .44 Magnum with 10-1/2-inch barrels and special silhouette sights. They began to show up at and win matches all over the country. Freedom Arms then designed a sixgun specifically for silhouetting with its .353 Casull. The .353 is nothing more than a .357 Magnum, however, the strength, tolerances, and five-shot cylinder of the Freedom Arms Casull revolver allows the .357 Magnum to be loaded up to the point that it will outperform the .357 Super-Mag. The only weak point in the chain is the .357 Magnum brass, however, it will handle 180 grain bullets to a full 1,700 feet per second.

Today, a look at the results of Revolver Class at the IHMSA Internationals reveals just how popular the Freedom Arms sixguns have become. It is rare to find any other sixgun in the top twenty scores.

During my more than ten years as a serious competitor in silhouetting, a number of sixguns were pressed into service: from Smith & Wesson, the 6-1/2- and 8-3/8-inch Model 29 .44 Magnum as well as the 10-1/2-inch Silhouette Model, and the 8-3/8-inch Model 27 .357 Magnum; from Ruger, the 7-1/2-inch Flat-Top Blackhawk .44 Magnum, the 10-1/2-inch Super Blackhawk .44 Magnum, and the superb 10-1/2-inch .357 Maximum. I have also used all Dan Wessons, 10-inch .357 Magnum, 8- and 10-inch .44 Magnums, and 8-inch SuperMags in .357 and .375; the 10-1/2-inch Seville .375 SuperMag; the 10-1/2-inch Abilene .44 Magnum; and finally the 10-1/2-inch Freedom Arms Silhouette sixguns in .454, .44 Magnum, and .353 Casull. It is a tribute to American gunmaking that all of these sixguns are capable of shooting a perfect 40 score.

Super Single Action Silhouette Sixguns: Top, Ruger 10-1/2-inch .357 Maximum; middle, Freedom Arms 10-1/2-inch .44 Magnum; bottom, Ruger 10-1/2-inch .44 Magnum. All stocks by Tedd Adamovich.

Long-range silhouette sixgun cartridges: The .357 Magnum, the .41 Magnum, the .44 Magnum, the .454 Casull, the .357 SuperMag, the .375 SuperMag, the very rare .414 SuperMag, and the .445 SuperMag.

Four .44 Magnums for silhouetting: A single action 10-1/2-inch Ruger Super Blackhawk with Pachmayr grips, a single action 10-1/2-inch Abilene with Eagle stocks, a 10-inch Dan Wesson Model 44 with factory stocks, and 10-1/2-inch Smith & Wesson Silhouette Model with Pachmayr grips.

Three .357 Magnums for silhouetting: Top, 8-inch Colt Python with BearHug stocks; middle, 10-inch Dan Wesson heavy barrel with Pachmayr grips; bottom, 8-3/8-inch Smith & Wesson Model 27 with BearHug stocks.

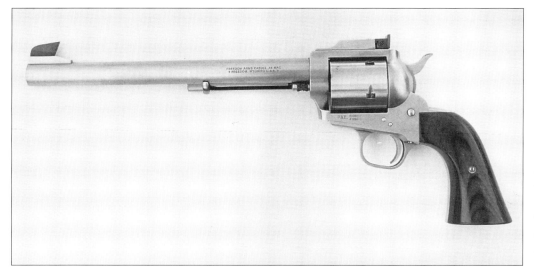

Freedom Arms Silhouette Sixgun with 10-1/2-inch barrel, special silhouette sights, factory stocks, and .44 Magnum chambering.

The 10-1/2-inch .375 SuperMag by Seville was an excellent sixgun for silhouetting.

Silhouetting is long-range shooting. The closest target is at 50 meters, about 55 yards, with other targets at 110, 165, and 225 yards. All targets are relatively small which is mind boggling to those who consider a sixgun a close-range weapon at best. Silhouetting has proven exactly what sixguns are capable of doing and, more importantly, to the silhouetter who is paying attention, what they are not capable of performing.

Silhouetting requires, as all shooting sports, that complete attention to sight alignment and trigger squeeze are carefully adhered to. This transfers positively to the hunting field. Silhouetting does not transfer positively to a hunting situation for that shooter who equates knocking down steel rams at 225 yards with doing the same thing in the game fields.

A bad hit in silhouetting usually results in the same reward as a good hit. The target goes down. I have

taken rams with horn hits, rear-end hits, leg hits, foot hits, some have even gone down that would still be standing if they were ewes. All of this is perfectly acceptable in silhouetting. It is not acceptable in hunting. We must not confuse the two sports. When the target is a live animal instead of steel, only those shots should be taken that ensure a quick, clean kill. To do otherwise is poor sportsmanship of the highest degree.

Silhouetting has had a tremendous effect on handgunning in general and sixgunning in particular. Without the advent of this popular sport in the 1970s, we would not have seen the tremendous advance in handguns and handgun sights we have experienced over the past two decades. It is now being challenged by the new kid on the block because sixgunners are flocking to the new game in town, Cowboy Action Shooting.

CHAPTER 12

COWBOY ACTION SHOOTING

Three men have, at various times in my life, been my heroes. None were born in the West, but all were real cowboys and left their marks on history in different ways: one in politics, one in the movies, and one in the world of sixgunning. First and foremost there was Theodore Roosevelt. Fortunately I had a most understanding teacher; while others in my ninth grade class were doing traditional book reports, mine was on *Hunting Trips of A Ranchman*. Although he was a New Yorker, TR proved he could survive in the Dakota Badlands in the 1880s. He went on to become the first president elected in the twentieth century and oh how we need someone cut from his cloth today!

Then there was The Duke, John Wayne. I have seen every one of his Western movies many times over. A comparison of *True Grit* with what is playing today shows just how far we have fallen. When he was once asked what he did he replied "I make Westerns." They were Westerns we could enjoy and never be embarrassed to take our families to see.

Finally, there was Elmer Keith. The Grand Old Master of Sixgunning. No one has ever caught the imagination of shooters as Keith did. The sixgun was his everyday tool from his days as bronc buster through his packing and guiding days to the decades he spent as the Dean of Gunwriters.

No, none of these men were born in the West. Roosevelt was from New York, The Duke from Iowa, and Keith was born in Missouri. They did, however have the cowboy spirit and all were true cowboys of one sort or another. Because of them, my heroes have always been cowboys. It was meant to be.

For all of us who grew up as the last generation to really have fun being kids, the early days of TV or the Saturday Afternoon Matinee at the local theater meant one thing—cowboys. My remembrance of my first trip to the movies conjures up the image of one

of my first heroes. There, bigger than life on the screen of the West theater, was John Wayne as gunfighter Quirt Evans in *The Angel and The Badman*. For weeks after that my cousin and I argued over who would be Quirt as we acted out our fantasies.

A few years later I can well remember coming out of the theater vowing that I would be just like the new hero I encountered. The most decorated hero of World War II was now a cowboy star and I would be just like Audie Murphy. Unfortunately for all those awaiting a new cowboy star, I was blessed with a physique more like Andy Devine than Audie Murphy.

St. Paul said "When I was a child I spoke as a child but when I became a man I put away childish things." For most of us, this is a given. We have to put our childhood behind us and go on to less pleasant duties. But now, thanks to the new sport in town, we can relive our childhood fantasies, do it with great style, and instead of being laughed at, we will be applauded. Applauded by a group of men and women who are doing the same thing, namely acting out their beliefs in the fact that their heroes have always been cowboys.

Most shooting sports require a gun, ammunition, shooting glasses, and ear protectors. The new sport in town requires all of this and much more. For the latest, and fastest growing shooting sport, it is necessary to dress like a real hero, a cowboy. Cowboy Action Shooting is *the* shooting sport of the 1990s. More than just a shooting competition, it literally requires that the participant dress like his or her favorite cowboy or cowgirl hero or even badman if such be your bent.

A few evenings back, after the grandkids were put to bed, my son-in-law and I settled down to watch the classic, and extremely violent, Peckinpaugh Western *The Wild Bunch*. For two and one half hours we watched Deke, Pike, Freddie, Angel, and the Gorch brothers go from bad to worse, until finally a spark of

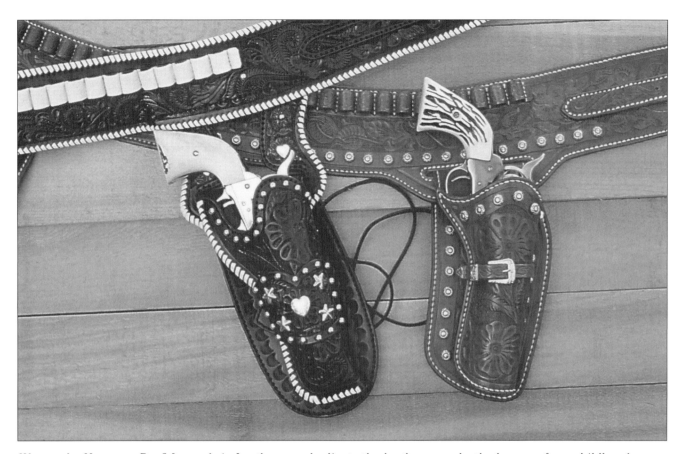

Want to be Hoppy or Roy? Legends in Leather can duplicate the leather worn by the heroes of our childhood.

something ignites and they accomplish the one positive act in their outlaw lives as they rid the Mexican farmers of their slavemasters. For most of us watching the film, enjoying good triumphing is enough. For a group of shooters in California, it was not.

In the 1970s, *The Wild Bunch* started shooting cowboy-style on a regular basis and the idea caught on and started to spread. The result is SASS, the Single Action Shooting Society, which is now an international organization. SASS sponsors monthly shoots all over the country and the world and stages the END OF TRAIL each spring in California. By its own words, SASS's purpose is to "…promulgate rules and procedures to ensure safety and consistency in Cowboy Action matches and seeks to protect its members' Second Amendment rights. SASS members share a common interest in preserving the history of the Old West and competitive shooting." SASS issues numbered badges to members, I'm #7517, and as this is written, badge #11,000 has been issued. SASS also estimates that no less than 50,000 shooters are regularly participating in Cowboy Action Shooting. A second national organization, though on a much smaller scale is NCOWS, the National Congress of Old West Shootists. There are differences in the two, and one

needs to know which set of rules or guidelines each local club operates under before investing a lot of money in guns and clothing.

Cowboy Action Shooting is more than a sport, it is a happening—an old time rendezvous. A step back in time to the period between the Civil War and the turn of the century. A spectacle of authentic costuming and weaponry. To really be involved means a great deal of time and money will be expended on both wardrobe and firearms.

Cowboy Action Shooting requires each participant to adopt a shooting alias. Again, the parameters of choice depend upon the parent organization. SASS is a "Spirit of the Old West" group in that each shooter may officially become someone from out of the nineteenth century West, or a Hollywood Western star, or a character from fiction, or even a made up character appropriate to the spirit of the game. NCOWS is much more narrow in its choice and tries to maintain historical purity. No Hollywood heroes allowed. In either case, your alias is registered and it becomes yours, or rather you become it. Or him. Or her. It is exclusively yours and registered in the national office. With the growing popularity of Cowboy Action Shooting, more and more imagination is required to come up with an

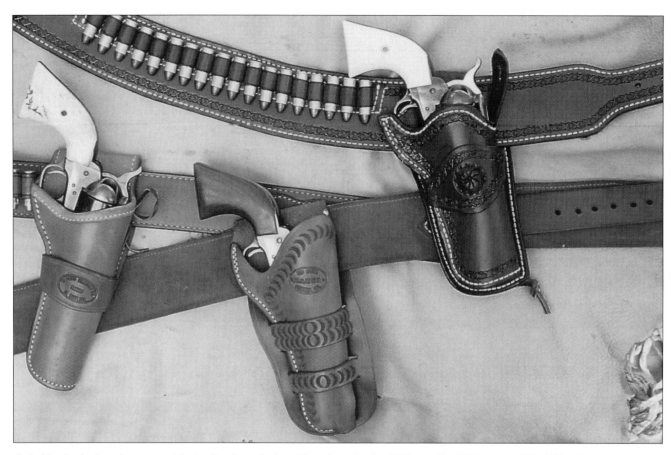

Colt Single Action Armys reside in Cowboy Action Shooting rigs by El Paso, Red River, and Ted Blocker.

Taffin shooting a pair of his favorite sixguns—Colt Single Action .45s with 7-1/2-inch barrels— for Cowboy Action Shooting.

Taffin shooting the Cimarron .44-40 with 7-1/2-inch barrel.

alias. You can bet Wyatt, Wild Bill, Roy, Hoppy, and Gene are all long gone!

As far as I know, there are no restrictions with SASS as to whether or not leather worn is out of the Old West or out of Hollywood; NCOWS bans drop loop holsters. SASS allows all single action sixguns; NCOWS bans the Cimarron New Thunderer with its Colt Lightning-style grip frame as being "un-authentic." NCOWS, however, allows the Ruger Vaquero, a fine shooting, feeling, and looking single action sixgun, but in no stretch of the imagination is it authentic, nor is it a replica of an Old West sixgun. Again, check with your local club before investing in equipment.

What, then, is Cowboy Action Shooting? There are rules that are mostly guidelines, however there is no set course of fire. Unlike IHMSA silhouetting, one may shoot Cowboy Action matches at a local club every month for a year and never repeat the same course of fire, depending upon the imagination of the club officers. This is what makes it so interesting. One never knows what the course will be until one arrives at the actual shooting area.

Targets may be cardboard or steel. Participants may be seated, standing, or required to move about. The stage of fire may start with the participant in a saddle mounted on a wooden frame or seated at a card table. Sixguns may be in the holster or lying on a table. Targets may be out in the open or in a window or across the table. Sometimes firearms will be loaded before the starting buzzer or each cowboy or cowgirl may be required to load while the clock is running. Reloading may or may not be required during each particular stage. Cowboy Action Shooting is not Fast Draw with blanks, but safe shooting with live ammunition. A fast draw is not allowed for obvious reasons.

Targets are usually fairly close with sixgun and shotgun targets under 25 yards and levergun targets within 50 yards. Targets are also fairly large with a size of 18 x 24 inches recommended and distances encouraged of 20 to 45 feet for sixguns, 25 to 50 feet for shotguns, and 40 to 150 feet for leverguns. One will be amazed at the fact that under the heat of competition, it is actually possible to miss targets. But it happens and it happens often. The emphasis is on speed as well as accuracy; speed of shooting, not of slapping leather. One's score is determined by the time required to complete each stage in addition to any penalties for missed targets.

For minimum participation, each contestant needs a single action sixgun, a lever-action rifle that fires pistol ammunition, and a double barreled or pump

Tony Kojis shooting the "Card Table" stage with Colt Single Action Armys in .357 Magnum.

shotgun of the type available before 1899. Most shooters will add a second sixgun because many stages require two revolvers. A Cowboy Action Shooter also needs a long-range rifle if the local club sponsors this part of cowboy shooting; .45-70s are the most popular in single-shot or levergun persuasion.

Cowboy Action Shooting has had a great effect on clothing available, and most western stores now carry authentic nineteenth century style clothing and boots. Part of the fun of Cowboy Action Shooting is planning the costume. It can be as simple as blue jeans, checkered shirt, boots, and hat or as involved as doing research to garner information as to exactly what was worn during the 1880s and gathering authentic vests, chaps, kerchiefs, gloves, etc.

Imagination also really helps to get into the Spirit of the Game. Targets can be inanimate steel or... The hard cases had been doggin' my trail for days. Now, here they were all lined up and liquored up and ready for a fight. There were five of them and I was alone, but I wouldn't have any choice in the matter. Suddenly it seemed as if they all went for their sixguns at once. My

hand dropped to my side and the Colt came up shooting. I was firing as fast as I could as bullets were flying through the air all around me. Working the hammer with blinding speed, I fired once, twice, three times and saw three men stumble and go down. Blackpowder smoke was everywhere as our shots echoed across the bar room. My fourth shot sounded just as the hombre to my left was fixin' to end my days. Only one to go. My last shot splintered wood from the wall above his head! I reached for the .45 in my shoulder holster as the last man was pulling down on me. I fired... What other shooting sport allows this much travel in a time machine?

Under SASS rules there are four, possibly five, shooting categories. A local club may use some or all of them. At the present time there are no classifications based on skill as there is in silhouetting. One simply takes part in whichever category or categories are desired. Categories are as follows:

FRONTIER BLACKPOWDER: This category allows the participant the choice of using a percussion revolver or a centerfire sixgun using blackpowder

Ken Durham of Rattlesnake Station Shootists is aptly equipped for Cowboy Action Shooting with a pair of stainless ivory-gripped Ruger Vaquero .45s—a 7-1/2 inch on the strong side, and a 5-1/2 inch in the cross-draw holster.

loads. Any authentic or replica single action percussion revolver of .36 caliber, or larger, or centerfire sixgun with fixed sights may be used including the Ruger Vaquero and Ruger Old Army with non-adjustable sights. Leverguns must also use blackpowder loads. The most popular cartridges for this category are .45 Colt and .44-40.

TRADITIONAL: This is the most popular category in Cowboy Action Shooting because it avoids the extra work involved in loading and clean-up with black-powder while still maintaining a true western atmosphere. Fixed-sighted single actions of .32 caliber or larger are required. The true traditionalist will use a sixgun chambered in .45 Colt, .44-40, or .38-40, however, rules allow the use of .357 Magnum, .38 Special, .44 Magnum, and .44 Special although they are not

from the 1860 to 1898 time period. All loads must be held under 1,000 feet per second in handguns and 1,400 feet per second in leverguns. This rule is both for safety and long target life and applies to all categories. All loads must also be assembled with cast bullets only. Jacketed bullets are not allowed in any of the categories whether using sixgun or levergun. Shotguns must use lead shot of #4 size or smaller.

Black Hills, Winchester, and Hornady are now offering Cowboy Action Shooting ammunition with flat-nosed lead bullets that are safe for the tube magazines of lever-action rifles. Black Hills covers all the bases with .45 Colt, .45 Schofield, .44-40, .44 Special, .44 Russian, .38-40, .38 Special, and .357 Magnum; Winchester's old style blue boxes come with .45 Colt, .44-40, .44 Special, and .38 Special; Hornady is now offering both .45 Colt and .44-40 loadings.

MODERN: This category is designed for those many shooters whose single action sixgun is a Ruger Blackhawk with adjustable sights in calibers .32 Magnum, .32-20, .30 Carbine, .357 Magnum, .41 Magnum, .44 Magnum, .38-40, .44-40, or .45 Colt. Both the Super Blackhawk and Bisley may also be used. Load restrictions remain the same.

DUELIST: This is an optional category that requires a traditional single action sixgun with blackpowder or smokeless loads. All shooting must be done one-handed. This category is espoused by those that wrongly believe that all the old time sixgunners used only one hand. I'm sure that sometime after the first sixgun came along, a sixgunner bent on survival learned that two hands were better than one for anything but across the table distances.

PLAINSMAN: This is a second optional category Mountain Man-style that requires two percussion revolvers, a single-shot rifle firing a blackpowder cartridge (a cartridge originally loaded with blackpowder), and a blackpowder shotgun.

Firearms for Cowboy Action Shooting must be the type available before 1899, either in original form or replicas thereof. One state organization, the Texas Historical Shootists Society has recently started a new phase of competition covering the period from 1900 to World War I. This allows the use of the 1917 Colt and Smith & Wesson .45 ACP sixguns with half-moon clips. It also opens up the long-range competition to the 1903 Springfield and 1917 Enfield .30-06 bolt action rifles.

Cowboy Action Shooting requires the use of six-gun, levergun, and shotgun, but it is basically big bore single action shooting. For the first time since the sport of fast draw spread across the country in the 1950s, the Single Action Sixgun is once again in the spotlight. Cowboy Action Shooting is now also the fastest growing competitive shooting sport in the country. What started with a small group of single action shooters in California has now spread across the United States and Canada. Just to keep things interesting and more western, rifle and shotgun shooting have been added to the course of fire, but the major emphasis is on the single action sixgun.

These Rattlesnake Station Shootists, all decked-out for competition, choose three different models of sixguns. Shooter on the left shoots Blackpowder with a Remington cap-n-ball .44 worn crossdraw, while the shootist in the middle opts for Ruger Blackhawk worn strong side for Modern Class, and the shooter on the right goes with a pair of Remington 1875 .45s for use in Traditional Class.

Blackpowder percussion pistols are popular for Cowboy Action Shooting as exemplified by Remington replicas in .36 and .44, Colt 1860 Army .44, and 1861 Navy .36. Leather by author.

Many competitors favor the .44-40 sixgun and rifle combination as illustrated here by Cimarron's 1873 levergun and EMF's Hartford .44-40s with 7-1/2-inch barrel.

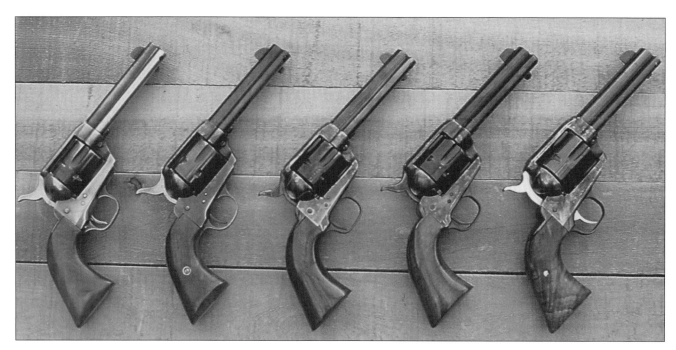

Gunfighter-length sixguns for Cowboy Action Shooting: Colt 4-3/4-inch 44 Special, Great Western 4-3/4-inch .45 Colt, EMF 4-3/4-inch .38-40, Cimarron 4-3/4-inch .44 Special, and Ruger 4-5/8-inch .45 Colt.

Winchester now offers special ammunition for Cowboy Action Shooting in .44 Special, .44-40, .45 Colt, and .38 Special. This Great Western sixgun has stag stocks by Tony Kojis.

For the Cowboy Action Shooter who prefers to use truly authentic sixguns of the time period in the Traditional or Blackpowder Class, the original Colt Single Action is the first choice. The Colt, however, was not the only single action sixgun available on the frontier. Others of note are the Smith & Wesson .45 Schofield and the .44 Russian New Model Number Three as well as Remington's Model 1875 and 1890.

Needless to say, all of the above mentioned single action sixguns, though favorites of the Cowboy Action Shooter who wishes to be as authentic as possible, are quite expensive and demand antique prices. Fortunately, there are sixguns available that are currently being produced which are excellent for Cowboy Action Shooting.

Colt Single Actions are now available through the Colt Custom Shop and in calibers .45 Colt, .44-40, and

.38-40, and barrel lengths of 4-3/4 and 5-1/2 inches. The standard Colt Single Action finish consisting of case-hardened frame with the balance of the gun blued, as well as a full nickel finish is offered. In fact the Colt Single Action Army is the only American made sixgun available today with a nickel finish. All currently produced Colt Single Action Armys are expensive and will run well over $1,000.

The mainstay of the Cowboy Action Shooter is the single action replica. Cimarron offers the three standard barrel lengths of 4-3/4, 5-1/2, and 7-1/2 inches in calibers .45 Colt, .44-40, .44 Special, .38-40, and .357 Magnum. All of these are available finished in standard blue and case coloring, nickel, or the nineteenth century charcoal or fire blue finish. The appropriately named Hartford Model is EMF's top of the line offering to the Cowboy Action Shooter. Like the Cimarron, all standard calibers and barrel lengths are offered. Navy Arms also offers Colt-style replicas but its big new sixgun is the Schofield, the first Smith & Wesson Single Action replica. The Schofield is cataloged with a standard barrel length of 7 inches and in calibers .45 Colt and .44-40. Cut the barrel to 5 inches and it becomes the Wells Fargo Model.

A new company, United States Patent Firearms Co., has recently emerged and also offers replicas of the Colt Single Action Army with a slightly different twist, actually two twists. These Italian made replica single actions are not only beautifully finished in this country, but are also coming out of the original Hartford plant that served as the basis for Colt Single Actions for more than one hundred years. The Company's catalog is straight out of the 1880s, and offers all the custom features that could be had by any Colt purchaser one hundred years ago.

A third replica available to Cowboy Action Shooters is the Remington in Models 1875 and 1890. Originally offered in .44 Remington and .44-40, the replica Remingtons are offered by Cimarron, Dixie Gun Works, EMF, and Navy Arms in .45 Colt and .44-40.

Ruger recognized early the growth of Cowboy Action Shooting and its resulting sixgun is the Vaquero. Basically a Blackhawk that has been sent back to the nineteenth century, the Vaquero features Colt Single Action-style sights, namely a hog wallow-style rear sight and a blade front sight, and a blue finish with a case-colored frame or a full stainless finish. Calibers offered are .45 Colt, .44 Magnum, and .44-40 with barrel lengths of 4-5/8, 5-1/2, or 7-1/2 inches as well as .357 Magnum in barrel lengths of 4-5/8 and 5-1/2 inches.

All of the preceding replica sixguns can be used for blackpowder participation or one may choose to go

Some events require shooting from a sitting position. This event started with shooter Dave Crandall "sleeping" on his saddle, then awakened to shoot his 7-1/2-inch Remington .45 Colt.

Three 7-1/2-inch .45 Colts for Cowboy Action Shooting: Great Western, Colt, and Cimarron Single Actions.

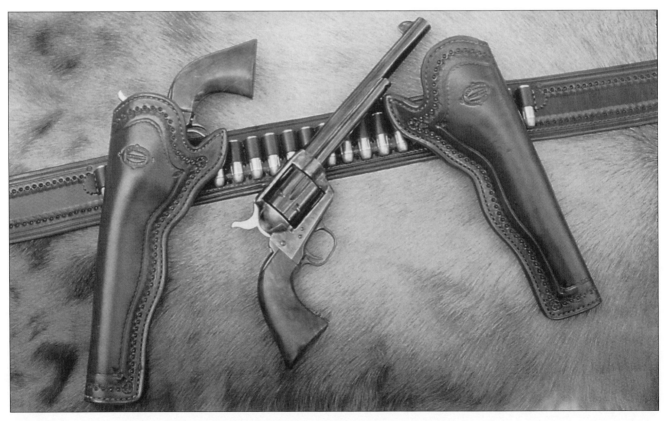

Favorites for silhouetting: A pair of Colt Single Action Army 45s with 7-1/2-inch barrels and one-piece stocks by Tedd Adamovich. Leather is San Pedro's Slim Jim Crossdraw double rig.

back even further than 1870 and choose a cap-n-ball sixgun that requires each chamber to be loaded with powder and ball and then a percussion cap placed on each nipple at the back of the cylinder. Cimarron, Dixie Gunworks, EMF, and Navy Arms all offer complete lines of replica percussion sixguns. The most popular are the .36 caliber 1851 Navy Colt, .44 caliber 1858 Remington, and the .44 caliber Colt Walker, Colt Dragoon, and Colt 1860 Army. The Ruger Old Army, the first "modern" blackpowder revolver, introduced in the early 1970s, is made of easy to care for stainless steel and boasts adjustable sights. Along with the Vaquero, it has now become a second sixgun from Ruger designed specifically for Cowboy Action Shooters as the fixed sighted Old Army.

During the 1870s and 1880s, cap-n-ball sixguns were gradually replaced by the new cartridge firing sixguns. All did not choose to discard their perfectly good percussion revolvers, but instead have them converted to cartridge use. Many Remington and Colt cap-n-balls had their cylinders altered or replaced and the loading lever replaced by an ejector rod, and Colt even offered a 1872 Model which was the 1860 Army designed to fire cartridges. A brand new company, American Frontier Firearms, will be importing metallic cartridge conversion replicas from Italy. The company now has the prototypes of several models and should have guns available in .38 Special, .44 Special, .44-40, and .45 Colt as you read this. These guns are made of modern steels and will be safe with reasonable smokeless powder loads.

Most single action sixguns will come from the factory with stiff hammer springs, heavy trigger pulls, and gritty actions. All interior parts should be thoroughly cleaned to eliminate metal shavings and then lubricated with a high quality gun grease. Colt-type mainsprings can be lightened by placing a leather washer pad on the mainspring screw between the mainspring and the frame. New Model Rugers will have their trigger pull improved by removing one of the dog legs of the trigger return spring from its post on the grip frame.

If you are one of those fortunate enough to own a Prewar Colt Single Action Army (and that particular sixgun needs parts to bring it into perfect shooting shape), Peacemaker Specialists maintains a complete line of both Prewar and Postwar Colt Single Action parts, and provides a complete restoration service.

Cimarron's engraved and stag-gripped 7-1/2-inch .44-40 with its full carved Mexican-style rig is a fancy rig for Cowboy Action Shooting.

Mario Hanel specializes in truly authentic leather for Cowboy Action Shooters. These sixguns are the Cimarron 7-1/2-inch .44-40, the Great Western 5-1/2-inch .45 Colt, the 7-inch Navy Arms .45 Schofield, and the Navy Arms .36 1851 Navy.

For a really smooth shooting and handling single action sixgun, an expert's touch is needed. Recently Ed Janis of Peacemaker Specialists tuned the action and adjusted the sights on a Colt Single Action nickel-plated 4-3/4-inch .44-40. This sixgun came from the factory with the front sight tilted, the action was sluggish, and the mainspring was definitely overly heavy. Now the Colt's performance matches its great looks and feel as it has been tuned and is perfectly ready for Cowboy Action Shooting.

For those who wish to make their trip back in time even more complete, brand new Third Generation Colts can be remarked on barrel and frame to match Colts from the 1870 to 1890 period and even made to look more than one hundred years old by an aging of the finish.

Janis works only on the genuine article, the Colt Single Action Armys, while Bob Munden performs his magic on all single actions. Munden's specialty is tuning the actions of Colt, Great Western, Ruger, and modern replica single action sixguns. Actions are smoothed and springs are replaced on those manufactured by Munden.

When I journeyed to Montana to visit Munden last year, a new in-the-box Ruger Vaquero that needed an expert's touch accompanied me. The action was tuned, and then we went shooting. Within minutes, Munden had the .45 Vaquero shooting right to point of aim. It has proven to be a superbly accurate gun. In fact, with full-house blackpowder loads consisting of a 260 grain lead bullet over 38.5 grains of FFFg Goex blackpowder, this new-old sixgun will place all five shots in one hole at 25 yards.

Anyone with a big bore single action sixgun can find a place in Cowboy Action Shooting, and in all probability find a match taking place within easy driving distance. I fully expect it to continue to grow and become the biggest competitive handgun sport ever.

CHAPTER 13

REPLICA SINGLE ACTION SIXGUNS

By the 1930s, the Colt Single Action was breathing its last gasp. Factory records show that some months the production figures of the grand old sixgun that had been in continuous production since 1873 were in single digits, with not all of these guns leaving the factory, but rather becoming part of inventory. All that remained was for the coffin to be closed, nailed shut, and buried.

As the war storm clouds gathered throughout Europe and the Pacific, it was obvious to all with their eyes open that we would eventually be involved in war on a major scale with all of our peacetime production being changed over to provide war materials. At Colt, this meant suspension of both the double action New Service and the Single Action Army. They would never return. At least all but the die-hard Peacemaker fans knew this to be carved in stone. The days of the big bore Colts were over. Smith had the .357 Magnum and Colt had the 1911 Government Model .45. The modern age had arrived, leaving little room for a relic from the frontier.

Britain was in the War long before we entered in December of 1941. The last major group of Colt Single Actions assembled went across the Atlantic to provide firearms to the disarmed Britons to help them defend their homeland. These Prewar Colt Single Actions are known to collectors as the "Battle of Britain" Single Actions.

It is a common myth that these were "Magnums For the Battle of Britain" with Colt sending .357 Magnums to the British. Factory records show that 163 Colt Single Actions left Hartford in June 1940. Of these, 108 were in .45 Colt chambering, 36 were .38 Specials and only 19 were .357 Magnums. All standard barrel lengths, 4-3/4, 5-1/2, and 7-1/2 inches were represented and 63 of the Single Actions were nickeled. It is obvious from looking at the diverse group of Single Actions that went to Britain, that many had been in the inventory at Colt for several years, even decades. Thirteen of the Colt Single Action sixguns were 7-1/2-inch nickel- plated .38 Specials, hardly what one would think of as a battle pistol. Of these thirteen examples, eleven had been assembled by Colt more than ten years earlier.

After the War, Colt began assembling Single Actions from the leftover parts inventory. These Prewar Colts built after the War comprise a very strange story indeed. More than five hundred Postwar sixguns were put together from Prewar parts, and the last example was not shipped until 1972, or more than fifteen years after the Second Generation of Colt Single Actions emerged.

The Colt Single Action Army was pronounced dead after 1940. It was not to be. In the late 1940s, a strange glow appeared in living rooms in the East and slowly began to spread across the country as TV arrived. To fill the airwaves, the movie archives were dug into and a whole new generation of viewers discovered "B" Westerns and, in some cases, as bad as they were, they would have to be called "C" and "D" Westerns. It made no difference. Americans were in love with the new medium.

Suddenly, shooters and would-be shooters rediscovered the Single Action sixgun and a demand was created for a gun that no longer existed. As The Three Mesquiteers, Tim McCoy, Buck Jones, Hopalong Cassidy, and the like, galloped across the small screen, prices on Prewar Colt Single Actions rose with the demand. It was time for the Single Action to be resurrected. In 1953, Ruger introduced a modern version of the Single Action Army with the Single-Six .22. It was not a Colt, but it was an immediate success.

About the same time, the first replica of the Colt Single Action appeared. As Single-Sixes came forth from Connecticut, Great Western began producing near perfect copies of the Colt Single Action Army

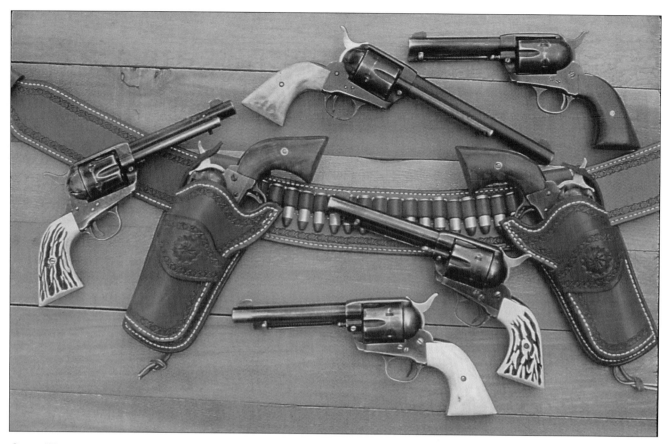

Great Western and Thell Reed double rig by Ted Blocker. Top sixguns are a stag-stocked 7-1/2-inch .38 Special and walnut-gripped 4-3/4-inch .44 Magnum; sixguns in holsters are 4-3/4-inch .44 Special and .45 Colt with walnut stocks; bottom sixgun is 5-1/2-inch .45 Colt with stag stocks. All stocks are by Charles Able except pair of 5-1/2-inch sixguns with original factory imitation stocks.

from its plant in California. The first Great Western Frontier Model emerged in 1954. In January 1955, the first magazine dedicated to guns and aptly titled *Guns* hit the newsstand for the first time. That first issue pictured a pair of .45 Colt Great Westerns on the cover. Both John Wayne and Audie Murphy promoted the new single action as Great Western caught the wave just right with the first big bore single action in fifteen years.

Ruger had modernized the Colt Single Action Army by replacing all the flat springs with unbreakable coils and a frame-mounted firing pin instead of placing the firing pin on the hammer like the original Colt. Great Western made one change in the old Colt: mounting the firing pin in the frame. For years, Christy Gun Works had been converting Colt Single Actions to this style especially with those chambered in the high pressure .357 Magnum. Perhaps Great Western received their inspiration from Christy.

Apart from the frame-mounted firing pin which resulted in a strange looking hammer profile, Great Western had very subtle differences compared to the

Colt such as the angle of the grip frame. They were, however, close enough to the Colt to allow the early advertising to use pictures of actual Colt Single Action Armys. If one watches TV Westerns from the 1950s closely, Great Westerns can be spotted on Single Actions that are cocked revealing the different hammer profile.

Standard Great Westerns carried the same imitation stag grips that were found on the Colts in the holsters of many "B" Western movies stars from the 1930s and 1940s. Genuine stag, pearl, or ivory stocks were available at extra cost. Barrel lengths offered were the standard Colt offerings of 4-3/4, 5-1/2, and 7-1/2 inches as well as the 12-inch Buntline length. Other barrel lengths were offered on a custom basis. The finish was deluxe blue with a case-hardened frame, definitely second-rate when compared to the genuine article as found on a Colt Single Army, offered at extra cost. A satin blue finish, like that found on the Smith & Wesson .357 Highway Patrolman of the same time period, was also offered. Nickeled sixguns were also offered at extra cost. A special

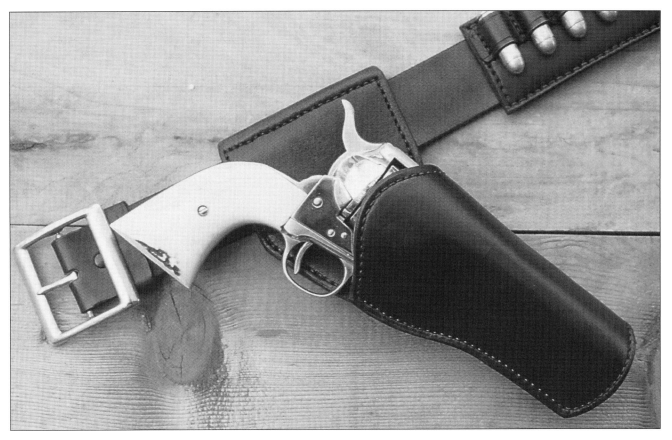

During the 1950s, the hero of the TV Westerns, Bat Masterson, carried a Great Western .45 in a rig like this replica from Legends in Leather.

Fast Draw Model with brass backstrap and trigger-guard and tuned action was available for the Fast Draw shooters of the 1950s.

Great Western ignored the frontier chamberings of .32-20, .38-40, and .44-40 found in the Prewar Colt Single Action Army and instead concentrated on the big bores of the time, .357 Magnum, .44 Special, and .45 Colt as well as .22 LR and .38 Special. Colt has never offered its Single Action Army in .44 Magnum, how-ever, the Great Western Frontier Model was also chambered in .44 Magnum with the same size cylinder and frame as found on the .44 Special and .45 Colt in both Colt and Great Western Single Actions. I have a .44 Magnum Great Western and, although its finish shows it has had much use by its original owner or owners, I will not fire it with full-house .44 Magnums, because I feel much safer using .44 Special loads. Cylinders were made of 4140 steel and Great Western claimed their tests showed they would withstand 100,000 pounds pressure, but I still prefer to walk carefully.

The 4-inch barreled Deputy Model with adjustable sights and full ribbed barrel is a very rare Great West-ern. These were chambered in .22, .38 Special, .357,

and .44 Special. Elmer Keith had a 4-3/4-inch .44 Spe-cial Great Western with adjustable sights that he pro-nounced to be an excellent sixgun.

Another rare Great Western is the ".357 Atomic," as they are so marked on the barrel.

They are, however, simply .357 Magnums that were used with a special Great Western hot loading of the .357 Magnum consisting of 16 grains of #2400 under a 158 grain bullet.

Some Great Westerns, especially the early ones, were poorly timed and fitted and others were as good, or better than, the Colt Single Action. I have two Great Westerns, one a .45 Colt and the other in .44 Special, that Hamilton Bowen went through with a critical eye and measuring tools, and confirmed they were extremely well-built single actions.

In the recent past, Great Westerns have normally gone for bargain prices at gun shows and in gun shops. Within the past five years, my .44 Magnum Great Western was picked up for $100 and I pur-chased a 5-1/2-inch .45 Colt and a 7-1/2-inch .38 Spe-cial, both for a total of $250. Apparently, with the coming of Cowboy Action Shooting, the Great West-erns have been rediscovered and prices are rising

Replica single actions from Italy: 7-1/2-inch .44-40, 5-1/2-inch .44 Special, 4-3/4-inch .45 Colt, and 4-inch Pinkerton Model .45 Colt.

Replicas work fine with blackpowder loads: Taffin shoots the 5-1/2-inch Cimarron .45 Colt with full blackpowder loads.

rapidly. I have fired Great Westerns extensively in calibers .38 Special, .357 Atomic, .44 Special, and .45 Colt. All proved to be excellent shooters. If you find one that is tight, well-timed, and at a good price, my advice is simply Buy It!

The popularity of the Ruger and Great Western Single Actions caught the attention of Colt and the Second Generation Colt Single Action was introduced in 1956 in .38 Special and .45 Colt, soon to be followed with chamberings in .357 Magnum, and .44 Special. This, coupled with the new Ruger Blackhawk produced in .357 Magnum in 1955 and .44 Magnum in 1956, was apparently too much for the Great Western and it disappeared in 1962. This, however, was not to be the end of replica single actions.

During the 1950s, replica single actions began to arrive here from Belgium and Italy. The first guns were cap-n-ball sixguns on both the Colt and Remington pattern and replica sixguns could be had in Remington's Model 1858 and Colt's 1860 Army, both in .44 caliber. Both were faithful re-creations of the originals.

When the cartridge firing replica sixguns started to arrive, they were found wanting because they were not nearly as faithful reproductions as the cap-n-ball sixguns. The replica Colt Single Actions from the 1960s, 1970s, and well into the 1980s, carried brass backstraps and triggerguards and poorly executed case-colored frames. Much less expensive than original Colts, they were solid sixguns and many sixgunners began their shooting lives with one of these Italian made Colts. These spaghetti sixguns, as I call

them, filled the screens of the period as most of the Westerns of the time were spaghetti Westerns made in Italy or Spain.

In the early 1970s, Iver Johnson began importing both Cattleman and Buckhorn Single Actions from Italy. The former were standard Colt copies with fixed sights, while the latter had flat-topped frames with adjustable sights. The standard sixguns were in .357 Magnum and .45 Colt with a larger-framed model available in .44 Magnum.

The Italian made sixgun copies of the Colt Single Action Army have been imported under a number of names such as Allen Firearms and Replica Arms. Today, however, the number one importers of replicas of frontier sixguns are Cimarron Firearms, EMF, Navy Arms, and Uberti U.S.A. Most of these sixguns come out of two factories in Italy, Armi San Marco and Uberti. The replicas fall into three categories: copies of the Colt Single Action Army, the 1875 and 1890 Remington Frontier Model, and the Smith & Wesson Schofield.

The early Colt Single Action replicas may have been second-rate copies, but now all that has changed thanks mainly to the efforts of Val Forgett of Navy Arms, Mike Harvey of Cimarron, and Boyd Davis of EMF. All of these men have worked to make authenticity job one. Gone are the brass backstraps and triggerguards. The blue finish is deep and case colors are not only as good as any ever seen on Colt Single Actions, but the hammers are also case-colored just like those found on the original Colts. Grip frames feel like Colts and one-piece-style

Three basic single action replicas available today are represented by these .45 Colts: Cimarron's 7- 1/2-inch Cavalry Model, Navy Arms 7-inch Schofield, Navy Arms 7-1/2-inch Remington 1875, and Cimarron's 5-1/2-inch Remington 1890.

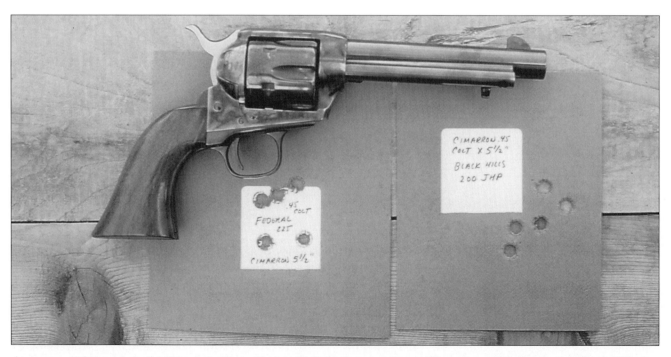

Accuracy of Cimarron's 5-1/2-inch Artillery Model .45 Colt: Groups shot at 25 yards with Federal and Black Hills factory loads.

walnut grips are very well shaped and rounded in the right places with no square blocky feel or high spots. The fit and finish and feel of grips have to be rated as excellent.

Just like the original Colt Single Actions, three standard barrel lengths are offered: 4-3/4, 5-1/2, and 7-1/2 inches. Chamberings are .357 Magnum, .38-40 (.38 WCF), .44-40 (.44 WCF), .44 Special, and .45 Colt. The .45 Colt was the most popular chambering in the original Colt Single Action. It is also the number one favorite with Cowboy Action Shooters which is reflected in the fact that it is the top choice in the replicas.

Replicas are available as Blackpowder Models with a screw in the front of the frame to retain the cylinder pin and a Bullseye ejector rod head, or as a Prewar Model with half-moon ejector rod head and spring-loaded cross pin cylinder latch. Blackpowder Models are not relegated to the exclusive use of blackpowder only. Although they work well with blackpowder or Pyrodex loaded cartridges, they are built of modern steel and are also safe with smokeless powder loads.

Most Italian imports of past years came with stingy front sights, that is, the front sights were too low, which caused the sixgun to shoot high. That has been changed and today's replica single actions will shoot low for most shooters. A sixgun that shoots low can be easily adjusted to its owner's hold, sight picture, and load with a little file work applied to the top of the front sight.

Both Cimarron and EMF offer something just a little different in their Single Actions with the New Thunderer and Pinkerton Model, respectively. Mike Harvey of Cimarron took a long look at the single action grip and changed it by fitting the 1873 Colt-style single action triggerguard with a backstrap that is a deadringer for the 1877 Colt .38 Lightning or .41 Thunderer double actions.

The New Thunderer grip frame starts out as a round butt, but as it curves up, a pronounced double action-style hump is encountered. It looks strange at first, but it is highly functional in controlling standard .45 Colt loads in the short barreled New Thunderer. Instead of the rolling-in-the-hand feeling afforded by the standard single action grip, the New Thunderer feels more like a double action grip and the sixgun does not twist or roll in the hand.

Originally, the New Thunderer was dubbed the Peacekeeper, a name I felt was really apropos. There was, however, a great deal of confusion with customer's ordering Peacekeepers and Peacemakers, so the New Thunderer label was applied to the Peacekeeper. It still remains an easy to conceal and handle big bore single action.

EMF's "Pocket Pistol" Frontier Style, the Pinkerton, mates a Colt-style triggerguard with a rounded backstrap, resulting in the old bird's head shape. This style of grip also fits well in the hand and reduces felt recoil on .44 Special and .45 Colt loads.

Both EMF and Cimarron also offer short barreled 3-1/2- and 4-inch single action sixguns with or without ejector rod housings. Originally offered by Colt without ejector rod housings, they have often been called Sheriff's Models. No lawman with any sense of survival would carry a sixgun that could not have its empties immediately removed. The ejectorless models were more appropriately named the Storekeeper's Model.

Cimarron's New Thunderer .45 in the middle blends the triggerguard of the 1873 Colt Single Action (top) with the backstrap of the 1877 Colt Lightning (bottom).

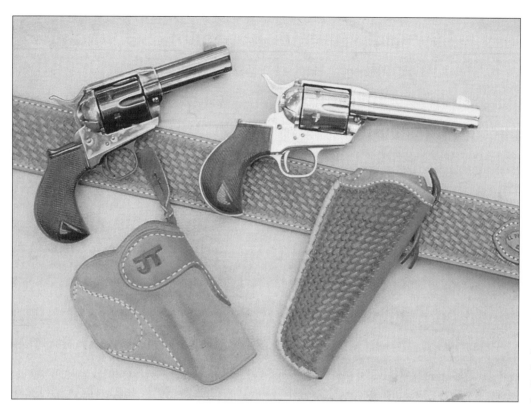

Cimarron's New Thunderer is available with either a 3-1/2- or 4-3/4-inch barrel and in blue case color of nickel finish. Leather inscribed JT is by Thad Rybka, and basket weave belt and holster are by El Paso.

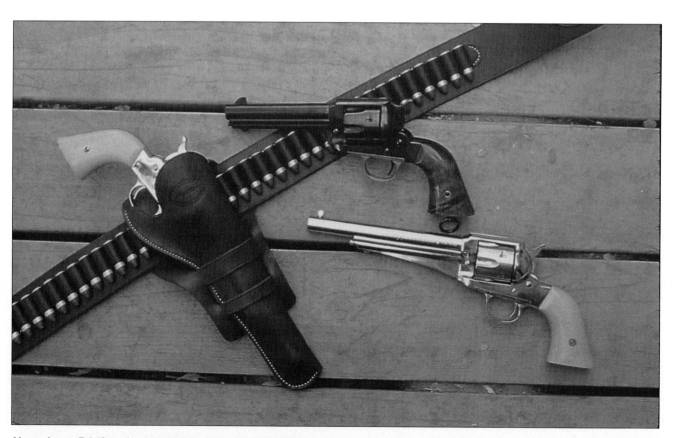

Navy Arms 7-1/2-inch nickel-plated Remington 1875s with ivory micarta stocks by Charles Able, and Cimarron's 5-1/2-inch Remington 1890 .45 Colt with Tombstone leather.

The first replica Smith & Wesson—Navy Arms 7-inch .45 Colt Schofield.

This beautiful Colt Single Action replica is a 4-3/4-inch .44-40 by United States Patent Firearms Co. and has one-piece walnut stocks, and a blue finish with case-colored hammer and main frame.

The modern replicas, especially with ejector rod housings are quite attractive sixguns and balance well for quick handling.

The Colt Single Action was not the only sixgun on the frontier. Although Remington did not produce anywhere near the number of that produced by Colt, it did provide both .45 and .44 caliber sixguns for the nineteenth century sixgunner. At first glance, the Remington Single Action looks a lot like a Colt, but there are several differences. The grip frame of the Remington is part of the main frame, resulting in a more solid and possibly stronger sixgun. The triggerguard is separate from the main frame and does not form part of the front grip strap as on the Colt. The Remington achieves its most distinctive appearance from a web under the barrel which runs from the end of ejector housing to the front of the frame. When the 1875 was upgraded to the 1890 Model, this web was streamlined, causing the latter model to have more of a Colt look. For most sixgunners, the Remington Single Action is not quite up to the Colt Single Action as far as feel or balance is concerned. The hammer on the Remington angles differently and has a shorter spur than found on the Colt, and is thus not as easy to reach, while the space behind the triggerguard is also slightly smaller and imparts almost a pinched feel to my hands when compared to a Colt Single Action.

Thanks to Navy Arms' Val Forgett, a Smith & Wesson single action replica now joins the Colt and Remington types. The Model 1875 Schofield is manufactured by Uberti, and is quite faithful to the original Schofield except the cylinder is longer and it is chambered, not for the obsolete .45 Smith & Wesson Schofield, but for the .45 Colt. Starline now offers .45 Schofield brass and Black Hills loads the .45 Schofield for Cowboy Action Shooting so perhaps we will see a Schofield in the future with a cylinder bored for the original offering of the shorter .45, the .45 Smith & Wesson Schofield. Cimarron also has a Schofield in the works that will have the original-sized cylinder and it is scheduled to be offered in both .45 Schofield and .44 Special, perhaps even .44 Russian. Navy Arms Schofields are available in both 5- and 7-inch barrel lengths and in .45 Colt, .44-40 and .44 Special. The 7-inch guns are U.S. Cavalry Models, while the 5-inch guns are cataloged as the Wells Fargo Model. The blued finish of the Schofield is nicely set off with a case-colored triggerguard, hammer, and latching system.

Both the Colt and Remington replicas, like their original ancestors, are loaded and unloaded by placing the hammer on half-cock, opening the loading gate, using the ejector rod to push out the empties, and then placing new cartridges in each chamber, closing the gate, and then for safety, lowering the hammer on an empty chamber. To operate the Schofield, the hammer is

placed on half-cock, the thumb pushes on the barrel catch, the barrel is swung open and down with the off hand, which causes the automatic ejector to eject all cases, and then return to battery. To reload, the new cartridges are placed in the cylinder and the barrel is moved up and latched tightly. If one desires to remove less than a whole cylinder full of cartridges, the barrel is opened just enough to start the ejector upward and the desired cases can be removed. The spent cartridges can be replaced and the action closed with the unfired cartridges still safely in place.

Shooting the Schofield gives quite a different feel than shooting a single action with a Colt-type grip. It is quite pleasant to shoot and balances well with the 7-inch barrel with excellent pointability.

As with all traditional single action sixguns, the Schofield should be carried with only five rounds and the hammer resting on an empty chamber at all times. The half-cock is not a safety and engaging it will allow the cylinder to rotate, possibly bringing a live round under the hammer, instead of having the hammer remain on an empty chamber.

The latest replicas of the Colt Single Action Army are from United States Patent Firearms Company of Hartford, Connecticut. These sixguns, manufactured by Uberti, are finished in this country in the old Colt factory. USPFA sixguns are of the 1870s blackpowder-style with a bullseye ejector rod head and a screw through the front of the frame to secure the cylinder pin. The serial number is found in three places, again in 1870s-style, on the front of the triggerguard behind the front screw, on the bottom of the frame in front of the triggerguard, and also on the butt. All sights are of the V-notch rear and narrow front blade, again like those in the 1870s.

USPFA sixguns are beautifully finished with a deep blue back finish mated up with mouthwatering case colors on the main frame and hammer. A full nickel finish is also available and standard barrel lengths of 4-3/4, 5-1/2, and 7-1/2 inches are offered along with the 12-inch Buntline length and other lengths on a custom basis. In fact, USPFA offers anything that was available in the 1870s and 1880s in terms of finish, engraving, special stocks, and so forth. Calibers offered are .38-40, .44-40, .44 Special, and .45 Colt. The .44 Special is most interesting because it is marked just like the early .44 Special Colt Single Actions with the barrel reading "RUSSIAN AND S&W SPECIAL .44."

It is with a great deal of pleasure that I see the grand revival of interest in single action sixguns. Much of this interest is due to the upgrading of the replicas along with the rise of Cowboy Action Shooting. The replicas shoot as well as, and perhaps even better than, their nineteenth century blackpowder

1920s-style "RUSSIAN AND S&W SPECIAL .44" with 7-1/2-inch barrel from United States Patent Firearms Co. Groups shot with Cowboy Action Shooting factory loads from Black Hills and Winchester.

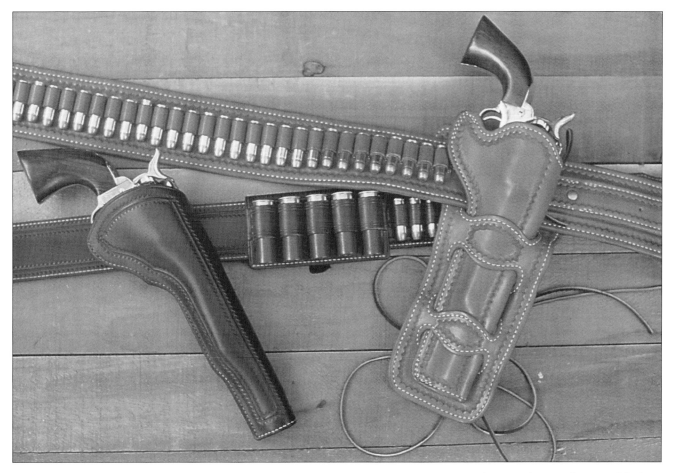

EMF's 7-1/2-inch Hartford Models in Slim Jim holster by Von Ringler and double Mexican loop holster and belt by The Leather Arsenal.

Cimarron's U.S. Cavalry 7-1/2-inch .45 Colt with charcoal blue finish mates up with Cimarron's carved, double loop holster and wide cartridge belt with double row of bullet loops to hold two boxes of cartridges.

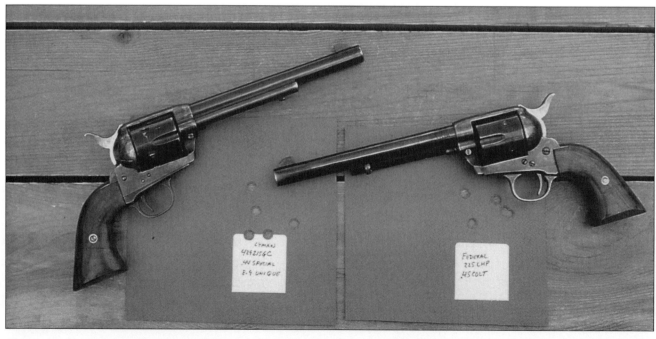

These groups were shot at 25 yards with Great Western's 7-1/2-inch .44 Special (handload) and .45 Colt (Federal factory load). Stocks by Charles Able.

Navy Arms 7-1/2-inch nickel-plated Remington 1875s in .44-40 and .45 Colt. Stocks by Charles Able.

counterparts. Every replica I have tried (several dozen over the past two decades) has been a good shootin' sixgun. I would not push them, that is, I recommend only standard loads be used. Stay within the Cowboy Action Shooting parameters of loads under 1,000 feet per second and the replica single action, be it Colt-, Remington-, or Smith & Wesson-style, should give many years of good service. Along with the newfound interest in single action sixguns both in original and replica form has also come a demand for authentic leather. A number of talented individuals are now offering belts and holsters that are either based upon, or are exact copies of, leather found between 1860 and 1898. Elmer McEvoy of The Leather Arsenal, well- known for inside the pants holsters for semi-automatics, has now branched out and is offering both single and double looped holsters with matching belts. All are border stamped, fully lined, and made of the best leather available.

Von Ringler has built hunting holsters for more than a decade doing some of his best work for John Linebaugh's big sixguns. Now both Mexican loop-style and Slim Jim holsters made of lightweight leather are carried out to perfection for single actions. Big Ed of San Pedro Saddlery also offers excellent loop-style Old West holsters and Slim Jim holsters with matching belts, all

fully lined. I use a pair of San Pedro's crossdraw Slim Jims for two 7-1/2-inch Single Actions in Cowboy Action Shooting.

Mario Hanel is more than a leatherworker. He is an Old West artist and carries out his designs in authentic leather to the smallest detail. All of his designs are 100 percent authentic. They are not only replicas of actual authentic Old West rigs, but are also made of old style lightweight leather. Whether they are made lined or of single weight leather, Mario "antiques" each piece so that it looks like it has been around for a century or more.

While the above mentioned artisans all look to original frontier leather for their inspiration, Jim Lockwood of Legends in Leather takes a different approach. Lockwood duplicates the rigs worn by the "B" Western stars as well as many TV cowboys. Whether the choice is a Roy Rogers' double carved rig, or Wild Bill Elliot's butt-to-the-front Red Ryder double outfit, or the crossdraw belt and holster worn by the dapper Bat Masterson as portrayed by Gene Barry, Legends in Leather can duplicate it exactly.

Very few of us can afford the highly collectible sixguns and leather from the past century, but we can all have access to highly authentic replicas that allow us to enjoy the past and catch the Spirit of the Old West.

CHAPTER 14

CAP-N-BALL SIXGUNS

It is dirty. It is smelly. It fouls sixguns badly. It is a mess to clean. When a better way arrived, it should have been deep-sixed. Instead of disappearing from use, it is more popular than ever. It is blackpowder and it should come with a warning label because it is highly addictive.

Once the hammer is dropped on that first percussion cap, once the sixgunner feels that ever so slight hesitation before the gun fires, once one is surrounded by smoke, and finally, once the nostrils are filled with the smell of sulphur, nothing short of a treatment center can cure the habit. Blackpowder will invade the heart, mind, soul, and spirit with its magical powers. Fire your first round of blackpowder. If you don't feel the ground move from horses hooves as the U.S. Cavalry comes to the rescue, if you don't smell purple sagebrush as the wind moves across the prairie, if you don't see the battle flag of the Ranger Company blowing in the breeze, if you don't hear the plaintive cry of the Indian fighting to protect his way of life, if none of this takes place, you may be in worse shape than thought possible. Take to your bed and call the doctor.

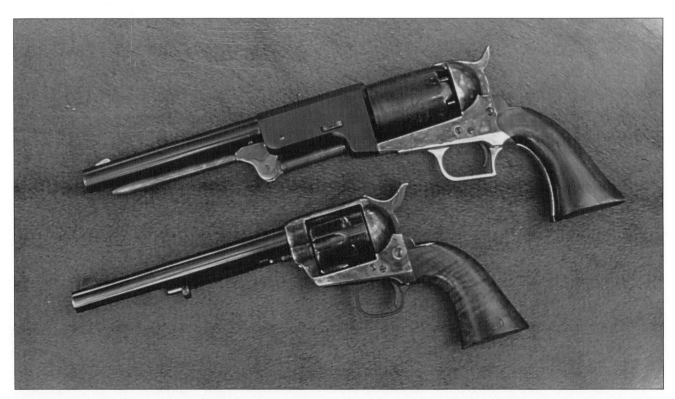

The EMF 1847 Walker .44 dwarfs the Colt Single Action replica, a Cimarron 7-1/2-inch Cavalry .45 Colt.

Blackpowder is definitely not smokeless, as shown by this full charge of FFFg from the 1858 Remington.

Most shooting sports count their active participants in the thousands, yet blackpowder has captured the soul and imagination of millions of shooters. Whether it be with percussion or flintlock rifles, blackpowder cartridge firing buffalo rifles or sixguns, or cap-n-ball sixguns from the middle of the nineteenth century, blackpowder raises a lot of smoke every year. I won't go as far as some who say "smokeless powder is a passing fad," but I will say anyone who is not taking part in shooting blackpowder sixguns, is missing a great deal of pure enjoyment and also missing out on an important part of sixgun history.

The first big bore centerfire sixgun did not arrive on the civilian market until sometime in the early 1870s. This was after the War with Mexico, after the Civil War, well after the Gunfighter period had begun, and long after Jesse James had robbed his first train. James Butler Hickok, Wild Bill, was one of the deadliest of all the gunfighters. No one could face him head on and come out ahead. When he was shot in the back of the head by Jack McCall in Deadwood, South Dakota, in 1876, he was not wearing a pair of the modern cartridge firing single action sixguns. The two sixguns stashed cross-draw-style in his waistband were ivory gripped .36 caliber 1851 Colt Navys.

Hickok, born in 1837, would have arrived at a gun carrying age at just about the time the 1851 Navy was the best fighting sixgun that could be had. It was, in fact, the first sixgun that made a man as dangerous with the gun in his holster as in his hand. Perhaps even more so. The age of the gunfighter arrived with the advent of the easy handling .36 Navy. The Smith & Wesson .44 and Colt Single Action .45 were surely found around the gold fields and card tables of Deadwood, but Hickok held on to his .36 Navys. They had been found tried and true and Hickok saw no reason to trade his cap-n-ball sixguns in for newer cartridge firing revolvers. After shooting a trio of these sixguns extensively, I can understand why.

As a teenager fresh out of high school in 1956, I purchased a mechanically excellent 1860 Colt Army .44 cap-n-ball sixgun with very good original wooden grips. At that time every Prewar sixgun had not yet attained automatic collector status and could be picked up quite reasonably. I knew nothing about percussion pistols or the value of a revolver that was nearly one hundred years old and—this will make you cry—I had it reblued! Then to make matters worse, I traded it for a Ruger .357 Blackhawk that sold for $87.50 at the time. A wise man said, and very rightly so, "We grow too soon old, and too late smart."

Sometime around 1960, I picked up one of the first replica cap-n-ball sixguns, a Navy Arms copy of the Remington 1858 .44 cap-n-ball revolver. Val Forgett of

The first Colt revolvers are represented by this Cimarron 1836 .36 Paterson and the first real fighting handgun, the 1847 Walker .44 from EMF.

Perhaps the best of all the frontier cap-n-ball sixguns was the 1858 .44 Remington as represented by the Navy Arms Deluxe Model.

Navy Arms deserves a lot of credit for the profusion of blackpowder arms and shooters today as he was one of the first to start importing blackpowder firearms for resale in this country. I never really appreciated that early Remington copy, mainly due to the fact that I was not very knowledgeable in the use of blackpowder. Somewhere along the line it was traded for something else. I wish I had both the Remington copy and the original 1860 Colt back. Yes, it really is true, we do grow too soon old and too late smart.

Today's shooters have a great smorgasbord to choose from when it comes to cap-n-ball sixguns. In addition to Ruger's Old Army series, available in both stainless and blued steel and with or without adjustable sights, there is a veritable feast of blackpowder sixguns waiting for the sixgunner, especially both Colt and Remington look-alikes. Colt replicas abound, including the 1836 Paterson, 1847 Walker, 1848 to 1850 First, Second, and Third Dragoons, 1851 Navy, 1860 Army, 1861 Navy, and Colt's last percussion sixgun, the five-shot 1862 New Police. Remingtons were available in several variations before the Civil War. Today, Remington replicas offered are the 1858 Army .44 and the Police Model .36. These sixguns are offered by

Cimarron, EMF, and Navy Arms. In addition, Navy Arms also serves up a few side dishes with the Rogers & Spencer and Griswold & Gunnison .44s and Spiller & Burr .36, and also the very unusual LeMat with a cylinder that holds nine (!) .451 round balls plus a .65 caliber shotgun single shot barrel under the standard barrel—a most formidable weapon indeed.

Many of the above models are also offered in stainless finish and with adjustable target sights. I prefer, however, to stay with the traditional models that are spitting images of the sixguns of the last century. There are also those offered as replicas that never existed as originals. These include long-barreled Buntline types, .44 caliber Navys, 1858 Remingtons, or 1860 Colt Armys with brass frames.

My blackpowder sixgun experience doesn't cover all the models available, but I do have extensive shooting knowledge of replicas of the 1847 Colt Walker .44, the 1850 Colt Third Model Dragoon .44, the 1851 Colt Navy .36, the 1860 Colt Army .44, the 1861 Colt Navy .36, the 1862 Colt New Police .36, and the 1858 Remington .44 and .36 Police, with examples of most models from both EMF and Navy Arms plus the Ruger Old Army in both fixed sight and adjustable

Three main sixguns of the Civil War and beyond: EMF's 1851 .36 Navy, 1858 .44 Remington, and 1860 .44 Army.

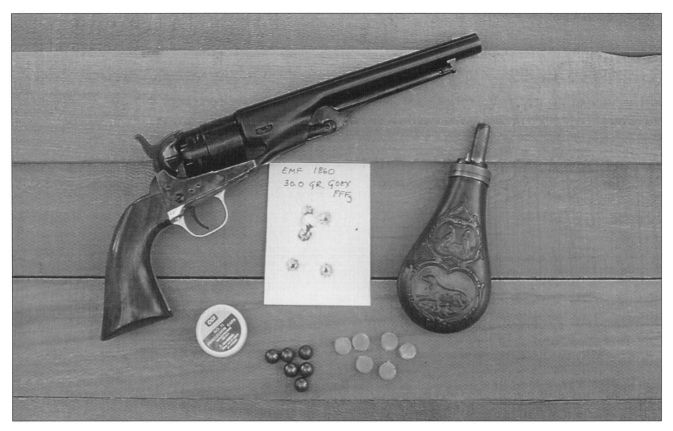

EMF's 1860 Army with all that is needed for accurate shooting: Flask with measuring spout for 30 grains of FFFg, Ox Yoke Wonder Wads, and Speer's .451-inch round ball and #11 percussion caps.

sight version. Every single cap-n-ball sixgun, without exception, will shoot and shoot well when properly managed. By managed, I mean more than just dumping in some powder and a round ball and hoping it will shoot. In blackpowder shooting, hoping will not get you very far at all.

All cap-n-ball sixguns are loaded the same way, that is, the powder charge is placed in the cylinder chamber, a wad is placed over the powder if desired, and an oversized round ball is seated using the built in rammer under the sixgun barrel. Forty-four cap-n-ball sixguns actually use .45 caliber round balls. As the ball is seated in the chamber, two things happen. The oversized ball is swaged down sealing the chamber, and the sides of the ball conform to the chamber resulting in a shape that looks like a cylinder with a hemisphere at each end. This flattened area gives a solid place for the barrel rifling to fit into.

Before any percussion pistol is loaded, and especially after it has been stored in an oiled condition, several percussion caps should be placed on each nipple and fired to clear the charge holes. If this is not done, there is a good chance that the loading of powder and ball will push even more oil into the nipple charge hole and the gun will not fire.

To load, powder is poured from a powder measure into each chamber. For experimenting with several sixguns and loads, I find the new see-through powder flask and adjustable powder measure from Thompson/Center to be invaluable. Clear plastic was never found on the frontier, so once a load is settled upon for extended use, I prefer a traditional brass powder flask with a spout that throws the desired charge. Different sized spouts from 20 grains up in 5 grain increments are available to fit most flasks.

Once the charge has been placed in the chamber, a lubed wad is then pushed into the front of the chamber by hand. These are available from either Ox-Yoke or Thompson Lube. A round ball is then set over the wad, the cylinder rotates under the rammer and the ball is solidly seated, and the powder and wad are compressed in the process. I then leave the rammer in the front of the chamber because it holds everything just right while I place the next powder charge, wad, and bullet.

Speer offers perfectly swaged round lead balls in diameters of .375 inch, .451 inch, .454 inch, and .457 inch. The former has worked well in all .36 caliber sixguns I have used, while the .44 cap-n-balls require experimenting to find the proper diameter round ball.

For example, the Colt 1860s use balls of .451 inch, the Remingtons are at their best with the .454-inch size, and the two Walkers I tried are individuals with one going for the .457-inch ball while the other must have .454-inch diameter balls to prevent damage to the loading lever. Use of a generously oversized round ball can break the relatively fragile "loading press" that the rammer under the sixgun barrel of each cap-n-ball sixgun actually is. It is better not to put undue strain on the loading lever.

Once **all** chambers are loaded, then, and only then, are the percussion caps placed on all nipples with the sixgun pointing safely down range. It is easy to see why as the gun is facing towards the shooter as the powder, wad, and bullet are put in place, and one who enjoys life does not want a loaded gun facing towards oneself with a cap on the nipple.

The use of the lubed wads performs three important functions. They help to compress the powder in less than maximum loads, they provide lubricant for the barrel which in turn reduces fouling, and most importantly, they seal each chamber against a flash traveling to the next chamber setting it off as well as

the chamber under the hammer. It is possible for two or even three chambers to ignite nearly at once with one ball going down the barrel and the others coming from the front of the cylinder alongside the frame. This is caused by a spark that jumps across the front of the cylinder and invades the next chamber. The wad seals the chamber against this possibility.

If one desires to go full-house, using as much powder as possible, there is not enough room left in the chamber for a wad. In this case, the front of each chamber is sealed with grease. I confiscate Crisco from my wife's kitchen and apply it with a cake decorating-type applicator from CVA. With a squirt into each chamber, and then smoothing them off with a finger or a knife blade, the chambers are sealed. This is done to each chamber before the percussion caps are applied to the nipples. Selection of percussion caps is critical to ease of operation with each cap-n-ball sixgun, and again, experimentation is necessary. If the caps are not tight enough, they will fall off as the cylinder is rotated. They must be a press fit on the nipple. I use both Speer #11 and Remington #10 caps and keep both in my shooting box. A fired cap

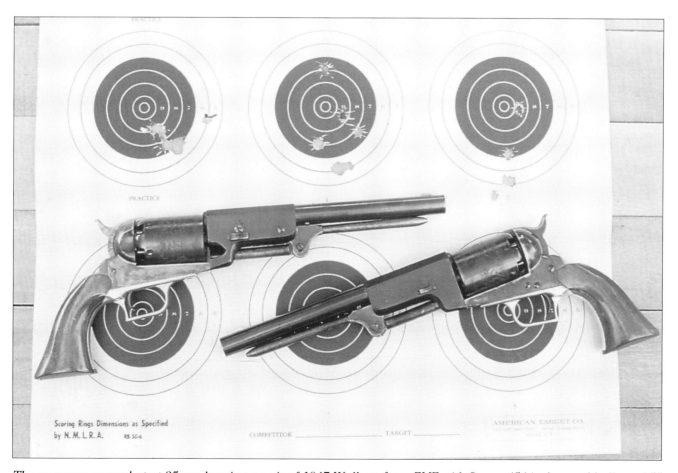

These groups were shot at 25 yards using a pair of 1847 Walkers from EMF with Speer .454-inch round balls and 55 grains of FFFg blackpowder. This load's muzzle velocity is over 1,200 fps.

that is too loose also has the tendency to fall into the action exposed by a cocked hammer. The only malfunctions likely to be encountered with cap-n-ball sixguns is binding caused by caps falling in between hammer and frame. If this occurs, the sixgun can be put out of action and locked up tight making disassembly necessary to remove the fired caps.

Not only do I confiscate Crisco from my wife's kitchen for blackpowder or Pyrodex shooting, but also the cleaning solution that keeps the cap-n-balls shooting. Windex contains ammonia and cuts blackpowder fouling right now. During long shooting sessions I spray a little Windex at the front and back of the cylinder and run a Windex soaked patch down the barrel. This keeps them shooting all day.

Blackpowder is highly corrosive and sixguns must be cleaned immediately after shooting, not several days later. When I am finished shooting a particular sixgun, the cylinder is removed and sprayed front and back with Windex, and a couple of the Windex soaked patches are run through the bore. Then, upon returning home, very little cleaning is necessary to come up with a perfectly clean barrel and cylinder using hot soapy water. To reach all the small areas such as around the hammer face, I use Q-Tips sprayed with Windex or soaked in blackpowder solvent. The sixgun is then allowed to dry and then thoroughly oiled to prevent rust and corrosion. I prefer Outer's Metal Seal because it displaces any water that may have been left behind in the drying process. After every three or four sessions, or before long time storage, every cap-n-ball sixgun should be completely disassembled and the lockwork thoroughly cleaned and oiled.

Replica Remingtons are available both as an 8-inch barreled .44 Army and a 6-1/2-inch barreled .36 Police Model. Unlike Colt replicas, the frame of the Remington is solid with a barrel that is permanently screwed into the frame. Colt cap-n-ball replicas, as the originals, are all open-topped with removable barrels that are held in place by two small pins at the bottom front of the frame and a wedge pin that entered the barrel assembly from the side.

The sighting arrangement on the Remington consists of a rear sight that is a "V" cut through the top of the frame mated up with an easy to see front sight that is shaped much like a rounded and upside down "V."

Remingtons are true sixguns; they are safe to carry fully loaded because both the .44 and .36 caliber models carry notches between cylinder chambers for the hammer to rest within. Recoil is very mild with both the .44 and .36 caliber sixguns. EMF's .44 Remington shoots 2-1/2 to 3-1/2 inches high at 50

feet with groups averaging 2-1/2 inches. Both point of impact and groups size are fine for Cowboy Action Shooting.

The Navy Arms Deluxe Model is especially tuned with a very tight smooth action and also carries a barrel with gain twist rifling for target shooting. It retails for twice as much as the standard model, however, it pays its way as groups average less than 1 inch with this superb model. Using Hodgdon's excellent blackpowder substitute, Pyrodex, and a 35 grain volume blackpowder measure, a Speer .454-inch round ball, sealed with Crisco and ignited by a Remington #10 percussion cap, velocity is 820 feet per second with five shots going into 3/4 inch at 50 feet. There are many modern sixguns that cannot duplicate this performance.

For use in Cowboy Action Shooting, I made my own traditional-type leather for carrying these two .44 Remingtons consisting of a Slim Jim holster to be worn crossdraw on the left side and a double looped Mexican-style holster to be worn on the strong side. Both are carried on a sturdy 2-1/2-inch wide belt.

I found the .36 caliber Remington 1858 I use in Cabela's Fall Catalog for a sale price of only $104! Now that kind of money doesn't buy much these days, however, Cabela's offering is a well-finished, well-timed sixgun that also certainly shoots well enough for Cowboy Action Shooting with groups averaging 2 inches at the Cowboy Action Shooting distance of 50 feet. With 25 grains of Pyrodex by volume, and using Speer's .375 round ball, muzzle velocity is 935 feet per second and five shots will stay well within 2 inches at 50 feet.

Everything mentioned about blackpowder's use and clean-up also applies to Pyrodex, Hodgdon's blackpowder substitute. Pyrodex is not measured by weight, but by volume. If one uses a 30 grain measure for blackpowder, the same measure should be used for Pyrodex. Actual weight of Pyrodex is about 80 percent that of blackpowder, so if Pyrodex is weighed it should be used in quantities that are 80 percent that of blackpowder, weight wise. For all of my blackpowder pistol shooting I use Goex FFFg, "Triple F," or Pyrodex P.

Some blackpowder cap-n-ball sixguns are so tight that they will only operate smoothly with the least fouling powder, which is Pyrodex. EMF's 1858 .44 is one such sixgun; it binds before a cylinder full of blackpowder can be run through it, yet it works fine with Pyrodex. When using both Remington .44's for Cowboy Action Shooting, I simply stay with Pyrodex for both guns.

Colt's first sixgun, actually a five-shooter, was the Paterson. Manufactured in New Jersey, it immediately

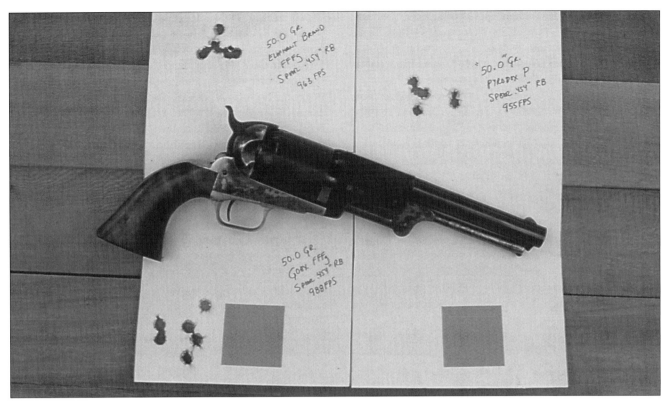

Uberti's .44 Third Model Dragoon is an excellent shooting sixgun with 50 grains of either Goex FFFg (by weight) or Pyrodex (by volume), and Speer's .454-inch round ball as these groups shot at 50 feet attest.

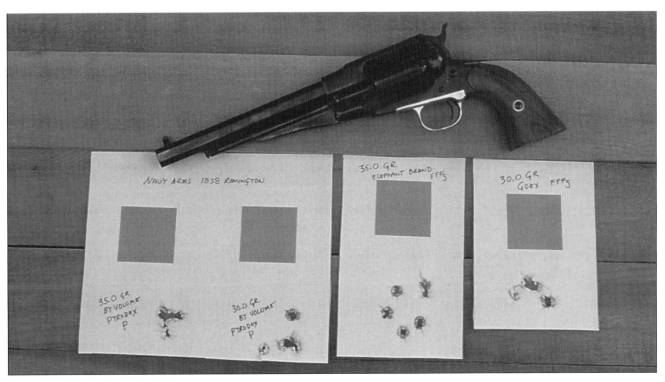

These groups shot at 50 feet are typical of the groups possible with the Navy Arms .44 Remington. These loads used 35 and 30 grains of Pyrodex, and 35 and 30 grains of Goex FFFg with Speer's .454-inch round ball. Orange squares are 2 x 2 inches. How many modern sixguns will shoot this well?

found favor with the Texas Rangers who used the long-barreled Texas Paterson quite effectively. In 1844 Texas Rangers Jack Hays, Sam Walker, and fourteen others all armed with Texas Patersons, fought more than eighty Comanches, and killed thirty-three of them.

Today's Paterson in replica form is available from Navy Arms. It can be had with or without a loading lever and in .36 caliber only. It is a most interesting design and a real part of history, however, due to the lack of a triggerguard and the fragile folding trigger, I look to other cap-n-ball sixguns for Cowboy Action Shooting.

In 1846, Sam Colt and Sam Walker met together with the goal of improving the basic Paterson design. The fragile folding trigger was replaced by a stationary trigger surrounded by a triggerguard, a situation that can only be appreciated if one has fired a sixgun without the triggerguard in place. The cylinder was enlarged to hold six .44 caliber chambers all of which would accept a full 60 grains of blackpowder. This was a fighting sixgun to be sure! Sam Walker considered the sixgun that bore his name "effective as a common rifle at 200 yards."

The Walker is a huge sixgun with a 9-inch barrel weighing more than 4-1/2 pounds. Walkers from EMF or Navy Arms are furnished with one-piece walnut grips, brass backstrap and triggerguard, case coloring on frame, hammer, and loading lever, and with very smooth actions. Walkers seem to do their best with 55 grains of Goex FFFg and a Speer .454 round ball lubed with a Thompson wad for a muzzle velocity of 1,224 feet per second or 60 grains of Pyrodex P lubed with Crisco for 1,109 feet per second. Groups average 2-1/2 inches at 50 feet.

Walkers are so heavy that they are very difficult to use in Cowboy Action Shooting when the course of fire requires a sixgun be fired in both hands or in the weak hand. Replica Walkers are complete in detail, so much so, that they continue the design flaw of the originals in that the loading lever often drops upon recoil. This was to be corrected in Colt's next group of sixguns, the Dragoons.

The Walker was good, but the Dragoon was better. The loading lever latch was improved, the barrel was shortened by 1-1/2 inches, the cylinder by 1/4 inch, and the grip shape improved, all resulting in the 4 pound First Model Dragoon in 1848. One year later, the cylinder locking bolt and slots were changed from oval shape to rectangular shape and the Second Model Dragoon appeared. By 1851, the square-backed triggerguard was dropped in favor of a rounded triggerguard and the Third Model Dragoon had arrived.

All Dragoons are now available in replica form, however, my preference and experience is with the Third Model Dragoon. It is much easier to handle than the Walker, but is about at the limit for both a holster pistol and a one-handed sixgun. Uberti's Third Model Dragoon carries a brass backstrap and triggerguard with a case-colored frame, hammer, and trigger. The one-piece walnut grips are well fitted and comfortably shaped. The action is very smooth and tight. Like the Walker, a pin protrudes from the back of the cylinder between chambers and a hole in the face of the hammer accepts this pin, allowing the hammer to be let down between chambers and the carrying of six shots safely.

The Third Model Dragoon shoots exceptionally well with the best loads being a full 50 grains of Goex FFFg or the same volume of Pyrodex P under a Speer .454 round ball ignited by Speer #11 percussion caps. Both loads shoot well under 2 inches with velocities at 950 to 990 feet per second.

After the Walker and the Dragoons, Colt made a complete turnaround with the advent of the 1851 Navy. Chambered in .36 caliber rather than .44, the Colt Navy was lighter, faster, and slicker handling. This was a real gunfighter's sixgun. For the first time, real speed from leather was possible. It is not unusual to find old military leather for the Navy Colt that had been surgically altered by the use of a sharp knife to remove any leather that interfered with a frontier fast draw.

Both the Armi San Marco 1851 Navy from EMF and its counterpart by Pietta via Navy Arms are 7-1/2-inch octagon-barreled, well-balanced sixguns with one-piece walnut grips, and case coloring on frame, hammer, and loading lever. While the Navy Arms example has a brass backstrap and triggerguard and shotgun-style gold bead front sight, EMF's 1851 has a silver colored backstrap and triggerguard and a front sight that fits into a dovetail sight. Actions are smooth and tight on both examples.

Both guns shoot well with either Goex FFFg or Pyrodex P and the Speer .375 round ball, however nipple sizes are different requiring #10 caps from Remington on one and Speer's #11 percussion caps on the other. These are mildly recoiling weapons with an 86 grain round ball at less than 900 feet per second. This certainly contributed to their popularity on the frontier. Quick to get into action, mild recoil, and good accuracy make them a natural for Cowboy Action Shooting.

Colt had the .44 Dragoon and the 1851 Navy .36—if only the .44 power could be packaged in the 1851 Navy! In 1860, Colt introduced its last .44 caliber cap-n-ball sixgun. Some would call it the finest of all the percussion pistols. Only slightly larger than the 1851 Navy, the Colt 1860 Army .44 carries a Dragoon-sized grip frame on a Navy main frame with a rebated cylin-

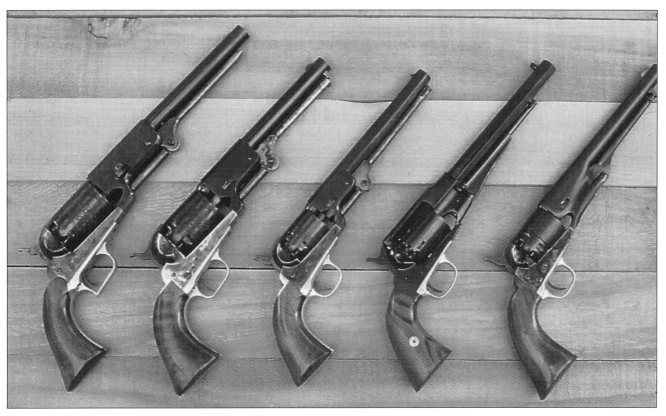

Evolution of cap-n-ball fightin' sixguns: 1847 Colt Walker .44, 1850 .44 Colt Third Model Dragoon, 1851 Colt .36 Navy, 1858 .44 Remington, and 1860 Colt .44 Army.

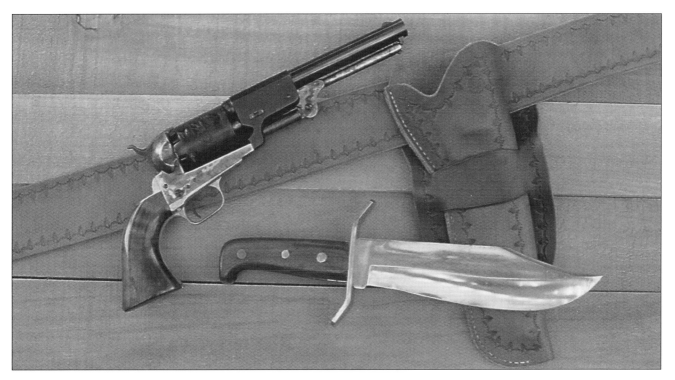

The well-armed man of 1850 could do no better than to carry a .44 Third Model Dragoon and a Bowie knife. Leather by the author.

der larger at the front to be able to hold a full 40 grains of blackpowder under a .44 caliber ball. The barrel length is 8 inches. My highest velocity recorded with the 1860 Army is only 35 feet per second slower than the Dragoon. This is accomplished with 15 grains less powder in a sixgun that weighs a full pound less.

Colt 1860 replicas are available from both EMF and Navy Arms. I have shot both examples extensively and both will group within 2 inches at 50 feet with either Pyrodex or FFFg. Like the originals, both the Navy Arms and EMF 1860s carry one-piece walnut grips, both have blued backstraps with a brass triggerguard on the Navy Arms example and a silver finish on EMF's example, and both sixguns are cut for a shoulder stock, have case-colored frames, loading levers, and hammers, and actions that are smooth and tight.

Colt was to do one final blending of two models before the cap-n-ball era ended. In 1861, the size and caliber of the 1851 Navy was combined with the round barrel and streamlined loading lever of the 1860 Army. The result, the 1861 Navy .36, is certainly one the best looking and easiest handling of all the sixguns to come forth during the cap-n-ball era.

EMF's 1861 carries a brass backstrap and triggerguard, beautifully shaped one-piece walnut grips, case-colored frame, hammer, and loading lever, mated with a smooth action that locks up tight. This final example of cap-n-ball sixguns proved to be the most accurate of all the Colt replicas tested. Whether using Pyrodex P or Goex FFFg, all loads average less than 1-1/4 inches for five shots at 50 feet. It simply doesn't get much better than this even with modern sixguns.

All Colt replicas share the same problem. They shoot high. Anywhere from 2 to 12 inches. This means for serious shooting, the front sight must be replaced with a higher sight or the rear sight lowered or both. Colt's rear sight is a notch cut into the hammer that is brought into play when the gun is at full cock. The notch can be cut deeper and the top of the hammer/rear sight filed to lower impact. All replica sixguns of the Colt pattern I have tested shoot well enough to warrant this step.

During the 1970s, Colt offered replica cap-n-ball sixguns that were assembled and finished in this

The best of the fightin' handguns before the advent of the Colt Single Action Army are represented by Remington 1858 .44s from EMF and Navy Arms and Colt 1860 Army .44s also from EMF and Navy Arms. Leather by the author.

Ruger's easy to clean stainless Old Army is available with either adjustable or fixed sights. Charles Able ivory micarta grips; top gun is fitted with a Super Blackhawk grip frame.

country from Italian parts. When Colt briefly halted the run of Colt Single Actions during this time, the percussion revolvers were also dropped. They are now back and Colt Blackpowder Arms, under special licensing from Colt, is offering the Walker, the Dragoons, the 1851 and 1861 Navy, the 1860 Army, as well as several pocket models. I have not had the opportunity to fire these guns but I have handled them and they are beautifully finished and fitted.

Ruger's Old Army sixguns are not replicas of nineteenth century firearms, but rather a blending of Ruger's improved single action lockwork consisting of all coil springs mated with a traditional look to bring forth what is probably the finest cap-n-ball sixgun ever offered. Since it is not a replica in the strictest sense of the word, I choose to go stainless with this sixgun for ease of cleaning.

Ruger introduced its stainless Old Army in 1975 with a number of most desirable features in addition to a virtually indestructible lockwork. The loading lever is positively locked into place and will not drop down upon firing as happens with some Colt replicas. The loading lever, rammer, and cylinder base pin are an interrelated assembly that can be removed from

the sixgun with the simple turn of a screw in the front of the frame. The Old Army is also a true sixgun in that it can be safely carried fully loaded with six shots as the hammer nose rests in the slot provided between the chambers at the rear of the cylinder. The chambers of the Old Army cylinder provide a very tight bullet-to-chamber seal when .457 inch round balls are used.

Ruger's newest cap-n-ball, the Old Army with fixed sights, will cut one ragged hole at 50 feet using either Pyrodex P or Goex FFFg and round balls. Realizing I am repeating myself, I again say the accuracy with today's cap-n-ball revolvers is excellent and old timers were certainly at no great disadvantage if the originals shot anywhere near as good as the replicas.

Cap-n-ball sixguns have long been popular for informal shooting or used in side events at blackpowder rifle matches. They are real bargains when compared price-wise to cartridge firing sixguns and certainly much less expensive to shoot. As Cowboy Action Shooting continues to spread we will see more and more sixgunners competing with the percussion pistols of the 1850s and 1860s.

CHAPTER 15

TEXAS LONGHORN ARMS— 'RIGHT-HANDED' SIXGUNS

Ever get the feeling that you were standing on hallowed ground? I feel somewhat that way as I load some very special .44 Special rounds. The brass, known as balloon head style, is old. This brass, which dates back to the pre-World Was II era, was so called because the primer pocket stuck up inside the case in these pre-solid head cases. The standard heavy load for the .44 Special from the 1930s through the 1940s prior to the introduction of modern solid brass was known simply as the Keith Load.

Elmer Keith's first .44 Special sixgun was to his way of thinking also the finest. The perfect sixgun. Dubbed the #5, Keith's idea of perfection was a 5-1/2-inch barreled Colt Single Action Army that was a far cry from the standard Colts of the day and was destined to serve as a model for single action gunmakers of the second half of the century.

The best gunsmiths of the time, Croft, Houchins, O'Meara, and Sedgley, all had a part in creating #5. It was named the #5 simply because Croft had showed Keith four prototype single actions that were hand stamped on the grip frame 1, 2, 3, and 4. In the late 1920s, Keith considered the .44 Special the King of Sixgun Cartridges, so naturally the #5 was chambered in what was to remain his favorite cartridge for thirty years. The frame was flat-topped and fitted with adjustable sights, with the front sight being the easy to see Patridge-style. The hammer was the wide Bisley-style, and the grip was made by combining a shortened Bisley backstrap bent to a Single Action angle with a Single Action triggerguard. Combined with the wide hammer, a wide trigger followed the curve of the triggerguard and set back as far as possible in the triggerguard.

A very special touch was the treatment given to the base, or cylinder pin. Anyone who has shot Magnum chambered single actions extensively will relate to chasing base pins that have come loose under recoil. Apparently it was also a problem in the pre-Magnum days of the 1920s because Keith and the gunsmiths on the project took care of the problem. Keith said: "The new type base pin has a large head that is easily grasped to remove the pin, instead of the regular head that one usually had to use the head of a shell on to pull it out. Unless the Single Action is fitted with an extra strong spring in the base-pin catch, the recoil will drive the pin forward, and in some cases tie up the gun. This new catch is a lever that swings into a square cut in the base pin and no amount of firing can loosen the pin. At the same time it is very easy to remove the pin for cleaning. A spring plunger locks the lever."

Being a special sixgun, a real one of a kind, the #5 was fully engraved and fitted with carved ivory stocks. I have seen and handled and fondled and drooled over and dreamt about the #5. It is truly perfection carried out in a sixgun.

A new bullet, which is still known as the Keith bullet, was designed for use in the #5. First made by Ideal, and later by Lyman and known as #429421, the semi-wadcutter Keith bullet has been offered by every mould company and is now held closest to the original by some Lyman #429421 moulds as well as NEI's #260.429 Keith and RCBS with the #44-250 Keith. First loaded with #80 powder, the charge became the well-known 18.5 grains of #2400 when this powder became available in the 1930s. **This charge should not be used with modern solid head brass which has less case capacity.**

Keith offered his improvements on the Colt Single Action Army to Colt seventy years ago. One can only wonder what would have been if Colt had listened. The influence of Keith can be seen in all of the single action sixguns from Ruger over the past forty years. Bill Ruger obviously was a student of Elmer Keith.

Top sixgun is Improved Number Five, engraved and ivory-stocked, to duplicate Elmer Keith's original #5 .44 Special. Bottom sixgun is standard Improved Number Five from Texas Longhorn Arms. Both sixguns are 5-1/2-inch .44 Magnums.

That was then and this is now and now is Texas Longhorn Arms Improved Number Five. This is the six-gun I load the old original Keith .44 Special load for using balloon head brass. Bill Grover is also a student

Close-up detail of cylinder latch on Improved Number Five: Master machinist and gunsmith Keith De Hart reproduced a mirror image of the lever and latch found on Keith's #5.

of Elmer Keith and set out to honor him by building an improved version of his #5. Keith preferred the nomenclature "#5" while Texas Longhorn Arms goes with Number Five. Grover did not have the original sixgun to work with, but did have photos and line drawings and he did manage to keep the flavor of the original sixgun with his added improvements.

In 1964, Keith sent Grover an autographed copy of his monumental work *Sixguns*. Grover was fascinated by the #5SA pictured and described in Keith's book and tried numerous times to duplicate the old gun without success. Grover's company is known for making right-handed single actions; that is, the loading gate and ejector rod are on the left side of Texas Longhorn Arm's Single Actions, which allows right-handed sixgunners to keep the guns in their right hand as it is loaded and unloaded with the left hand. Grover claims that Sam Colt was obviously left-handed or he would not have made his single actions backwards. Because Sam Colt died before the advent of the Colt Single Action Army, it really didn't make any difference if he was left-handed, right-handed, or ambidextrous.

In 1986, at the SHOT Show, Grover met Dan Love of Arthur, Iowa. Love had the detailed pattern for the grip of the #5SA as drawn for him by Keith himself when Love visited Keith in 1971. Love contacted Ted Keith and received numerous black and white photos of the #5SA. During the summer of '86, Grover, using the black & white photos and the patterns from Dan Love, began in earnest to try once again to build the Improved Number Five. In 1987, at the SHOT Show, a number of like-minded individuals gathered at the Texas Longhorn Arms booth to discuss the Improved Number Five. They decided to make it a reality and all gathered at Texas Longhorn Arms after SHOT.

Grover relates: "In two weeks time, we had the complete 'Grover's Improved Number Five' gun made! To start with a block of steel, machining parts, making workable patterns, spring, sights, and screws, and countless other items took all the men's time. We had Bill Oakes from Lancaster, Kentucky, Dan Love from Arthur, Iowa, Bill Konig, a renowned gripmaker from Centerville, Tennessee, and Robert Luna from Pleak, Texas, a very fine h and polisher. I sat down and drew out the plans as to what each would be doing, All work and design was done in the Texas Longhorn Arms factory. To do a pilot model from scratch in two weeks is quite an accomplishment. It took the entire crew to get it out in short order. I machined the frame and cylinder out. As they were being fitted and polished, Glenn Foley of Alice made the barrel. Grip maker, Bill Konig, was working with Dan Love and myself on the newest one-piece type grip that would fit on the Improved Number Five with no screw holes going through either side. The

one-piece look gives the gun a much better appearance. As all this was going on, I turned to Master Machinist and Designer, Keith DeHart for assistance with the base pin and lever latch. I showed DeHart what I wanted, along with the drawings from Dan Love, and the pictures that Ted Keith had sent. I pointed out that we had to make this in reverse as our new right-handed single actions were the opposite of the Colts and the original #5SA is a Colt."

Bill Grover's goal was not to copy the Keith #5SA, but to really improve upon it while keeping the original flavor. The grip straps, grip contour, base pin, and lever latch are all identical to Elmer's original #5SA. I have been fortunate enough to handle both sixguns at the same time. The grip frame feels and looks the same. The lever latch, other than being a mirror image on the Improved Number Five, is identical.

Is Grover's Improved Number Five really an improvement over Keith's #5? I do believe even Keith would say so. The flat springs of the Colt Single Action are gone and replaced with a lockwork consisting of all music wire coil springs. A round triggerguard like that found on the Prewar Colts is used and the trigger itself is rounded like a shotgun trigger and sets back in the uttermost rear of the triggerguard, moving only very slightly when the gun is cocked.

The checkered hammer spur is low and wide which makes it easy to reach with plenty of room in front of the checkering so the thumb can roll with the hammer as it is cocked. This allows for fast and easy cocking both from the leather and when deliberately shooting at targets or game.

Because the loading gate and ejector rod are on the left side, a right-handed shooter can load, shoot, empty, and reload without ever taking the gun out of the right hand. As a single action sixgunner of forty years, I always place a traditional single action sixgun in my left hand, open the loading gate with my right thumb, rotate the cylinder with my left hand, remove empties, and shove in loaded rounds with my right hand. With the Improved Number Five, once the routine is learned, the sixgun stays in the right hand, the right thumb opens the loading gate and the left hand is used to remove empties and replace them with loaded rounds.

The front sight on the Improved Number Five is a flat black post and is mated with a rear sight that is fully adjustable and of the old Micro-style with the rounded front found on the early flat-top Ruger Single Actions. The top strap is a heavy, wide flat-top-style also. The firing pin is of the rebounding style, frame mounted rather than on the hammer itself to better handle heavy loads.

These groups were shot at 25 yards with Texas Longhorn Arms 5-1/2-inch .44 Magnum Improved Number Five and Keith's standard load of 250 grain Lyman #429421 bullet over 22 grains of #2400.

The entire Improved Number Five is made of #4140 Certified Aircraft Steel. The cylinder is double heat-treated to ensure strength, and both the cylinder and the frame are larger and stronger than the original #5SA. Keith chose the best cartridge for his #5SA, the .44 Special. The Improved Number Five is chambered for Keith's favorite cartridge from 1956 to his disabling stroke in 1981, the .44 Magnum.

The first Improved Number Five was serial numbered K-1. The "K" of course stands for Keith and my Number Five is appropriately numbered K-44. Although the Improved Number Five is larger than its predecessor it does not feel either too large or heavy at 44 ounces; the balance is perfect. The first time I ever shot a Texas Longhorn Arms Number Five, I was totally impressed. Not only did it feel right and look great with its highly polished deep blue black finish, the first five shots got my attention real fast. Yes, this sixgun is a five-shooter and, as with all Colt Single Action Armys and Old Model Ruger Single Actions, should be carried with an empty chamber under the hammer. Five rounds of 250 grain hard cast Keith bullets over 20 grains of #2400 in Winchester's .44 Magnum brass, a load in the 1,200 to 1,300 feet per second category, shot into less than 1 inch at 25 yards.

When holding the Improved Number Five, I certainly conjure up spirits of the past and the old time sixgunners who preceded me. Keith was definitely right. The grip on the Number Five, either original or Improved, is a perfect single action grip. Colt's standard grip is per-

fect for standard loads, Keith took us to the level for Magnum-type loads, and the Freedom Arms grip frame with much the same feel is the final development for .454-type loads. Move into the area of John Linebaugh's wildcats, the .475 and .500 and the Ruger Bisley, a modification of Keith's original #5 grip becomes the solution for heavy recoil.

The Number Five grip is quite small (its size is the same as a standard Colt Single Action grip) and my little finger curls under the butt. One might feel it is inadequate for heavy loads, but I have used it with 250 grain bullets at 1,500 feet per second plus and 300 grain bullets at 1,300 feet per second plus and it works fine.

The Improved Number Five is an excellent handlin' and shootin' sixgun. My standard for a great sixgun is one that with at least one selected load gets right into the "five-shots-at-twenty-five-yards in-one-inch" category. The Number Five does it with both handloads and factory loads and with jacketed bullets as well as cast bullets. Particularly accurate loads are Hornady's 240 XTP over 25 grains of WW296 at 1,543 feet per second, H&G's Keith bullet over 10 grains of AA#2 at 1,226 feet per second, 10.5 grains of Herco at 1,132 feet per second, and 12 grains of HS-6 for 1,041 feet per second. My workin' load of 8.5 grains of Unique with the 240 Bull-X bullet is the second most accurate load in the Number Five with five shots in 1-1/8 inches at 25 yards. It just doesn't get much better than this.

The above mentioned load of the Bull-X 240 semi-wadcutter over 8.5 grains of Unique is my .44 Magnum "workin' load" because it does about 95 percent of what I want a sixgun to do. The same bullet is used over 7.5 grains of Unique in .44 Special sixguns as an every day load. It isn't necessary to always run my thirty year old El Dorado Cadillac with its 500 cubic inch engine at full throttle nor is it necessary to do the same with big bore sixguns. In fact, some of my greatest pleasures experienced with both are when I am just amblin' along.

Texas Longhorn Arms Improved Number Five is a limited edition; however, variations on the standard item are already being offered. One such sixgun is the Express Model with a standard rear sight for 25 yard shooting flanked by folding leafs for 100 and 200 yard shooting—great idea! The Express is made of 17-4 stainless, the front sight is on a barrel band in front of the ejector rod housing, the cylinder latch is a duplicate of the Number Five's, and the grip frame can be of the Border Special or West Texas Flat-Top Target-style.

In addition to the Improved Number Five, Texas Longhorn Arms is offering right-handed Single Actions in three other models: The West Texas Flat-Top Target, which just as the name implies is a target-sighted single action sixgun; The South Texas Army, a fixed sighted Single Action which looks quite a bit like a mirror image of a standard Colt SA; and The Texas Border Special which is a 4-inch- barreled "Sheriff's Model"-style sixgun.

The Improved Number Five has the ingenious locking arrangement of the original #5 for the cylinder base pin. Each of Texas Longhorn Arms' other sixguns are fitted with a large base pin, something custom gunsmiths have done for years on Colt SAs, plus, the pin is held in place with a screw at the front of the frame rather than the spring loaded "modern" setup which fails so often with heavy loads.

For better handling, the grip straps on The West Texas Flat-Top Target and The South Texas Army have been extended by 3/16 inch, allowing more room for the little finger. This doesn't sound like much difference, but it is enough that all four of my fingers will fit the grip rather than the little finger curling under the butt. Each Texas Longhorn Arms sixgun is fitted with a low wide hammer, deep cut in front of the spur to allow for ease of cocking with no need to change the grip when cocking the hammer.

All Texas Longhorn Arms cylinders completely fill the cylinder window in the main frame. Tolerances are kept very close with barrel/cylinder gaps held at .0015 to .002 inch, and a blending of modern technology with tradition can be seen in the serial numbers which are all hand stamped with original-style Colt stamps.

Texas Longhorn Arms's Border Special is a 4-inch, round-butted sixgun chambered in .44 Special, .45 Colt, and .44 Magnum. Shooting a .44 Magnum in a short barreled, 38-1/2-ounce sixgun is normally not a very pleas-

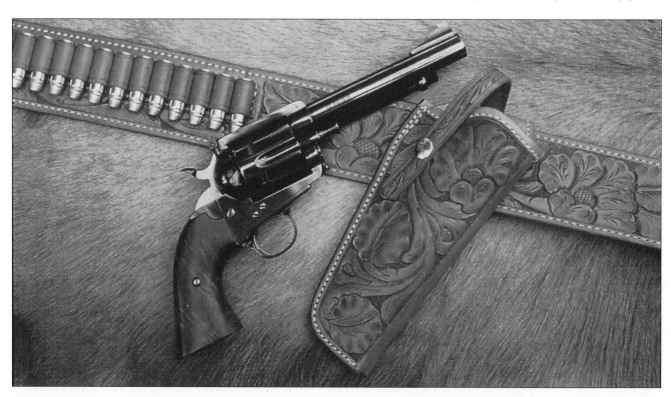

Texas Longhorn Arms Improved Number Five 5-1/2-inch .44 Magnum and El Paso Tom Threepersons flower-carved holster and belt.

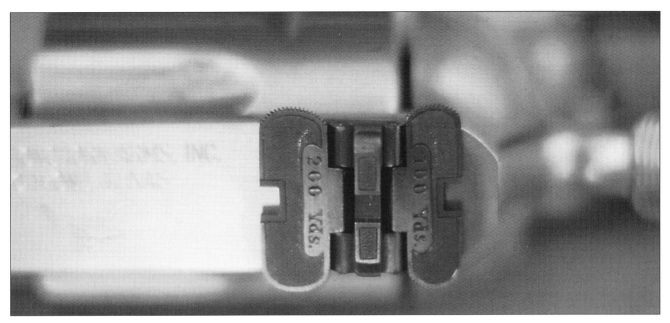

Detail of rear sight on Express Model: The center blade is for 100 yard shooting, and the folding blades are for 200 and 300 yards.

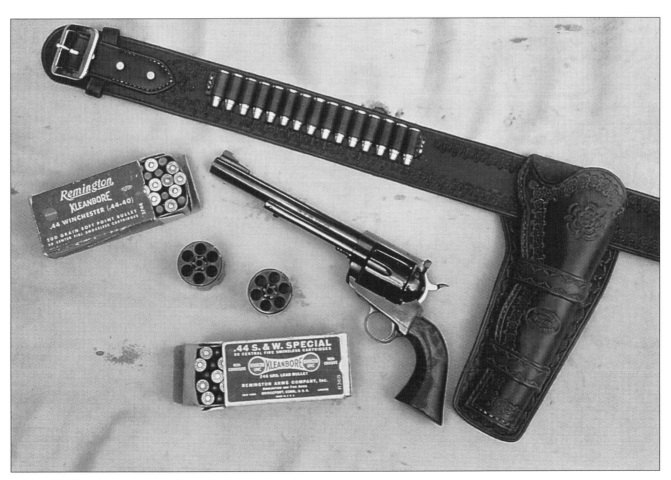

A modern classic: The Texas Longhorn Arms 7-1/2-inch West Texas Flat-Top Target with three cylinders in .44 Magnum, .44 Special, and .44-40 with Bull-X's Chaparral rig.

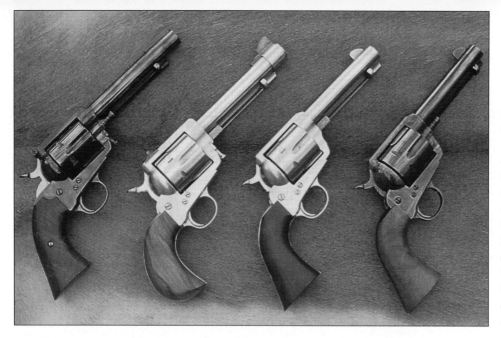

Blue steel and stainless steel by Texas Longhorn Arms: The 5-1/2-inch .44 Magnum Improved Number Five with walnut stocks, the 5-1/2-inch stainless Express Model Number Five with express sights, Border Special grip frame and maple stocks, the Stainless South Texas Army 4-3/4-inch .45 Colt with ebony stocks, and the blued South Texas Army 4-3/4-inch .44 Special, mesquite stocks.

ant experience. I prepared myself for an unpleasant experience, and as the little sixgun went off, I was pleasantly surprised to experience no pain. The little Border Special, even with full-house .44 Magnum loads, does not punish the shooter. The reason for the lack of felt recoil is the fact that The Texas Border Special is fitted with a grip style known as bird's head. The original design may be more than one hundred years old, but Grover's modification certainly takes the sting out of .44 Magnum loads.

This is a traditional defensive single action sixgun that packs very easily in a hip holster, shoulder holster, or waist band. The low wide hammer makes cocking for the first shot very fast and is easy to get to for repeat shots. Winchester's medium velocity .44 Magnum loading with a 240 grain bullet at 950 feet per second is ideal for this little big bore. Speer's new Gold Dot .44 Special load has an 85 percent effective rating as a one-shot stopper in defensive situations, and would be a good choice for use in the Border Special.

Only 1,000 Border Specials will be made and, as this is written, the serial numbers are in the 8XX range. Border Specials are offered by Texas Longhorn Arms in full blue or blued with case-colored frame and with or without adjustable sights.

Texas Longhorn Arms third right-handed single action offering is the South Texas Army, which is basically Grover's answer to the standard Colt Single Action Army. Only 1,000 of these will be made in either blue or blue with case-colored frame, but they will be carried on with the stainless version that Texas Longhorn Arms calls Grover's Northpaw. Both versions of the South Texas Army have a wide front sight matched with a square rear sight, a combination that is much easier to pick up than the original narrow notch and front sight found on a Colt. Call it a fixed target sight. The base pin head is much larger than that found on a Colt or Ruger and is also knurled for ease of removal.

Although Grover's other sixguns are limited to a production run of 1,000 units, the Northpaw is a standard catalog item. It is made completely of 17-4 heat-treated stainless steel. This is one fine looking, fine feeling sixgun.

My favorite of all of Grover's sixguns is the West Texas Flat-Top Target. A few years back Grover let me borrow his personal West Texas Flat-Top Target chambered in .44 Special. I simply cannot pass up a good .44 Special. This was more than good—it was a great .44 Special. It took some convincing, I may have even gone so far as to tell Grover that he wasn't going to get it back, so it would be wise on his part to set a price.

Bill Grover is a master gunmaker and I do believe his Flat-Top Target is his finest effort. I do believe if I am pressed to the wall that I would have to say that 7-1/2-inch single actions are my favorite sixguns. Begin with the Colt Single Action Army, to the original Ruger .44 Blackhawk, to the Colt New Frontier, to the Ruger Bisley, to the Freedom Arms Casull, all with a .44 or .45 hole in the barrel whose length is 7-1/2 inches and one just may have the perfect sixgun. To that list we now add the West Texas Flat-Top Target. To add to its versatility as a big bore sixgun, the Flat-Top Target was returned to Texas Longhorn Arms and fitted with two more cylinders, one in .44 Magnum and the other in .44-40.

There are a few .44 Magnum factory loadings available for hunting deer-sized game, but nothing in .44-40 or .44 Special, so it was to the loading bench. For the .44-40, the Speer 225 grain pure lead hollowpoint in a copper cup over 10 grains of Unique was decided upon as a load that could do the job. Muzzle velocity is 1,150 feet per second and five shots group into 1-1/8 inches at 25 yards. For the .44 Special, the new Hornady 200 grain XTP was loaded over 18.5 grains of #2400. This load gives a muzzle velocity of 1,375 and puts five shots into 1-1/4 inches at 25 yards. The Keith .44 Special load,

The West Texas Flat-Top Target from Texas Longhorn Arms, like the Improved Number Five, is a right-handed single action—the ejector rod housing and loading gate are on the left side.

Taffin shooting the 7-1/2-inch Texas Longhorn Arms West Texas Flat-Top Target.

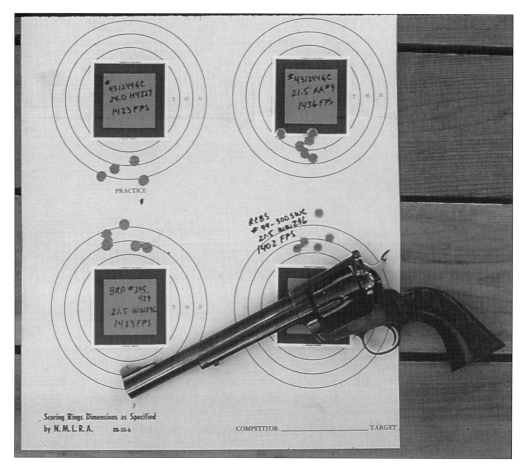

Representative loads fired at 25 yards with cast bullets in the .44 Magnum 7-1/2-inch Texas Longhorn Arms West Texas Flat-Top Target. Top loads use Lyman's 255 grain Thompson gas check #431244GC; bottom, 300 grain bullet loads with BRP's 295 grain gas check and RCBS's #44-300 SWC.

17 grains of #2400 in solid head brass and 250 grain RCBS Keith bullet, does over 1,300 feet per second muzzle velocity and will stay under 1 inch for five shots at 25 yards. These loads are not necessarily recommended for any other sixguns but this one. I found that the .44-40 load and the .44 Magnum were dead on with the rear sight bottomed out and three fourths of a turn up brought the lighter .44 Special bullet to point of aim.

When the Texas Longhorn Arms West Texas Flat-Top Target came back with all three cylinders, Grover also included one of his Texas High Rider Holster systems. The High Rider works with any single action sixgun and is especially handy with 7-1/2-inch barrel lengths. It is worn high either strong side or crossdraw and consists of a holster proper and a belt slide. The holster fits inside the belt slide and locks into place with the bottom end of a loop on the front of the holster that snaps to the belt slide. To remove the holster, simply unsnap and raise the holster out of the belt slide.

Each of the .44 cylinders in the West Texas Flat-Top Target has been used to harvest game. The West Texas Flat-Top Target, as offered by Texas Longhorn Arms with a barrel length of 7-1/2 inches and all steel construction, weighs in at 45 ounces. The grip frame is a longer 3/16 inch Colt Single Action-style and fitted with

one-piece figured walnut stocks that are perfectly shaped for my hand.

The triggerguard is smaller and more rounded than found on most Colt Single Action Armys and, as with all Texas Longhorn Arms sixguns, the shotgun-style trigger sits far back in the rear of the triggerguard. The hammer is wide and checkered and deep enough in the front to allow the thumb to slip naturally when cocking. Sights are fully adjustable with a melted Micro-style set at the rear of the flat-top frame. The rear sight is mated with a Patridge front sight which gives a sharp black sight picture that I prefer for most sixgun applications. The finish is highly polished deep blue black and all metal-to-metal and metal-to-wood fit is excellent. Again, as with all Texas Longhorn Arms single actions, the action and lockwork of the Flat-Top Target consists totally of music wire coil springs. Operation is smooth and positive and the cylinder locks up tight with any of the three cylinders in place.

The Texas Longhorn Arms West Texas Flat-Top Target shoots both .44-40s and .44 Specials in 1 inch or less, and also does the same thing with the .44 Magnum. In fact, the .44 Magnum, loaded with Lyman's #431244GC bullet over 21.5 grains of AA#9 at 1,436 feet per second, outshot both the .44-40 and the .44 Special

The four main models of Texas Longhorn Arms right-handed single actions: blued 7-1/2-inch .44 Special West Texas Flat-Top Target with one-piece walnut stocks; blued 5-1/2-inch .44 Magnum Improved Number Five with walnut stocks, blued and case-colored; 4-3/4-inch .44 Special South Texas Army with one-piece mesquite stocks; blued and case-colored 4-inch .45 Colt Border Special with one-piece walnut stocks.

with five shots in 3/4 inch at 25 yards. If it got any better than this I could not stand it.

As we stand ready to enter the twenty-first century, I must admit that I am not a great fan of the twentieth century, especially the second half. I do believe mankind, in general, would be better off if the calendar had stuck at around 1881. We are, in too many instances, more slave to than master of the great advances in technology.

Two categories that stand out in these strange times are medicine and single action sixguns. Medicine keeps us alive and single action sixguns make living worthwhile. For the first fifty years one could have any single action sixgun as long as it was a Colt. Now the sixgunner faces a veritable candy store of great sixguns. After World War II, Great Western was the first manufacturer to offer big bore single action sixguns. They are long gone, but at least six classes of single action sixguns remain.

The single action fancier can still purchase a Colt Single Action Army that has basically remained unchanged since 1873. Quality replicas abound. In addition to more than a dozen cap-n-ball models, one can also choose from Colt, Remington, and Smith & Wesson copies. Ruger, the greatest producer of single actions of all time, offers the shooter the most for the least money expended with the Blackhawk, Super Blackhawk, Bisley, and Vaquero Models.

For those who wish to have a fine custom single action, determined only by the imagination and the amount of money available to invest, sixgunsmiths such as Hamilton Bowen, David Clements, John Gallagher, Andy Horvath, Milt Morrison, John Linebaugh, and Jim Stroh can take the Ruger Single Action to the height of perfection in everything from an eight-shot .32-20 to a five-shot .500 Linebaugh.

Finally, we come to the manufacturers that offer what are in essence factory-built custom single actions. Freedom Arms and Texas Longhorn Arms both fall into this category. Freedom Arms offers five-shot stainless steel sixguns, first in .454 Casull, but also in .44 Magnum, .357 Magnum, .50AE, and a soon to be unveiled fifth big bore chambering in the Casull revolver. Look for Freedom Arms to also introduce a brand new sixgun.

Unique is a term that is highly misused. An item can be unique. It cannot be most unique or more unique. Or even unique-est. Only unique. With that clearly understood, we come to the single actions of Texas Longhorn Arms. Bill Grover chose to take a different path. His single actions with the loading gate and ejector rod on the left side for use by right-handers are certainly unique. Not only are they different, but they are also examples of the best of the gunmaker's art.

Replica Single Actions. Colt Single Actions. Ruger Blackhawks. Freedom Arms Casulls. Texas Longhorn Arms Right-Handed Single Actions. Maybe the twentieth century isn't so bad after all.

CHAPTER 16

HUNTING WITH SIXGUNS

As I sat on the hillside I could see it was a big buck. Even with my naked eyes I could easily make out his antlers glistening in the sun. It would be a simple matter to take a good rest with a good rifle and a good scope. A good shot with a good flat shooting load could easily take him cleanly. The problem was that I had none of the above.

It was hunting season and I was hunting, but my weapon of choice was not a rifle, or even a long-range single-shot pistol. My shoulder holster contained a sixgun, a .44 Magnum single action sixgun, with iron sights. As such, the buck on the opposite wall of the canyon was at least 400 yards beyond my effective range. He would be safe from me this day, a fact that every sixgun hunter must often accept.

The first sixgun hunter was probably a Texas Ranger who took fresh meat with his new Colt Walker .44 in the late 1840s. As veterans headed home after the War Between the States, those fortunate enough to maintain their sidearms certainly were able to feed them-

Taffin takes a steady rest with the Freedom Arms .454 Casull. Available rest should be used when hunting with sixguns or any handgun.

selves with their Remington and Colt cap-n-ball sixguns. Buffalo, deer, antelope, even grizzly bear, all were taken with Colt and Smith & Wesson Single Actions in .44 Russian, .44-40, and most certainly .45 Colt during the last quarter of the nineteenth century. These men did not deliberately set out to hunt with their sixguns. It was simply a matter of convenience. When the game appeared the tried and true big bore sixgun was at hand, riding on the hip.

Elmer Keith was the number one advocate for hunting with a sixgun from the 1920s through the 1970s. Keith, however, was not a handgun hunter. He was simply a hunter who always had a handgun. As with the men mentioned above, it was a matter of convenience. Keith spent many years packing a sixgun as he said "buckled on as naturally as buckling on my pants." For thirty years he served as a packer, guide, outfitter, and rancher with a sixgun, either a .45 Colt or, more often, a .44 Special on his hip. When he ventured forth with hunting as the sole purpose in mind, he carried a rifle, a big bore rifle.

One of the earliest proponents of handgun hunting was Col. D.B. Wesson of Smith & Wesson. With the advent of the .357 Magnum in 1935, Col. Wesson sallied forth with an 8-3/8-inch .357 Magnum and took all manner of big game, including moose, to promote the new sixgun and cartridge. In the 1950s, Al Goerg, author of *Pioneering Handgun Hunting*, mounted a 1X Weaver scope on a Smith & Wesson .44 Magnum and proceeded to take many species of big game including a beautiful full curl Dall ram.

It is only within the last twenty years that handgun hunting has really come into its own as a viable way of taking big game. Such men as J.D. Jones of SSK Industries and Larry Kelly of Mag-Na-Port have promoted handgun hunting as well as provided the equipment needed to be successful. Jones also founded Handgun Hunters International which publishes a bi-monthly paper, *The Sixgunner*, a most valuable reference for handgun hunters.

All manner of big game, including the big bears of Alaska and the Big Five of Africa (elephant, Cape buffalo, rhino, lion, and leopard) have all been taken quickly and cleanly with a sixgun. Heavy loaded .44 Magnum, .45 Colt, and .454 Casull sixguns in the hands of dedicated sixgunners have proven that anything that walks can be taken with a sixgun just as efficiently as with a rifle.

I would not call the sixgunner handicapped when it comes to a comparison with a rifle hunter, however, there are certain parameters that must be considered. Sixgun hunting is not long-range shooting. The

Taffin takes a solid rest with the Dan Wesson 8-inch .44 Magnum.

A solid rest can be taken by drawing the knees up and placing elbows inside the knees. Taffin shoots the 10-inch .454 Casull.

number one rule is get close and then get closer. How close is close? This varies from hunter to hunter. I prefer to be within 50 yards for using an open-sighted sixgun and 75 yards is my maximum range. In either case, a solid rest is a necessity.

If one is familiar with long-range silhouetting, the above distances may seem conservative, to say the least, because the long-range ram in silhouetting is taken at 225 yards. I shot silhouettes for many years and my favorite competition was with the iron-sighted big bore sixgun. One thing I definitely learned was silhouetting did not transfer positively to hunting. Any shot that takes down the target counts in silhouetting. A leg shot, a gut shot, tail shot, it doesn't make any difference as long as the target falls. This is definitely not true in a hunting situation. I respect every animal I hunt. I will not take a shot that does not reasonably assure me a clean kill.

Silhouetting does not readily transfer to hunting, however, Blackie Sleeva, five-time winner of the Pistol Division of the Buckmasters Tournament, has come up with a course that sharpens the skills of handgun hunters. Sleeva is a dedicated handgun hunter as well as one of the world's best shots with a sixgun. He is also a good friend and it has been my good fortune to be invited to take part in both the First and Second Annual World's Championship Pistol Shoot on the Y.O. Ranch in Texas each of the last

two years. Sleeva's course consists of metal animal silhouettes just like in long-range silhouetting, however, there are various kinds of targets including both big game and varmints set at various distances from close in to 150 yards or so. The distances are unknown and the targets are engaged as one walks through the woods. Varmints count wherever they are hit; big game only counts if the kill zone is hit. This past year, Blackie even came up with a running target of a deer that required a hit in the kill zone to count.

Targets must be found as well as taken. Some allow a rest from a nearby tree; others can only be shot off-hand or kneeling. Some degree of skill is needed to simply locate the targets. This year's course consisted of sixty targets. As I finished, I had forty-four empty cartridge cases which simply means either I did not see sixteen targets or I passed them up to get a better shot as I advanced and then found they were out of my line of sight. One is not allowed to retreat backwards in the course. A most challenging and practical course of fire for handgun hunters.

An excellent way to determine one's maximum range with a sixgun is simply to practice using paper plates as targets. The kill zone on a big game animal is about the size of a paper plate. By shooting at such a target with both a solid rest and off-hand, both with iron sights and with a scope, one easily, and honestly establishes his effective range. Only when the plate can be hit consistently shot after shot, can one establish his or her true clean kill distance. If the plate cannot be hit every time at 50 yards in practice under ideal conditions, do not expect the appearance of game to suddenly change everything. As sixgunners we must, absolutely must, be fair to the animal we are hunting and either be reasonably assured of a clean kill or watch it walk away unharmed. There is no acceptable in-between.

With a scoped sixgun, I feel I can stretch my range out slightly. With a .44 Magnum that means possibly 100 yards, depending upon the animal and conditions. With the .454 Casull, I will go out to 150 yards, again only when conditions are right and I have a solid rest.

Robert Ruark, noted author and African big game hunter, wrote a book entitled *Use Enough Gun*. His advice is certainly appropriate for the sixgun hunter. The best sixguns for hunting are those chambered for the really big bores, with the .44 Magnum being the

bottom choice followed by the .45 Colt in sixguns that will accept heavy loads, the .454 Casull, and the .475 and .500 Linebaughs. There are no other choices available in standard-sized sixguns for really big game, except possibly the Freedom Arms revolver chambered in .50AE.

For deer-sized game, the picture expands bringing in the .41 Magnum, the .44 Special, and the .44-40 with the latter two requiring handloads as there are no factory loadings available suitable for hunting. Finally, there is the .357 Magnum. I have personally taken deer-sized game with factory chamberings using the .357 Magnum in the .353 Casull persuasion, .41 Magnum, .44 Special, .44-40, .44 Magnum, .45 Colt, .454 Casull, and .50AE. With close-range broadside lung shots I see no appreciable difference in any of the above calibers. All will take deer-sized game cleanly, quickly, and efficiently. The picture changes dramatically when really big game is encountered. In this case penetration, deep penetration, is needed and the best choices are the .44 Magnum, .45 Colt, and

Freedom Arms' Bob Baker took this Missouri whitetail while testing the prototype .353 Casull. Four-power scope is mounted on SSK T'SOB mount. Note SSK bipod mounted on the barrel.

This large Texas wild hog fell to Hal Swiggett's .44 handload from the Taurus .44 Magnum with Nikon scope. Range was more than 70 yards.

Texas Longhorn Arms' Bill Grover took this Sika buck on the Y.O. Ranch using his Improved Number Five and Black Hills .44 Magnum load.

.454 Casull, all in proper loadings. Let's take a look at sixguns and loads available in each of the above calibers:

.357 MAGNUM: I will not recommend the .357 Magnum for hunting anything other than small game. If it were all I had I would probably use it, but it isn't, so I won't. My good friend Joe Penner was a real fan of the .357 Magnum until he shot a small black bear with one. The bear was up a tree and a 140 grain bullet in the center of his chest did not penetrate to the spine. Penner is an excellent and careful shot and got by with the .357 Magnum. When I saw the size of the bear and the lack of penetration, I presented him with a .45 Colt sixgun. He now carries that Ruger New Model .45 Colt loaded with 300 grain hard cast bullets at 1,100 feet per second. They penetrate.

.353 CASULL: Freedom Arms' .353 Casull is nothing more than a hot-loaded .357 Magnum with 158 grain bullets at 1,700 feet per second and 180s at 1,600 feet per second. Factory loads are available from Cor-Bon in a 180 grain bonded core soft point at 1,650 feet per second. For handloads I would use the Hornady 180 grain XTP. In either case, this cartridge is only for broadside shots on 100 to 150 pound deer-sized game.

.41 MAGNUM: Now we get into the big bores for hunting. The .41 Magnum is an excellent cartridge, perhaps the best choice for deer hunting with a sixgun because it offers high velocity and penetration combined with recoil that doesn't punish the shooter excessively. For a hunting sixgun in this caliber, I prefer the Ruger Bisley with a 7-1/2-inch barrel or the Smith & Wesson Model 57 with an 8-3/8-inch barrel because I seem to do my best shooting with the longer barrel lengths.

Lyman's recommended maximum load with its Keith bullet #410459 is 20 grains of #2400. This is a little hot in my sixguns, so I drop back to 19.5 grains. Velocity for the 220 grain hard cast bullet is 1,600 feet per second from the Smith & Wesson long-barreled sixgun and 1,550 feet per second from the Ruger Bisley with complete penetration afforded on deer-sized game on broadside shots. I am a firm believer in complete penetration with a big hole in and a big hole out. This allows bleeding from both sides and a good blood trail to follow. Death normally results within 100 yards. There are those that maintain that a bullet that does not completely penetrate somehow "expends all of its energy" within the animal. I have no idea what this is supposed to mean.

Cor-Bon now offers a .41 Magnum loading with a 265 hard cast bullet at 1,300 feet per second. The .41 Magnum is very inconsistent accuracy-wise with heavy weight bullets, however, the Cor-Bon load performs exceptionally well in the Dan Wesson .41 Magnum. I would prefer this load if the .41 Magnum is to be used for anything larger and tougher than deer, such as wild boar.

.44 SPECIAL: For nearly three decades the .44 Special was *the* sixgun for hunting. Loaded with 250 grain hard cast bullets at 1,200 feet per second muzzle velocity, it was definitely superior to the .357 Magnum in actual results, not paper ballistics. Since the 1950s, it has largely if not totally been supplanted by its bigger and better brother, the .44 Magnum. There are no currently manufactured .44 Special sixguns available from Colt or Smith & Wesson and Ruger has never offered a sixgun in this fine old chambering.

On the used gun market, the picture is much brighter. Adjustable-sighted Colt New Frontiers are available at much lower prices than their Single Action Army counterparts. Smith & Wesson made a run of both blue Model 24 and stainless Model 624 .44 Specials in the 1980s and these also are readily found on the gun show and gun shop circuit. Texas Longhorn Arms will chamber its sixguns in .44 Special. These are bull strong .44 Specials; they are made on the same frame and cylinder as the .44 Magnum.

My favorite loading for the .44 Special for hunting consists of the Speer 225 grain pure lead hollowpoint bullet with a full copper cup-shaped jacket at around 1,200 feet per second. This loading is for expansion, not penetration, and only standing broadside shots are taken and only on deer-sized game.

.44-40: More deer have fallen to the .44-40 than any of the other cartridges listed, simply due to the fact that it was chambered in the Winchester Models 1873 and 1892. By modern standards, however, the .44-40 is mild loading, to say the least, with a 200 grain bullet at under 1,000 feet per second from a sixgun. Couple this with the fact that there are no adjustable-sighted sixguns available and the .44-40 is at the bottom of the totem pole as a hunting sixgun. However, when extra cylinders are fitted to a Colt New Frontier .44 Special or a Texas Longhorn Arms .44 Magnum Flat-Top Target, the .44-40 becomes a viable hunting handgun. There are no factory .44-40 loads available that are suitable for hunting.

I prefer the same 225 grain Speer bullet as with the .44 Special loaded to around 1,100 feet per second in the .44-40. Again, this is not a powerful loading for big game but a deer cartridge for the careful, close in hunter. It may not be very practical, but it certainly is nostalgic. I like it.

.44 MAGNUM: For four decades the .44 Magnum has been the big bore sixgun by which all other sixguns have been judged. In the 1950s we knew we had reached the ultimate. There was simply no way to put any more power in a portable sixgun. The .44 Magnum has been eclipsed power-wise, but it has taken revolvers with five-shot cylinders to do the job. Such "sixguns" are the Freedom Arms .454 Casull and .50AE as well as custom sixguns with five-shot cylinders in .45 Colt, .475 Linebaugh, and .500 Linebaugh.

There are many great sixguns chambered for the .44 Magnum. On the double action scene we have the Smith & Wesson in both blue and stainless models and with standard or heavy underlugged barrels of 6-1/2- or 8-3/8-inch length, Colt contributes the Anaconda in stainless with both 6- and 8-inch length barrels, and Ruger offers both the 7-1/2-inch Redhawk and 9-1/2-inch Super Redhawk. Dan Wessons are out of production as this is written, but are readily available on the used gun market at good prices in both blue and stainless versions and in barrel lengths up to 10 inches. The Dan Wesson .44 Magnum at 4 pounds is the easiest shooting of all the .44 Magnums.

Single action .44 Magnums are heavily favored by handgun hunters and the Ruger Super Blackhawk is the top favorite. Available in both blue and stainless and barrel lengths of 5-1/2, 7-1/2, and 10-1/2 inches, the Ruger Super Blackhawk is simply the best bargain available to handgun hunters today. No other sixgun delivers so much for such a small financial expenditure. In addition to the Super Blackhawk, Ruger's Bisley Model Blackhawk is an outstanding hunting sixgun.

Finally, factory-wise, there are the finest .44 Magnums ever offered, the Improved Number Five and Flat-Top Target Models from Texas Longhorn Arms and the Freedom Arms revolver chambered in .44 Magnum. The latter is offered in stainless only in barrel lengths, suitable for hunting, of 6, 7-1/2, and 10 inches. Texas Longhorn Arms standard lengths are 5-1/2 inches for the Number Five and 7-1/2 inches for the Flat-Top.

Most all models mentioned are also offered in shorter barrel lengths of 4 inches for double action models and 4-3/4 inches in single actions. These are great for packin' but I prefer the longer sight radius as well as the increased muzzle velocity for hunting. This is strictly a personal preference and there are no other reasons for not using the shorter barrels if preferred, however, check local regulations. Would you believe in some states a 4-inch .44 Magnum is not legal for hunting big game but a 5-inch .357 Magnum is allowed? I would like to meet someone who can explain the logic of this law!

A few years back it was impossible to find factory loads suitable for hunting anything other than deer-

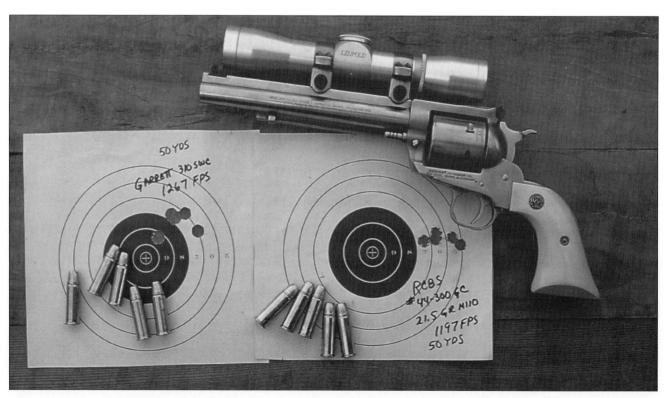

The Ruger Super Blackhawk Hunter Model, set up with Leupold 4X scope and Ruger rings, is an excellent hunting sixgun. Targets shot at 50 yards.

Sika buck taken on the Annual Handgun Hunters Against Hunger Hunt on the Y.O. Ranch to benefit the Salvation Army. Sixgun is Freedom Arms .44 Magnum with Leupold 2X scope.

These sixguns, with proper loads, will handle the largest of game animals. Top, Freedom Arms 10-inch .454; bottom, Custom Ruger New Model 10-inch .44 Magnum. Both wear Leupold 2X scopes.

sized game with the .44 Magnum. All of the 240 grain soft point and hollowpoint factory loadings are deer cartridges. For use on bigger and tougher game, bigger and tougher bullets are needed. Garrett Cartridges led the way with its 310 grain Keith-style hard cast bullet load at 1,300 feet per second. This is an excellent load, suitable for big critters such as elk and moose, or smaller heavy muscled examples such as wild hogs that require deep penetration. Cor-Bon offers a 260 Bonded Core as well as loadings with the 300 grain Hornady XTP and a 320 grain hard cast bullet both at 1,300 feet per second. Finally, Hornady loads its own XTP bullets in both 260 and 300 grain weights, Black Hills offers the 300 grain Hornady XTP in a .44 Magnum loading, and Speer now has a 270 grain Gold Dot loading. Black Hills has just recently added a .44 Magnum loading with a 320 grain hard cast bullet.

.45 COLT: The old .45 Colt is, to say the least, a most versatile sixgun cartridge. A few decades back it was written off as dead by all except diehard traditionalists. Today it is the most popular caliber for Cowboy Action Shooting and is also one of the best hunting cartridges **when used in the proper sixgun**. I cannot emphasize the latter enough. For years the .45 Colt cartridge carried the myth of weak brass—not so—only certain sixguns chambered for the .45 Colt are weak.

There are actually three levels of .45 Colt sixguns when it comes to hunting. At Level One we place the Colt New Frontier and the Smith & Wesson Model 25-5. For these sixguns, a 260 grain hard cast bullet at 1,050 feet per second is the main course. It kills all out of proportion to its paper ballistics and will penetrate deer completely on broadside shots.

Moving up to Level Two we have the .44 Magnum frame-sized .45 Colts, the Ruger Blackhawk and Bisley, the Texas Longhorn Arms Improved Number Five and Flat-Top Target, the Colt Anaconda, and the Dan Wesson. For these sixguns, a 300 grain bullet at 1,200 feet per second muzzle velocity puts us into the larger game category. For this loading level I prefer 21.5 grains of either H110 or WW296. Loading manuals go to 23 grains with jacketed bullets, so I feel perfectly safe with cast bullets and 1-1/2 grains less powder.

Finally, Level Three finds us with the five-shot custom sixguns built on Ruger Blackhawks and Bisleys by sixgunsmiths such as Hamilton Bowen, David Clements, John Linebaugh, and Jim Stroh. All of these men are masters at building custom sixguns. With these sixguns built in the fivegun persuasion, .45 Colt loads with either 260 or 300 grain bullets at 1,500 feet per second are easily and safely attained.

Heavy-duty hunting loads for the .45 Colt are just starting to appear. Cor-Bon's offering is a 300 grain jacketed soft point at 1,300 feet per second. Needless to say, this is only for modern heavy-framed sixguns in excellent condition.

.454 CASULL: Offered only in the superb Freedom Arms revolver, the .454 Casull is without a doubt the finest factory sixgun ever offered for the handgun

Alaskan brown bear? No. Grizzly bear? No. This is the first Yugoslavian brown bear taken by a handgun. Hunter Jerry Danuser took his bear with a .454 Casull mounted with an Ultra Dot scope.

The 10-inch .454 Casull carries well with a sling and factory-installed swivels.

hunter. For hunting, the Casull can be had with a 6-, 7-1/2-, or 10-inch barrel, as well as an easy packin' 4-3/4-inch length. Factory ammo, a 260 grain flat-point at 1,700 feet per second or a 300 grain flat-point at 1,600 feet per second, is available from either Freedom Arms or Winchester. Black Hills also has a milder loading using Hornady's XTP bullet that falls in between the standard .454 and the .44 Magnum.

Cor-Bon's .454 offerings consist of a 300 grain Bonded Core at 1,650 feet per second, a 320 grain Penetrator at 1,600 feet per second, and a 360 grain Penetrator at 1,500 feet per second. Friend Jerry Danuser used the 320 grain Cor-Bon .454 on a Cape buffalo and reports complete penetration. I backed up friend Tedd Adamovich as he hunted the American bison, or buffalo, with the .454 using a 300 grain hard cast bullet from BRP. This is a flat-point gas-checked bullet designed by Dick Casull for his .454. At the shot I knew it was all over. The buffalo ran about 30 yards, flopped over on its back with all four legs in the air and died. I do believe we felt the ground shake as it fell. The 300 grain bullet penetrated completely going through the heart in the process.

.50AE: As a sixgun cartridge, the .50AE is offered only in the Freedom Arms revolver. Originally chambered in the Desert Eagle semi-automatic, the .50AE is a rimless cartridge so it presents special reloading problems when used in a revolver cylinder. As a rimless cartridge it headspaces on the mouth of the case making a heavy crimp impossible. Reloaders have to experiment to find a load with a heavy bullet that won't jump the crimp. In the meanwhile Speer's 325 grain jacketed hollowpoint at 1,300 feet per second performs about as well as a 300 grain .44 Magnum bullet at the same velocity.

The most popular sixguns for hunting are in .44 and .45 caliber. As I have mentioned, factory loadings in the .44 Magnum with 240 grain bullets are for deer only. For bigger game, the best hunting loads for such sixguns are assembled with heavyweight bullets. Heavyweight bullets of 300 grains weight or more seem to shoot better in most sixguns as compared to their standard weight counterparts and they certainly penetrate deeper. Twenty years ago it was impossible to find 300 grain bullets for these cartridges, so sixgunners who favored the Ruger .45 Colt Blackhawk-sized .45-70 rifle bullets down to .452 inch

Bud McDonald used the Ruger Redhawk .44 Magnum with 300 grain hard cast bullet to harvest this Colorado bull elk.

Tedd Adamovich and guide Frank Pulkrabek are all smiles after Tedd took this bison at 35 yards with one shot using the Freedom Arms .454 and his handload using the BRP 300 grain cast bullet.

Taffin and South African warthog taken with Freedom Arms .454 Casull and 260 grain factory load. Scope on 7-1/2-inch .454 is 2X Leupold on SSK T'SOB mount.

used them with great success in the .45 Colt case. Today, all of the major mould manufacturers, LBT, Lyman, NEI, and RCBS, offer blocks that drop heavyweight bullets in both .44 and .45 calibers with the latter being applicable to the .454 Casull as well.

Favored bullets from these moulds include the Keith-style from NEI with a .44 caliber 295 grain gas check #295.429, and 310 and 325 grain plain base Keith-style .45 bullets bearing numbers 310.451 and 325.454. NEI also makes the mould for the first, and still one of the best .44 heavyweight bullets available, namely J.D. Jones' 320 grain #311.429, as well as Jones' .45 offering the flat-point 340 grain #345.451.

LBT offers a full line of heavyweight bullets in all calibers in both LFN (Long Flat Nose) and WFN (Wide Flat Nose) styles. All LBT bullets are designed to carry most of the weight in the nose thus affording maximum case capacity. I particularly prefer LBT's .45 caliber #454.300 LFN and #454.325 WFN as well as the 280 grain .44 bullet #432.280 LFN. LBT also offers heavyweight bullets for the .41 Magnum with the #411.250 LFN and #410.250 WFN. Both of these bullets shoot exceptionally well in the Dan Wesson .41 Magnum.

Lyman's first heavyweight .45 bullet mould was manufactured specifically for Freedom Arms with a 300 grain gas check flat-nosed bullet #454629. This is the bullet offered by BRP that Tedd Adamovich used

on his buffalo. Designed by Dick Casull, this is a superb bullet for hunting or long-range shooting in either the .454 or .45 Colt. Lyman's latest heavyweight bullet offerings are the 300 grain .44 #429649 and the 325 grain .45 #452651. Both of these are gas-checked designs.

Finally, from RCBS, we have two excellent heavyweight designs, the .44 Keith-style #44-300 SWC and the .45 Keith-style #45-300 SWC. Both of these are also gas-checked designs and exceptionally accurate.

Those who prefer heavyweight jacketed bullets are not left wanting. Freedom Arms offers 300 grain heavy-duty bullets with an .032 inch copper jacket in both .44 and .45 caliber. Hornady's 300 grain XTP design has proven itself in the game fields in both .44 and .45 caliber, Speer's 300 grain flat-point is a .44 bullet designed for deep penetration, and Sierra's 300 grain hollowpoint gets the nod when expansion is the number one desired trait.

For those who prefer hard cast heavyweight bullets without casting their own, BRP offers both the NEI #429.295 and the Lyman/Freedom Arms #454629 and Cast Performance Bullet Company and Fusilier both offer a full line of heavyweight hard cast bullets, and Bull-X has both .44 and .45 plain based 300 grain bullets.

Many sixguns now come scope ready. Some Ruger Redhawks and all Super Redhawks come with scal-

Jim Wilson, Shooting Times and Handgunning Field Editor, took this Texas whitetail with a Freedom Arms .44 Magnum. Scope is 2X Leupold, load was Speer's 270 Gold Dot.

loped barrels or frame and barrel to accept Ruger rings. All Smith & Wesson large-framed sixguns are now drilled and tapped to accept mounts such as those offered by Weigand, and the Freedom Arms rear sight assembly removes to accept a special scope mount. Dan Wessons were designed to allow the removal of the iron-sighted shroud to be replaced by a shroud with a scope base mounted.

Most of my sixguns that are scope-mounted carry Bausch & Lomb, Burris, Leupold, or Simmons scopes. Because sixguns are not long-range hunting weapons, we don't need high magnification. Two power is fine, and four power is not quite as fast, but it works. The fastest scopes are actually the non-magnifiers, the red dot electronic scopes such as the Tasco ProPoint or Weaver QuikPoint. A completely new concept is the Bushnell HoloSight that gives one the illusion of looking at a screen. All of these electronic scopes work equally as well on sixguns, single-shot pistols, rifles, and shotguns. In fact, I am able to shoot aerial targets with a shotgun for the first time in my life using a HoloSight.

Modern pistol scopes are tough. The only scope failure I have ever had occurred when I neglected to snap the safety strap on my shoulder holster after shooting an African warthog. The bullet penetrated completely and, as I was looking for it in the mud, my .454 tumbled out, the scope hit the only rock close by, and I could no longer stay on paper with that sixgun at 100 yards. When I got home I found my sixgun was shooting 18 inches to the right from the bump.

Scopes take a terrific beating on a sixgun and I highly recommend the SSK mounting system consisting of the T'SOB mount and three rings. SSK can adopt this mount to any sixgun with adjustable sights. It will not come off! SSK can also perform a complete action job on any hunting handgun. Mag-Na-Port also specializes in mounting scopes on Smith & Wesson, Ruger, and Freedom Arms sixguns and, in addition to cutting its muzzle jump reducing porting slots, builds complete hunting packages such as its

A most successful aoudad hunt: Ted Adamovich took the Number One Handgun Record Book aoudad with the .353 Casull, Rick Von der Heide used a T/C .35 Remington for Number Thirteen, and Taffin collected Number Seven with the Ruger Hunter Model .44 Magnum. Note the three types of handguns for hunting: the scoped revolver, the scoped single-shot, and the iron-sighted revolver.

Stalker Package with scope, sling swivels, action job, and even fancy embellishments like highly polished cylinder flutes, or special high polish bands around barrel and/or cylinder.

For those who prefer to hunt with iron sights, Mag-Na-Port offers the C-More sight system consisting of fluorescent front sights in orange, green, red, blue, or hot pink. Those who own sixguns with a C-More front sight may take a little ribbin' from their friends but they will see the sights better than the standard offering affords. Both SSK and Mag-Na-Port are as important to a sixgunner as a doctor is to a sick man.

Ready to take up handgun hunting? If you have never hunted with a sixgun, think seriously about taking the plunge. Once the decision is made to use a sixgun, then really use it. Don't simply take it along as a second choice. Leave the rifle at home and concentrate on using the sixgun.

Most handgun hunters are better than the average rifle hunters simply due to the fact they practice more and shoot more often. The average rifle hunter takes his or her rifle out twice a year—once to sight

in and the other to actually hunt. Sixguns demand more attention than this. Once the decision is made, one must get to know the sixgun and load of choice, really know it, that is. Sixgunners must also know what they can do at various distances and how well they can hit both with a rest and without. One must also be totally honest with oneself at this time. If the sixgun can't be shot well, one owes it to the game and oneself not to use a sixgun for hunting.

As a little extra help for the handgun hunter, John Underwood supplies a lightweight portable set of cross sticks that are invaluable for the handgun hunter. They are available in lengths that are applicable to both standing and kneeling situations and they also collapse to a very small package that can be carried in a pouch with very little weight and bulk added to what the hunter normally carries.

The decision has been made and the homework has been done as far as practice. Now what? Check the game rules in your area and see what can be hunted with a sixgun. Most states allow the use of handguns that meet certain energy and caliber cri-

SSK's J.D. Jones took these warthogs with his 320 grain hard cast bullet .44 Magnum loads.

teria for hunting. The white-tailed deer is the number one game animal for most hunters, be it rifle or handgun style. A second option available in many areas is wild hogs. They are tough critters with heavy muscles and are not only hard to kill, they can also be dangerous. Some have called them the Poor Man's Grizzly, a most appropriate title.

I also enjoy hunting exotics with a sixgun. Exotics are non-native animals that were mostly imported into Texas in the 1930s and are now available to the hunter on private land in many areas. Some such as Barbary sheep and Blackbuck antelope are real challenges to the handgun hunter. Others such as Corsican rams and Catalina goats are usually much easier to approach.

Both cougar and black bear are also available in many areas and offer sufficient challenges to the handgun hunter to make their pursuit worthwhile.

Finally we have the really big game such as elk, moose, and the big bears on this continent and a varied supply of both dangerous and non-dangerous game in Africa. Consider these the post graduate course after the others have been mastered.

The greatest attribute connected to hunting with a sixgun is that it is sufficiently challenging to make every animal taken a trophy. It is one type of hunting thrill to take a trophy animal at 300 yards with a flat-shooting rifle; it is quite another to take an animal at 50 yards or less with a sixgun.

Finally, an 8-pound rifle gets mighty heavy and cumbersome after a day afield, while a 3-pound sixgun in a properly designed shoulder holster is hardly noticeable. I hunt with both single-shot pistols and sixguns. With sixguns I use both scope-sighted and iron-sighted examples. The latter certainly gives the most enjoyment and sense of accomplishment.

CHAPTER 17

SIXGUN STOCKS

Pachmayr calls 'em grips. Roy Fishpaw calls 'em grips. Guy Hogue calls 'em grips. BearHug's Deacon Deason called 'em grips. But Steve Herrett called 'em stocks, and I prefer stocks. Deason and I went around on this all the time. "The grip is what I provide when I grasp the sixgun," said I. "What is that thing on the rifle stock behind the triggerguard?" said he. And before I could answer I would hear: "It's the pistol grip. You stock a rifle, but you grip a pistol." "No. I shoulder a rifle and I grip the pistol's stocks!" And on and on and on.

We may never settle whether they are grips or stocks, but this I know: I am a grip connoisseur. I like good ones. Normally I prefer stocks that are beautiful as well as functional, but quite often, I have to settle for functional only. There is nothing beautiful about finger groove rubber grips, but they are highly functional. Normally I prefer a blue gun with grips of ivory or fancy woods, however, there are conditions that demand a stainless gun and synthetic grips such as outdoor or law enforcement use in which the sixgun and the grips are constantly exposed to the elements.

We will take a look at some of the best grips available today. I do not pretend to cover all available stocks. I can only share with you the ones that I have found highly functional, spirit and soul stirring, or both. For the past forty years I have been wrapping my hands around every conceivable style of sixgun stocks. Experience is definitely the best teacher. With that in mind I hereby endeavor to transfer some of that experience to other sixgunners. Sixgun stocks are so important to me that normally the first modification I perform to any personal sixgun is the application of a screwdriver to the stock screw and the tossing of the factory stocks in a box. Most factory stocks do not appeal to me either aesthetically or physically. I prefer a stock that fits my hand, looks good, and also one that adds a touch of my personal taste to each of my sixguns. The latter is one of the most important reasons to restock a sixgun and one of the easiest ways to personalize a pistol.

Most factory stocks are pretty plain, but there is a vast array of materials available when one considers custom sixgun stocks. At the top of the list is ivory. Nothing looks richer or feels better than real ivory, especially ivory that looks milky and has aged somewhat, yellowing in the process and adding tiny cracks. Nearly as fine a material as ivory for sixgun stocks is ram's horn from any of the American mountain sheep such as Bighorn, Desert, Dall, or Stone sheep. This very hard to come by material makes into yellow colored stocks that almost appear translucent. It is, as expected, very expensive.

Mother-of-pearl may have been shunned by General Patton, but many others have used it with fine success on real business-type sixguns over the years; it is often found on Colt Single Actions carried by lawmen of the Southwest. One of my favorite materials is reworked staghorn. Most stag grips for single action sixguns come too thick and too rough for serious use. When they are slimmed down, however, they take on a much better feel and also the appearance of bone, almost like ivory, with the added bonus of being much tougher. Some pieces will be completely white while others will have just a trace of the brown mottled stag appearance remaining.

After grip, or stock, materials such as real ivory, mother-of-pearl, or staghorn, come such exotic woods as fancy figured walnut, ebony, cordia, kingswood, tulipwood, bloodwood, morodilla, and zebrawood. One can find a vast array of colors in fancy woods all the way from the near black of ebony to the deep red of bloodwood.

Finally we have the synthetic materials for sixgun stocks. Polymer looks a lot like ivory but costs about 1/10 as much with the extra added bonus of being very tough, which makes it a good choice when the going is difficult. The same can be said for micarta. Micarta is a material that came from the electrical

Single Action grip frames. Left side: Colt Single Action Army, Colt Bisley Model, and Texas Longhorn Arms Improved Number Five; right side: Ruger Super Blackhawk, Ruger Bisley, and Freedom Arms .454 .

Nothing looks better than one-piece ivory stocks on a Colt Single Action. Eddie Janis of Peacemaker Specialists tuned and gripped this sixgun.

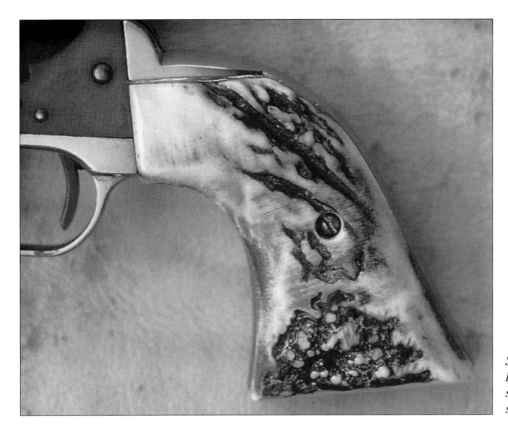

Stag stocks, as shown on this Ruger .45 Colt, are normally supplied with a very rough surface.

industry, and I believe is made from paper fibers strongly pressed together. Both ivory and black micarta look exceptionally good on blue, nickel, or stainless sixguns and make a very tough durable sixgun grip. Micarta is a favorite on heavy recoiling sixguns such as the Freedom Arms .454 or the custom sixguns in .475 and .500 Linebaugh. Micarta seems impervious to recoil and also stands up to tough outdoor use.

Cost is often a factor when choosing sixgun stocks. Custom-designed and -fitted stocks are certainly more expensive than those made to a standard pattern. Material-wise, ivory, mother-of-pearl, and ram's horn are the most expensive and one should expect to pay in the $300 to $400 range. Exotic woods from the custom makers can approach $200 while micarta or stag is usually under $100. The most reasonably priced are the under $50 wood or polymer off-the-shelf stocks from such suppliers as Ajax, Eagle, and Hogue.

Why would anyone want to spend extra money to do away with a pair of factory grips and replace them with what are normally expensive custom grips? There are a number of reasons. We have already mentioned some of the materials that can be used for grips; personal taste in material is a large factor. Exotic woods, ivory, staghorn, micarta, all add greatly to the looks and pride of ownership of a fine sixgun.

Lessening felt recoil is another important reason for going to custom grips. Most factory grips of the past twenty years or so accentuate, rather than reduce, recoil. There are some noticeable exceptions such as the smooth factory grips found on Dan Wesson revolvers. These are the only factory double action sixgun grips that I have found that are totally acceptable as they came from the factory.

At one time, many of the grips found on single action sixguns were excellent. For whatever the reason, over the years they have become more flared at the bottom, resulting in a grip that really accentuates recoil. Check a Flat-top Ruger .357 or .44 against a New Model Ruger in any caliber and notice the great difference in the feel of the grips. This is also true of early Ruger Super Blackhawks compared to later New Model Super Blackhawks. The best shaped grips found on Colt Single Actions since the 1950s have been the hard rubber stocks. These seem to be a thing of the past as the Third Generation Single Actions carried the thicker eagle-style grips and the latest Custom Shop Single Actions are equipped with the plainest un-contoured wood imaginable.

For my hand, the Ruger Super Blackhawk is punishing as it slaps me hard on the knuckle of my middle finger, while the standard Colt Single Action shape, designed for blackpowder loads, is fine up to muzzle velocities with 250 grain bullets of about 1,100 feet per

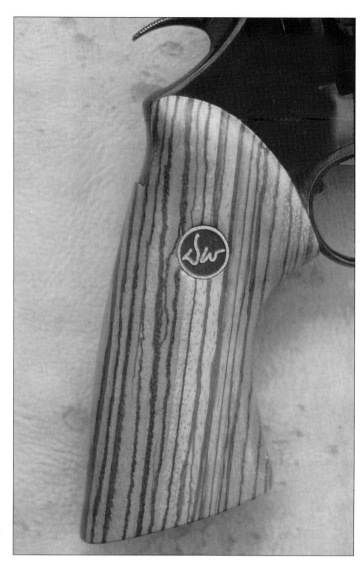

The best factory double action stock ever offered is found on the Dan Wesson .44 Magnum.

second. After that, recoil begins to work on me. There are some noticeable exceptions in the single action sixgun grip shapes available. In the 1920s, Elmer Keith, working with custom gunsmith Harold Croft, came up with what he considered the perfect single action grip. Keith apparently found the Colt Single Action grip shape wanting with heavy loads also. Mating a Colt Bisley backstrap with a Colt Single Action trigger-guard, Keith and Croft gave us the #5 Single Action Grip. This grip was on a 5-1/2-inch barreled .44 Special Single Action Colt with adjustable sights that Keith considered the perfect sixgun. Keith gave all of his ideas to the Colt factory, both grip improvements and other design improvements, but to no avail.

The #5 grip shape still exists, though—not on a Colt Single Action, but its influence can be found in three single actions that are available today. First, it is available exactly as designed by Keith on the Improved Number Five Single Actions from Texas Longhorn Arms. Bill Grover started with the idea of original Keith #5 and upgraded it to a .44 Magnum sixgun with loading gate and ejector rod on the left side. I would like to see Texas Longhorn Arms make this grip frame available as an option for Ruger Blackhawks and Colt Single Actions.

Dick Casull is a Colt Single Action buff from way back and the influence of Keith's #5 grip shape can be found in the Freedom Arms .454 Casull revolver he designed. The same can be said for the grips found on the Ruger Bisley Single Actions. Unlike the major media, I will admit my bias and state that, in my opinion, the Ruger Bisley and the Freedom Arms Casull are the finest single action grip shapes to ever come from a factory when it comes to handling heavy recoil. They both work well because they come up high in the back like the original Keith #5 grip shape. This helps prevent the grip from twisting in the hand when firing heavy loads.

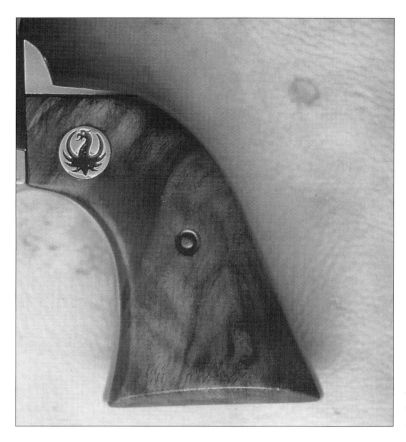

Believe it or not, these are fancy walnut factory stocks on an early 1960s 10-inch Ruger Blackhawk .44 Magnum!

Note the difference in shape between these two stocks for Smith & Wesson N-frame sixguns. BearHug's custom grip is shaped for comfort in shooting, while the factory stock is too blocky to control felt recoil well.

Bloodwood BearHug Target grips on a Smith & Wesson 8-3/8-inch .41 Magnum.

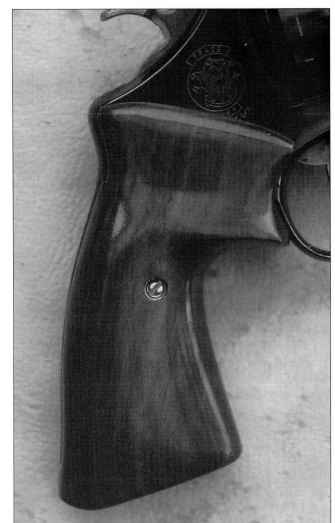

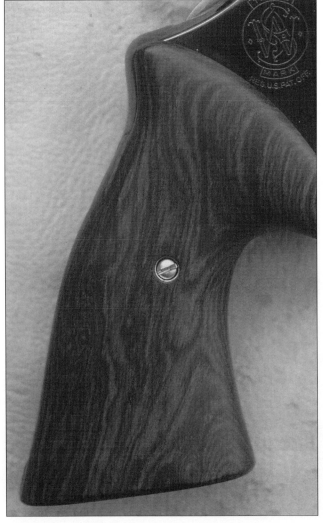

This .44 Special Smith & Wesson is personalized with BearHug Skeeter Skelton rosewood stocks.

Smith & Wesson double actions are some of my favorite sixguns. I particularly like the looks and feel of the standard 4-inch big bore N-frames and the 4-inch K-frame Model 19. The Model 29 has to be rated as one of the three or four best lookin' sixguns of all time, and most of the time that I pack a double action revolver, it is an N-frame Smith & Wesson in .44 Magnum, .45 Colt, .41 Magnum, .44 Special, or even .45 ACP.

Smith & Wesson sixguns are great favorites, however, the standard Smith & Wesson Target grips are the worst grips ever offered on a big bore sixgun. Everything about them is wrong. They are too wide, flared too much at the bottom, deeply checkered, and do not have enough material behind the triggerguard. Add to this their poor fit of wood to grip frame and one has the worst possible scenario in grip making.

It was not always this way, though. Target grips found on early .357 Magnums and .44 Specials and later on the .44 Magnum were not nearly so square-shaped but rather smoothly rounded in the right places, the checkering was much more subdued, and they were also available in a smooth finish. They even mated well with my stubby fingers.

Smith & Wesson has seen the error of its ways and now most Smith & Wesson sixguns have come through fitted with Hogue's or Uncle Mike's synthetic finger groove grips, which creates a great improvement for most shooters. They lack the beauty of natural wood, but they are highly functional and, due to their finger grooves and soft material, they also handle recoil quite well.

A few years back any number of custom gunsmiths were offering round butt configurations on N-frame sixguns. This consisted of changing the shape of the grip frame from an N-frame square butt to a K-frame round butt. About fifteen years ago, I had a 4-inch Model 29 done by Mag-Na-Port and now equipped with BearHug round butt grips, it is one of my favorite packin' sixguns.

Most Smith & Wesson sixguns are now furnished only in the round butt style. Round butts are great on sixguns with short standard barrels, especially on those sixguns that are going to be carried concealed. The finger groove grips found on the round butt, heavy barrel Smiths are a big improvement over the standard grips, especially when it comes to felt recoil. Round butt grip frames also allow the owner to fit his or her sixgun with a personally styled grip that is much smaller than the original square butt Target grips as furnished on Smith & Wesson N-frame sixguns for nearly forty years.

Sixgun grips are very personal and what is set down here is nothing but one longtime sixgunner's preferences. Grips should have great aesthetic appeal to the eye and emotions, feel good to the hand, and provide significant help in taming felt recoil. Most grips covered fit all these categories, however, some of the synthetics, especially the rubber ones, make up in functional qualities what they lack in aesthetic value.

My good friend Deacon Deason passed away while I was hunting in Africa in June 1994. It is my hope that someone will pick up where Deacon left off in the manufacture of sixgun stocks because nothing feels better in my hand than the BearHug Skeeter Skelton design on a Smith & Wesson K-frame such as the Model 19 .357 Magnum. The BearHug Skeeter Skelton style for the Smith & Wesson N-frame is a mite larger, but feels very good in this sixgunner's hand.

Skeeter Skelton was a longtime lawman who served in the Border Patrol and also spent time as a Texas Sheriff and Narcotics Agent. From personal experience he knew what serious gun handling was all about and his grip design for double action sixguns proves it. These are simply fast handlin', defensive grips with nothing that will get in the way of slick shooting and quick handling, but still designed to control recoil.

Skelton took the Roper design, which was an improvement on the Smith & Wesson Target design way back when it was a usable grip, and modified it slightly in an effort to contour and angle it to fit his hand for law enforcement work, hunting, and sixgunnin'. BearHug Grips carried Skeeter's idea out to perfection with Deason and Skelton working hand-in-hand to produce the Skeeter Skelton-style grip.

For both my emotional and physical well-being, the Skeeter Skelton style is my favorite grip for Smith & Wesson N- and K-frame sixguns, especially. I have a large hand with stubby fingers and the BearHug Skeeter Skelton grip fits my hand as well as any sixgun stock design I have ever tried. When I first bolted a pair of Skeeter Skelton stocks on a .44 Magnum Smith & Wesson, I remembered how factory Target stocks felt and I expected the open backstrap to result in the same accentuated felt recoil. It did not and does not. They are especially comfortable on the K-frame 4-inch Model 19 Combat Magnum .357 and L-frame .357 Magnums right up through the N-frame .41 and .44 Magnums.

CHARLES ABLE

BearHug may be out of production as this is written, but there are several individuals and companies that have taken up the slack in offering not only double action sixgun stocks, but also single action perfection

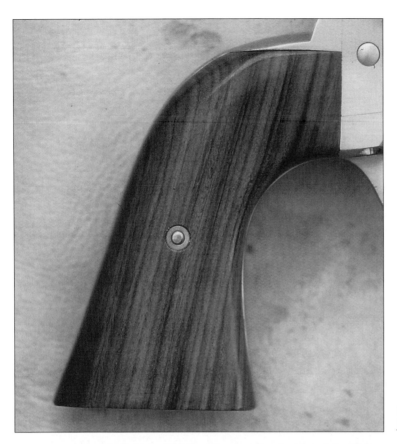

Charles Able's fancy walnut stocks are on a Freedom Arms .44 Magnum.

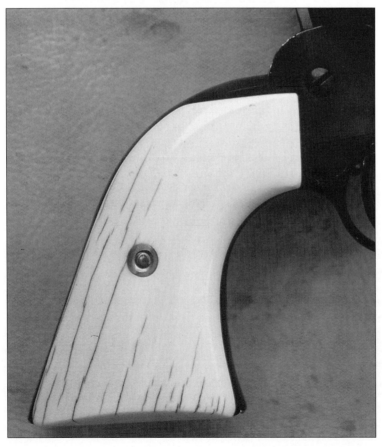

Aged ivory grips by Charles Able on a Ruger Old Model .45 Colt.

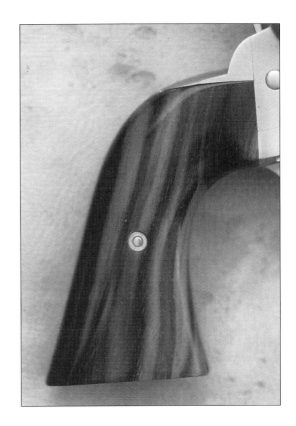

Ebony stocks by Charles Able on a Freedom Arms .44 Magnum.

as well. Charles Able loves single action sixguns, especially Ruger and Freedom Arms revolvers, and builds stocks only for these great sixguns except on that rare occasion when he might be convinced to make a pair of Ruger Redhawk stocks. By specializing in single action grips, Able has become a master craftsman working in exotic woods such as fancy walnut, rosewood, and ebony, plus staghorn and ivory, when available. Able not only fits grips perfectly to the grip frame, but he also has an excellent understanding of how grips should feel to the shooter's hand. Single Action stocks must be just the right thickness, have just the right taper, and be rounded just so. Able understands all of this perfectly. If you want the best fitting grips possible for a single action simply order grips "to feel the way Taffin likes 'em."

All of Able's grips are completely hand made, one at a time—no factory production here. He has been a source for single action grips that could not be found anywhere else such as those needed for the long-out-of-production Great Western Single Actions and the Remington 1875 sixguns. Even my Ruger Bisleys, which came with usable grips made of very good wood, have mostly been custom fitted with Able fancy walnut stocks.

AJAX CUSTOM GRIPS

Ajax Custom Grips offers a full line of custom stocks for sixgunners crafted of both natural and synthetic materials. Ajax also offers staghorn stocks from the Indian Sambar deer. Two pair now ride on my single actions, one on a Ruger Super Blackhawk and the other a Colt Single Action Army. The former now reside on a 7-1/2-inch Hunter Model Ruger, while the latter, supplied with a Colt Factory medallion fitted, compliment a 4-3/4-inch nickel-plated .44-40 used perfectly for Cowboy Action Shooting.

We have mentioned that most stag grips I have seen offered have been overly thick and so very sharp that they were unusable, which is why I started having stag stocks slimmed down considerably and smoothed to an almost ivory-like appearance. Ajax's stag grips are already of the proper width without the rough surface found on many stag stocks.

Stag grips have always been very popular for use on single action sixguns. They not only look good, but they are also much less fragile than either ivory or mother-of-pearl and are less costly. The Ruger Vaquero, especially the highly polished stainless steel model, has great appeal when equipped with stag grips.

Ajax also offers grips made of four synthetic materials, ivory polymer, pearlite, black pearlite, and staglite, all designed to replace the costlier ivory, pearl, and stag stocks. Ivory polymer grips are especially popular for hard kickin' single action sixguns because they are tough and smooth to the hand. The grips provided by Ajax are slightly oversized to be hand fitted to each

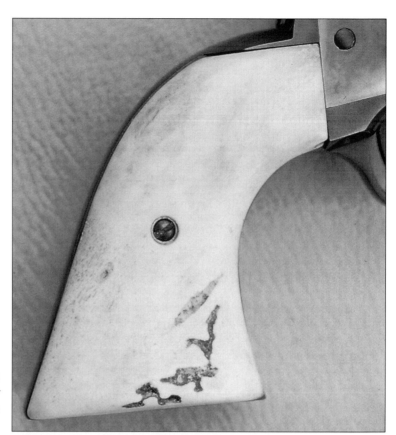

Charles Able supplies stag stocks that are smooth and have the appearance of bone or ivory like the stocks on this Colt Single Action .44 Special.

Single Action grips by Ajax from top left clockwise: Stags on Ruger Hunter Model 7-1/2-inch .44 Magnum, ivory polymer on Colt New Frontier 5-1/2-inch .44 Special, stags on Colt Single Action 4-3/4-inch .44-40, and ivory polymer on 4-3/4-inch .44 Magnum Ruger Super Blackhawk with Old Model grip frame.

individual grip frame. There is considerable variation in the dimensions of factory grip frames on both Colt and Ruger single actions. I have had a pair of Ajax ivory polymers fitted to a Colt New Frontier .44 Special x 5-1/2 inches by gunsmith David Clements. This sixgun was originally a 7-1/2-inch model, however, Clements also expertly cut the barrel at the time he was fitting the grips. The combination of 5-1/2-inch barrel and Ajax grips turned this sixgun into a favorite packin' pistol.

A second set of Ajax smooth ivory polymers have been fitted to a custom Ruger Super Blackhawk. Worked over by Mag-Na-Port, this sixgun is now fitted with a standard grip frame, ported 4-5/8-inch barrel, and Ajax ivory polymer stocks. Don't confuse these polymer grips with the imitation ivory grips available in the past. These grips do not have that cheap look and are of the proper width without being bulky.

Ajax also offers a line of wood grips for most revolvers in walnut, cherry wood, and black silverwood. For those who want the best in grip materials, genuine ivory cannot be topped. Ajax is one of the few sources for this rare material. Made of African elephant ivory, these grips must be special ordered and custom fit to each individual handgun. Finally, for those who would like to add a little weight as well as fancy-up their Ruger Blackhawk, Ajax offers carved pewter grips in several scroll patterns. Ajax is also one of the few suppliers I know of that can fit the original Ruger Blackhawks, the XR-3 grip frames, that were standard on the Single-Six and .357 and .44 Magnum Blackhawks from 1953 to 1963.

TEDD ADAMOVICH–BLUMAGNUM

Deacon Deason's good friend, Tedd Adamovich, learned to make stocks from BearHug and offers stocks for all single action sixguns under the name BluMagnum. Custom single action grips of plain and fancy walnut, maple, and exotic woods when available, are now offered by BluMagnum. I worked with Adamovich in making a custom stock for the heavy recoiling .454 Casull. He subsequently sent me the prototype, which I found to be too large for my liking.

After making a few sketches and marking the stocks with a felt tip pen, I sent them back with my suggestions for improvement. Adamovich made the desired modifications and sent the improved stocks back for testing. Using them on a short-barreled .454 Casull, they removed the problem I encounter with all heavy recoiling handguns, knuckle-dusting. There is no more pain on the middle finger of my shooting

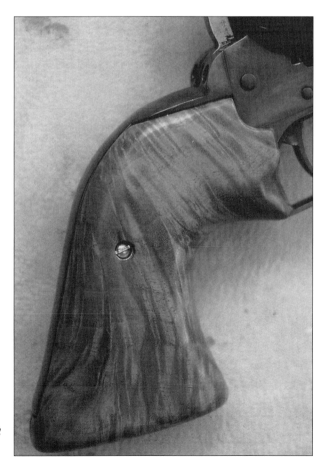

BluMagnum stocks of flame-grained walnut on a 10-1/2-inch Ruger .357 Maximum. Note filler behind the triggerguard.

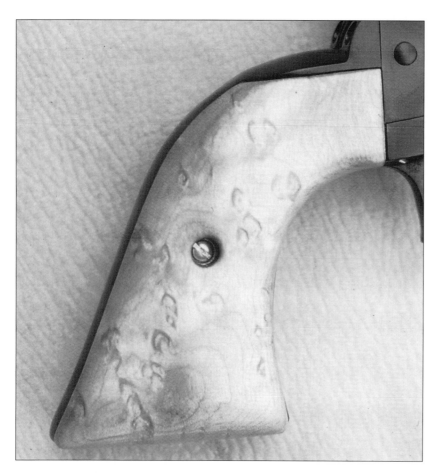

Birdseye maple stocks by BluMagnum adorn this Ruger 5-1/2-inch .44 Magnum Super Blackhawk.

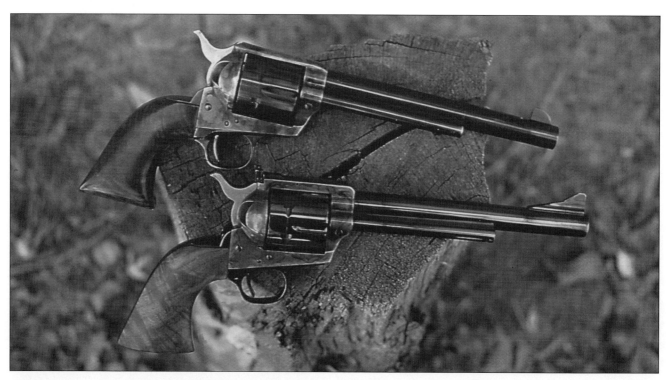

These .45 Colts, a 7-1/2-inch Single Action and a 7-1/2-inch New Frontier, are stocked with one-piece walnut grips by BluMagnum.

hand when using 340 grain bullets at 1,700 feet per second muzzle velocity.

The BluMagnum design for the Freedom Arms revolvers has now been finalized and are just about perfect in both design, fit, and wood selection. Made of fancy figured walnut, they feel very good, to say the least. Even though the frontstrap has a filler behind the triggerguard, these stocks do not have a bulky feeling. BluMagnum does it right.

In addition to the filler stocks for the Freedom Arms line of revolvers, BluMagnum offers the same grip style for the Ruger Super Blackhawk. This style grip now rides on three of my favorite long-range sixguns, a Ruger 10-1/2-inch stainless .44 Super Blackhawk, a Ruger 10-1/2-inch .357 Maximum which was supplied by the factory with the Super Blackhawk grip frame, and a Freedom Arms 10-inch .44 Magnum. The stocks supplied for the .357 Maximum are made out of one of the most striking pieces of flame-grained walnut I have ever encountered. BluMagnum is also offering grips for Colt Single Actions and the Ruger Blackhawk and Bisley Models. Four styles are available for most single action sixguns: factory replacement stocks, the same with extended butt, stocks with a filler behind triggerguard, and the same with finger grooves.

The original Colt Single Actions of the 1870s came equipped with one-piece wooden stocks. These grips were inletted to accept the backstrap and triggerguard and required the removal of the backstrap to install. This type of grip is very hard to find today.

BluMagnum can, however, supply them for any single action equipped with the two-piece grip frame.

EAGLE GRIPS

Eagle Grips offers a full line of stocks for single action and double action sixguns in a choice of several materials. I have already mentioned the BearHug Skeeter Skelton grips I have preferred for Smith & Wesson double actions above all others. Eagle catalogs oversized stocks in both rosewood and ebony wood for double action sixguns. These are very close to the Skeeter Skelton style; a pair of smooth rosewood Eagle stocks on a Smith & Wesson K-frame look good, feel like the Skeeter Skelton style, and fit perfectly on an old nickel-plated .357 Combat Magnum. I particularly like the contrast of the dark rosewood with the nickel plating of the .357 Magnum Model 19.

Oversized stocks are available in both checkered or smooth finger groove-style in addition to standard smooth grips. As handguns have become heavier, I have learned to appreciate the added element of control offered by finger groove grips. Finger groove checkered rosewood Eagle grips now reside on a 5-inch Smith & Wesson Model 629 .44 Magnum while their smooth counterpart has found a home with a 6-inch heavy underlugged barrel Model 686 .357 Magnum. These rosewood stocks look exceptionally good on stainless steel sixguns.

Eagle also offers genuine staghorn, buffalo horn, and mother-of-pearl grips for most handguns. All

Eagle grips on Smith & Wesson sixguns: Oversized rosewood on 4-inch nickel .357 Model 19, ebony Secret Service on 4-inch stainless .45 ACP Springfield Armory Commemorative, and finger groove rosewood on 6-inch stainless .357 M686.

stag grips come from India's Sambar deer, buffalo horn grips, usually a deep shiny black color, also come from India, and mother-of-pearl grips are offered for that extra fancy sixgun. Eagle recommends the fragile and expensive mother-of-pearl for presentation sixguns only and suggests that they be removed if the gun is to be fired.

Of special interest to me is the concealment stock design from Eagle known as the Secret Service line. These tiny grips are of the boot grip finger groove-style in rosewood or ebony, with or without checkering. This design has been extremely well thought out; they combine a small size for concealment and finger grooves for control. The backstrap and bottom of the butt are left open while two finger grooves fill in the frontstrap. They are the smallest grips I have ever encountered for the round-butted large Smith & Wessons such as the Mountain Gun. The Secret Service grip style from Eagle conceals easily without printing on the jacket lining and is as small as a grip can be and still be practical for shooting a big bore sixgun.

Not all sixguns are equal when it comes to grip frame size with single actions being the least likely of all to be of uniform size. Colt Single Actions are found to be quite different in grip frame dimensions when the First, Second, and Third Generation guns are compared size-wise. The same is true of Ruger Blackhawks. Old Models, New Models, Vaqueros, and Old Armys should all have the same size and shape of grip frame. They don't always. Eagle also custom fits sixgun grips.

ROY FISHPAW

Roy Fishpaw is *the* stock maker by which all other grip makers are judged. He is simply a superb craftsman and a complete grip maker in that he offers grips for all single action and double action revolvers. In addition to offering top quality grips, Fishpaw also offers a complete line of grip materials that includes exotic woods, aged elephant ivory, and the very rare ram's horn.

My experience with Fishpaw sixgun grips consists of figured walnut grips from his establishment, Custom Gun Grips, on a 3-1/2-inch Smith & Wesson Model 27 .357 Magnum, and a 4-5/8-inch Ruger Blackhawk custom .44 Special. In both cases, the gun was shipped to Fishpaw for precise fitting to the frame. The stocks provided for the Smith .357 are of the modified Roper design and come down further behind the triggerguard and also have less material filling in the area between triggerguard and frontstrap than the Skeeter Skelton style of grip. They feel exceptionally good. There is no more businesslike-

looking big bore defensive sixgun than the 3-1/2-inch .357 Magnum and the addition of Fishpaw grips simply adds to this appearance.

Fishpaw will not make grips unless he has the gun frame to custom fit the grips. He does not print a brochure, but rather prefers to work with each individual customer. He requires hand patterns and the use of the gun for individual fitting for about one month. He is normally heavily back-logged and each customer is put on the calendar so one's gun is not tied up for a long period of time. His grips are well worth the wait.

HERRETT STOCKS

Around 1960, a check for $12 went off to Herrett's Stocks for my first pair of custom stocks. I still have those original Herrett stocks that have been used on several Smith & Wessons over the past four decades. They are still in excellent shape. The Herrett Trooper stocks arrived just at the right time. They were first used on a Smith & Wesson .357 Magnum Highway Patrolman and then switched to my first Smith & Wesson .44 Magnum.

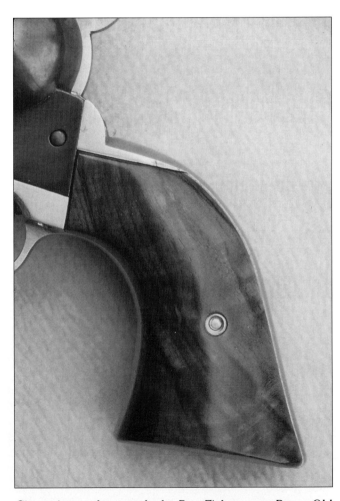

Circassian walnut stocks by Roy Fishpaw on Ruger Old Model Blackhawk.

The factory grips supplied on the early .44 Magnums were bigger at the bottom and smaller at the top than they should have been. Later examples would be even worse! The .44 Magnum was the first sixgun that really kicked and the stocks supplied with it emphasized recoil that needed to be minimized.

Steve Herrett was a dedicated sixgunner. It shows in his thin Trooper stocks that fill in behind the top of the backstrap to prevent the .44 from being driven deep into the hand upon firing, and the area behind the triggerguard was filled in perfectly.

Herrett teamed up with Bill Jordan to design a second set of stocks for the double action sixgun. Originally designed for fast work from the holster, the smooth finished Jordan Trooper completely enclosed the grip frame of the Smith & Wesson .357 or .44 Magnum. Jordan had designed this special grip for his K-framed Combat Magnum. They have proven to be a set of stocks that also work well on the .44 Magnum in the field.

Walter Roper was a well-known handgunner and experimenter before World War II and designer of the stocks that bear his name. Target stocks from Smith & Wesson are Roper-style, but are made much too large and bulky. Roper's stocks fill in behind the triggerguard and under the butt of a double action revolver while leaving the backstrap open. Skeeter Skelton used the Roper grip as the basis for his stocks. He simply changed the angle behind the triggerguard slightly and slimmed them down overall. I have seen later Roper stocks that were deadringers for Skeeter's idea of an improved design. Today, Herrett offers Roper stocks as a standard catalog item.

Originally designed for the small framed .38s from Smith & Wesson and Colt, Herrett's Detective stocks also work quite well on large-framed Smith & Wessons with round butts, which come from the factory fitted with rubber finger groove grips. The Detective stocks fill in behind the triggerguard, but with their open-backed feature do not add to the bulk of the sixgun. They also extend far enough below the bottom of the butt to accept three fingers perfectly or they can be ordered to just extend below the butt for ease of concealment. I like the longer grip for use with heavy-underlugged barreled .44 Magnums from Smith & Wesson.

One of my favorite Herrett stocks is that designed by Rod Herrett, Steve's son and head man at Herrett's. Rod took the Jordan Trooper and made it for the large-framed Dan Wesson. Because the Dan Wessons do not have a traditional grip frame but a stud that accepts a one-piece grip, Herrett was able to carve this stock much smaller than the Jordan and, at the same time, improve upon the factory stocks provided on the large-framed Dan Wesson. They are smooth walnut and help immensely in handling the heavy weight and felt recoil of the Dan Wesson .44 Magnum and .45 Colt.

HOGUE GRIPS

Guy Hogue started the grip company that bears his name more than twenty-five years ago and is now carried on by his two sons. Hogue is synonymous with finger grooves and the Monogrip concept which allows one-piece-style grips to be fitted to double action revolvers from the bottom through the use of a special stirrup that fits over the grip pin on the bottom of double action grip frames.

The grip is slipped up and over the stirrup and then bolted on solidly from the bottom. This creates a very smooth look and a solid setup. Hogue grips are available in the original pebble-grained rubber design as well as the more aesthetically pleasing style in exotic woods such as Goncala Alves, Pau Ferro, rosewood, kingwood, mesquite, tulipwood, and Coco Bolo.

Hogue grips are normally found in a large finger groove-style, however, they can be made smaller and without finger grooves upon special request. I find the medium frame finger groove grips fit me extremely well and one of my silhouette revolvers, a 10-inch Dan Wesson .357 Magnum, wears Pau Ferro Hogue Monogrips. The long, heavy barrel of the .357 Dan Wesson tends to pull the gun down and the finger grooves help to counteract this trend immensely. The fastest man with a double action sixgun, now or probably ever, Jerry Miculek, uses a specially designed pair of Hogue Monogrips that look much like Jordan Troopers on his 8-3/8-inch Model 27 .357 Magnum.

With the great rise in single action interest, especially since the advent of Cowboy Action Shooting, Hogue has now branched out into this field and is offering standard single action stocks for Colt Single Actions, Ruger Blackhawks, and Ruger Vaqueros. Available in both ivory and black micarta, plus such exotic woods as tulipwood, kingwood, Goncala Alves, and rosewood, these latest additions to Hogue's line-up are designed to add that special touch to a single action sixgun.

Anyone who has worked with single action grip frames knows very well the variation that exists in grip dimensions from frame to frame. To accomplish a precise fit, Hogue's stocks are supplied oversized without the grip pin hole being drilled. Instructions are included for drilling the pin holes. Each individual can then sand and polish the grips to size, or they can be properly marked and returned to Hogue for custom fitting for a modest sum of $10.

Herrett's stocks on Smith & Wessons, from top left: Jordan Trooper on 4-inch .44 Special, Trooper on 6-1/2-inch .44 Magnum, Detective on 4-inch .45, and Roper on 5-inch .357 Magnum.

Hogue's fancy wood monogrips on 6-inch .357 Colt Python, 10-1/2-inch .44 Magnum Ruger Super Blackhawk, and Smith & Wesson 6-inch .357 Magnum M686.

Both Pachmayr and Hogue supply highly serviceable rubber grips. Top, Pachmayr on Dan Wesson .357 and Smith & Wesson .45; bottom, Hogue on Dan Wesson .357 and Smith & Wesson .44 Magnum.

BOB LESKOVEC–PRECISION PRO GRIPS

I always wondered how Elmer Keith could shoot his 4-inch .44 Magnum with the standard Magna grips. I tried and I just could not control the recoil. Then I was given the wonderful opportunity of examining Keith's sixguns after his death and I found out just how gun-wise the old boy was. On the right grip panel of each of his most used sixguns was a carving strategically placed to fill in the palm of the hand and keep the sixgun from twisting in recoil.

I sent pictures of these original Keith grips off to Bob Leskovec at Precision Pro Grips to see if he could duplicate both a pair of double action N-frame and Colt Single Action Army grips with the carving placed exactly as on the Keith sixguns.

The pictures sent to Leskovec were of three special Keith sixguns. His 5-1/2-inch #5 .44 Special Single Action that inspired Texas Longhorn Arms Improved Number Five, a 7-1/2-inch .44 Special Colt Single Action Army worked over by King in the 1920s, and a 4-inch .44 Magnum Smith & Wesson that Keith carried daily before his stroke in 1981. The one thing they all had in common, besides being in .44 caliber, was the carved ivory stocks.

Having anything made like this today in genuine ivory would be cost prohibitive, for me at least. Leskovec works not only in ivory, but also in an antique ivory polymer that looks more like ivory than the ivory grips I do have. I sent off the original grips, backstrap, and triggerguard of a Colt New Frontier .45 and the original Magna grips from a 4-inch Elmer Keith Commemorative .44 Magnum

Smith & Wesson. Leskovec copied the fit exactly and made the grips the width I wanted, much thinner than the factory grips, and most importantly carried out the carved steer heads to perfection.

Precision Pro Grips can supply custom grips in ivory or antique ivory acrylic, plain or carved, and also in exotic woods, plain or inlaid. In addition to the steerhead carving on my grips, I also had Leskovec carve my initials in the opposite grip for each sixgun. Precision Pro Grips does not turn out stocks on a factory basis but rather prefers to work with each sixgunner individually.

SYNTHETIC GRIPS

Finally we come to the synthetic grips offered by Hogue, Uncle Mike's, and Pachmayr. They won't do anything to fancy up a fine sixgun, but they are relatively inexpensive, highly durable, and normally a top choice for handling felt recoil. A sixgun that is packed openly can destroy a pair of expensive stocks very quickly especially if the sixgun's grip frame is subject to being bumped on hard objects. The synthetic grips from these three manufacturers take the bumps in stride. They are also perfect when the weather is wet because they still provide a positive gripping surface. For silhouette shooting there is no better choice.

Rifles and shotguns, like computers and claw hammers, are, for the most part, highly efficient tools. Sixguns, however, are soul-stirring personal firearms that deserve a personal touch. There is no easier way to personalize a great sixgun than by adding custom stocks.

CHAPTER 18

SIXGUN LEATHER

Sixguns have neither the range of a rifle, nor the easy-to-hit qualities of the shotgun. They do, however, have one major attribute that the others do not possess—handiness. With all the reasons we love sixguns so, this one stands above all else. Sixguns are personal weapons. Weapons that are always handy and convenient because they are always on or about the body.

With the single-shot flintlock and percussion pistols of the eighteenth and early nineteenth century, the standard procedure was simply to tuck said pistol in a sash around the waist, which is not too terribly different from the modern pistolero who tucks a slab-sided semi-automatic in his waistband.

As weapons became larger, the mounted Dragoon of the early 1800s carried his single-shot .54 caliber pistols and later, the 4 pound Walker Colt .44s in specially designed holsters, so-called pommel holsters because they were designed in pairs with a center section that was cut out to fit over the pommel of a saddle. The soldier carried his sword around his waist while his pair of pistols, and later sixguns, were conveniently at hand riding in front of him on both sides of his horse. With the coming of the First Model Colt Dragoon .44 in 1848 followed almost immediately by the Second and Third Models and then by the 1851 Navy .36 and 1860 Army .44, the military switched from saddle holsters to belt holsters with these early cap-n-ball sixguns being worn butt forward in full flap holsters. Certainly someone with a sharp knife and a sharp mind noticed early on that all that leather wasn't needed and quickly realized the convenience of being able to rapidly draw a sixgun from a less cumbersome rig than the military flap holster and the age of the gunfighter began.

Actually, the possibility of drawing a sixgun with some haste probably began to some extent before the War Between the States, because the California or Slim Jim holster emerged. This was an open top holster with the leather cut away from the grip and top of the triggerguard with the hammer of a single action still fully covered. Most of these holsters were made of flimsy leather (the best leather was reserved for saddles), however, one occasionally finds a California holster not only made of sturdy leather, but also modified to allow quick access to the hammer and trigger as the sixgun is drawn. There were definitely some very savvy sixgunners about in the 1850s.

There are those who will tell you that a quick draw was impossible from the old leather—not so. Speed is relative. True, sixgunners with modern holsters who know what they are about could certainly beat any one of the old-time gunfighters with their sixguns and rigs when it comes to shading leather, however, the old timers only had to be faster than their peers. Quite often they did not even have to be faster, but simply more accurate and able to stand up with lead whizzing around them and deliver the one deadly shot.

The quick draw, in reality, is nothing even close to the Hollywood hokum that has been spread throughout this century. Only a man contemplating suicide allowed the other man to draw first. Most gunfights probably began with the sixgun already in the hand, or given two equal opponents, the one who went for his sixgun first *always* won. The 1851 Navy Colt especially made it possible for a practiced sixgunner to be just as deadly with his sixgun in the leather as in his hand—perhaps even more so. I will guarantee that with a little practice using either the California holster or the Mexican style that followed it, a sixgunner can draw and fire before the average person can react. By the time realization sets in as to what is happening, it is too late.

With the advent of the cartridge firing sixgun, belts with sewn on cartridge loops became popular and the Mexican-style holster emerged to fit over the cartridge belts. Again, ignore the Hollywood influence. The drop loop holster, riding in a slot cut in a loop in the bottom of the belt, often seen on the silver screen began with the "B" Westerns of the 1930s, evolved into the low riding, metal-lined holsters of the 1950s. Such rigs never existed on the frontier. The norm was a belt that threaded through a loop, sewn on the back of the holster. Worn on a wide belt, a tight belt loop on the holster precluded any need for the Hollywood tie down for a faster draw.

The Mexican-style holster combined the California holster with a full backflap with slots that accepted the holster body. This is the most popular style seen in Cowboy Action Shooting today and is certainly the most authentic for the period from the 1870s to the turn of the century. A close look at the Mexican holsters surviving from this period again shows that a quick draw was indeed possible. Many of them were built for maximum security. Others, however, were cut away for quick access to the grip, hammer, and trigger of a single action sixgun.

At the turn of the century, creditable leather rigs were being turned out by such holster makers as H.H. Heiser of Colorado, George Lawrence of Oregon, and S.D. Myres of Texas. It remained for a Cherokee Indian from Oklahoma, one Tom Threepersons, to modernize the sixgun scabbard. Threepersons was a real gunfighter, a lawman who while serving on the El Paso Police Department, walked into S.D. Myres Saddle Shop in 1920 with the idea for a radical new holster. Myres was well-known and had been popular for decades among Texas Rangers who took their leather seriously.

Threepersons removed the backflap and instead used a belt loop designed to fit the belt tightly. All leather was cut away from the hammer, grip frame, and triggerguard area. In fact, the front of the sixgun's triggerguard rested on the top of a heavy welt, sewn in the back edge of the holster. There was no extra leather of any kind. Only the barrel, top strap, and part of the cylinder and main frame were covered. The leather used was of the finest saddle skirting, allowing the holster to be wet-moulded to the sixgun

This pair of Berns-Martin Speed Holsters and the 5-1/2-inch .44 Special Colt Single Action sixguns belonged to Elmer Keith.

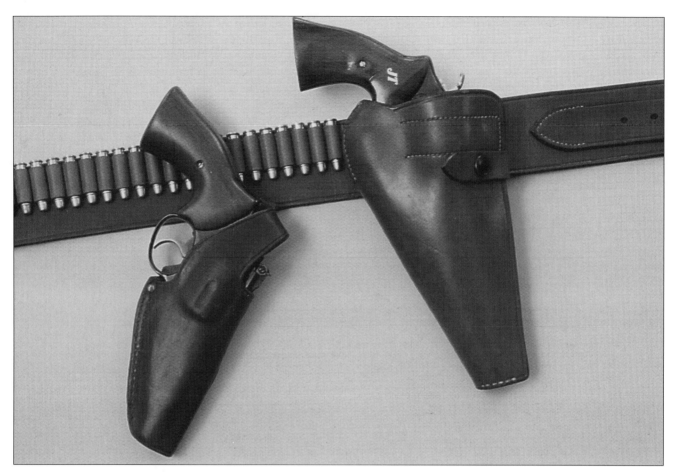

Classic holster designs: Chic Gaylord Thumb Snap with 4-inch Smith & Wesson .44 Magnum and Berns-Martin Speed Holster with 5-inch Smith & Wesson .357 Magnum.

The Hollywood Fast Draw holster, the original metal-lined holster designed by Arvo Ojala for TV and movie Western stars in the 1950s. This style rig appeared in virtually every Western movie of the time as well and was popular in the early days of Fast Draw.

so that when it dried slowly, the result would be a tight fit, requiring no safety straps of any kind while still allowing a fast draw due to the basic design. To aid in a fast draw, the holster was angled so the muzzle of the sixgun pointed to the rear at about 30 degrees in what is now known as an F.B.I. cant.

The Tom Threepersons holster is certainly the most famous holster of the twentieth century. It has been offered by virtually all holster makers including Lawrence's #120 Keith, Bianchi's #1 Lawman, and today, the original design is still available from the original location (El Paso Saddlery is the successor to S.D. Myres).

S.D. Myres also collaborated with another lawman to produce a classic holster in the 1950s. Border Patrolman Bill Jordan vastly improved the duty holster of the time by doing two things. The Border Patrol issue holster of the time rode below the belt by using a drop loop shank. Jordan did away with the flop-around, flimsy design and the shank of the holster was metal-lined to allow a tight fit on the belt and also to keep it in place when the sixgun was drawn. A Threepersons-style holster was then fit to the shank, and replaced the bulky style that covered the trigger-guard, and the Jordan holster was born. Until the advent of the "wondernines," the high capacity semi-automatics, amongst law enforcement personnel, the Jordan holster combined with a good sixgun was the rig of choice all around the country.

In the 1930s, while in the Navy, Jack Martin was stationed in the deep snows of Alaska and needed a holster for a 7-1/2-inch Colt Single Action .45 that allowed a fast draw while at the same time kept the long barrel out of the snow. The result was the revolutionary Berns-Martin holster. This holster consisted of a pouch that carried a spring and a completely open front. The sixgun was placed in the front of the holster barrel first and then snapped back into the spring. To withdraw the sixgun, one simply pressed down on the grip and then brought the gun straight out and up—very fast. Berns-Martin was eventually purchased by Bianchi and the holster became the Bianchi Breakfront.

In the 1950s, I well remember seeing a segment on the old *You Asked For It* TV show in which a man concealed twenty-six handguns on his person. The man was holster maker Chic Gaylord, who specialized in concealment rigs for undercover peace officers, diplomats, customs agents, and the like. From his shop in New York, Gaylord pioneered the creation of maximum concealment rigs with minimum leather used.

All of Gaylord's holsters were boned, that is, the sixgun was inserted while the leather was wet and

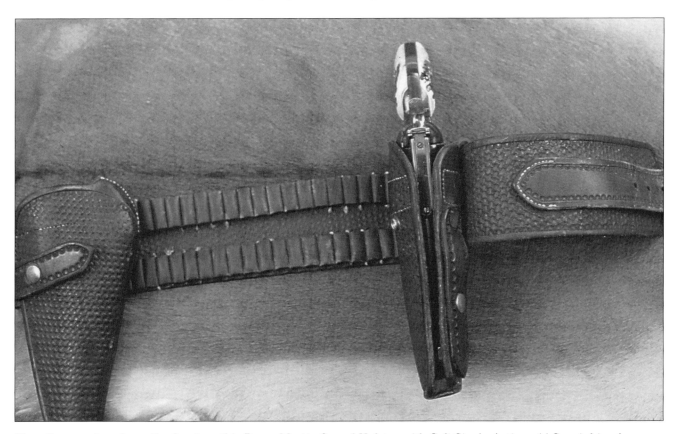

Note the opening down the front on this Berns-Martin Speed Holster with Colt Single Action .44 Special in place.

Border-stamped Half Breed by John Bianchi's Frontier Gunleather for Cimarron Model P. Note special conchos on holster flap and fancy buckle.

then a piece of plastic was used to carefully mould the holster to every contour of the gun. This allowed a fast draw from a secure holster with no straps. That same TV show later featured Bill Jordan demonstrating his fast draw. How times have changed.

It was also about this time that the TV Western emerged. Instead of today's mindless sitcoms, the airwaves of all networks were filled with Westerns.— every night—on every channel. The sport of Fast Draw sprang up and the man making much of the leather for both the TV Westerns and the new sport was Arvo Ojala.

Ojala took the drop loop belt of the "B" Western movies, added a holster with a longer shank that was metal-lined, and for the body of the holster, used a metal-lined Threeperson style that hung straight. The metal lining of the holster body allowed for tremendous speed from the leather as the single action sixgun could be cocked while in the leather. Then and now this method is only for the use of blanks. A single action sixgun with live rounds should **never**, repeat, **never, ever be cocked in the holster.**

Ojala's rigs were extremely popular. Mine, purchased in 1958, is for a 7-1/2-inch Colt or Great Western .45 and is finished in black basket stamping. It holds special significance for two reasons. First, it cost me a week and one-half's pay, and second, my first date with the girl who would be my wife within a few months was to the gun shop to pick up my newly arrived Ojala belt and holster. No one can say she wasn't warned as to what to expect in the future. I still have both the Ojala rig and the same wife, so it has worked.

An employee of Ojala's soon went out on his own and Andy Anderson introduced his Gunfighter rig. Anderson took the basic Ojala holster, brought it out of the belt loop and up high on the belt, slanted muzzle forward, for an even quicker draw. It was especially popular with those who fanned their sixguns in Fast Draw competition. Clint Eastwood favored the Anderson rig in most of his movies as did James Drury in the *Virginian* TV series.

About the same time that Ojala and Anderson were revolutionizing the Western rig, Roy Baker added leather to the Threepersons by cutting two pieces of leather in the shape of a pancake, sewing them together around the edges, and then sewing inside of the pancake to the form of the sixgun. He then added belt slots and his unique, and now universally copied, pancake holster was born. One of the great attributes of the pancake holster is the fact that a natural sight channel is formed at the front edge, allowing sixguns with post front sights to be carried without fear of the front sight digging into the leather as the sixgun is drawn.

FBI agent Hank Sloan took the basic Threepersons design, but did not want the insecurity of a holster without a safety strap. His ingenious idea was to add a moveable slot of leather to the holster welt, a piece held in place with an adjustable screw. This little strip of heavy leather bears against the bottom of the sixgun frame and holds the gun in place under most activity, but does not hinder a fast draw when the sixgun is needed quickly. Threepersons, Martin, Gaylord, Jordan, Baker, Ojala, Anderson, and Sloan are definitely men who greatly influenced holster design from the 1920s to the 1960s.

Like sixgun stocks, sixgun leather is highly personal. Today there are literally legions of excellent holster makers out there offering the best leather designs ever available. I will share some with which I am completely familiar for hunting, Cowboy Action Shooting, and for such great activities as desert roamin' and woods bummin'.

Forty years ago I purchased a Ruger .44 Magnum Flat-Top, the original Blackhawk, and ordered a cartridge belt and #120 Keith holster from the George Lawrence Company in Portland, Oregon. The sixgun and holster are still in service, but the belt has shrunk significantly over the past four decades. Since that time, I have been the perpetual experimenter both with sixguns and leather, with the latter being tried in virtually every persuasion both purchased from many excellent craftsman and homegrown.

I have learned what constitutes good leather in terms of design, material, and craftsmanship. I also have some definite ideas on what I like when it comes to carrying single action or double action sixguns, long or short barrels, in hunting situations, for concealed carry, for Cowboy Action Shooting, for Fast Draw, and just general use. I have found that cheap leather is too expensive and good leather is a bargain that will last indefinitely with proper care.

Just as there is no perfect sixgun for every situation, there is no perfect holster. That is what makes sixgunning so interesting. Every new sixgun and leather rig has the potential to reach into the very spirit and stir the soul. The great joy in life is never in finding the perfect anything, it is always in the pursuit. With that in mind, I share some great leather that I have experienced from several sources.

Bianchi/Frontier Gunleather

John Bianchi started making holsters in his garage during his off-duty hours as a California police officer. He became so successful, that he soon went into holster making full-time, and built Bianchi International into one of the largest holster making companies of all time. His Lawman holster alone has sold well over one million units. A few years back Bianchi "retired." He apparently did not miss corporate life, but he did miss the working of fine leather, so we now have John Bianchi's Frontier Gunleather.

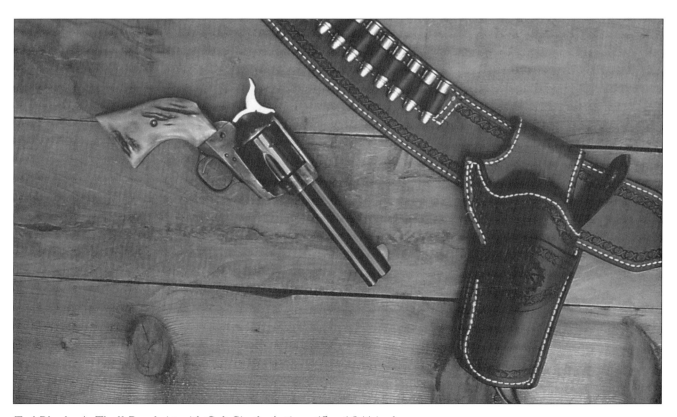

Ted Blocker's Thell Reed rig with Colt Single Action .45 x 4-3/4 inch.

No mass production here—every rig is custom-built to each customer's specifications. One can find Buscadero-style rigs with single or double holsters in everything from plain, smooth leather up to the fanciest presentation grade possible. His Half Breed and Plainsman rigs are more conventional Western-style rigs, consisting of holsters that slide over a cartridge belt. All rigs are double thickness leather and holsters can be made with or without full backflaps. Western leather just doesn't get any better than this.

Ted Blocker

One of the most practical Western rigs offered is the Thell Reed, designed by Ted Blocker for well-known and long-time sixgunner Thell Reed. The holsters ride high on the belt with a muzzle forward rake and are not only fast, but without metal lining, they are also both lightweight and comfortable to wear. The Thell Reed has an ingenious leather tab on the back of the holster to keep it tight on the belt and in place as the sixgun is drawn. It is one of the few fast holsters to provide an 1880s-style covered triggerguard. Blocker also continues the tradition of Gunfighter Leather by Andy Anderson with his drop loop and high riding Anderson Gunfighter-style Western rigs.

Ed Bohlin

During the heyday of the Western movies, especially during the time of Tom Mix, Buck Jones, Tim McCoy, and their peers, much of the Hollywood leather was turned out by Ed Bohlin. Bohlin's shop specialized in extra fancy leather gun rigs with floral carving and silver embellishments. During the 1960s Bohlin also offered some of the best Fast Draw leather including a rig that incorporated a very long drop loop in the belt while the holster was folded to form the backflap as high as the Tom Threepersons design.

Elmer Keith worked with Bohlin on the perfect sixgun rig that consisted of a Threepersons-style holster with a backflap, short drop loop, and a slotted belt. Known as the Elmer Keith Protect-A-Sight rig, the safety strap was spring loaded and came up and over the front of the holster with a built-in leather protector for the rear sight. Bohlin rigs can be found sporadically at gun shows.

Bull-X/Chaparral

Bull-X produces a full line of quality bullets including the proper designs and weights for Cowboy Action Shooters who load their own. Most of my everyday workloads for my sixguns are assembled with Bull-X's 240 grain .44 and 255 grain .45 semi-wadcutter bullets. Now Bull-X is also in the leather business and offers a very fine rig of single weight leather known as the Chaparral.

This is a very practical rig for either hunting or Cowboy Action Shooting. Mine has fifteen bullet

These holsters carried Elmer Keith's ivory-stocked 4-inch Smith & Wesson .44s. Leather by Sparks, Lawrence, Bohlin, and S.D. Myres.

Bull-X markets this single-weight leather Chaparral rig for all single action sixguns. The pictured sixgun is a 7-1/2-inch Great Western with stocks by Charles Able.

The Rooster by G.Wm. Davis is patterned after John Wayne's belt and holster. The sixgun is a 5-1/2-inch .44 Special that was tuned by Bob Munden and has Charles Able stag stocks.

loops on the left side while the holster carries a 7-1/2-inch single action. The holster and belt are both border stamped while the holster has a block at the toe and a full backflap—nice leather.

G.Wm. Davis/Trailhands-Gunslingers

G.Wm. Davis has long been known for quality leather and competition rigs, but my main interest is his best Western-style rig as offered under the Trail-hands and Gunslingers banner. While nearly every Western star of either movies or TV went the route of the heavy metal-lined drop loop holsters in the 1950s, one man did not. The Duke stayed with the traditional belt and lightweight holsters that slid on the cartridge belt rather than hanging low on the hip and tied down. The Rooster Rig, appropriately named after John Wayne's portrayal of Rooster Cogburn in *True Grit*, is such an outfit. My personal Rooster Rig is a rough-out lined belt and smooth finish-lined holster for a pet Colt Single Action 5-1/2-inch barreled .44 Special. I rank the Rooster as one of my favorite rigs.

El Paso Saddlery

Bobby McNellis of El Paso Saddlery offers not only plain smooth leather, but also supplies basket stamp-ing, done by hand not machine, that is particularly attractive. El Paso's basket stamping is also a small design, rather than a large one designed to cover a great deal of area in the smallest possible time. El Paso is also one of the few companies that offers real floral carving, both in the modern style and the old incised 1880s design. Floral carving from El Paso is affordable and is also even better than what used to be offered by Elmer Keith's favorite holster maker, the George Lawrence Company. El Paso also manages to get a very beautiful brown oiled color to its leather.

The mainstay of the El Paso line is the number 1920, a Tom Threepersons holster that the old law-man himself would be quite proud to use. For easier access to long-barreled sixguns for hunting, El Paso offers the Tom Threepersons in a crossdraw design that works exceptionally well with 7-1/2-inch single action and 8-3/8-inch double action sixguns. Also available is the Border Patrol, patterned after the rig pioneered by Bill Jordan that is particularly striking in floral carved design. I have one of the few floral carved Border Patrol holsters; it is a cherished pos-session.

The famous leather worn by General Patton came out of the El Paso shop of S.D. Myres, and El Paso

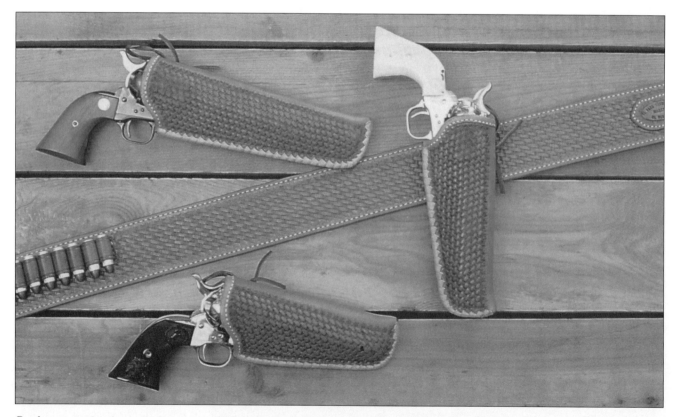

Basket stamping is carried out to perfection as these hand-stamped examples of the El Paso #1920 Tom Threepersons holsters show. Sixguns pictured are Colt Single Actions: A 7-1/2-inch .45 Colt, a 5-1/2-inch .45 Colt, and a 4-3/4-inch .44-40.

Modern floral-carved Tom Threepersons holster and matching belt from El Paso, with ivory- stocked 7-1/2-inch .44 Special Colt New Frontier. Compare this to Lawrence floral-carved #120 Keith from the 1960s that carries Colt New Frontier 7-1/2-inch .45 Colt with stocks by Bob Leskovec.

Saddlery carries on the tradition with this famous rig for both single and double action sixguns. El Paso's Duke rig is a copy of the belt and holster worn by John Wayne for more than thirty years. Complete with a rough-out money belt, this is one of the most comfortable rigs around. El Paso also offers the money belt in a smooth finish. Money belts are made of one piece of wide leather folded over with the smooth side or rough side up and then sewn on three sides to provide a lining plus an opening at one end for coins. They are quite comfortable to wear, especially after a long day in the field.

Authentic, old leather comes out of El Paso also in the shape of the favorite Texas Ranger holster, the 1930 Austin, and such 1880s styles as the Slim Jim, Ranger, and Sweetwater. The latter is a lower riding than normal Mexican loop-style holster that works particularly well with 7-1/2-inch single action sixguns. An 1895 Hardin, patterned after John Wesley Hardin's shoulder rig, is also available as well as a spring clip shoulder holster straight out of the Old West. Anyone who likes premium leather and cannot find it from El Paso is impossible to please.

Freedom Arms

Freedom Arms not only manufacturers the finest possible single action sixguns, but it also offers one of the best shoulder holster designs for the hunter. Made of double thickness leather with a suede lining that protects the sixgun's finish, this rig does not hang horizontally under the off-side arm, but rather rides across the abdomen with part of the weight being taken up by a strap on the back of the holster that accepts the pants belt. This divides the weight between shoulders and waist. Made for both scoped and iron-sighted single action sixguns, this rig is the hunter's friend.

Galco

Galco is heavily into police duty equipment and concealment rigs and its Yaqui Slide and S.O.B. (Small Of the Back) holsters are very well-known. Two of my favorite Galco rigs are a pair, left and

Freedom Arms markets this excellent shoulder holster for handgun hunters. It holds a scoped Freedom Arms 7-1/2-inch .454. Straps go over the shoulder and around the waist and the pants belt also hooks into the back of the holster.

Galco's Trail Boss is a faithful re-creation of a frontier sixgun rig made of double-leather. Here it carries a 5-1/2-inch Colt Single Action .44 Special.

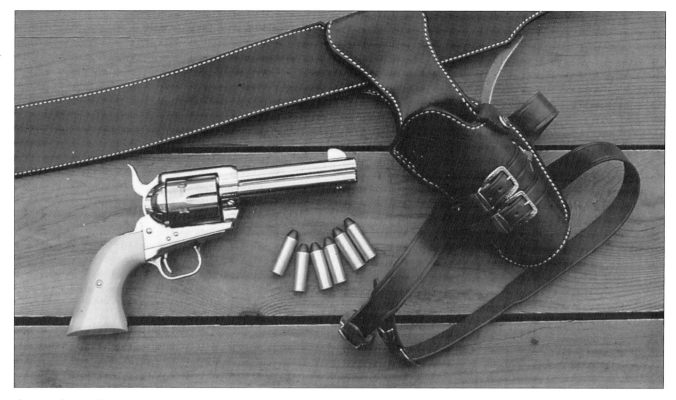

Galco's Speed Rig was designed by exhibition shooter Bob Munden. Munden also modified the Colt Single Action .45 to be used as a fanning sixgun. Note high swept hammer.

right hand, of Silhouettes for Smith & Wesson N-frames and a pair of Speed Masters for two Smith & Wesson 4-inch Model 19 .357 Magnums. The latter are entirely moulded to the sixgun and feature a completely covered triggerguard with no safety strap. They carry extremely well under a sport coat. The Silhouette, as its name indicates, is an abbreviated thumb snap holster that accepts any length barrel. It is also easy to conceal under a sports coat.

Galco's Trail Boss is an authentic Western rig of top-quality leather which consists of a Mexican-style holster and a 2-1/2-inch wide cartridge belt; both are fully lined. For those who want the fastest possible rig for Fast Draw with a Colt Single Action Army or replica thereof, Galco offers the Bob Munden Speed Rig designed by the Fastest Man Alive, Bob Munden. This rig is made of double- thickness leather with a forward rake holster, cut low in the front for speed. It works equally well with a straight draw or for the fanner who draws with one hand and fans the hammer with the other.

Al Goerg

Al Goerg was a pioneer handgun hunter in the 1950s who also designed a premium shoulder holster. He was killed in plane crash in Alaska nearly thirty years ago. I treasure a Goerg shoulder holster

for a 10-inch Ruger Flat-Top .44 Magnum. A few years ago I walked into a local pawn shop looking for bargain sixguns, as I often do, and saw nothing of interest, but as I turned to leave, I spotted something on the back shelf. There was a Goerg shoulder holster for a Smith & Wesson 6-1/2-inch .44 Magnum for only $30! Needless to say, it now carries my 6-1/2-inch .44 Magnum.

Goerg field tested everything himself on handgun hunting trips. His shoulder holster is a masterpiece. It is a spring clip holster, very lightweight with a cartridge carrier on the off-side that also serves as a belt slide to balance the weight. Most of the weight is carried by the hips rather than the shoulders. My original Goerg has logged many Idaho mountain miles with its 10-inch Flat-Top .44 Ruger in place. The only drawback is that the small shoulder straps make wearing a heavy shirt mandatory.

Mario Hanel

A look at old, authentic leather from the frontier days reveals that most of it was made of very lightweight leather and that some came not just from the shop of a craftsman, but a real artist. Today, this same type of leather is available from the shop of Mario Hanel. All of Hanel's rigs are made to duplicate old style leather to the smallest detail. Hanel also

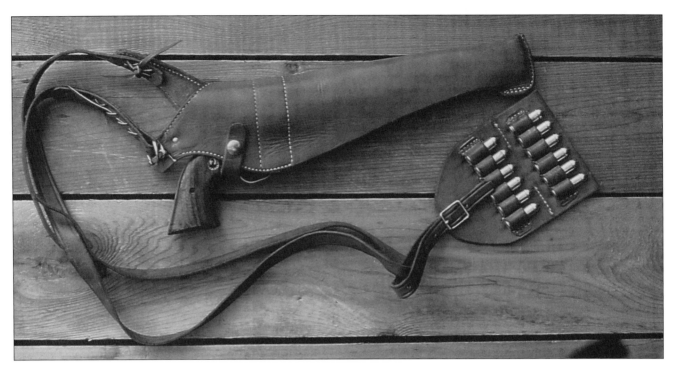

Handgun Hunter Al Goerg designed this shoulder rig. The sixgun is a 10-inch Ruger Flat-Top .44 Magnum.

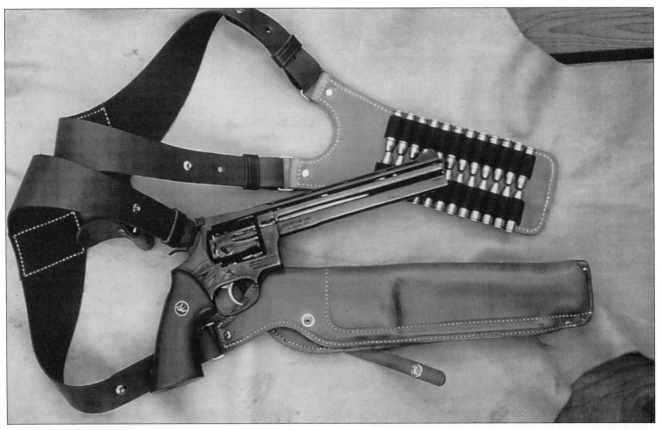

Idaho Leather's Deluxe Shoulder rig for the Dan Wesson 8-inch .44 Magnum is an improvement on the Goerg shoulder holster with wider, more comfortable carrying straps.

uses the leather like a canvas on which he creates intricate designs.

All of Hanel's leather is antiqued to look as if it has been around for a century or more and then finished in a very pleasing deep brown color. In addition to the artistry in leather, Hanel also carries his talent to the metal, including intricate patterns on buckles for both belts and spur straps. Hanel's leather is not the heavy-duty style one would pack on a week long hunting trip in bad weather. It is, however, the best available for the Cowboy Action Shooter who wants to be truly authentic.

Idaho Leather

It is not often one can improve on a great design, however, Idaho Leather has managed to improve on the Goerg shoulder holster by adding heavier, wider, and thus more comfortable, shoulder straps. This is a premium shoulder holster and is cataloged as number 41 Deluxe. The holster is lined, the offside cartridge carrier carries twelve or twenty-four cartridges horizontally, and it has a belt loop for weight distribution between shoulders and hips.

The bullet loops are made of elastic instead of leather, which means I can leave my hunting loads in the loops indefinitely without having the cartridge cases turn green like most will do when left in leather loops. Rather than having the shoulder harness loop together in the back, the 41 Deluxe has two separate wide shoulder harnesses, one for the holster and one for the cartridge carrier, that are attached with dee rings behind the back. This is the most comfortable way to build a shoulder holster.

I am not fan of nylon "leather," however, Idaho Leather offers a nylon shoulder holster design that I often use for hunting. Unlike other nylon designs, this holster is lined with leather, a soft suede leather, that protects the gun's finish. I use this design for all six-guns from 5-1/2 to 8-3/8 inches. It carries comfortably and securely, and provides maximum protection for the sixgun in bad weather situations. Idaho Leather also offers a high riding pancake-style holster that is double stitched, and carries the sixgun high and secure. Idaho Leather is one of the few shops that will not only do custom work, but will also do it in a short period of time.

Gould & Goodrich

The George Lawrence Company began offering leather to sixgunners way back in 1853. This was

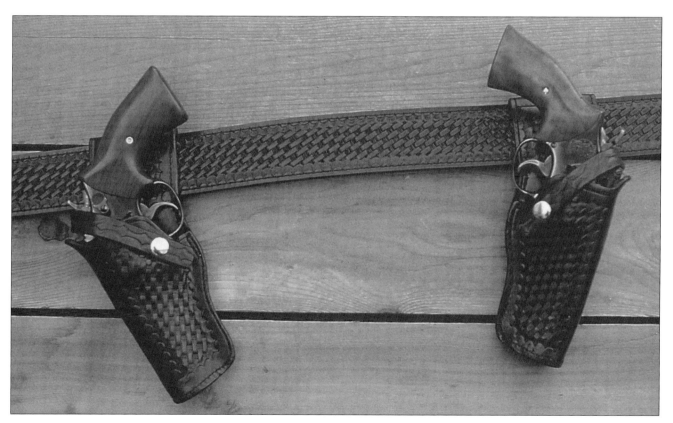

This double rig by Gould & Goodrich sports holsters designed by Bill Jordan and carries Bill Jordan-designed Smith & Wesson Model 19 .357 Magnums. The grips are BearHug's Skeeter Skelton design.

Elmer Keith's favorite leather supplier, and it offers the Keith #120 Tom Threepersons-style holster. In the 1980s, Lawrence was purchased by Gould & Goodrich. Subsequently, all of the Lawrence designs but one, the Gunslinger II, were dropped. Gould & Goodrich still offers its own line of police equipment, concealment rigs, and a very good-looking and comfortable across-the-chest padded hunting shoulder holster. My favorite Gould & Goodrich personal rig consists of a black basket weave, stamped, double set of Bill Jordan-style Border Patrol holsters and matching belt for a pair of Smith & Wesson 4-inch Model 19 .357 Magnums. As a teenager, I did a lot of two gun Fast Draw work with a pair of 7-1/2-inch Colt Single Action Army .45s from a Ray Howser double rig. Now I find 4-inch .357s are not only much easier to master, but practice with double action sixguns is certainly much more practical for, as they say, "serious social purposes."

Elmer McEvoy/Leather Arsenal

Elmer McEvoy of the Leather Arsenal has made his reputation with concealment rigs for semi-automatics. With the great wave of interest in Cowboy Action Shooting sweeping across the country, McEvoy has turned his considerable talents to Western-style leather.

Made of double thickness leather in either black or natural tan, the Leather Arsenal's Western rigs are made of top-quality leather and craftsmanship. Belts are 2-1/2 inches wide with full bullet loops, while holsters are of the Mexican style with one or two loops, depending upon barrel length, to hold the holster tight against the backflap. This is the only holster I know of that is designed to fit perfectly over the bullet loops. Both the belt and holster are border stamped and beautifully made.

Jim Lockwood/Legends in Leather

Like Mario Hanel, Jim Lockwood fills a unique niche in the leather field. Lockwood has had a long fascination with the heroes of the silver screen and has been especially enamored by the belts and holsters worn by everyone from William S. Hart to Briscoe County Jr. Lockwood studied under one of the leading holster makers, Bob Brown, who designed and made many of the rigs worn by the Hollywood cowboys of the 1930s and 1940s Saturday matinees .

Now Lockwood, as Legends In Leather, offers totally authentic "B" Western rigs. Roy Rogers, Hopalong Cassidy, Gene Autry, The Lone Ranger, you name 'em, and Lockwood can supply a duplicate of the rig

This Von Ringler Wyoming Combination rig is designed to be worn over the shoulder as a shoulder rig, on the strong side, or as a crossdraw on the weak side. The sixgun is a 5-1/2-inch Ruger Super Blackhawk.

they wore as they rode across the movie screen in those kinder, gentler days when we were kids. The carving on these rigs is taken from the original patterns of more than a half century ago. All of Lockwood's leather is double thickness, but very lightweight just like the originals. There were no metal linings in those days. For the Cowboy Action Shooter who prefers the look of the movie heroes to frontier characters, Lockwood can supply intricately detailed authentic leather.

Von Ringler

The Wyoming Combination Rig by Von Ringler is truly unique. The holster itself is basically a large "U" or "V" shape of two back-to-back pieces of high quality, but lightweight leather, and the belt part is attached at each wing of the "V." The whole outfit is designed so it can be worn on the strong side, crossdraw, or as a shoulder outfit. The Wyoming Combination really does work all three ways, is comfortable in any position, and can be shifted during the day from any position to the other as one desires. The sixgun fits into a specially-formed pocket that is as if it is moulded from the leather and cartridges are carried in a special pouch in front of the holster pocket.

Ringler also specializes in thumb break strong side holsters or crossdraw pancake-style holsters for the custom sixguns such as the .475 and .500 Linebaughs made on the Ruger Bisley frame. A Ringler pancake holster, heavy-duty pants belt, and a cartridge slide all made for a Bisley sixgun makes an extremely practical hunting rig. Ringler is also now into Cowboy Action Shooting leather and provides authentic-quality Western leather.

Thad Rybka

Thad Rybka masterfully combines the required three elements of good leather: leather quality, craftsmanship, and design. Thad is a dedicated disciple of Chic Gaylord and Andy Anderson and strives to provide minimum leather with maximum comfort and security. I have an M-81 Crossdraw that was custom made for a pet 4-inch Ruger Three-Screw Blackhawk converted to .44 Special that is absolutely perfect in execution. The M-81 rides high and the front half of the triggerguard is covered which helps to hold the Ruger .44 Special in close to the body—a very fast holster.

One of Rybka's best rigs for the hunter is the Tomahawk Crossdraw semi-flap holster. Mine were made for a pair of 4-3/4-inch single action sixguns, a Ruger Super Blackhawk .44 Magnum and a Freedom Arms .454 Casull. This hunting rig carries high, secure, and comfortable.

All of Rybka's leather is hand-made, that is, every piece of leather that Rybka turns out is hand-cut, hand-sewn, and custom-moulded to the exact gun it is to carry. Rybka leather is fitted so precisely that most designs hold the sixgun securely without the need for a safety strap. The provided safety straps are of a most ingenious braided design that adds to the quality of the holster. Thad is heavy on crossdraws and rough-out leather and believes that linings cause more prob-

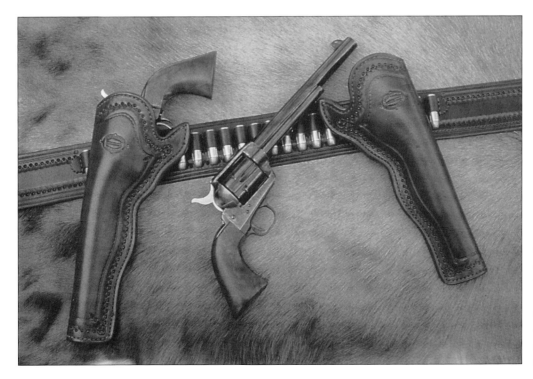

It doesn't get much better than this—a pair of Colt Single Action Army 7-1/2-inch .45s and Slim Jim holsters from San Pedro. Cowboy Action Shooting rig carried out to perfection.

lems than they solve. On most of his holsters, he reverses the leather and furnishes them with the smooth side in, resulting in a rough side out that wears well and is scratch resistant.

San Pedro Saddlery

San Pedro Saddlery offers Cowboy Action Shooters pigskin-lined leather for all single action sixguns with two basic designs. I have two rigs from San Pedro that I use for competition. For a 4-3/4-inch sixgun, San Pedro came up with a Mexican-style sheath with pigskin lining to be worn on the strong side while the second sixgun, a 7-1/2 inch is carried in a crossdraw Slim Jim holster, also pigskin- lined, on the weak side. The holsters and sixguns are carried on a single weight 2-1/2-inch wide belt with twenty-four cartridge loops across the center. Both holsters and belt are a light tan color and feature a most attractive small border design stamping.

My favorite Colt Single Actions for Cowboy Action Shooting, a pair of 7-1/2-inch .45s are used with a San Pedro rig consisting of two crossdraw Slim Jim holsters finished in an antique dark brown finish. This rig does double duty as a pair of nickel-plated EMF 7-1/2-inch .44-40s, complete with checkered ivory polymer eagle grips are also carried in this double set of crossdraw Slim Jim holsters. San Pedro leather is light weight and doesn't get heavy as the day of shooting wears on.

Milt Sparks

Elmer Keith collaborated with Milt Sparks in designing the Hank Sloan FBI holster by suggesting the addition of a hammer extension to protect the clothing from being eaten by an exposed hammer when a jacket or suit coat is worn. The Sloan holster by Sparks secures the sixgun by a screw adjustable leather tab that bears against the bottom of the gun frame and holds it securely in the holster under most activity. Keith carried his 4-inch .44 Magnum daily in a plain black Sparks Sloan holster which speaks highly of its desirability as a concealment rig. I personally use two Sparks Sloan holsters, one in plain black for a 4-inch .357 Combat Magnum, and a lined, basket weave for a 4-inch .44 Magnum. They are first-class in design, material, and craftsmanship.

Texas Longhorn Arms

Texas Longhorn Arms, maker of the fine Improved Number Five and West Texas Flat-Top Target sixguns, also offers a holster that comfortably carries one my favorite sixguns, the 7-1/2-inch single action, which is difficult to carry, especially concealed. The idea behind the Texas High Rider is to allow any barrel length to be carried high and comfortably and also to permit the holster to be easily removed without the necessity of unbuckling and removing the pants belt. All of this is done by combining a holster with a belt slide.

This homemade rig has carried the author's 7-1/2-inch Single Action Blackhawks and New Frontiers in comfort and safety for more than twenty years.

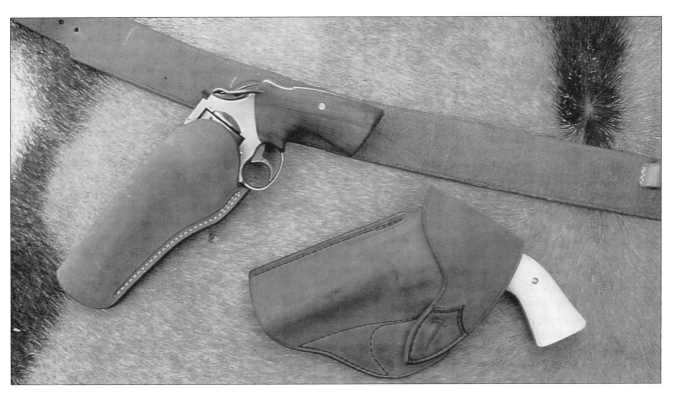

Outdoor rigs of rough-out design by Thad Rybka. Swivel holster on belt carries a .45 Colt Anaconda while the Tomahawk flap holster packs a .45 Ruger Bisley.

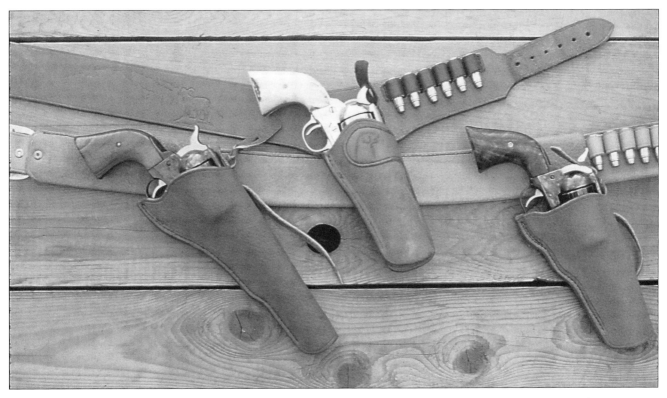

Rough-out leather designs by Thad Rybka for Ruger and Colt Single Actions. In this case, a 4-5/8-inch .45 Blackhawk, a 4-3/4-inch .45 Colt, and a 7-1/2-inch .45 Vaquero. All wear stocks by Blu-Magnum.

This Hank Sloan holster by Milt Sparks is perfect for concealment use with a Smith & Wesson 4-inch Model 19 .357 Magnum. The screw tension keeps the sixgun secure, but does not interfere with a fast draw.

These Texas Longhorn Arms High Rider holster systems are applicable to hunting or concealment use. The holster snaps loose from the belt strap in an instant. Sixguns are Colt Bisley .44 Specials with 4-3/4- and 7-1/2-inch barrels.

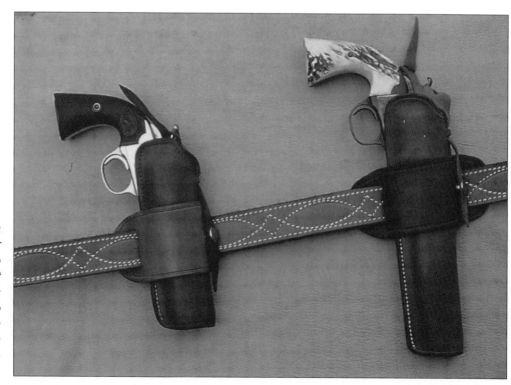

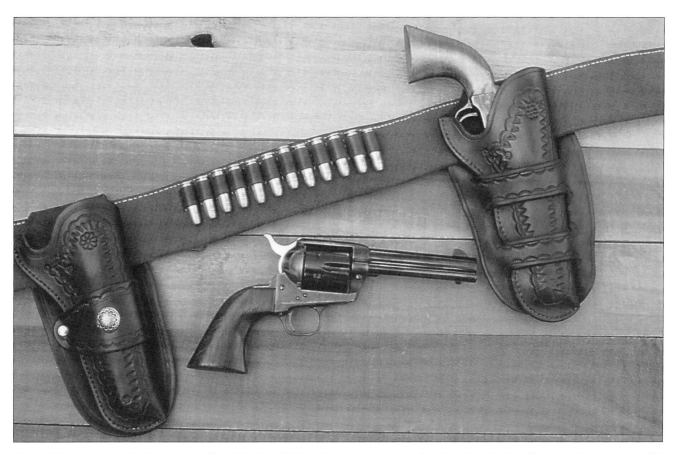

These Mexican-style holsters are offered by TrailRider for the frontier buff or Cowboy Action Shooter. Sixguns are .38-40s by Colt and EMF.

The holster fits into a belt slide and is locked into place by the bottom end of a loop on the front of the holster that contains a female snap that fits with a male snap on the front of the belt slide. The top end of the loop serves as a hammer safety strap. When removal of the holster is desired, one simply unsnaps the loop and the holster can be removed from the belt loop. While in the belt loop, the holster holds the sixgun high and tight to the body and allows even a 7-1/2-inch barreled single action to be worn while sitting. The High Rider can also be worn strong side or crossdraw—a most practical rig for hunting.

Jim Barnard/Trailrider

Trailrider offers the outdoor enthusiast a very heavy-duty, semi-flap crossdraw holster and matching belt. The triggerguard is covered as is most of the upper part of the gun. This is not a fast draw holster, but a secure holster for the hunter and horse rider.

Jim Barnard of Trailrider is heavily into the Old West and is one of the few men I know who shoots an original Spencer carbine. As a true student of the frontier, Barnard offers a complete line of authentic Western holsters for single action sixguns including Mexican style as well as military-style full and half flap designs, along with cartridge pouches, money belts, and old style belt buckles.

Thirty years ago when I strapped on a belt and holster, it was likely to be a 3-inch wide belt with full cartridge loops and a Mexican- or Threepersons-style holster. Maybe my tastes have changed, or maybe I've gotten smarter, or even possibly become a better shot, but today, my belt is more likely to be 2-1/2 inch wide with twelve to fifteen cartridge loops, however, my taste in holsters remains basically the same.

For serious hunting I find myself going more and more to a lightweight and very comfortable shoulder holster. Worn under a down vest, it is out of the way, the sixgun is protected from the elements, and I can even lie down to rest and the sixgun is not affected in any way.

We are blessed to be living in a time of so many great sixgun designs being available, along with a profusion of excellent leather. Great guns. Great stocks. Great leather. Yes, the twentieth century really hasn't been so bad after all.

CHAPTER 19

CUSTOM TOUCHES FOR THE BIG BORE SIXGUN

Sixguns are personal weapons and, as such, all truly serious sixgunners I know prefer to make their sixguns personally and uniquely theirs. One of the easiest ways, as we have already discussed, is to replace the factory stocks with those of ivory, stag, or fancy woods. There are also other ways to make one's sixgun personally unique and personify pride of ownership. Many of the touches we will cover can be done by the sixgunner with very little skill; others will require a gunsmith. My rule of thumb for any sixgun work is quite simple. I am an artist, not a mechanic, so if I, as fumble fingered as I am, can do it, anyone can do it. I also know when to seek the services of a good gunsmith.

In this chapter and the next we will look at custom touches and custom sixgunsmiths. There is not always a clear line between the two, that is, where custom touches end and custom sixgunsmithing begins, so there will be some overlapping and blending of the two.

Custom touches can make a sixgun look better, feel better, even shoot better. I simply cannot abide by an ugly sixgun. If I do not feel something spiritual with each sixgun, it simply will not shoot for me. Oftentimes it only takes a minor change to turn an ugly duckling sixgun into a good-looking sixgun that almost automatically shoots better than before. Of course, I know it is all in my mind, but no one will

Custom .45 New Model Blackhawks: Left gun is all steel with replaced ejector tube, grip frame and rear sight, with grips by BluMagnum; right gun was built in memory of Deacon Deason and totally smoothed out by Milt Morrison, with deluxe bluing, gold embellishments, and fitted with custom stocks by David Wayland. This sixgun, along with the Thad Rybka holster, was presented to the author by The Shootists as they celebrated their Tenth Anniversary.

A totally one-of-a-kind sixgun—a personalized Ruger New Model 4-5/8-inch .45 Blackhawk. It was action-tuned by Teddy Jacobsen, has a steel ejector tube from Texas Longhorn Arms, a locking base pin from Belt Mountain Enterprises, a Bowen rear sight, a steel grip frame, and engraving and stocks from BluMagnum.

ever really convince me that a sixgun with a pre-warning barrel does not shoot better than one with a warning label on the side!

I have just registered my pet peeve when it comes to sixguns. The bad news is that some gunmakers insist on stamping warning labels on the sides of their barrels; the good news is that they all don't do it—at least not yet. We can thank product liability decisions for this abomination. My stainless steel sixguns routinely have the barrel warning label polished off. Not only can this be accomplished, it can be done so that one doesn't even know it was there, and the barrel will not look slab-sided in the process. With blued sixguns it will be necessary to reblue the barrel when the polishing is complete so I usually have sight work or barrel shortening done at the same time.

Nearly every sixgun that comes from the factory needs an action or trigger job, or both. For Freedom Arms sixguns, I routinely have the factory experts do an action job and set the trigger pull at three pounds. For other sixguns, I often call upon Teddy Jacobsen of Actions By T, to smooth up a personal sixgun, especially one that will be carried concealed and used for defensive purposes. Jacobsen is a retired police officer, so he knows what to do to a sixgun and what not to do as far as liability is concerned. We live in a strange world where too many people try to turn black and white into varying shades of gray. Should one's sixgun ever be used in a defensive shooting, it is quite likely that some lawyers would probably do their best to prove the gun was worked over to make it more deadly. Of course, it doesn't make sense but such is the case with justice today. Jacobsen knows

how to avoid this problem by making sixguns smoother and better without leaving them open to ridiculous charges. A good gunsmith is like one's doctor—heed his advice.

Only a few minor changes are necessary with already nearly-perfect Smith & Wesson N-and K-frame sixguns to make them not only personal, but even better sixguns. I do not like wide, sharply checkered hammers and definitely do better double action work with smooth, rounded triggers. Wide target hammers can be reshaped to a more pleasing oval shape and the sharp checkering can be toned down in the process. For wide triggers, I simply have the triggers slimmed to a width no wider than the triggerguard, and then rounded and polished smooth. A rounded, smooth trigger that slips on the trigger finger seems to work much better for me in fast work.

When the Smith & Wesson double action is used with the Magna stocks that were standard on the .44 Specials and .357 Magnums until well into the 1960s, I find I need a filler behind the triggerguard. The answer doesn't have to be a completely new stock, simply a grip adaptor. Tyler's T-Grip is available in blue or polished aluminum for blue, stainless, or nickel sixguns in round butt- or square butt-style. Its use coupled with the standard, old style stocks aids controllability while not sacrificing concealability.

I am in the process of one more change on Smith & Wesson sixguns, especially those that are used for hunting with iron sights. The standard factory red ramp front sight does not work for me as well as a black post. It worked fine thirty years ago, but my eyes are thirty years older and not as sharp as they

Ruger New Model Super Blackhawk grip frames are now available with or without the square- backed triggerguard.

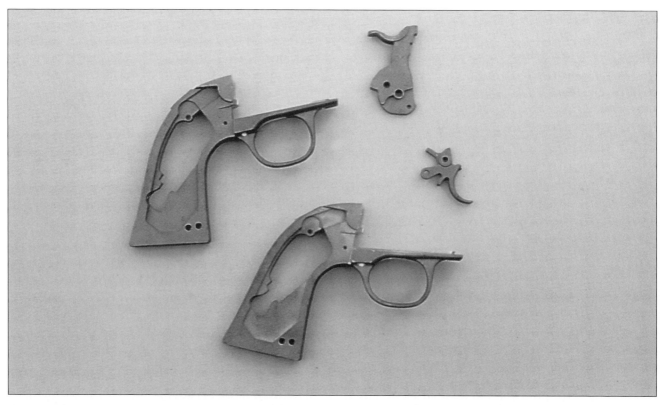

All New Model Blackhawks can be fitted with Bisley-style grip frames, hammers, and triggers as exemplified by these parts from Linebaugh Custom Sixguns.

The Ruger 4-5/8-inch .357 Black-hawk can be personalized with grip options such as round-butted Flat-Top and Old Model grip frames as well as a standard Old Model grip frame. Three-Screw Super Blackhawk grips frames will also fit.

once were. Smith & Wesson can supply the Patridge-style front sight and any competent local gunsmith can remove the red ramp and replace it with the much easier to see, for me at least, black post. These Patridge front sights can also be fitted to Ruger Black-hawks. I just recently had one added to a custom 4-3/4-inch Super Blackhawk that is also fitted with a standard grip frame, Mag-Na-Ported, and fitted with ivory polymer stocks from Ajax. All of this makes one fine packin' pistol even better.

Walt, the pistolsmith at Shapel's, our local gun shop, has been experimenting with another type of easy to see front sight. His solution for a quick front sight pick-up, especially in a hunting situation, is the replacement of the factory sight on Ruger Vaqueros with a fluorescent shotgun bead. It works.

Ruger big bore double action sixguns lend them-selves well to customizing and personalizing. The Redhawk .44 Magnum has been available only in the 7-1/2 and 5-1/2-inch barrel lengths. To make a much easier handling packin' pistol, the barrel can be cut to 4 inches by a local gunsmith, the front sight replaced with a Ron Power black post or ramp front sight, and to further carry out the ease of handling quality, the grip frame and factory stocks can be round-butted. Such a sixgun is not all that much bulkier than a 4-inch Smith & Wesson Model 29 and it will handle hunting loads using heavyweight 300 grain bullets with ease. The round butting seems to lessen felt recoil considerably. I can think of no better sixgun for packin' on the hip when wild hogs in heavy cover are on the hunting menu.

My first personalized sixgun was a Ruger Flat-Top .44 Magnum I purchased as a teenager, fresh out of high school in 1957. A first year production sixgun, the Ruger had the 6-1/2-inch barrel that must have been copied from Smith & Wesson, because no Colt Single Action ever came with such a barrel length as a standard offering. I could have lived with a 5-1/2- or 7-1/2-inch length, but 6-1/2 inches seemed to be neither fish nor fowl. Too long to be short and too short to be long, aesthetically speaking, it just did not seem to fit the sixgun. I had a local gunsmith cut the barrel even with the ejector rod housing and I requested a Super Blackhawk hammer and trigger from Ruger.

The hammer was easy to install, but the wider trig-ger took some work. To cut out the trigger slot in the grip frame, I drilled tiny holes and then used a needle file to open up the slot. The aluminum grip frame was then brightly polished. That sixgun was packed on most outings in a Lawrence #120 Keith holster for a decade before I had the barrel replaced by a longer 7-1/2-inch barrel, so I could steal the shorter barrel for another custom project.

Over the past thirty plus years, I have personal-ized several .44 Blackhawks and Super Blackhawks by simply shortening the barrels. It took Ruger more than thirty years to discover what sixgunners had learned very early: Ruger .44 Magnums make great packin' pistols with barrels cut to 5- 1/2 inches or even with the ejector tubes at 4-5/8 inches. The Super Blackhawk is now available in a factory model in blue or stainless with a 5-1/2-inch barrel and a standard grip frame, but would Ruger also consider offering

Ruger Blackhawks can be fitted with Colt-style grip frames that allow the use of one-piece grips as has been done to this custom .44 Special Flat-Top by Bill Grover.

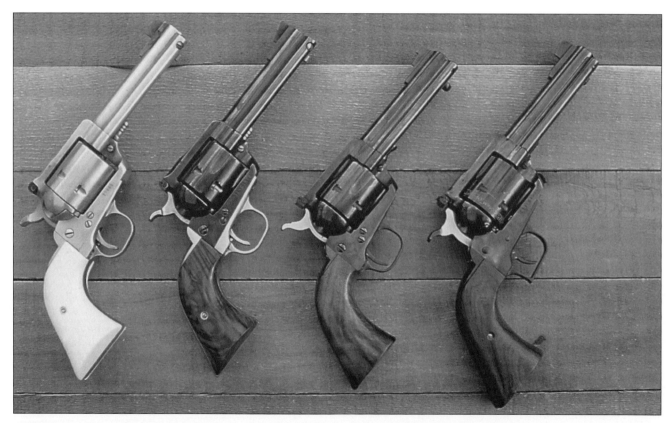

All of these Rugers wear grip frames that are not original: From the left, Ruger Super Blackhawk, barrel cut to 4-3/4 inches, Mag-Na-Ported, tuned, and fitted with an Old Model grip frame and Ajax ivory polymer grips; custom 4-3/4-inch .44 Special wears an Old Army stainless grip frame and Roy Fishpaw stocks; custom .44 Special wears Colt Single Action grip frame and one-piece grips by Bill Grover; 4-3/4-inch .38-40 New Model now is fitted with a Super Blackhawk grip frame.

the Bisley Model with both a 4-5/8- and a 5-1/2-inch barrel? Until it does, gunsmiths around the country are kept busy doing this simple chore.

Another step to customizing via the barrel route is to have the barrel cut even shorter than the ejector tube. A savvy gunsmith can cut the barrel to 4 inches and shorten both the ejector tube and the ejector rod in the process. This makes into a beautiful little sixgun and a very practical concealment rig.

Ruger Blackhawks also lend themselves well to other areas of customizing or personalizing. All Ruger sixguns on the basic single action pattern, the Single-Six, the original Blackhawks in .357 and .44 Magnum, the Old Models in .357, .45 Colt, .41 Magnum, and .30 Carbine, the Old Army, and the Old Model Super Blackhawk, are built on the same bolt pattern for grip frames so all grips frames are interchangeable from model to model. The original Flat-Tops and the Single-Six, produced from 1953 to 1963, carry an XR-3 number on their grip frames while the Old Models from 1963 to 1973 are marked XR-3RED. The former are the same size and shape as the Colt Single Action grip frames while the latter have more room between the frontstrap and back of the triggerguard. All of these sixguns can also be fitted with the wide trigger and hammer from the original Super Blackhawks. The factory no longer has the XR-3 or XR-3RED grip frames, but they can be found at gun shows along with the original Super Blackhawk hammers, trigger, and grip frames. All New Model Blackhawks and New Model Super Blackhawks have grip frames that are the same size and shape as the Old Models, however, the pattern inside is different to accept the New Model lockwork. Due to this change on the interior of Ruger sixguns, Old and New Model grip frames are not interchangeable. Ruger Bisley Blackhawks have a frame that is slightly deeper than the standard models. Bisley grip frames can be fitted to New Model Rugers, however, neither Super Blackhawk, nor standard grip frames, can be fitted to Bisley main frames.

What, then, are the possibilities when it comes to personalizing a Ruger by changing grip frames? Until very recently, all Blackhawk grip frames have been of an alloy rather than steel. We can add weight by using an Old Army stainless steel grip frame on any Ruger Blackhawk made from 1955 to 1973. It also makes a very attractive addition when compared to the easily scratched alloy frame. On the other hand, Ruger Super Blackhawks gain a whole new personality, and weight is reduced by adding either a stainless steel Old Army grip frame or an alloy grip frame from either a Flat-Top or Old Model Blackhawk.

The Ruger Super Blackhawk grip frame does not work for me with heavy recoiling loads, however, it works perfectly when placed on a .357 Magnum or similar sixgun. My favorite grip frame of all the Rugers is the original XR-3; it is the first item I look for at any gun show.

When it comes to the New Model Blackhawks, all alloy grip frames are interchangeable with the steel Vaquero grip frame or any of the New Model stainless steel grip frames. The Bisley grip frame, as previously stated, can be fitted to any of the New Model Blackhawks. I especially prefer it on any heavy kickin' Ruger such as a .44 Magnum or custom .45 Colt. When fitted to the Vaquero, the Bisley grip results in a most aesthetically pleasing sixgun, reminiscent of the old Colt Single Action Army Bisleys of one hundred years ago.

All Ruger Single Action grip frames can also be round-butted, which results in an easier to conceal and control sixgun. All current New Model and Bisley grips frames as well as the Old Army grip frame are available through the Ruger parts department. If one decides to go with a Bisley grip frame, a Bisley hammer, trigger, and backstrap screws are also required to make the transition. It is no great chore to fit the hammer and trigger, however it takes quite a bit of fitting and polishing to match the Bisley grip frame to the Blackhawk main frame. Both Qualite Pistol & Revolver and Linebaugh Custom Sixguns are offering Ruger grip frames, with Qualite having brass Blackhawk grip frames and Linebaugh now casting Bisley-style grip frames of brass, steel, and stainless steel. All grip frames whether they be from Qualite, Linebaugh, or Ruger, require final fitting, polishing, and finishing.

A unique application of a grip frame to a Ruger sixgun is the installation of a Colt backstrap and triggerguard. Ruger's grip frame is one piece and accepts only two-piece grips with a screw through the middle while Colt's two-piece-style allows the use of one-piece grips, which does away with the screw hole on a beautiful piece of wood. Installing the Colt grip straps requires relocating the front triggerguard screw only as all others line up perfectly. A shelf must also be welded to the inside back of the backstrap to accept the Ruger coil spring. The result is well worth the effort.

All blued Rugers, since the inception of the Old Model Blackhawks in 1963, have been fit with an alloy rather than a steel ejector rod housing. These can be replaced with a stainless steel housing, which to me looks out of place on a blued sixgun, or a replacement steel housing is available from either Qualite Pistol & Revolver or Texas Longhorn Arms. All Ruger sixguns are not equal when it comes to ejector tubes, so they must be ordered for a specific model. A steel ejector

Bowen's all steel rear sight easily replaces the factory alloy sight on a Ruger .45 Blackhawk.

Belt Mountain Enterprises supplies these locking base pins for all single actions. The head of the pin is larger and a screw bears against the bottom of the barrel to keep the pin in place under heavy recoil.

These three sixguns have all been touched and tuned by Bob Munden: A 4-inch Smith & Wesson Elmer Keith Commemorative .44 Magnum has had the hammer spur reshaped to a long oval, the trigger thinned, smoothed, and rounded, while the 5-1/2-inch .44 Special Colt has been completely rebuilt for Fast Draw work, and the 4-3/4-inch .45 Colt has been set up for fanning with a high hammer spur and a totally reworked action.

tube and a steel grip frame do wonders for my soul and spirit, not to mention the balance, on a Ruger single action sixgun.

The original Blackhawks were fit with Micro sights. By 1963, these were replaced with a less expensive alloy rear sight. Now even the rear sights can be replaced with a precise click, adjustable steel sight from Bowen Classic Arms. These sights will fit both Blackhawks and Redhawks with a minimum amount of fitting. Again, if I can fit one to a New Model Blackhawk, anyone can.

Anyone who has ever shot single action sixguns much knows that the cylinder pin, or base pin as it is often called, has a habit of loosening under recoil and working itself forward, sometimes to the point of actually leaving the sixgun upon firing. It is no great pleasure to look for a cylinder pin in the snow or sagebrush. Both Freedom Arms and custom gunsmiths handle this problem by fitting base pins with a small screw that tightens against the bottom of the barrel to prevent the pin from moving. Now all single actions can be fitted with the same type of base pin thanks to Belt Mountain Enterprises. Like ejector tubes, all base pins are not equal so the exact Model of Ruger or Colt that will be fitted with the new base pin must be specified.

A so-so New Model Blackhawk, when fitted with a steel grip frame, steel ejector rod housing, Bowen rear sight, and Belt Mountain base pin, becomes a very special sixgun. Add a pair of custom stocks of either fancy walnut or stag, and one is in sixgun heaven.

In the 1950s and early 1960s, both the Flat-Top Blackhawks in .357 and .44 were available with 10-

inch barrels. The Super Blackhawk .44 Magnum stayed standardized at 7-1/2 inches. When the New Model arrived in 1973, I had a Super Blackhawk made into a long-range sixgun by shipping it off to Trapper Gun to have a 10-inch barrel installed and the entire gun finished in a satin nickel to use as a weather resistant hunting handgun. Within a couple of years, Ruger would offer the New Model with a 10-1/2-inch barrel followed in the 1980s with a stainless 10-1/2-inch Super Blackhawk. Both were immediately very popular with silhouetters and hunters. I was simply ahead of my time.

When it comes to personalizing Colt Single Actions, Peacemaker Specialists is the outfit to know. Ed Janis can take a dog of a Colt, fit all new lockwork, a new cylinder and barrel, and refinish it to a thing of beauty again, or he can start with a new Colt and "antique" it, or make it look as if it has been around for one hundred years even though it is mechanically perfect. The latter is especially appealing to Cowboy Action Shooters.

Peacemaker Specialists stocks parts for all three generations of Colt Single Actions and also reworks Third Generation Colts to look like First Generation sixguns by reshaping the front sight and replacing the barrel markings. For example, Third Generation Single Actions are barrel marked "COLT SINGLE ACTION ARMY .45" while original Colts simply said ".45 COLT." Janis can send the new Colt back one hundred years by changing the caliber marking.

Janis also specializes in action jobs, with a Saddle Tramp package that lightens the hammer fall, sets trigger pull at 4 pounds, and deburrs all internal

These targets shot at 25 yards show Munden-tuned sixguns—a 4-inch Smith & Wesson .44 Magnum, a 4-3/4-inch Colt .45, and a 5-1/2-inch Colt .44 Special—will shoot.

parts, or a Gunslinger package that adds extra polishing of all internal parts plus specified trigger pull.

For Ruger, Colt, or replica single actions, Munden Enterprises offers Bob Munden's special actions jobs. Munden has been a Fast Draw exhibition shooter for nearly four decades and knows what works with single actions. He replaces springs with those of his own manufacture and will absolutely make your mouth water over the smoothness of his action jobs.

Fanning the hammer on a Colt Single Action Army looks good in the movies, but a stock single action will not withstand the kind of punishment dished out by this abuse. Munden builds sixguns specially for fanning complete with extended hammers that will stand up to the abuse. Guaranteed.

Munden Enterprises also provides custom single action grips by Mike Wallace and total gunsmithing from completely rebuilding a sixgun to making new cylinders by Jim Lewis. Wallace put a pair of fancy wood one-piece grips on a .44 Special New Frontier worked over by Munden, and the result is again sixgun perfection.

Munden is mostly known for single action work, however, he worked over a 4-inch Smith & Wesson .44 Magnum Elmer Keith Commemorative Model that the Old Master himself would be proud of. The trigger has been rounded and smoothed, the hammer spur reshaped to an oval, and the action smoothed and tuned. I added a set of stocks by Bob Leskovec that duplicates Elmer's ivory stocks with a carved steer head on the right side. The result is one fine double action packin' pistol.

Single action sixguns with fixed sights rarely ever shoot to point of aim. Chances are highly probable that they will either shoot high, low, left, right, or any combination thereof. Some adjustments can be made personally, others take a gunsmith. A sixgun that doesn't shoot close to point of aim is about as impersonal a sixgun as one can have. It just isn't worth a whole lot, especially if one has different sixguns that shoot to different points of aim and one is trying to remember them all.

Most single action sixguns, both foreign and domestic, are coming through now with enough front sight height that they are shooting low. This allows each individual shooter to personally adjust the front sight with the careful use of a file. If the sixgun in question shoots low, but is on for windage, it is necessary to lower the front sight to raise the impact of the bullet on target. To raise impact of the bullet on target, simply file the top of the front sight until the bullet strikes exactly where desired.

The sixgun barrel should be wrapped with tape just in case the file slips and hits the barrel. Metal that is removed cannot be replaced which makes every file stroke most important. It takes very little metal removed from the top of the front sight to drastically change the impact of the bullet on target. It is also necessary to choose the load that will be used with each particular sixgun and file the front sight for that load.

If the sixgun is shot from sandbags or a rest using two hands for sighting in, and then in actual use, fired from a standing position using one hand, chances are very good that the point of impact will be different. For me, the point of impact is higher from a standing one-handed position. The stance that will be used for most shooting should also be used as the front sight is filed in.

A gun that shoots left needs the front sight moved in the opposite direction that one would move the rear sight to change point of impact. The barrel is turned to the left to center the point of impact of a sixgun that shoots to the left. For most single action sixguns, the barrel is simply turned in tighter to move the impact and loosened slightly if the sixgun shoots to the right. Better gunsmiths are set up with a barrel vise that will not scratch the surface of the barrel. I have had numerous barrels turned by the gunsmiths at our local gun shop, Shapel's, with excellent results.

If a sixgun shoots high by several inches or more, the front sight must be changed, that is, replaced by one that is higher. Metal can be added to the front sight by someone who is an excellent welder, or a new sight can be shaped and attached to the barrel. Either will probably require refinishing of the barrel in the process. An easier way is to use a rifle-style front sight. Brownell's carries a full line of Williams Shorty Ramps that attach by drilling and tapping a hole in the top of the barrel and using a screw through the top of the ramp. Ramps are available in height sizes of 1/8 inch (.032), 3/16 inch (.0945), 9/32 inch (.188), and 3/8 inch (.282). Heights are measured from the top of the barrel to the bottom of the dovetail.

To match up with the Williams Shorty Ramps, Brownell's Marble Ramp Mounted Front Sights are offered in heights of .260, .290, .312, .343, .375, .410, .450, .500, and .538, all sizes in thousandths of an inch. Mating four ramps to nine front sights allows thirty-six possible height combinations, so how do we find the right height?

A simple proportion that is used is the change in impact desired (A) compares to the distance to the target in inches (B) as the change required in the front sight (X) compares to the sight radius (C), or $A/B = X/C$. Cross multiplying gives us $AC = BX$, and $X = A$ times C divided by B. Add this to the height of the

Shapel's Gun Shop fitted these two Rugers with shotgun front sights with high visibility fluorescent beads. The top gun is a .45 Colt Ruger Bisley, and the bottom sixgun is a 4-5/8-inch Vaquero fitted with an easy to reach Bisley hammer.

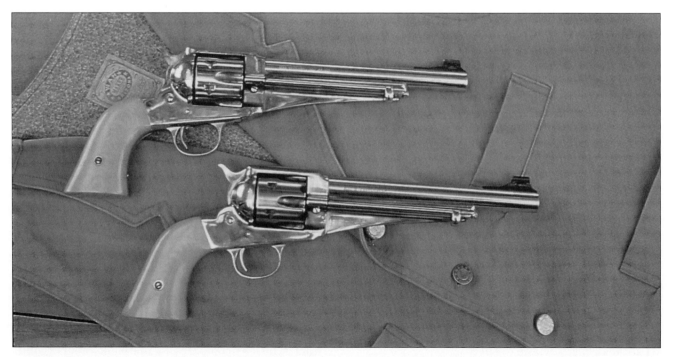

Shapel's Gun Shop brought these two Remington replicas to point of aim by fitting them with Williams Shorty ramps and Marble gold beads like those usually found on rifles.

Ruger Blackhawks can be fitted with post-style front sights, and in this case, Milt Morrison fitted a front sight with two gold beads on a 4-5/8-inch .45 Colt.

The standard Ruger ramp front sight can be re-shaped and painted with fluorescent paint for greatly improved visibility.

original front sight and we come up with the new front sight height. A 1-inch change with a 7-1/2-inch barreled .45 at 25 yards is accomplished by a front sight change of only .01 inch.

Marble bead front sights are available in both 1/16- and 3/32-inch diameters and in both gold and white; the larger beads are much easier to see for sixgun use. The Marble sight fits in a dovetail on the top of the Williams ramp, so windage can easily be adjusted by tapping the ramp front sights right or left.

Adding extra cylinders is one of the best ways to both personalize a sixgun and also maximize its use. Extra cylinders are a natural for single action sixguns. All that is necessary for installation is to remove the cylinder pin, take out the old cylinder, insert the new cylinder, and replace the cylinder pin, all in less time that it takes to tell it.

Freedom Arms'.454 Casull is, without a doubt, the finest revolver ever offered, bar none. One has the choice of adding to the versatility of the .454 with a factory installed cylinder bored for .45 Colt, .45 ACP, or .45 Winchester Magnum. Each cylinder, no matter what the choice of chambering, is line-bored exactly like the original cylinder. That is, the cylinder is chambered locked in the frame for near- perfect alignment of each chamber with the barrel.

One of the most important items around here is my parts box that contains sights, grips, grip frames, barrels, and cylinders that I find at good prices in gun shops or on gun show tables. When I need it I normally have it. With the advent of the Third Generation Colt Single Action in the late 1970s, I ordered an extra .44 Special cylinder. The order was filled incorrectly and I was sent a .44-40 cylinder instead. It went into the parts box and stayed there for years, until I decided to dual cylinder a 7-1/2-inch Colt New Frontier. The original chambering in .44 Special combined with its adjustable sights made it a natural for a .44-40

Freedom Arms offers a personal touch for its .454 Casull by providing three auxiliary cylinders. This 4-3/4-inch Premier Grade with stocks by Charles Able now shoots all four .45s, the .454 Casull, the .45 Colt, the .45 WinMag, and the .45 ACP.

addition. The New Frontier went off to Hamilton Bowen who set the barrel back to minimize the over-sized factory barrel/cylinder gap, and then expertly installed the .44-40 cylinder.

One day I wandered into Shapel's and came out with a great supply of original once-fired .44 Russian brass. The Russian was the forerunner of the Special; the Russian was lengthened to become the Special in 1907 and the Special was lengthened to become the Magnum in 1955. It just seemed a waste to shoot this old rare brass in a .44 Special or .44 Magnum cylinder. A used Third Generation .357 Magnum cylinder in excellent shape went off to Hamilton Bowen to become a .44 Russian cylinder. My New Frontier Colt is now doubly personal. I use .44 Specials with 250 grain hard cast bullets at 1,200 feet per second. Change cylinders and it is .44-40 200 grain bullets at 1,000 feet per second. One more change and the .44 Russian is fed a steady diet of 250 grain bullets at 750 feet per second. New .44 Russian brass is now available because Starline is producing the forerunner of the Special and Magnum.

Texas Longhorn Arms will also personalize its six-guns by adding extra cylinders. My West Texas Flat-Top Target started life as a .44 Special and now has extra cylinders in both .44-40 and .44 Magnum. It may even go back some day to be fitted with a .44 Russian cylinder.

I mentioned the 10-inch New Model that I had fin-ished in a satin nickel to provide a weatherproof finish.

In these days of easily available stainless sixguns, that doesn't seem quite so important. However, blued six-guns can still receive the plating process with firms such as Mag-Na-Port which produces a Mag-Na-Life fin-ish as well as barrel porting. We will look more at Mag-Na-Port's custom services in detail in the next chapter.

One final touch that really personalizes a sixgun is engraving. I have had Texan Jim Riggs do two sixguns for me with full coverage. Actually, my wife had the first one done, a 4-inch Smith & Wesson Model 29 .44 Magnum, as a birthday present for me. Deacon Deason of BearHug added a pair of Skeeter Skelton grips of ivory micarta to complete the special package. Deason said he would never make a set of grips from micarta again because they were too difficult to work with his equipment, but he eventually relented and I also have the only other pair ever turned out by BearHug. You can bet they are as cherished as anything I own.

Recently, Riggs completed my second sixgun, a match to the Smith & Wesson by engraving a 4-3/4-inch Colt Single Action .45, which also carries authen-tic ivory stocks. Both sixguns have been finished in an antique nickel to highlight the engraving. I trust my grandsons will enjoy these two special sixguns as much as I do.

Tedd Adamovich of BluMagnum also does engrav-ing and has personalized two sixguns for me, both Rugers. The first is a 4-inch custom .44 Special Black-hawk done by Andy Horvath (more on his work shortly), and the second is on a 4-5/8-inch .45 Colt

This 7-1/2-inch Colt New Frontier .44 Special does triple-duty because it has been fitted with an extra cylinder in .44-40 plus a third cylinder in .44 Russian. The latter was rechambered by Hamilton Bowen from .357 Magnum.

This 7-1/2-inch Texas Longhorn Arms Flat-Top Target began life as a .44 Special and has now been retro-fitted with extra cylinders in .44-40 and .44 Magnum.

Sixgun backstraps can be easily personalized with name, date, event, or motto.

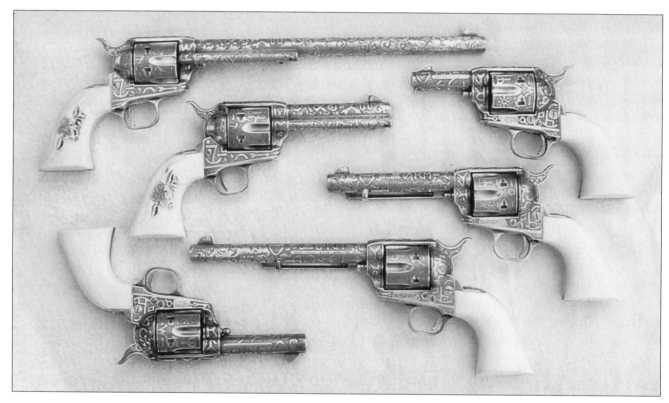

John Adams has expertly engraved and ivory-stocked all of these Colt Single Action .45s in barrel lengths of 3, 4, 4-3/4, 5-1/2, 7-1/2, and 12 inches.

New Model. These two sixguns both feature "A" or half coverage and are blued. They are also part of the Don't Sell group of sixguns.

A stroll through history reveals that sixgunners from outlaws to Texas Rangers to General Patton took pride in personalizing their sixguns. Tom Threepersons even fitted his nickel-plated, pearl-stocked 4-3/4-inch Colt Single Action with a post front sight long before almost anyone else ever thought of it. Ed McGivern experimented with all types of sights as well as enlarged triggerguards to facilitate double action shooting. Colt's Fitz chopped New Service Colt barrels, removed the front of the triggerguard, and shortened the butt to make Fitz Specials, his personal pocket pistols. And of course, Elmer Keith personalized his sixguns matter of factly. Those of us who want to be just a mite different than the mainstream are in good company.

CHAPTER 20

CUSTOM SIXGUNSMITHS

We are indeed fortunate as sixgunners to be living at a time when so many excellent factory sixguns are not only readily available, but are also affordable. When I graduated from high school, one could find, with a great deal of luck, a .357 Magnum chambered in either the Ruger Blackhawk or a Smith & Wesson Highway Patrolman. Both Ruger and Smith & Wesson cataloged a .44 Magnum, but none had yet arrived in my area and the Colt Single Action was hinted at, but who had seen one?

As I write this, there are two gun shops within walking distance stocking hundreds of sixguns. If I don't find what I want, either can have it for me in a few short days. In spite of the best efforts of the anti-gunners, we definitely live in a veritable sixgunner's heaven.

Along with the proliferation of great sixguns, especially since the 1970s, we have also seen a tremendous rise in interest in custom sixguns. We are doubly fortunate, for we not only have access to so many great sixguns, but we also are living at the time of the greatest number of premier sixgunsmiths. Always in search of that perfect sixgun, it has been my privilege to see, handle, test-fire, and even own some of the finest sixguns ever produced by the most talented group of metalsmiths imaginable.

In my business, I am privileged to be able to shoot all the new guns that come along, test all the latest equipment, and often be in on the ground floor of new developments. All of this is wonderful, however, the greatest advantage to my profession as a gunwriter is not things, but people. The fine men and women I meet and work with and shoot with and discuss ideas with, are what make my job so interesting and fruitful.

The American Pistolsmith's Guild was formed to promote the best in pistolsmithing ideals and professionalism. Most of the sixgunsmiths whose work I will be discussing here are members. Many have been named as Pistolsmith of the Year by their peers. I have met all of these craftsmen personally save one. I count them among my cherished friends and I stand in awe at their talent for taking a great sixgun and making it even better. We have discussed both John Linebaugh and Bill Grover in earlier chapters. I definitely include them with this fine group. There are others out there who are also gunmakers and sixgunsmiths who are equals to the members of this group, but I can only report on those whose work I have experienced personally.

To build a great sixgun requires a solid foundation. It is not surprising, then, to find most custom sixgun work today is performed on Ruger products. The Blackhawk and Redhawk comprise solid basic designs that are bull strong and relatively inexpensive. Consider the fact that a Ruger .44 Magnum listed for $96 in 1956. Today, a Super Blackhawk retails for $413. Compare that to the price of a car or home. A full-sized automobile was under $2,000 in the early 1950s, while a very good house could be had for $10,000, or less. Both of these have inflated to a least ten times their cost of forty years ago, while the Ruger sticker reads less than five times what it was in the 1950s.

JIM STROH–ALPHA PRECISION

Alpha Precision is Jim Stroh, who without a doubt, is one of the premier metalsmiths in the business. Stroh is a complete pistolsmith who works in all phases and takes time from his busy schedule to also teach classes for gunsmiths in training. Stroh does some of his finest work with Ruger Single Actions. I had been wanting a truly custom .45 Colt for a number of years, so a New Model Super Blackhawk was sent off with the request to turn it into a first-class .45 Colt. This would be my "easy" sixgun with the two most important attributes being a 5-1/2-inch barrel for easy packin' and an easy to see post front sight.

Jim Stroh of Alpha Precision converted this six-shot .44 Magnum Ruger Super Blackhawk to a five-shot .45 Colt with a new cylinder and barrel, rounded triggerguard, and custom sights. Rosewood grips by BluMagnum.

Close-up of front sight on custom .45 Colt sixgun by Jim Stroh highlights the easy to see post front sight, which is provided with interchangeable blades of differing heights.

Stroh's custom five-shot cylinder is fitted to the frame with an oversized base pin. The head of the base pin is larger than conventional factory pins, and Stroh uses a special heavy-duty spring-loaded latch to prevent movement of the pin under stress of recoil. The base pin snaps in with authority and locks into place. The cylinder on this .45 Colt by Stroh has absolutely no end shake or side-to-side play whatsoever. An interior support is added to the locking bolt to further insure that locking bolt and slots do not receive excessive wear under the forces of recoil.

The transfer bar safety is maintained and the cylinder rotates once the loading gate is opened—both ways, meaning the cylinder rotates both clockwise and counter clockwise. This is a great asset for those who shoot sixguns, because sooner or later, a bullet will jump the crimp, stick out past the front of the cylinder, and stop operation of the gun as the bullet hits the left side of the barrel protruding through the rear of the frame. With the Stroh action, it is a simple matter to rotate the cylinder backwards and bring the cartridge case under the loading gate and remove it with the ejector rod.

For those sixgunners who were raised on the traditional Colt Single Action and Ruger Flat-Tops, Stroh has placed a half-cock notch on the Super Blackhawk hammer allowing the hammer to be placed in this old style loading position and the cylinder will rotate just as it always did from 1836 to the arrival of the transfer bar in 1973.

All Stroh sixguns are line-bored, that is, the cylinder is fit to the frame and each chamber is then cut as it is precisely aligned with the barrel. Stroh cuts his cylinders with a diameter of .452 inch at the chamber mouths matched with minimum tolerances that prevent the case from excessive expansion. This results in increased accuracy and long case life.

The heart of every sixgun is the cylinder, and like all knowledgeable sixgunsmiths, Stroh builds his 4140 cylinders as large as possible, in this case, with a diameter of 1.780 inches. This is the maximum diameter that can be used within the cylinder window of the Ruger Super Blackhawk without weakening the frame.

With the popularity of heavyweight bullets in both the .45 Colt and .44 Magnum, it is a rare gun whose sights will handle a wide range of bullet weights from 240 up to 340 grains. The rear sight simply does not have enough adjustment. Either the lighter weights will shoot low or the heavier weights will shoot high. By adding adjustment to the front sight, this problem is easily taken care of. To this end, Stroh provides an interchangeable front sight system with the blade front sight being locked into place with an Allen screw that enters from the front of the sight base.

We have a large range of bullet moulds for the .45 Colt in weights of 260, 300, 325, and 340 grains that are perfectly useable in both Ruger Blackhawks and Bisleys in .45 Colt as well as in custom five- and six-shot revolvers. The Ruger factory guns will handle 300 grain bullets to 1,200 feet per second muzzle velocity. This custom five-shooter will easily handle all bullet weights to a full 1,500 feet per second. I received a test target shot with my Stroh .45 using 350 grain LBT bullets at around 1,200 feet per second muzzle velocity. Shot from a Ransom Rest, all five shots comprise a 50-yard group of 1-1/2 inches. That is excellent performance from a really big bore sixgun.

The Super Blackhawk is one of the great sixgun designs of all time, a true classic, however, I have never been a fan of the square-backed triggerguard of the Super Blackhawk, a design that was dropped by Colt before the Civil War. It looks good, but it nails me with heavy loads; the square-backed triggerguard bounces off the knuckle on my middle finger. To avoid this, I stayed with the Super Blackhawk grip frame and asked Stroh to cut and weld the triggerguard to give it a rounded contour. This helped alleviate the problem, but with heavy loads, namely 300 grain bullets in excess of 1,200 feet per second muzzle velocity, the Super Blackhawk grip frame does not come up high enough in the back to prevent twisting in the hand. This custom fivegun is now back with Alpha Precision and is being fitted with a Ruger Bisley grip frame, hammer, and trigger. The original parts will go on a Ruger Vaquero to give it a slightly different feel and appearance.

Jim Stroh is a complete sixgunsmith who works on all revolvers as well as semi-automatics. He can build the finest sixgun imaginable with custom barrel contours. My good friend and brother, the late Jack Pender, always spoke in awe of his "Stroh Gun." I now know what he meant.

HAMILTON BOWEN–BOWEN CLASSIC ARMS

I first met Hamilton Bowen of Bowen Classic Arms at the second gathering of The Shootists in 1987. Bowen brought some samples of his work, which covered the entire spectrum of big bore sixguns: one of the guns was a .500 Linebaugh on a Ruger Redhawk and the other a .41 Special on a Ruger Security-Six. I may not be the smartest sixgunner in the world, but it didn't take me long to realize this was one talented sixgunsmith.

Over the past ten years, it has been my good pleasure to test several dozen Bowen sixguns and to have several guns built to my personal specifications. As far as I know, the .41 Special Colt Single Action mentioned in the chapter on the .41 Magnum is the first ever Colt Single Action built for the cartridge that was never offered commercially, but should have been. Along the same line, Bowen has also built several sixguns for me that never were but should have been, including .44 Specials on Ruger .357 Flat-Tops and Three-Screw Old Model Blackhawks. These have also been previously covered.

I do believe the work Bowen did for me on the Ruger .357 Blackhawks got him interested in this fine sixgun as a basis for building custom revolvers. Witness his .38-40 on the Blackhawk, the first sixgun to test some really great ideas he has about sixguns. The top strap has been slimmed down, the Ruger rear sight has been replaced with a Smith & Wesson adjustable rear sight and mated up with the Smith & Wesson rear sight that goes all the way to the front of the frame is a barrel that has an integral rib that becomes the front sight base. For this innovation on a single action Bowen has used a Smith & Wesson barrel with the underlug that receives the ejector rod of the double action Smith & Wesson machined off. Topped off with a flat black post front sight, the result is one of the best looking top strap/rear sight/barrel combinations I have ever seen.

To convert a .357 to .38-40, Bowen first had the original Ruger .357 barrel rebored to the .400 inch, cut to 4 inches, then slimmed much like a Dan Wesson barrel. He followed this by making the Smith & Wesson barrel into a permanent shroud. The original Ruger .357 cylinder has been rechambered to .38-40 .

The original Ruger grip frame has also been discarded on this single action and replaced with a New Thunderer grip frame from Cimarron Arms. This double action-style grip shape gives a completely different feel to a single action sixgun and allows one to maintain a solid grip with the low recoiling .38-40. A most unusual sixgun and one that stirs the emotions as the result is an easy packin', easy shootin', easy to look at single action in a chambering and feel that conjures up images of the Old West.

Bowen and I have often discussed converting a Ruger Flat-Top Blackhawk .357 Magnum to .45 Colt. Our main concern has been the amount of metal that would be removed to transform a .357 cylinder to a .45 Colt. Bowen also shared the same concern, so when he finally did a .45 Colt on a Flat-Top Blackhawk, he made a new oversized six-shot cylinder that is 1.691 inches in diameter as opposed to the 1.665 inches of the cylinder of a Colt .45 I measured. This is

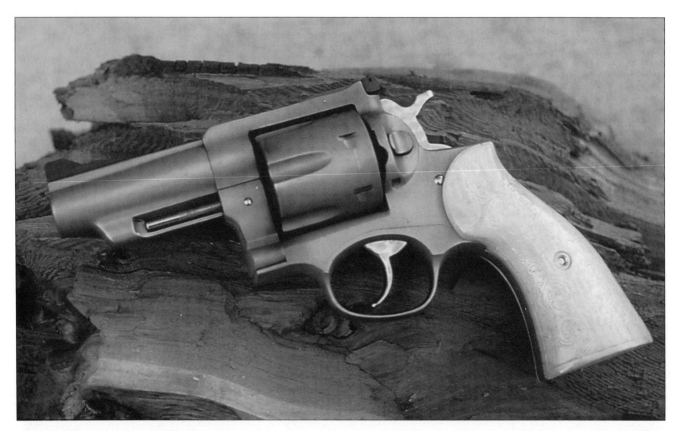

The .44 Magnum Ruger Redhawk makes into a compact 3-1/2-inch sixgun as can be seen in this example by Hamilton Bowen with bead-blasted finish, Ron Power front sight, tuned action, and ivory micarta grips by Charles Able.

Hamilton Bowen six-shot .45 Colt on Redhawk uses original cylinder with Dan Wesson-style interchangeable 4- and 6-inch barrels. Grips are by BearHug.

not a .45 for heavy loads. This sixgun, as is the case with the Colt Single Action Army .45, should only be used with standard loads.

The original grip frame has been replaced by an EMF backstrap and triggerguard to allow the use of dark, beautifully grained walnut one-piece grips by the master himself, Roy Fishpaw. The cylinder has tight, minimum-sized .45 Colt chambers, the 5-1/2-inch Douglas barrel is fit with a Ruger-style ramp with a Bowen front sight, while the rear sight is the original Micro like that found on the Flat-Top Ruger .357 Blackhawks. A .45 sixgun that any sixgunner would be proud to belt on each day.

Bowen has used double action Rugers as the basis for several custom revolver designs. The little gun of the Redhawk conversions from Bowen Classic Arms is left as a standard .44 Magnum with the personal touches that make it more practical as a defensive sixgun. The factory barrel is shortened to 3-1/2-inches and fitted with a Power Custom front sight which is a serrated Baughman-style on a ramp that is held to the barrel with an Allen screw. The entire gun is finished in a bead-blasted satin nickel and highlighted with nickel-plated trigger, hammer, ejector rod, and pins.

The trigger is slightly rounded and smoothly polished, the sides of the hammer and trigger are jeweled, and the action is smoothed to provide easy shootin' either double or single action-style. The grip frame is left as is or round-butted. The entire package weighs in at 2 ounces shy of 3 pounds, is not much larger than a 4-inch Smith & Wesson Model 29, and handles heavy loads with ease.

Bowen advertises his round butt conversion on the Redhawk as being well-suited to those shooters with smaller hands. Even those who have larger hands will find the Redhawk much easier to control, especially in double action shooting, with a rounded butt.

The .45 Colt is one of the finest sixgun cartridges of all time. In the past I've run Bowen Classic Arms five-shot .45 Colt conversions to 1,600 feet per second with both 310 and 325 grain bullets. Cases extracted easily with no excessive pressure signs. Recoil called a halt, not the inability of gun or cartridge case to handle more.

Bowen's .45 Colt Redhawk is rebarreled with a 6-inch heavy barrel with a full underlug. The heavy barrel coupled with a non-fluted five-shot cylinder brings the weight of this fivegun up to a recoil taming 56

Five-shot Bowen-built .50AE on Ruger Super Blackhawk with five-shot cylinder, ported barrel, and BluMagnum grips to soften recoil.

ounces. The cylinder is larger in diameter than factory size, completely fills the frame window, and the bolt notches are between the chambers further adding to the strength of this .45 Colt.

Bowen also offers the .45 Colt conversion on Ruger Blackhawks with five-shot cylinders and custom barrels. Six-shot .45 Colt conversions utilize a rechambered factory cylinder and can be found with either a completely custom barrel or the factory barrel can be relined or rebored. A double action Redhawk made into a 3-1/2-inch .45 Colt sixgun with a round butt is an eminently practical defensive gun.

To come up with a truly big bore sixgun that is also easy shooting, Bowen created the .50 Special. As its name implies, the .50 Special cartridge, which is the same length as the .38 Special and .44 Special, is designed for muzzle velocities of 700 to 900 feet per second with 300 to 400 grain bullets. Bowen's .50 Special Redhawk is fitted with a five-shot cylinder that completely fills the frame window, the 4-inch heavy barrel is full underlug style and the machined ramp holds a Baughman-style front sight that is pinned in. At a weight of 1 ounce over 3 pounds, Bowen's .50 Special Redhawk combines big bore feel without big bore recoil.

The advent of the .50 Action Express in the Desert Eagle semi-automatic opened new possibilities for the largest semi-automatic cartridge in a sixgun chambering. Freedom Arms now chambers its Casull revolver for .50AE, and Bowen converts both Ruger Redhawk and Super Blackhawks to the Big Fifty. Bowen has recently taken a new path with the .50AE. He builds powerful sixguns as small and light as possible, sixguns that can be easily packed and still come up shooting powerful ammunition.

Bowen's Lightweight Fifty on the Blackhawk is an all steel 4-inch barreled fivegun with a new cylinder installed and the barrel being made from a rebored N-frame barrel. The factory alloy grip frame and the ejector rod housing are replaced with steel parts and the loading gate and recoil shield are dished out to save weight. To save even more weight, the Featherweight .50AE Bowen retains the alloy grip frame and ejector rod housing. To overcome felt recoil, the Featherweight Fifty has two Mag-Na-Port slots, one on each side of the front sight plus one behind the front sight.

Both guns have been fit with Ruger Bisley hammers and Bowen custom cylinder pins that are held in place by an Allen screw that bears against the bot-

Three conversions on the Ruger Redhawk by Hamilton Bowen: Blued .45 Colt with 4-inch heavy barrel, stainless .45 Colt with 6-inch heavy barrel set up for scope mounting, and stainless .44 Magnum with ivory micarta stocks by Charles Able. Both .45s feature five-shot cylinders to handle the heaviest loads.

tom of the barrel. Weight-wise, the lightweight comes in at 39 ounces, and the Featherweight at 34 ounces.

These are two-handed guns, to be sure, but they do not deliver the punishing recoil of some of the other custom .50 caliber sixguns such as a full-house .500 Linebaugh or .500 Maximum. Muzzle velocity using Speer's 325 grain jacketed hollow-point .50AE factory ammunition is right at 1,200 feet per second. These little sixguns should be especially appealing to the rifleman or woman or bowhunter who wishes to carry a potent backup gun or even the woods loafer, hiker, or one who fishes who wants to carry a dependable, but small, powerful sixgun.

For those who want the most powerful but packable sixguns for hunting really big game, Bowen can also build five-shot conversions on the Redhawk or Bisley chambered for the really big cartridges, the .475 and .500 Linebaughs.

DAVID CLEMENTS

I first became acquainted with David Clements through our mutual love and admiration for the .44 Special, especially conversions on Ruger Three-Screw

Blackhawks. Clements came up with one of those "ridden hard and put up wet" gun show special sixguns that was good for little else except as a candidate for a complete rebuild. The factory barrel was discarded and a Shilen chrome moly barrel 5 inches in length was fitted along with a screw on interchangeable blade front sight. The cylinder was rechambered to .44 Special and fitted with an oversized locking bolt and base pin. At a 5-inch barrel length, it was necessary to machine a special ejector rod housing for the .357 Magnum turned .44 Special in order to have the ejector tube extend the full length of the barrel. The combination of 5-inch heavy barrel and steel ejector tube gives this .44 Special a definite muzzle heavy feel that comes onto target fast. This is one classy .44 Special sixgun.

Starting with a Flat-Top or Old Model Ruger Blackhawk, Clements can build a first-class sixgun in .44 Special, 10MM, or .40 Smith & Wesson. Moving up to the larger-framed New Model Blackhawk gives many more choices such as .44-40, .38-40, .45 Colt, and .45 ACP. Five-shot .45 Colt and .475 and .500 Linebaugh conversions are built on either the Ruger Bisley, New Model Blackhawk, Redhawk, or Super Redhawk. The Bisley is the best choice for the really hard kickin' six-

Custom sixguns by David Clements, clockwise from top left: Ruger .41 Magnum with custom 7-1/2-inch barrel; 5-1/2-inch .475 Linebaugh on Ruger Bisley; .445 SuperMag built up on Seville .375 SuperMag; Redhawk .45 Colt with full underlug barrel.

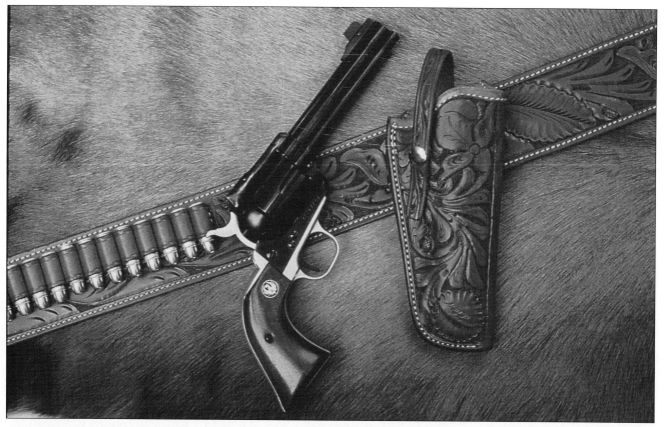

David Clements custom .44 Special on a Ruger .357 Old Model Blackhawk with heavyweight 5-inch barrel, tuned action, polished grip frame, and post front sight. Floral-carved leather is by El Paso.

guns, because its grip frames handle felt recoil the easiest of all Ruger grip frames.

Minimum tolerances in all sixguns built by Clements Custom Guns are adhered to throughout, with no side play or endshake in the cylinder. All chambers are line-bored with the barrel. With six-shot conversions, the cylinder is rechambered, a new barrel fitted, along with an oversized base pin, heavy-duty base pin catch spring, oversized locking bolt, and interchangeable front sight system. The action is completely smoothed and tuned. Five-shot conversions feature an oversized cylinder that completely fills in the frame window. Both conversions come with a steel ejector rod housing.

Clements Custom Guns handles all phases of sixgunsmithing. I have just received two sixguns back that were sent to him for some personal touches. A 7-1/2-inch Colt New Frontier .44 Special is now an easy to pack 5-1/2 inches with Ajax ivory polymer grips expertly fitted, and a 5-1/2-inch .44 Magnum Super Blackhawk now wears Ruger Bisley parts, including the grip frame, hammer, and trigger, plus an easy to see post front sight, resulting in two easy to pack and easy to shoot big bore .44s.

ANDY HORVATH

In 1986, I sent a Ruger Three-Screw .357 Magnum Blackhawk off to Andy Horvath with the request to make it into a 4-inch sixgun with a rounded butt and chambered in .44 Special. The result was even better than I had expected. The bluing was deep and perfect and the round-butted grip felt even better than I had hoped for. Horvath had polished the standard aluminum grip frame and round-butted it so it slipped into my hand perfectly. The grips were also rounded and tapered just right. The sides of the hammer and trigger were jeweled while the cylinder pin was machined with a flat face to allow maximum ejector rod travel to fully extract empties.

Since that time, Horvath has been doing a thriving business building these little Rugers on both Old and New Model Blackhawks in calibers of .44 Special, .41 Magnum, and .45 Colt. When I wrote of these little guns in *American Handgunner*, Hollywood took notice and I received a call one afternoon. One of the stars of a new movie had seen my article and wanted my personal gun for use in the movie. Now this little sixgun had not only been built to perfection by Horvath, it had also been engraved by BluMagnum. I've seen enough movies to know what they do with guns when they are empty—they always throw them!—so I graciously declined the use of my gun but did put them in touch with Horvath. He wound up making seven little Rugers for the movie as well as personal sixguns for the stars, Mickey Rourke and Don Johnson.

Round-butted Little Rugers redefine the shooting of big bore single action sixguns. The simple act of round butting the grip frame changes the perceived recoil significantly and the heavy loads can be shot in relative comfort. Since Horvath did these sixguns, both Cimarron and EMF now offer single actions with modified grip frames. Cimarron's New Thunderer Colt Lightning-style and a true round butt is now found on EMF's Pinkerton Model.

The short barrels make them particularly fast out of a properly designed holster while the rounded butt helps to control recoil. I would certainly not feel that I was giving anything away to those armed with semi-autos or double action revolvers, at least for the first shot. No gun is any faster from the leather for the first shot than a single action sixgun. With a big bore single action, a second shot is rarely needed.

Horvath does all the standard sixgun work, trigger jobs, action tuning, custom barrels, sights, and so forth. He can also provide steel ejector rod housings for those who, like myself, detest alloy housings on single action sixguns.

MAG-NA-PORT

Mag-Na-Port has been building hunting sixguns for well over two decades. Mag-Na-Port's founder, Larry Kelly, is the ultimate handgun hunter who has taken virtually everything everywhere. He was the first man to take all of the Big Five of Africa, Cape buffalo, elephant, rhino, lion, and leopard, with a handgun. He knows what constitutes a good sixgun for the handgun hunter. His premium offering is the Stalker.

The Stalker series was conceived by Kelly as the perfect revolver for serious handgun hunting, and the first Stalker, a Ruger Super Blackhawk .44 Magnum, has been used by Kelly all over the globe to take many big game trophies. Kelly describes the Stalker as "a very special gun offered to meet the requirements of the hunting fraternity—the dedicated handgun hunters. The Stalker was developed to meet the requirements of these men and women. It's a gun designed by hunters, for hunters. The Stalker is the result of many years hunting experience by the people here. We are proud of the gun, and sincerely convinced it is everything a serious hunter requires, whatever the game."

Stalker conversions start with stainless steel sixguns, the Ruger Super Blackhawk, the Ruger Super Redhawk, the Smith & Wesson Model 629, and the .454 Casull from Freedom Arms. All Stalker conversions have a number of things in common, including an 8-3/8-inch barrel, an inverted muzzle crown that I

Mag-Na-Port supplies this inverted crown on its custom sixguns to prevent any dings from cutting into the rifling.

would like to have on every sixgun I own, Mag-Na-Porting, Velvet Hone finish, polished hammer and trigger, a superb action job, Pachmayr grips, SSK scope mount base (except Super Redhawk), 2X Leupold scope, swivels and studs, and a carrying sling.

An especially appreciated touch to the Stalker series is the numbering of each chamber on the back of the cylinder. Quite often one revolver chamber will be a little out of synch with the rest resulting in fliers. Numbering of each chamber makes the culprit easy to identify and avoid. Silhouetters, who do it with five from a sixgun, would definitely like to see all factory revolvers with this feature.

The Super Blackhawk was the obvious choice for the first Mag-Na-Port Stalker because it has been a favorite of handgun hunters for nearly forty years. Kelly simply takes a good hunting handgun and makes it even better. There are many handgun hunters who still manage to make do with iron sights, however, many of us often need the extra help that a scope gives. Kelly has chosen the excellent Leupold 2X long eye relief scope as standard equipment for his Stalker series. As I looked at a mounted elephant in The Hand-gunners Museum, I could see how critical bullet placement would be with such a mammoth creature, and a scope would be mandatory.

On the Super Blackhawk, in addition to the polished trigger and hammer, the cylinder pin, ejector rod head, cylinder release pin, and the screws, are all polished. The subdued Velvet Hone finish contrasts nicely with the polished parts.

The newest addition to the Mag-Na-Port Stalker lineup is the .454 Casull. Starting with the 10-inch Premium Grade .454, Mag-Na-Port cuts the barrel to the standard Stalker length of 8-3/8 inches and adds the deep inverted muzzle crown that protects the muzzle from any dings.

Because of the increased recoil of the .454 full-house loads over .44 Magnum loads, the two standard trapezoidal Mag-Na-Port slots are aided by two smaller hexagonal slots, one on each side of the barrel behind the standard slots. They work, certainly more so than my heavier 10-inch un-ported, but scoped .454 Casull. This is certainly the most pleasant .454 I have ever shot. The latter has now been tamed by being fitted with Mag-Na-Port's muzzle brake, the Mag-Na-Brake.

Carrying a Stalker, like any scoped revolver, can be a problem. Some hunters prefer to use the nylon carrying sling provided, others use shoulder holsters of various configurations, some even stick the gun in the pants belt behind the back, and still others use the original carrier, the hand. As far as transporting the Stalker, the problem has been solved with the combining of the ideas of Kelly and leather genius Thad Rybka. Kelly transports his Stalkers in one of Rybka's "Packmule" rigs. The Packmule is a full flap holster, with the flap padded to protect the scope. On the front of the rig, one finds pouches for ammo and a folding knife, and the holster itself, in addition to a belt loop, has three dee rings to allow the rig to be used with a shoulder strap, tied to pack frame or lashed to a saddle. Kelly uses only top-quality leather.

One of the handiest sixguns available is the Mag-Na-Port short-barreled fast handlin' Predator. The Predator starts out as a Stainless Super Blackhawk. The barrel is cut to 4-5/8 inches and given Mag-Na-Porting and the inverted muzzle crown exactly as found on the Stalker series.

The Predator also has the standard Velvet Hone finish, action job, polished hammer, trigger, cylinder pin release, cylinder pin, ejector rod head, and screws. Since the Predator is not designed as a primary hunting handgun, but a back-up, it is fitted with a C-More colored front sight and white outline rear. C-More sights are available in blue, green, pink, red, and yellow; I have them on three of my short-barreled sixguns. Instead of an insert, the C-More front sight takes the place of front sights and is pinned on through the ramp base. I sent two of these three sixguns to Mag-Na-Port several years ago. One started life as a blued 7-1/2-inch Super Blackhawk and the other as a blued 4-inch Smith & Wesson Model 29. The Blackhawk's barrel was cut to 4-3/4 inches, and both guns were tuned, Mag-Na-Ported, and given a stainless steel-style finish that is designated as Mag-Na-Life. The Model 29 was also round-butted before the Smith & Wesson factory discovered round butt-

ing. These are now two very practical, powerful, and portable sixguns.

Larry Kelly is now semi-retired, allowing more time for hunting and fishing, while son Ken Kelly now ably heads up Mag-Na-Port. In addition to porting all manner of sixguns, muzzle brakes are now available, as well as action jobs on all sixguns as well as Mini-Guns built on such sixguns as the Smith & Wesson and Colt Anaconda .44 Magnums. The Mini-Guns use 3-inch barrels for maximum concealment.

Over the past two decades, Mag-Na-Port has issued Limited Editions, most of which have been built on Ruger Super Blackhawks. These have become instant collector's items. Many limited offerings consist of a number limited to how many can be sold. This is not so with Mag-Na-Port. Its latest limited edition, the Silver Six, commemorates the 25th Anniversary of Mag-Na-Port and it is a true limited edition of 200 pieces. This stainless Super Blackhawk Silver Six is a 6-inch .44 Magnum with all of the niceties mentioned above on the Predator as well as the special 25th Anniversary etching and the Handgun Hunter's Hall of Fame logo. It is a beautiful sixgun.

Each year, Mag-Na-Port builds several very limited editions for special occasions. This year, three identi-

Taffin discusses a handgun project with Ken Kelly, president of Mag-Na-Port.

Custom .44 Magnums from Mag-Na-Port, clockwise from top right: Smith & Wesson 629 Stalker conversion with full length rib, 4-inch round-butted Model 29 with Mag-Na-Life finish, 4-5/8-inch Ruger Super Blackhawk with Mag-Na-Life finish, and Stalker conversion on a Ruger Super Blackhawk .44 Magnum. All feature Mag-Na-Ported barrels and tuned actions.

cal, except for serial numbers, sixguns were built to celebrate the Annual Handgun Hunters Against Hunger Hunt on the Y.O. Ranch in Texas, the Annual Handgun Only Hunt on the White Oak Plantation in Alabama, and finally the third gun in the series will be raffled off at the 25th Anniversary of the Outstanding American Handgunner Awards Foundation Banquet. Freedom Arms provided the .353 Casull's, Bushnell the HoloSights, SSK the T'SOB scope bases, and Mag-Na-Port did all the custom work. These are fitting tributes for three special events.

MILT MORRISON–QUALITE PISTOL & REVOLVER

Milt Morrison, along with his wife Karen, head up Qualite Pistol & Revolver. They describe Qualite as a complete handgun service center, and Milt has been involved in pistolsmithing and the training of peace officers for the past twenty years. In addition to general service work, Morrison also specializes in custom sixguns built on both Ruger and Smith & Wesson platforms. His favorite conversions begin with big bore Ruger Blackhawks and Super Blackhawks.

The Western Hunter can be accomplished on any blue Blackhawk or Super Blackhawk. The factory barrel is replaced with a .900-inch custom moly steel barrel and fitted with a Qualite Pistol & Revolver custom compensator. The actual barrel length is only 4-1/4 inches and the comp. adds about 1 inch to this total length, which results in a practical packin' pistol for hunting big game close up.

Steel is the watchword here as the alloy grip frame is replaced with a steel Ruger grip frame and the alloy ejector rod housing has been replaced by a Qualite steel ejector rod housing. These steel housings are now being offered by Qualite to those sixgunners who would like to upgrade their Ruger Single Actions.

The Western Hunter is set up with an easy to see Patridge-style front sight of .100 inch. The barrel, cylinder, and grip frame are finished in Qualite's high lustre blue and the frame is color case hardened. Morrison tops off the bright blue and color case finish with custom grips made of ivory micarta or fancy walnut.

In 1995, at the 10th Anniversary gathering of The Shootists, I was caught completely off guard as this fine group of men presented me with a custom sixgun from Qualite. It was my good fortune to gather what became The Shootists for the first time in 1986,

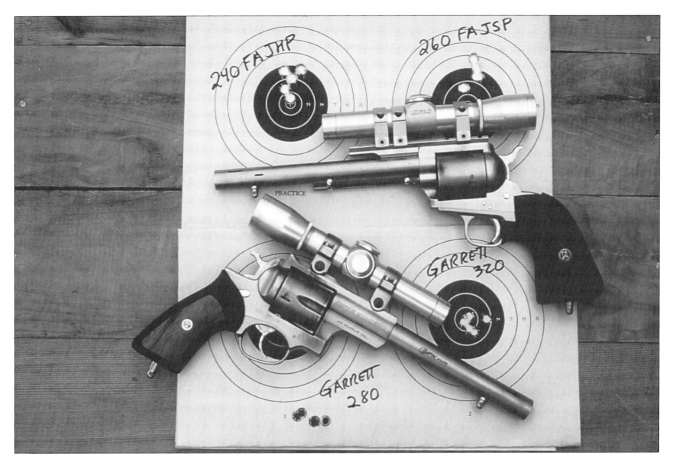

Targets shot at 50 yards with hunting loads in the Mag-Na-Port Stalker conversions on the Freedom Arms .454 and Ruger .44 Magnum Super Redhawk. Loads are factory 240 and 260 .454s and Garrett 280 and 320 grain .44 Magnums.

Mag-Na-Port specializes in handguns for hunters as exemplified by these Stalker conversions. Top, Ruger Super Redhawk; bottom, Freedom Arms .454 Casull. Both have Mag-Na-Ported 8-3/8-inch barrels, Velvet Hone finish, tuned and tightened action, sling swivels, and 2X Leupold scopes.

Mag-Na-Port's 25th Anniversary Silver Six Ruger Blackhawk carries all of the Mag-Na-Port custom features, smoothed and tightened action, antiqued stocks, C-More front sight, plus both a 25th Anniversary logo on the cylinder and a Handgun Hunter's logo on the top strap.

This Western Hunter Custom Ruger is from the shop of Qualite Pistol & Revolver. It features a high lustre blue finish with case-colored frame, tuned action, compensated barrel, post front sight, and ivory mi-carta grips.

and also become the first chairman of this group. Since then, The Shootists Holiday has become an annual event bringing sixgunners together from around the country to share ideas, fellowship, shoot together, and once in a great while, tell a few lies.

The 10th Anniversary Shootists presentation sixgun by Qualite started life as a Ruger New Model .45 Blackhawk. It has been completely tuned, polished and finished in a high lustre blue with gold embellishments including a special marking on the butt with my logo and the top strap being marked in memory of Deacon Deason, my good friend and chairman of The Shootists when he was called Home in 1994. Two gold beads are set in the face of the Patridge front sight. Dave Wayland made the fancy walnut grips. This sixgun is too pretty to shoot, but my orders were to shoot it and shoot it I do.

J.D. JONES–SSK INDUSTRIES

SSK Industries has offered the SSK HandCannon line of Custom Thompson/Center Contenders and barrels for a long time. The head of SSK, J.D. Jones, like Larry Kelly, has hunted all over the world and knows what constitutes a good hunting handgun.

While most of SSK's work is with custom calibers such as the .257JDJ, the 6.5JDJ, and the best single-shot handgun chambering for big game hunting, the .375JDJ, SSK also builds custom sixguns on the super-strong Ruger Super Redhawk.

J.D. believes in minimum tolerances. Barrels are reset and rethroated with the barrel/cylinder gap set at less than .002 inch. Jones also likes custom barrel contours such as a tapered octagon, round at the frame for about 1/4 inch and tapered into the octagonal flats. To combat recoil, barrels have the standard Mag-Na-Porting trapezoidal slots and two extra hexagonal slots on both sides of the barrel. The Mag-Na-Porting and the added weight of a Leupold 2X scope brings total weight to 57 ounces, making an SSK .44 Magnum very easy to shoot even with full-house 300 grain bullets. SSK calls this conversion the Beauty. It is also available rechambered to .45 Colt with the Ruger barrel replaced with a Shilen .45 Colt barrel. For a heavier barrel, SSK uses a 7-1/2-inch octagonal barrel.

To transform the Beauty into the Beast, SSK provides an interchangeable barrel feature. These SSK Custom sixguns are not meant to have the barrels

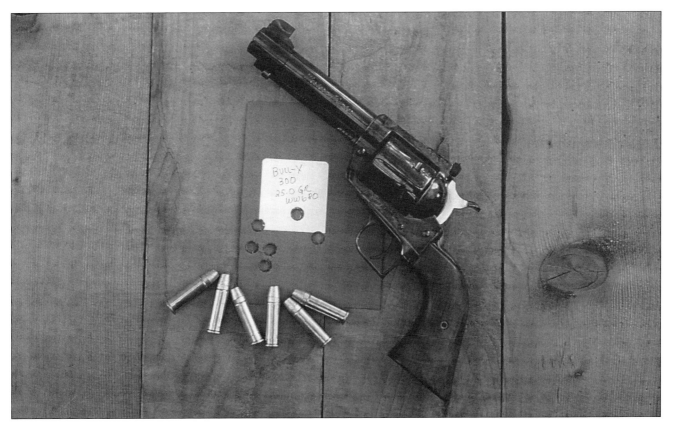

Target shot at 25 yards using Bull-X's 300 grain bullet and heavy hunting load in Western Hunter .44 Magnum by Qualite Pistol & Revolver. This sixgun features high lustre blue finish with post front sight, compensated barrel, and tuned action.

changed in the field like the Dan Wesson series of revolvers. A bench vise is required. The barrel is cinched up in the vise, barrel padded of course, the set screw is backed out, and the barrel is then easily turned off by hand.

The rounded, compensated Beast barrel is hand-tightened as far as possible, then clamped in the padded vise, and the frame is tightened on to the barrel. Barrels for both the .44 Magnum and .45 Colt Beasts are made from Shilen blanks and length on the .45 Colt and .44 Magnum Compensated SSK Redhawks are both 4-1/2 inches for the barrel proper with the expansion chamber bringing the total length up to 6-1/4 inches. Barrels are one-piece, with the expansion chamber machined as part of the barrel which is of the heavy bull barrel type, .962 inch in diameter. With the extended frame of the Super Redhawk, only 3-5/8 inches of barrel and compensator extend beyond the end of the Redhawk frame. The .44 "Beast" weighs in at 52 ounces with the .45 Colt version going 1 ounce more.

Using only heavy loads of 300 grain bullets in the .44 Magnum at 1,300 plus feet per second, and the same weight bullets in the .45 Colt at 1,100 plus feet per second, I have no problem staying on targets shooting two-handed double action with either gun. Photographs taken of me firing both sixguns at the same time double action shows the guns virtually level.

RICHARD MCCANN–MCCANN'S MACHINE SHOP

Richard McCann of McCann's Machine Shop also builds sixguns with interchangeable barrels, but McCann goes one step further and provides interchangeable cylinders. Using the Ruger Blackhawk as a platform, McCann can provide a .44 Magnum sixgun that transforms into a .41 Magnum by removing the barrel with special wrench, installing the optional barrel, and then changing cylinders. If we ever get to the point that we are restricted to a limited number of sixguns—God forbid—McCann's process allows one frame to be used with .45 Colt, .44 Magnum, .41 Magnum, and .357 Magnum barrel cylinder combinations. By controlling the length of the cylinder and the amount of barrel portion that protrudes through the rear of the frame, it is possible to prevent a larger

Custom Super Redhawks by SSK Industries. Left sixgun is original .44 Magnum fitted with a slim barrel with Mag-Na-Porting, tuned action, and tightening; right sixgun has been converted to .45 Colt with a Mag-Na-Ported octagon barrel. Both barrels are designed to be removed and replaced with a shorter compensated barrel. Scopes are 2X Leupold on Ruger rings.

SSK's Custom .45 Colt on A Ruger Super Redhawk is the Beauty with long barrel and scope installed. When shorter compensated barrel is installed, it becomes the Beast.

Taffin shooting the SSK .45 Colt Beast by SSK on the Ruger Super Redhawk. Notice the mild recoil.

.44 MAG
SSK
310

1328
FPS
DOUBLE
ACTION

.45 COLT
BRP 300
1109
FPS
DOUBLE
ACTION

SSK's Custom .45 Colt on A Ruger Super Redhawk is the Beauty with long barrel and scope installed. When shorter compensated barrel is installed, it becomes the Beast.

Richard McCann's switch barrel conversion allows both .44 Magnum and .41 Magnum to be used on the same sixgun frame by switching barrels and cylinders.

cylinder from being matched with a smaller caliber barrel.

JIM CLARK

With any big bore sixgun, especially those chambered in anything from .44 Magnum and upwards, recoil becomes a real factor. I have always enjoyed shooting the heavy-barreled Dan Wesson .44 Magnum because it is the most comfortable .44 Magnum to shoot—until now. Compensators are really coming into their own, and two sixgunsmiths, both of which are dedicated handgun hunters, have tamed the .44 Magnum. Jim Clark prefers the Smith & Wesson .44 Magnum for hunting. His custom version features a bull barrel with a built-in compensator. The action is tuned, the trigger is polished smooth, a Patridge front sight is installed, and the entire package is set off with Hogue grips without finger grooves.

RON POWER

Ron Power starts with the Ruger Super Redhawk, smooths and tunes the action, and then rebarrels Big Red with a bull barrel of his design with a built-in compensator in front of the front sight. Add Hogue pebble grained Monogrips and one has a .44 Magnum that can actually be double-tapped, that is, fired with more than one shot quickly and still stay on target.

Both of these custom .44 Magnums were fired alongside a pair of Dan Wesson .44 Magnums, one with an 8-inch heavy barrel and the other with a 10-inch standard barrel. These have been the sixguns that I have used to shoot heavy loads, that is 300 grain or heavier weight bullets, when I did not want recoil to be a factor. I was most pleasantly surprised to find both the Clark and Power sixguns actually shoot easier than these old favorites. Every heavy-weight bulleted .44 Magnum factory load and hand-load I had on hand were fired in both sixguns with .38 Special comfort. These compensators combined with heavy barrels really work.

Ports and compensators do work to reduce muzzle flip and felt recoil, but there are trade-offs. Both are noisy and the risk of hearing loss is increased with their use. **ALWAYS** wear hearing protection when compensated or ported sixguns, or for that matter any sixgun, are fired, unless caught in an emergency situation. One must be especially careful when firing such altered sixguns around other people. They are not exactly welcomed guests at most public ranges.

As a ported or compensated sixgun is fired, what has been called muzzle blast in the past actually exits through the ports. Gases, flame, and pieces of lead or copper can all exit upwards or to the side of the barrel. It should go without saying that this can be extremely dangerous if the sixgun is fired close to one's body or face. Firing a compensated sixgun in a cardboard box will give testimony to the material that can exit the ports.

These .44 Magnums have been totally tamed by installing heavy barrels with built-in compensators. Jimmy Clark conversion on a Smith & Wesson Model 29 (top) and Ron Power conversion on a Ruger Super Redhawk (bottom).

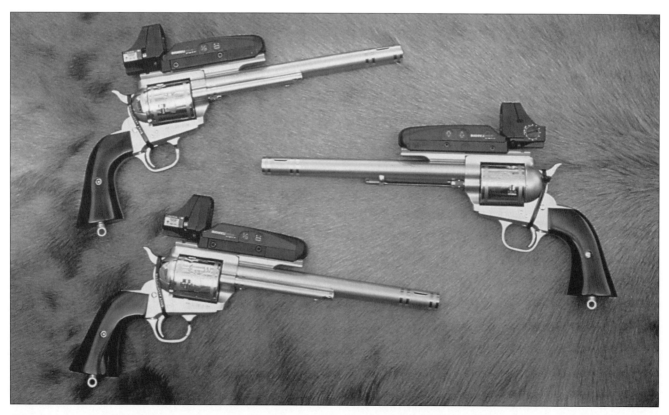

Three custom .353 Casulls by Mag-Na-Port celebrate the Annual Handgun Hunters Against Hunger Hunt on the Y.O. Ranch, the Handgun Only Hunt on the White Oak Plantation, and the 25th Anniversary of the Outstanding American Handgunner Awards Foundation.

On a sixgun designed for defensive use, the flame that exits from the ports or compensator can be a real detriment if the sixgun is fired in low light or darkness momentarily causing vision problems as occurs when looking into a bright light. Both the porting and compensating of a sixgun can be a real aid to effective shooting but they both must be used with the foregoing in mind.

JOHN GALLAGHER

A relative newcomer to the sixgunsmithing scene is John Gallagher. Gallagher's friends, Gary Sitton and Jim Wilson, both highly recommended his workmanship and have written about him in various gun magazines. At the 1996 Shootist Holiday, I had a chance to experience Gallagher's customsmithing first hand. Two of the most interesting single actions were a .32-20 on a Ruger Blackhawk with an eight-shot cylinder, a most practical idea, and a very small big bore sixgun.

This latter sixgun that really caught my attention was a Single-Six converted to a five-shot .41 Special. This is about as big a sixgun as one can get on small frame. My Single-Six is now being converted by Gallagher. I have also sent him a .357 Magnum Highway Patrolman along with an in the white Smith & Wesson 6-1/2-inch 1950 Target .45 ACP barrel. Gallagher is combining these parts into a 5-inch .45 Colt that will have the Mountain Gun barrel profile that is so popular now mated with a standard square butt grip frame.

BILL GROVER–TEXAS LONGHORN ARMS

Bill Grover of Texas Longhorn Arms is a master gunmaker who offers sixgunners his "Right-Handed Single Actions" with the Improved Number Five, the West Texas Flat-Top Target, the South Texas Army, and the Border Special. Grover has also converted two Ruger .357 Magnum Blackhawks to .44 Special for me. Grover's occupation is building sixguns. In his spare time, he builds custom guns.

It recently struck Grover that since his sixguns are right-handed, that is, the loading gate and ejector rod are on the left side, he ought to build a pair of sixguns that are identical, except one is the mirror image of the other. These two engraved Flat-Top Targets use the Number Five frame which means the cylinder pins are held in place by the lever latch design of the Number Five, however, one rotates to the left and the other to the right.

Both sixguns are 7-1/2-inch .44 Magnums, serial numbers LH-1 and RH-1, engraved by Dan Love, finished in antique nickel by Jim Riggs and John Adams, and the African ebony grips are set off by steer head ivory carvings by Dennis Holland. I was so struck by the uniqueness of these pieces, and since I am always in search of that perfect sixgun, Grover has been commissioned to build me a pair of .44 Specials, one left-hand and the other right-hand, with 5-1/2-inch barrels.

Most of today's sixguns are built to a price. They have to be or none of the major firearms manufacturers would still be in business. Most shooters can be satisfied with standard factory offerings with perhaps the addition of an action job and custom grips. For the discriminating sixgunner who is always in search of that perfect sixgun, custom gunsmiths can provide the special finish, or barrel contour, or rechambering that will satisfy us until we get another idea for another perfect sixgun. It is all part of what makes sixgunning so interesting and enjoyable.

We have not mentioned the cost of custom sixguns. They are not quite in the if-you-have-to-ask-you-can't-afford-it category, but one should approach the idea off a custom sixgun with the realization that these are sixguns that are built by demanding craftsman that only accept perfection or as close as it is humanly possible to approach it. Expect to pay $1,500 to $2,000 for a full-blown custom sixgun with a new cylinder, barrel, finish, and altering and strengthening of the interior lockwork. I learned long ago that cheap was too expensive in the long run, and bargain basement prices resulted in bargain basement sixguns. A custom sixgun is more than a lifetime investment. If properly treated, it will be passed on and enjoyed for many generations.

CHAPTER 21

PLAYIN' FAVORITES

Solomon was the wisest man who ever lived and quite possibly even the richest ruler of all times. He had seven hundred wives and, in such a situation, was probably wise enough not to play favorites. Not being as wise as Solomon and certainly not having as many sixguns as he had wives, I have been thinking during the course of this book about which sixguns are really my favorites. If a sixgun looks good, feels good, and shoots well, I like it. Picking favorites is not an easy task.

Not only do I have the great privilege of testing all the new sixguns that arrive each year, I am also constantly on the lookout for certain classic sixguns, especially big bore sixguns from Colt, Ruger, and Smith & Wesson. For the past forty years, I have been faithfully attending local gun shows and regularly searching local gun shops for sixguns that stir the heart, mind, soul, and spirit.

As I prepared to list my real favorites, I left out specialty guns, those sixguns that are scoped for hunting, such as the 7-1/2-inch Freedom Arms sixguns chambered in .44 Magnum and .454 Casull, the long-range sixguns for silhouetting, personified by the 10-1/2-inch Rugers, .357 Maximum and .44 Magnum and also the slicked-up little sixguns for concealment use carried out to perfection in the Smith & Wessons, the Models 60 and 65 .357 Magnums. I've also excluded the custom-chambered sixguns by Hamilton Bowen, Bill Grover, Andy Horvath, John Linebaugh, and Jim Stroh. It goes without saying that these are favorites. The big bore sixguns listed and pictured here are all around sixguns that can be belted on any day for practically any purpose.

I'll always have a special place in my heart for my first two centerfire sixguns, a 4-5/8-inch Ruger Flat-Top .357 Blackhawk and a 4-3/4-inch Colt Single Action .38-40. The Ruger was brand new in 1956, the Colt was nearly sixty years old. Both cost about the same, $87.50 for the Ruger, a flat $90 for the Colt. That was BIG money then, especially for one making all of 90 cents an hour.

The first two leather rigs I ever made were belts and holsters for those two ".38s." In the foolishness of my youth, I let both of them get away. I was, in fact, doubly foolish with the Ruger as I let it get away twice after it had come back to me in another trade. I don't trade sixguns much anymore. I've learned to keep the good ones.

Those two early sixguns may have gotten away, but they have been replaced. Four Flat-Top Rugers entered here as .357s over the years, however, they have all been converted to .44 Special along the way. It was time to have one in .357 Magnum and left that way, so at the last gun show a 1956 manufactured .357 Ruger Blackhawk cost me $399. The .38-40 is also home now. A brand new Third Generation .38-40 Colt Single Action may be very pricey, but at least it shoots better than the original.

I have found my favorites list to be rather narrow as to caliber. Only the .44s and .45s made it, and, they seem to stay. Since those first two mistakes, when I've acquired something I like, I tend to hold on to it. I've been married to the same woman for thirty-eight years, all the credit for this feat goes to her, I've lived in the same house for twenty-eight years, and my Bronco is fifteen years old, so it is not surprising to find that among my favorite sixguns, the average tenure in my hands is eighteen years with the elder statesman having been a faithful companion for a full forty years. I was, as they say, still wet behind the ears when I purchased it. Today, it is illegal for a teenager to start off with such a handgun purchase. Come to think of it, by today's standards, I was too young then to even purchase a .22 rifle!

I remember well a few years ago one of our esteemed national lawmakers wanted to outlaw guns with the notion that even though there were many guns in existence, they would all eventually break and all guns would be totally out of commission within ten years. My forty year old .44 is as good today as it was the day it left the factory—actually better. Lawmakers should be more knowledgeable about everything before they attempt to pass foolish legislation. I can only conclude if they are this ignorant about firearms they are also possessed of the same ignorance about every other topic that comes before them.

I've spent way too much money on sixguns, if such a thing is possible, however, I've also made up for it by spending very little, relatively speaking, on anything else. There are a few unscrupulous characters around who have learned my weakness. They know that a sixgun that has ".44 SPECIAL" or ".45 COLT" or ".44 MAGNUM" accompanied with "COLT" or "RUGER" or "SMITH & WESSON" inscribed upon it will very likely have me reaching for my wallet.

Apparently it is a family trait now. A few years back a friend dropped by to tempt me with a 7-1/2-inch Great Western Single Action .45 Colt. "I'd really like to have that sixgun but I am sorry, I am really broke right now." My wife went into the bedroom, came back with the money, and paid the friend who sat there speechless at the thought that there were really women like this around. It must have really affected him. He had been a confirmed bachelor up to that point. Shortly thereafter he met a woman with three kids, wound up marrying her, and now they have three more of their own. All because of a Great Western .45! That's the real power of a sixgun.

In 1956, after fifteen years of being out of production, the Colt Single Action Army .45 came back as the run of Second Generation Colt Single Actions commenced. About the same time, .44 Magnums from Ruger and Smith & Wesson began to appear in gun shops around the country. I purchased the first Colt, a 7-1/2-inch blue model with case-hardened frame, to

The Colt Single Action Army 4-3/4 inch—the best lookin' sixgun ever built. These favorite Second Generation Colts are the .45 Colt engraved by Jim Riggs, factory ivories with Colt medallion, El Paso floral-carved #1920 Tom Threepersons rig (top) and the .44 Special, Pau Ferro stocks by Tony Kojis, basket stamped #1920 Tom Threepersons rig (bottom).

A favorite sixgun for forty years has been the 7-1/2-inch Colt Single Action Army .45 Colt that is here represented by a pair of Third Generation sixguns. Top, a blackpowder-style frame with a screw in front of the frame that secures the cylinder pin and a bullseye-shaped ejector rod head; bottom, the more modern style with a spring-loaded cylinder pin catch and a half-moon-shaped ejector rod head. Both wear one-piece fancy walnut stocks by BluMagnum.

This Colt New Frontier 7-1/2-inch .44 Special with extra cylinders chambered in .44-40 and .44 Russian does triple-duty. Ivory stocks by Charles Able.

Colt's Classic New Frontiers: Left, 7-1/2-inch .45 Colt with carved steer head ivory polymer stocks by Bob Leskovec; right, 7-1/2-inch .44 Special, with Charles Able ivory stocks.

show up in my area. A second Colt was added by rebuilding an 1899 Single Action with a new Second Generation cylinder and 7-1/2-inch barrel—boy, do I wish I had that one back!

A pair of Mexican-style holsters from Lawrence were worn on double-crossed belts and I practiced fast draw with those Colts every day for hours on end. A black Buscadero rig from Ray Houser was added—still more practice. When I really got serious about fast draw, an Arvo Ojala rig with the full metal-lined holster became the rig of choice. It would be several years before I even thought of using any Colt Single Action barrel length but 7-1/2 inches. The 4-3/4 inch may have been the choice of Fast Draw buffs and old time gunfighters, but the 7-1/2-inch gun had the balance and easy shooting qualities that I preferred. It was just as fast out of the leather for me as a shorter sixgun.

My first explorations into the then mysterious arena of handloading began with the 7-1/2-inch .45 Colt. It also almost ended there. I didn't have a powder scale, only a powder measure. I set it the way the chart read for the desired charge, something I would

never do today. Always, absolutely always, use a powder scale to set a powder measure. Factory loads had been very mild. My first handloads with the old DuPont #5066 powder were anything but. At the shot the long barrel of the Colt stood straight up in the air as the grip slammed back into my hand. To compound my original error, I did not stop and pull the rest of my loads. I shot them all. The Good Lord surely takes care of fools and sixgunners, especially when they are one in the same.

That first Colt Single Action helped me to really appreciate the grand old .45 Colt cartridge as well as develop an almost spiritual bond with the 7-1/2-inch single action sixgun. Two other long-barreled .45 Colts emerged after the Colt Single Action Army that also make my Favorite List. In 1962, Colt flat-topped the frame of the Single Action, added adjustable sights and the New Frontier was born. It was introduced by Colt to celebrate the advent of the New Frontier of President Kennedy.

About eight years later, the .45 Colt would be further modernized when Ruger came forth with the first heavy-framed .45 Colt, the Old Model Blackhawk.

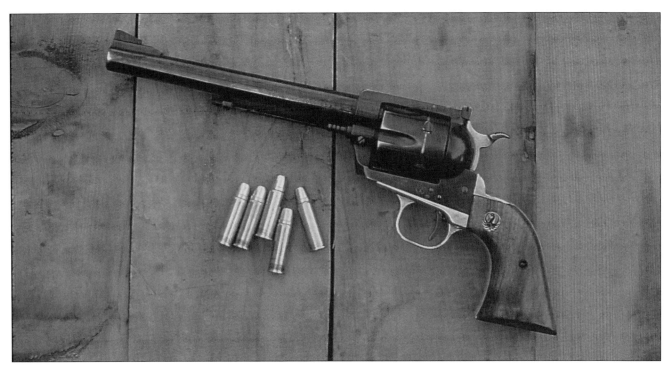

Taffin's first true big bore, Ruger's .44 Magnum Flat-Top Blackhawk. A favorite for forty years, it has been a 6-1/2-, a 4-5/8-, and a 7-1/2-inch sixgun during this time.

Ruger's original Super Blackhawk Three-Screw Model: This early 7-1/2-inch .44 Magnum becomes a favorite when the Super Blackhawk grip frame is replaced with an original Flat-Top grip frame and stocks.

Suddenly we had a single action that turned the .45 into a real hunting handgun with the capability of handling 300 grain bullets at 1,200 feet per second muzzle velocities.

One final .45 makes the List. It is the Colt Single Action Army that graces the dust jacket of this book. I will state without hesitation that the 4-3/4-inch Colt Single Action is the best looking sixgun of all time. It is definitely worthy of decoration such as engraving by Jim Riggs and the factory ivory stocks. The lines are simply classic and just holding one conjures up all sorts of images, sounds, and smells.

Pick one up, slowly cock the hammer, and see gunfighters advancing towards each other in a dusty street, hear the thundering of the hooves of thousands of cattle, smell the bacon and beans over an open campfire. If a Colt doesn't have this effect on you, you are in deep trouble. You've been working too hard, taking life too seriously. It is time to relax and enjoy the finer things.

The first .44 Magnum to appear in our area was a 4-inch Smith & Wesson. The gun shop did not put it up for sale, but instead rented it out to be shot so everyone could get the feel of the new Magnum. And feel it we did. We all shot it. We all lied and said it wasn't bad. We were all secretly happy to go back to our .357s, .44 Specials, and .45 Colts.

Shortly thereafter a Ruger .44 Magnum appeared, the original Flat-Top Blackhawk with a 6-1/2-inch barrel. This would surely be the answer. I loaded the cylinder with Remington factory 240s, squeezed off the first shot, and then realized I had just purchased a .44 Magnum that kicked even worse than the Smith & Wesson .44! Not only did it hurt, but the hammer also came back and dug a piece of skin out of the area between my thumb and trigger finger. In my defense, I will say that .44 Magnum factory loads were a whole lot hotter than they are today, 200 to 300 feet per second muzzle velocity hotter. I also had not yet learned that I had two hands, nor that custom grips were available. Most importantly, I had to learn that it took a definite mind set to handle really big bore sixguns.

That sixgun was eventually conquered by shooting a whole lot of .44 Special loads, then working up to the Keith .44 Special load, and finally full-power .44 Magnum loads. The barrel was cut to 4-5/8 inch for easy packin' in a Lawrence #120 Keith holster. My hunting buddies never worried if the rifles were out of reach while we camped or slept as long as I had the "Bear Buster," as they called the Ruger .44. When the short barrel was needed for my first .357 to .44 Special conversion, the .44 Flat-Top was returned to the factory and rebarreled with the 7-1/2-inch barrel that it still wears today.

Today, this favorite sixgun lives in a kinder, gentler world. Once in great while, just to remind it of its past glory, I'll fire a few cylindersful of full .44 Magnum loads always with Keith hard cast bullets and always with Alliant #2400 powder. It certainly is hard not to say Hercules #2400 after all these years, but for the most part, the old Ruger .44 enjoys life with a hard cast bullet, 250 or 300 grains, over 10 grains of Unique. This is an 1,150 foot per second load that guarantees both me and the Ruger .44 will last a lot longer. It is powerful but easy shootin'.

Ruger came very close to building the perfect sixgun with the original Blackhawk .44 Magnum. Only two things, at least in my mind, kept it from perfection. For years double action sixguns had been equipped with front sights that were designed to be fast from the leather, namely Baughman ramp front sights that were sloped to prevent any snagging on leather as they came forth. Ruger Blackhawks were sixguns for the outdoorsman and woman, but they came with Baughman instead of Patridge-style, flat black post front sights. The same situation exists today except with the long-barreled .44s designed for silhouetting.

The Blackhawk was a great improvement design-wise over the Colt Single Action Army with coil spring lockwork, wide hammer and trigger, flat-top main frame and adjustable sights. These were all great steps forward and then came one giant step back. The grip frame was an alloy instead of steel. Three years later, the .44 Blackhawk was improved with the advent of the Super Blackhawk. The sights remained the same, except for added protective ears around the rear sight, but the grip frame was now real steel.

For most the larger Dragoon-style grip frame was a great improvement; for me the material was right, but the shape was not. Mine was eventually sent off to Mag-Na-Port in the 1970s and made into an extremely practical packin' pistol. The barrel was cut to 4-3/4 inch, Mag-Na-Ported, the action was slicked, the entire sixgun was finished in the stainless steel-style Mag-Na-Life finish. I swapped grip frames with a stainless steel Old Army and had a favorite sixgun that is very close to the short-barreled Super Blackhawks available today.

My final favorite Ruger .44 is another early Super Blackhawk. I found someone who had a Flat-Top, but did not like the shape of the grip frame. A parts trade was made and we now have grip frames that fit our hands and attitudes. Basically, the only difference in the two Ruger 7-1/2-inch .44 Magnums on my Favorite List now is the unfluted cylinder of the Super.

Other .44s also make the List. The Smith & Wesson .44 Magnum in its original configuration before the

Hard to beat for self defense or plain woods loafin' are these 4-inch .44 Specials from Smith & Wesson: The Highway Patrolman converted to .44 with rosewood Magna stocks, the Model 624 stainless, scrimshawed ivory stocks by Twyla Taylor, and the 1950 Target with factory Magna stocks. All wear Tyler T-grip adapters.

These favorite sixguns are powerful and easy to pack, clockwise from top left: Smith & Wesson 4-inch .44 Magnum Elmer Keith Commemorative with ivory polymer stocks by Bob Leskovec, Colt SAA 4-3/4-inch .44 Special with stocks by Tony Kojis, Colt SAA 4-3/4-inch .45 Colt engraved by Jim Riggs and with factory ivories, and Smith & Wesson 4-inch Model 29 .44 Magnum engraved by Jim Riggs with BearHug ivory micarta stocks.

The best in .44s from Smith & Wesson: Top, late 1950s 6-1/2-inch .44 Magnum; bottom, 1980s resurrection of the 1950 Target, the 6-1/2-inch Model 24 .44 Special. Both wear BearHug Skeeter Skelton stocks of fancy walnut (top) and rosewood (bottom).

days of heavy underlugged barrels and round-butted grip frames, is surely the best looking double action sixgun ever to come from a factory. Smith started with the fine .44 Special that basically dated all the way back to 1907 with the Triple-Lock, added a bull barrel and full length cylinder, and the result was, again, near perfection in a sixgun. Four-inch Smith & Wesson .44 Magnums are fine for easy packin' and when properly loaded, ideal for defensive use. They are also classic enough to deserve engraving. My original 4-inch .44, also pictured on the dust jacket, has been engraved and finished in antique nickel by Jim Riggs and stocked by BearHug. It is definitely a favorite.

That original 4-inch .44 has now been joined by a second 4-inch Smith & Wesson from a special run of 2,500 sixguns designated the Elmer Keith Commemorative. Embellished in gold to celebrate highlights of the Old Master's life, the 4-inch .44 has also been tuned to perfection by Bob Munden, including slimming, smoothing and rounding the trigger for better double action control, and also stocked by Bob Leskovec with ivory polymer grips with the steer head carving favored by Keith. All this sixgun needs is an easy to see black post front sight and it will personify perfection in a double action big bore sixgun.

Finally, there is the first Smith & Wesson, the 6-1/2-inch barreled Smith that is so practical for hunting and long-range shooting. The advent of the .44 Magnum in both the Ruger single action and Smith & Wesson double action really made handgun hunting feasible and practical. Early on, the argument began as to which was the best because both had to be cocked for hunting use. The double action certainly had the best single action trigger, however, today there are any number of sixgunsmiths who can tune triggers on single action sixguns to equal or surpass the finest found on any double action.

With the coming of the .454 Casull and the .475 and .500 Linebaughs, the single action definitely became the king of the hunting handguns. Now several sixgunsmiths offer first-class conversions on the double action Super Redhawk to .475 and .500, so the old argument continues. Which is best for hunting? Single action or double action? It all comes right down to personal preference. I like 'em both. If there is any advantage to one or the other, it is simply that the single action is usually easier to holster as it is inherently better balanced for ease of carrying. Then again, this may also simply be personal preference.

Seniority-wise, my old Smith .44 Magnum takes a back seat only to the Ruger .44 Flat-Top as it has been

Hard to beat for close-range hunting is this Freedom Arms 6-inch .44 Magnum with grips by Charles Able. It carries easily and securely in this leather-lined nylon rig by Idaho Leather.

a part of my sixgunnin' life for over thirty-five years. Stocked by BearHug with Skeeter Skelton stocks of walnut smoothed out in all the right places, it definitely makes the Taffin Team of Big Bore Sixguns. It has earned its easier life and is now treated the same as the Flat-Top Ruger when it comes to .44 Magnum loads. If I want to shoot a long string of heavy loads I will reach for a Ruger Redhawk or Dan Wesson .44; if I want to enjoy life, I will go with the Smith & Wesson.

The last two .44 Magnums on the Favorite List are relative newcomers. While Colt and Smith & Wesson were both established firearms makers before Lincoln was president, and Ruger will soon be celebrating its Golden Anniversary, Freedom Arms and Texas Longhorn Arms are relative newcomers both having begun producing quality sixguns in the 1980s. Both offer superb single action .44 Magnums, possibly the finest ever produced.

Freedom Arms' .44 is simply its .454 with smaller holes in cylinder and barrel. In the 6-inch length, it carries easily in a shoulder holster, and is a most practical close-range hunting handgun. Texas Longhorn Arms Improved Number Five is a modern descendant of the "perfect" sixgun designed by Keith

and Harold Croft in the 1920s. The latter was a customized 5-1/2-inch Colt in .44 Special, the former duplicates the grip frame of the Keith/Croft #5 and uses a slightly larger frame and cylinder to handle the .44 Magnum. Mine was ordered early and bears serial number K-44. It has now been joined by an identical sixgun chambered in .45 Colt. All three of these big bore sixguns easily make the Favorite List.

In my youthful sixgunning days, the .44 Special was even harder to find than the .44 Magnum. My first modern .44 Special came two years after the Magnums when my wife presented me with a 6-1/2-inch Smith & Wesson 1950 Target .44 Special for our first Christmas together. One year later I was in college, our first baby was due, and all we could afford was a bottle of Hoppe's #9 for Christmas!

That .44 Special was a real favorite sixgun in those days, however, by the time I was well into my third year of college, we had three hungry kids, tuition was due, and something had to give. It turned out to be the Smith & Wesson .44 Special. My 7-1/2-inch .45 Colt Single Action, a Model 94 Winchester, and the .44 Special were all taken to the local gun shop and sold for a grand total of $100! As we left, my wife was sobbing

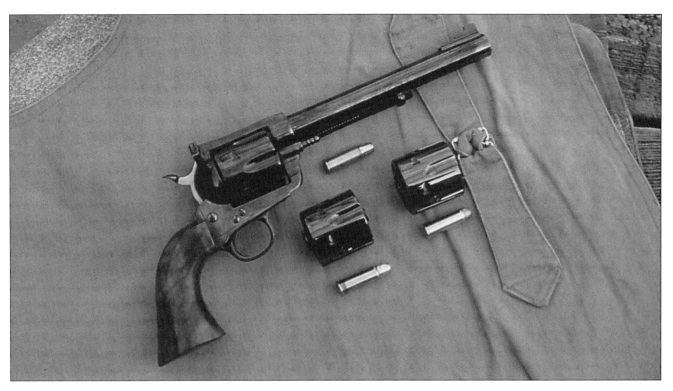

All the .44 bases are covered by this Texas Longhorn Arms Flat-Top Target 7-1/2-inch .44 Special with extra cylinders chambered in .44 Magnum and .44-40.

Favored short-barreled sixguns for rough going: Top, Freedom Arms .454 Casull with ivory micarta grips by Charles Able; bottom, Ruger .44 Magnum Super Blackhawk cut to 4-3/4 inches, tuned, Mag-Na-Ported, Mag-Na-Life finish, and standard grip frame with Ajax ivory polymer grips.

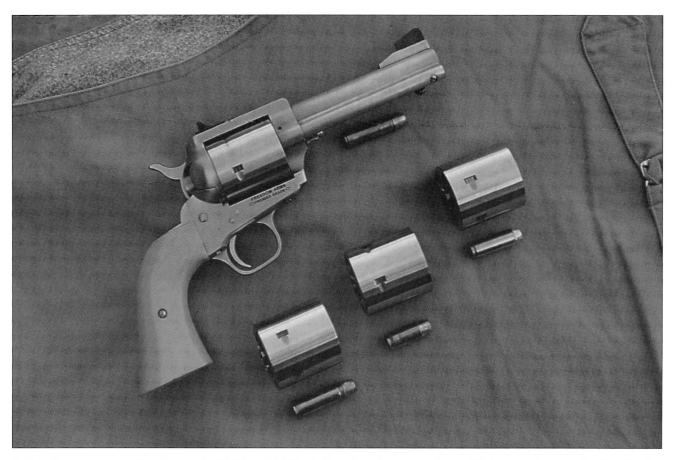

Is this the most versatile sixgun of all? This 4-3/4-inch Freedom Arms revolver with ivory micarta grips by Charles Able is chambered in .454 with extra cylinders in .45 Colt, .45 WinMag, and .45 ACP.

and said to me: "You will never, ever have to do that again." She was right!

Both the .44 Special and the .45 Colt have been replaced. A later Model 1950 Target .44 Special was cut to 4 inches and became an ideal carry-gun. In the 1980s Smith made a new run of .44 Specials in both stainless and blued versions. The 6-1/2-inch blued .44 Special is every bit as good a sixgun as the original, while the 4-inch stainless version could do well in a contest to determine the finest double action carry gun.

Single Actions are perfect vehicles for the .44 Special and three make my Favorite List. An early Second Generation Colt Single Action Army cut to 4-3/4-inch length, fitted with one-piece Pau Ferro grips by friend Tony Kojis is way up at the top of the List. Most of the bluing is gone or very faded, the case colors are gray, and the action is silky smooth, all of which makes this one of the most distinguished-looking Colts around. If ever a sixgun was a time machine to travel back to the past it is this .44 Special. It is impossible to pick it up without the mind and spirit going back ninety years or more. It is good therapy for the soul.

The other two .44 Specials are both 7-1/2-inch six-guns. First is the Colt New Frontier with ivory stocks by Charles Able and extra cylinders chambered in .44-40 and .44 Russian. The Texas Longhorn Arms .44 Special West Texas Flat-Top Target has the same sized frame as the Improved Number Five, which allows it to be fitted with a second cylinder in .44 Magnum as well as a .44-40 cylinder. Both of these sixguns are versatile, to say the least, and the Flat-Top Target may well be that all elusive perfect six-gun or as close as we are likely to come. It corrected both of the "faults" of the original Ruger .44 Black-hawk, namely the steel grip frame and post front sight. The grip frame is slightly longer than the standard single action frame making it easier to handle heavy loads.

Finally, we come to the .454 Casull. This finest made sixgun ever to leave a factory is offered in barrel lengths of 4-3/4, 6, 7-1/2 and 10 inches, with most lengths also available with fixed or adjustable sights. The .454 that finds its way on the List is the easy packin' 4-3/4-inch Premier Grade with ivory micarta stocks by Charles Able. It is simply impossible to

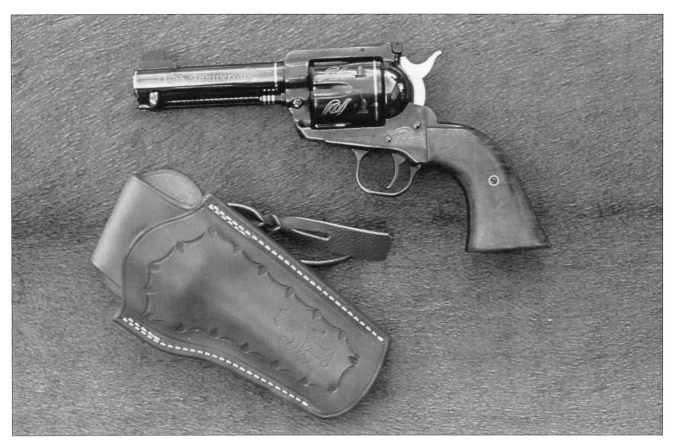

A favorite sixgun, emotionally and otherwise, is this sixgun that The Shootists presented to Taffin—a 4-5/8-inch New Model Ruger .45 Blackhawk. Dave Wayland stocked this completely tuned, high polished blued, and Qualite Pistol & Revolver-embellished sixgun.

pack any more power than this in such a portable sixgun. It is also highly versatile.

Freedom Arms offers auxiliary cylinders for its .454 in .45 Colt, .45 ACP, and .45 WinMag which in reality gives a person two, three, or even four sixguns for relatively little extra expense above the cost of the original sixgun. Consider the fact that it is possible to fire four different .45s through this little sixgun from 185 grain hollowpoints all the way up to 350 grain hard cast bullets. No rear sight has enough adjustment to handle this wide range of bullet weights, so the Freedom Arms .454 proves again how adaptable it is to any situation by the use of interchangeable front sights of varying heights and configurations. This sixgun is surely well at the top of the List.

The final sixgun to make the List is highly emotional. In 1985, I wrote a fictional article with a dozen real people who brought their favorite sixguns for a Shootists Holiday. Those who were involved through my imagination said we should really do it, really all gather together for a week of shooting and sharing information.

That first Shootist Holiday was held in Freedom, Wyoming, in 1986. We have continued to meet and grow ever since and the annual event has become the Mecca for sixgunners. We do in person what the old .44 Associates did by mail more than fifty years ago. Not only has a lot of shooting and sharing gone on, but also real, solid lasting friendships have been formed. In 1995, at our 10th Annual gathering, I was totally caught off guard when members presented me with a 10th Anniversary sixgun. Qualite Pistol & Revolver was commissioned to build this special sixgun. A Ruger 4-5/8-inch .45 Colt New Model Blackhawk was totally tuned to perfection, highly polished and blued, gold embellished, and fitted with custom fancy walnut stocks by Dave Wayland. Both Milt Morrison of Qualite and Dave Wayland are members of The Shootists, so that adds to the special feeling I have for this sixgun presented to me by such a special group of sixgunners.

We've looked at quite a few favorite sixguns, single action and double action, short barrel- and long barrel-style. If pinned to the wall and forced to choose only one, I would not hesitate to go with a 7-1/2-inch single action. It would have to be equipped with

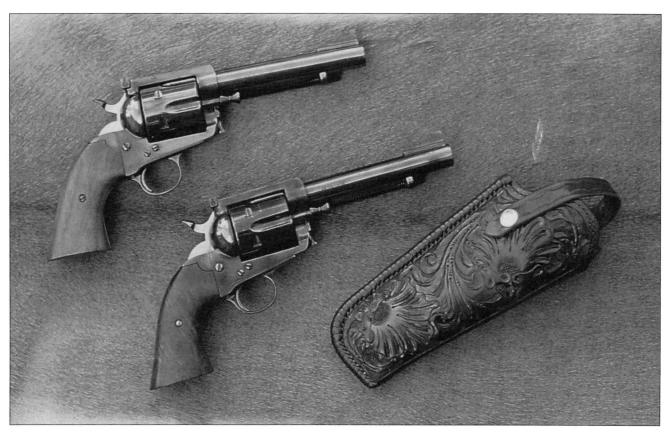

These Texas Longhorn Arms Improved Number Fives were inspired by Elmer Keith's custom Colt Single Action of the 1920s: Top, 5-1/2-inch .45 Colt; bottom, 5-1/2-inch .44 Magnum. Holster is one of the last, and probably the last, to come out of the old Lawrence Leather Co.

adjustable sights and chambered in .44 or .45. That narrows the choice down considerably.

Although I shudder at the thought of having only one sixgun, I could be quite happy with a Freedom Arms .44 Magnum or .454 Casull or Texas Longhorn Arms Flat-Top Target in .44 Special/.44 Magnum or .45 Colt. From the used gun market there is the Colt New Frontier in .44 Special or .45 Colt, Ruger's Flat-Top .44 Magnum, Old Model Super Blackhawk .44 Magnum fitted with a standard grip frame, or the Old Model .45 Colt Blackhawk.

Ruger's current crop of Blackhawks, the New Models, are all of the transfer bar safety-style and while being safer than the old style sixguns, they do need sixgunsmithing to operate as smoothly as the older guns. The Bisley .44 Magnum or .45 Colt, Blackhawk .45 Colt, and the .44 Super Blackhawk, all can be tuned, warning label polished from the left side of the barrel, and fitted with a Patridge front sight. The Freedom Arms sixguns have a distinct advantage over all the others in that they are easily scoped and just as easily returned to iron sights.

It has been a long road traveled since a seventeen year old purchased his first sixgun, a Ruger .22 Single-Six in 1956. Big bore sixguns have been my consuming passion since I dropped the hammer shortly thereafter on that first Magnum round from the Ruger Flat-Top .357 Blackhawk. Along the way I have shot all the great sixguns, and more importantly, met a whole bunch of great sixgunners. To be able to have received so much enjoyment thus far in life, I realize I have been truly blessed. To you the reader, I leave the two greatest wishes I am able to offer. Good Shootin' and God Bless.

DIRECTORY OF SERVICES FOR SIXGUNNERS

SIXGUNS—U.S. MFGD., REPLICAS, AND ANTIQUES

American Frontier Firearms, 40725 Brook Trails Way, Aguanga, CA 92536

Cimarron Arms, P.O. Box 906, Fredericksburg, TX 78624

Colt's Mfg., P.O. Box 1868, Hartford, CT 06144

EMF, 1900 E. Warner, Suite 1-D, Santa Ana, CA 92705

Freedom Arms, P.O. Box 150, Freedom, WY 83120

Navy Arms, 689 Bergen Blvd., Ridgefield, NJ 07657

Old Town Station Ltd., P.O. Box 15351, Lenexa, KS 66285

Sturm, Ruger & Co., Lacey Place, Southport, CT 06490

Smith & Wesson, 2100 Roosevelt Ave., Springfield, MA 01102

Taurus International, 16175 NW 49th Ave., Miami, FL 33014

USPFA Co., P.O. Box 1901, Hartford, CT 06106

CUSTOM SIXGUNSMITHS, PARTS, AND ENGRAVING

Actions By T, 16315 Redwood Forest Ct., Sugar Land, TX 77478

Adams & Son Engravers, 87 Acorn St., Dennis, MA 02638

Alpha Precision, 2765-B Preston Rd., Good Hope, GA 30641

Belt Mtn. Enterprises, P.O. Box 3202, Bozeman, MT 59772

Bowen Classic Arms, P.O. Box 67, Louisville, TN 37777

Brownell's, 200 S. Front St., Montezuma, IA 50171

Clements Custom Guns, 60338 Hatley Rd., Amory, MS 38821

Clark Custom Guns, 336 Shootout Lane, Princeton, LA 71067

John Gallagher, 306 Highway 78 West, Jasper, AL 35501

Andy Horvath, 14131 Diagonal Rd., LaGrange, OH 44050

Linebaugh Custom Sixguns, Rt 2, Box 100, Maryville, MO 64468

Mag-Na-Port, 41302 Executive Dr., Harrison TWP, MI 48045

Richard McCann, P.O. Box 641, Spanaway, WA 98387

Munden Enterprises, 1621 Samson St., Butte, MT 59701

Peacemaker Specialists, P.O. Box 157, Whitmore, CA 96096

Power Custom, RR2 Box 756AB, Gravois Mills, MO 65037

Qualite Pistol & Revolver, 5580 Havana #6A, Denver, CO 80239

Jim Riggs, 206 Azalea, Boerne, TX 78006

Shapel's Gun Shop, 1708 N. Liberty, Boise, ID 83704

SSK Industries, 721 Woodvue Lane, Wintersville, OH 43952

Texas Longhorn Arms, 5959 W. Loop South, Suite 424, Bellaire, TX 77401

SIXGUN STOCKS

Charles Able, 205 N. 1st. St., Carlsbad, NM 88020

Ajax Custom Grips, 9130 Viscount Row, Dallas, TX 75247

BluMagnum, 5960 Wilson Rd., Colorado Springs, CO 80919

Eagle Grips, 460 Randy Rd., Carol Stream, IL 60188

Roy Fishpaw, 101 Primrose Ln., Lynchburg, VA 24501

Herrett Stocks, P.O. Box 741, Twin Falls, ID 83303

Hogue Grips, P.O. Box 1138, Paso Robles, CA 93447

Pachmayr Ltd., 1875 S. Mtn. Ave., Monrovia, CA 91016

Precision Pro Grips, 4429 Stanton Ave., Pittsburgh, PA 15201

Uncle Mike's, P.O. Box 13010, Portland, OR 97213

SIXGUN LEATHER

John Bianchi, P.O. Box 2038, Rancho Mirage, CA 92270

Ted Blocker, 14787 S.E. 82nd Dr., Clackamas, OR 97015

Bull-X, Inc., 520 N. Main St., Farmer City, IL 61842

G. Wm. Davis, 3995 Valley Blvd. Unit D, Walnut, CA 91789

El Paso Saddlery, P.O. Box 27194, El Paso, TX 79926

Galco International, 2019 W. Quail Ave., Phoenix, AZ 85027

Gould & Goodrich, P.O. Box 1479, Lillington, NC 27546

Mario Hanel, 1189 N. 5th Ave., Stayton, OR 97383

Idaho Leather, 18 S. Orchard, Boise, ID 83705

The Leather Arsenal, 27549 Middleton Rd., Middleton, ID 83644

Legends in Leather, 1353 Coyote Rd., Prescott, AZ 86303

Arvo Ojala, P.O. Box 98, N. Hollywood, CA 91603

Thad Rybka, 134 Havilah Hill, Odenville, AL 35120

San Pedro Saddlery, 506 E. Fremont, Tombstone, AZ 85638

Milt Sparks, 605 E. 44th St., Boise, ID 83714

TrailRider, P.O. Box 2284, Littleton, CO 80161

Von Ringler, 31 Shining Mtn. Rd., Powell, WY 82435

Texas Longhorn Arms, 5959 W. Loop South, Suite 424, Bellaire, TX 77401

AMMUNITION, BULLETS, BULLET MOULDS, MISCELLANEOUS

Black Hills Ammunition, P.O. Box 3090, Rapid City, SD 57709

BRP Bullets, 1210 Alexander Rd., Colorado Springs, CO 80909

Bull-X Bullets, 520 N. Main St., Farmer City, IL 61842

CCI/Speer, P.O. Box 856, Lewiston, ID 83501

Cor-Bon, 1311 Industry Rd., Sturgis, SD 57785

Federal Cartridge, 900 Ehlen Dr., Anoka, MN 55303

Ben Forkin, 107 10th Ave., White Sulphur Springs, MT 59645

Fusilier Bullets, 10010 N. 600 W., Highland, UT 84003

Garrett Cartridges, P.O. Box 178, Chehalis, WA 98532

Hornady, P.O. Box 1848, Grand Island, NE 68802

LBT, HCR 62, Box 145, Moyie Springs, ID 83845

Lyman, 475 Smith St., Middleton, CT 06457

NEI, 51583 Columbia River Hwy., Scappoose, OR 97056

RCBS, 605 Oro Dam Blvd., Oroville, CA 95965

Remington, P.O. Box 700, Madison, NC 27025

Sierra Bullets, 1400 W. Henry St., Sedalia, MO 65301

Winchester Div., Olin Corp., 427 N. Shamrock, E. Alton, IL 62024

SIXGUN SCOPES

Burris, P.O. 1747, Greeley, CO 80631

Bushnell, 9200 Cody, Overland Park, KS 66214

Leupold & Stevens, P.O. Box 688, Beaverton, OR 97075

Redfield, 5800 E. Jewell Ave., Denver, CO 80224

Simmons, 2120 Kilarnery Way, Tallahassee, FL 32308

Thompson/Center, P.O. Box 5002, Rochester, NH 03866

Weaver, Blount Inc, P.O. Box 856, Lewiston, ID 83501

INDEX